PETER PARKER

HOUSMAN COUNTRY

Peter Parker is the author of *The Old Lie: The Great War and the Public-School Ethos*, biographies of J. R. Ackerley and Christopher Isherwood, and *The Last Veteran: Harry Patch and the Legacy of War*. He edited (and wrote much of) *A Reader's Guide to the Twentieth-Century Novel* and *A Reader's Guide to Twentieth-Century Writers*. He was also an associate editor of the *Oxford Dictionary of National Biography*, and his edition of G. F. Green's 1952 novel *In the Making* was published as a Penguin Modern Classic in 2012. A Fellow of the Royal Society of Literature, he has written for *The Telegraph*, *The Spectator*, *Apollo*, and *The Times Literary Supplement*. Born on a Herefordshire farm, he now lives in London's East End.

ALSO BY PETER PARKER

The Old Lie:
The Great War and the Public-School Ethos

Ackerley:
A Life of J. R. Ackerley

A Reader's Guide to the Twentieth-Century Novel

A Reader's Guide to Twentieth-Century Writers

Isherwood:
A Life Revealed

The Last Veteran:
Harry Patch and the Legacy of War

HOUSMAN
COUNTRY

Housman photographed by Henry Van der Weyde, *c.* 1894

HOUSMAN COUNTRY

INTO THE HEART OF ENGLAND

PETER PARKER

FARRAR, STRAUS AND GIROUX   NEW YORK

Farrar, Straus and Giroux
175 Varick Street, New York 10014

Printed in the United States of America
Originally published in 2016 by Little, Brown, Great Britain
Published in the United States in 2017 by Farrar, Straus and Giroux
First American paperback edition, 2018

The Library of Congress has cataloged the hardcover edition as follows:
Names: Parker, Peter, 1954– author.
Title: Housman country : into the heart of England / Peter Parker.
Description: New York : Farrar, Straus and Giroux, 2017. | Includes bibliographical
  references and index.
Identifiers: LCCN 2016045041 | ISBN 9780374173043 (hardback) |
  ISBN 9780374709358 (e-book)
Subjects: LCSH: Housman, A. E. (Alfred Edward), 1859–1936—Criticism and
  interpretation. | Housman, A. E. (Alfred Edward), 1859–1936. Shropshire lad. |
  English poetry—19th century—History and criticism. | National characteristics,
  English, in literature. | BISAC: LITERARY CRITICISM / European / English, Irish,
  Scottish, Welsh. | BIOGRAPHY & AUTOBIOGRAPHY / Literary.
Classification: LCC PR4809.H15 P37 2017 | DDC 821/.912—dc23
LC record available at https://lccn.loc.gov/2016045041

Paperback ISBN: 978-0-374-53786-9

Our books may be purchased in bulk for promotional, educational, or business use.
Please contact your local bookseller or the Macmillan Corporate and Premium Sales
Department at 1-800-221-7945, extension 5442, or by e-mail at
MacmillanSpecialMarkets@macmillan.com.

www.fsgbooks.com
www.twitter.com/fsgbooks • www.facebook.com/fsgbooks

For
Sue
in memory
of
Pat & Teddy

CONTENTS

PREFACE

In her introduction to Grant Richards's memoir of her brother, Katharine Symons described the book as 'not a complete biography of A.E. Housman but a nearly complete biography of his poems'. *Housman Country* is neither of these things, though it might be described as an account of the life and times of *A Shropshire Lad*. It is for this reason that the text of Housman's first volume has been included in this book, and those poems discussed in the text are additionally identified by the Roman numeral each of them bears in order to make them easy to locate. Since many of the poems published in later volumes were drafted or written at the same time as those in *A Shropshire Lad* or otherwise bear on the narrative, I have often referred to or discussed them. There are innumerable editions of Housman's collected poems, but all quotations from them in this book are taken from *A Shropshire Lad and Other Poems* (2010), authoritatively edited by Archie Burnett and readily available as a Penguin paperback or as an e-book. These poems are identified in the notes, once again by the Roman numerals used by Housman, which will make them easy to locate in any edition.

There remain whole areas of Housman's life and work – notably his career as a classicist – that do not come into this book. Several biographies of Housman, referred to in the text and listed in the bibliography, supply a more comprehensive account for anyone seeking one. Equally, at a time when questions of national identity are being much discussed, 'Englishness' here describes something that seemed rather more clearly identifiable during Housman's lifetime, although it is still recognisable today. My principal intention has been to investigate what I have called 'Housman Country', an English sensibility in which literature, landscape, music and emotion all play their part, and which finds one of its most perfect expressions in Housman's poetry.

Peter Parker, London E3, March 2016

HOUSMAN
COUNTRY

I

ENGLAND IN YOUR POCKET

> He is a strange phenomenon, but to my mind the most
> perfect expression of something deeply English and a whole
> mood of English history – a true master.
>
> Ted Hughes on A.E. Housman

Towards the end of February 1896 a small volume of sixty-three poems was published by Kegan Paul, Trench, Trübner & Co. Ltd in an edition of 500 copies at half a crown each. The author was a thirty-seven-year-old professor of Latin at University College, London, named Alfred Edward Housman, and he had been obliged to pay £30 towards the cost of publication. A small, slow trickle of reviews was led by *The Times*, which in its brief round-up of 'Books of the Week' on 27 March noted: 'Mr Housman has a true sense of the sweetness of country life and of its tragedies too, and his gift of melodious expression is genuine.' Other reviewers were less faint in their praise, but there is little in their verdicts to suggest that *A Shropshire Lad* would become, and remain, one of the best-loved volumes of poetry in the language. By the end of the year its combined sales in Britain and America amounted to only 381 copies, and the first edition did not sell out until two years later – and only then because Housman's brother Laurence bought up the remaining copies.

It took the enthusiasm and persistence of a young publisher called Grant Richards to rescue the book from this faltering start. Richards had reviewed *A Shropshire Lad* in W.T. Stead's *Review of Reviews*, rightly describing Housman as 'a very real poet, and a very English one at that'. On 1 January 1897 he set up his own publishing company, Grant Richards Ltd, with premises on Henrietta Street in Covent Garden, declaring that '*A Shropshire Lad* was perhaps of all books the one I most wanted on my list.' Housman took some persuading, but a new edition of 500 copies was published by Richards on 14 September 1898. Although sales were not exactly brisk, the little book's reputation gradually grew and it soon went into further editions. In America, meanwhile, the poems had found more immediate popularity after 161 copies of the first edition were imported and published under the John Lane (New York) imprint in 1897. The book was widely pirated and, although Lane reprinted his edition several times, innumerable unauthorised editions were issued from 1902 onwards, continuing to appear even after Henry Holt & Co. published the first authorised US edition in 1922. Housman took a lenient view of piracy, complaining only when books were badly produced or poems misprinted. 'Vanity, not avarice, is my ruling passion,' he told Richards; 'and so long as young men write to me from America saying that they would rather part with their hair than with their copy of my book, I do not feel the need of food and drink.'

Apart from eliminating misprints, Housman's principal concern was that his book should remain affordable, and in order to ensure this he declined royalties. 'I only stipulate for simplicity of design and moderateness of price,' he told Richards. Having for his first edition raised the original cover price by one shilling to 3s 6d – 'perhaps the largest sum which can be called moderate, but I suppose it deserves the name', Housman grumbled – Richards lowered it to 3s for his second. In December 1899 the publisher suggested a new size for the third edition. 'I rather like the notion of a pocket edition,' Housman commented. 'Large paper and illustrations are things I have not much affection for.' An octavo edition was therefore published in January 1903, priced at 1s.

In 1904 Richards 'gave full weight to the author's strong preference for a really cheap book' and published what he called a 'waistcoat pocket edition (at sixpence with a cloth cover; at a shilling bound in leather)'. This edition was unfortunately full of misprints, though Housman felt 'bound to say however that the leather binding makes a very pretty book', and it sold well, serving as 'a pleasant and inexpensive Christmas card' for the literary minded. The poet Edward Shanks recalled buying a copy of this edition in a Falmouth bookshop in 1907 when he was fifteen: 'It was not for its reputation that I bought it, for I had never heard of either A.E. Housman or *A Shropshire Lad*. I like to think now that I must have turned over the pages as I stood in the shop and recognized the quality of the verses. The more probable supposition, however, is that I was seduced by the price. It was only sixpence, and I hadn't much more, and it was a very low price indeed to pay for such an attractive-looking little book.'

The growth in the book's popularity was most marked during the early years of the twentieth century: in 1905 it sold 886 copies, but by 1911 the average yearly sale was an astonishing 13,500 copies. Sales were undoubtedly boosted by the large number of composers who made settings of Housman's poems during this period, which had seen a renaissance in English music and a rediscovery of traditional English folk song. In Housman, English composers felt they had found their own Heine or Müller, and *A Shropshire Lad* provided ideal texts for the forging of a truly English equivalent of the lieder tradition. According to the poet Robert Nichols, by the outbreak of the First World War, Housman's little book was 'in every pocket'. Poems describing the quiet places of an idealised rural England, a 'land of lost content' to which one could never return, struck a chord with those huddled in trenches amid the shattered landscapes of France and Belgium. Housman's themes of love and loss and of 'lads that will die in their glory and never be old' seemed additionally poignant and of the moment to those left at home when their men marched away.

The book's popularity was maintained after the war, with Grant Richards producing numerous further editions during the 1920s and 1930s. In 1929 alone he issued 5000 copies of the small edition and 2000 of the larger one, with another reprint of 5000 copies of the smaller edition the following year. Housman felt sure that his insistence upon the book's availability in inexpensive editions was largely responsible for its continuing sales, proudly telling an admirer who wrote to him in 1934 that 'for the last thirty years or more it has been procurable for eighteenpence'.

By the fiftieth anniversary of its first publication, *A Shropshire Lad* had gone through forty-eight editions in Britain and had become securely embedded in the national culture. In 1935 Eugene Goossens, who was at that time conductor of the Cincinnati Symphony Orchestra and described himself as 'a terrific lover of the Shropshire Lad poems', had insisted that 'The particular psychology they express is something which belongs only to Englishmen and it is idle to expect an American (as I know from experience) to try and understand the underlying idiom of these poems. Nobody who hasn't lived somewhere near the Wrekin or Bredon Hill or, to go a little farther afield, the Cotswold country, as I have, could ever hope to relish these works and their peculiar "aura".' That this was not the case may be judged by the fact that forty-seven American editions (not including mere reprints or imported volumes) were listed in a 1946 bibliography, and that a note in the US edition of Housman's *Selected Poems*, published three years earlier, stated: 'No contemporary poet has been so widely read or appreciated as this quiet scholar, whose verse has the accent of immortality and who always prized quality above quantity.'

Similarly, Morton D. Zabel, the literary critic and academic who became Professor of English at the University of Chicago, could confidently assert on the fiftieth anniversary of *A Shropshire Lad*'s original publication that 'no book of poetry published in the past half-century has attained a greater popularity.' One unusual mark of that popularity was that Yardley could use two lines from one of the poems to advertise its Orchis perfume in the *New Yorker* in 1931. *A Shropshire Lad* has been reprinted continually ever since its half-centenary and individual lines of the poems remain familiar even to those who have never read the book. In the 120 years since its original publication it has never once been out of print.

The unlikely author of this enduringly popular volume of poetry was not himself a Shropshire Lad. 'I was born in Worcestershire, not Shropshire, where I have never spent much time,' he confessed in 1933. 'I had a sentimental feeling for Shropshire because its hills were our

Western horizon.' That horizon was visible from Fockbury, the small Worcestershire hamlet where A.E. Housman was born on 26 March 1859. He was the eldest of the seven children of a genial but financially improvident solicitor, and he spent his childhood at Perry Hall, a large family house in nearby Bromsgrove. It was here that his siblings were born: Robert (1860), Clemence (1861), Katharine (always known as Kate, 1862), Basil (1864), Laurence (1865) and Herbert (1868). Already weakened by this swift succession of childbirths, Housman's beloved mother, Sarah Jane, developed breast cancer shortly after the birth of Herbert and by 1870 had become an invalid, unable any longer to manage the household. A cousin, Mary Housman, came to take on the role, while the older children took it in turns to read aloud to and write letters for their stricken mother. When it became clear that Sarah Jane was dying, Housman was sent to stay with his godmother at Woodchester in rural Gloucestershire. It was here that news of his mother's death reached him on his twelfth birthday. Housman had been brought up as a devout Christian, but the loss of his mother began a process which led him to reject Christianity altogether and become a convinced atheist at the age of twenty-one.

Housman had gone as a scholar to his local public school, King Edward's in Bromsgrove, where he excelled at Classics and won several prizes for Greek, Latin and English verse. In 1877 he was awarded an open classical scholarship to St John's College, Oxford, where he was generally regarded as exceptional, and where he met a fellow student called Moses Jackson, with whom he fell unrequitedly in love. To everyone's astonishment, having gained a first in Moderations, the exam taken at the end of his second year, he entirely failed his finals. Instead of embarking on the academic career everyone had predicted, he was obliged to sit the Civil Service Examination, and as a result accepted in 1882 a comparatively lowly job as a clerk in the Patent Office in London. He did not abandon his studies, however; he spent his evenings and weekends working on classical texts in the reading room of the British Museum, and the articles he began contributing to scholarly magazines gradually acquired him a considerable reputation in his field. When in 1892 the Chair of Latin fell vacant at University College, London, he was able to provide seventeen testimonials in support of his application for the post, to which he was duly appointed. He had written poetry since childhood, mostly light verse, but in the late 1880s, while living in Highgate, north London, he began writing the poems that would eventually be published in *A Shropshire Lad*, the majority of them in a sudden burst of creativity in 1895.

The success of *A Shropshire Lad* led many people to enquire when a second volume of poems might be ready for the press. Housman was disinclined to oblige, concentrating instead on scholarly publications, notably his edition of Manilius's *Astronomica*, which appeared (at his own expense) in five volumes between 1903 and 1930. He had been appointed Kennedy Professor of Latin at the University of Cambridge in 1911, and would remain there as a Fellow of Trinity College until his death. He continued, somewhat costively, to write new poems and revise those he had excluded from *A Shropshire Lad*. Another burst of creativity led him to announce to his delighted publisher in April 1922 that he hoped to have a second volume ready for the autumn. The decisively but as it turned out inaccurately titled *Last Poems* appeared on 19 October 1922 and attracted widespread notice and very good sales.

Housman had left it to his brother Laurence, himself a renowned poet and playwright, to decide what should be published after his death. Most of the poems were contained in four notebooks and the only instruction Housman left was that Laurence should publish 'nothing which [he] considered inferior to anything that had already appeared'. After Housman died on 30 April 1936, Laurence selected forty-eight items to publish as *More Poems* in October of that year. The following year an additional eighteen poems appeared in his memoir *A.E.H.*, alongside some 'light verse and parodies' and a selection of letters. In a note explaining his reasons for publishing what became known as the 'Additional Poems', Laurence argued that although the three previous volumes now constituted 'the canon' of his brother's poetry, nothing he was now publishing was 'of a lower standard' than the one Housman had set. Five more poems, three of them 'rescued from periodicals', were appended to these *Additional Poems* when they were subsumed into the canon as part of the first *Collected Poems*, published in 1939. This volume excluded the light verse and parodies, but contained three previously published translations from the Greek.

Setting aside these translations, the light verse, and the assorted fragments that have subsequently been published, the collected edition of Housman's poetry remains small: 170 numbered poems with the addition of the two used as epigraphs for *Last Poems* and *More Poems*. Few of these take up more than a page and many of them consist of as few as two or three four-line stanzas. It seems very little on which to rest a considerable reputation, but if Housman had published nothing after *A Shropshire Lad*, he would still have earned his place in literary history. This is the volume that people always associate with him and it has retained the affection of readers from all backgrounds over many years. At the time of writing it is available in thirty-one editions.

There will continue to be arguments over the literary merits of *A Shropshire Lad*, but although Housman was not entirely indifferent to the views of critics and academics, and had a robust sense of his own literary standing, he wrote for ordinary people rather than his scholarly peers. 'My chief object in publishing my verses was to give pleasure to a few young men here and there,' he once said (women, young or old, tending not to enter his calculations very often). It is to the young that the poems' prevailing mood of romantic melancholy, their depiction of thwarted or unrequited love, and their railing against the injustices of life have always had a special appeal. 'I don't know how it is with the young today,' wrote W.H. Auden in 1972, 'but to my generation no other English poet seemed so perfectly to express the sensibility of a male adolescent.' George Orwell concurred, describing Housman as 'the writer who had the deepest hold upon the thinking young' in the years between 1910 and 1925. He described the poems' themes as 'adolescent': 'murder, suicide, unhappy love, early death' – though by that reckoning the plays of Shakespeare might equally be deemed adolescent in their preoccupations. One sees, however, his point, and it is in adolescence that poetry tends to strike home most forcefully, even among those who may never read it thereafter. Orwell claimed to have had the whole of *A Shropshire Lad* by heart while at Eton: 'these are the poems that I and my contemporaries used to recite to ourselves, over and over, in a kind of ecstasy'. Orwell further felt that young people were attracted by the 'blasphemous, antinomian, "cynical" strain' of Housman's poetry, particularly in the wake of the First World War, as the result of which a huge gulf had opened up between the generations. Housman, he wrote, 'stood for a kind of bitter, defiant paganism, a conviction that life is short and the gods are against you, which exactly fitted the prevailing mood of the young'. Orwell would become disenchanted with Housman, but others did not, and Cyril Connolly's brutal reassessment of the poems in the *New Statesman* shortly after Housman's death caused howls of outrage – an indication of how far Housman retained his hold upon readers well beyond their impressionable youth.

Housman believed that poetry had other functions beyond the principal one of giving pleasure to young men. In a letter of condolence to his sister Kate, one of whose sons had been killed in the First World War, he wrote: 'I do not know that I can do better than send you some verses that I wrote many years ago; because the essential business of poetry, as it has been said, is to harmonise the sadness of the universe, and it is somehow more sustaining and more healing than prose.' The person who gave this definition was Sir Leslie Stephen in his *A History of English Thought in the Eighteenth Century* (1876), and Housman had copied the observation into a notebook, along with the statement that immediately preceded it: 'Nothing is less poetical than optimism.' Optimism is certainly not something the reader encounters very often in *A Shropshire Lad*, which at times seems almost comically glum. In 'Twice a week the winter thorough' (XVII), for example, Housman depicts a lad in summer 'trying to be glad' as he strides out onto a cricket pitch:

> Try I will; no harm in trying:
>   Wonder 'tis how little mirth
> Keeps the bones of man from lying
>   On the bed of earth.

This is the sort of poem that has always made Housman a popular target for parodists, though it is unclear quite how seriously we are supposed to take it. It seems the sort of verse against which a protest is raised in the book's penultimate poem, 'Terence, this is stupid stuff' (LXII). Indeed, in that poem's reply to the criticism of a friend there is a near echo of the earlier one in the undermining aside: 'Therefore, since the world has still / Much good, but much less good than ill . . .'

8

Well aware of the reputation for gloominess his poetry had gained, Housman once agreed to a request that *Last Poems* should appear in a Braille edition on the grounds that 'The blind want cheering up.' As this remark shows, Housman could be very funny in his dry ironic way. He firmly rebutted the suggestion that he had at any time suffered 'a crisis of pessimism', insisting that he was not a pessimist but a 'pejorist', which is to say someone who believes the world is getting worse rather than better – adding (not entirely truthfully) 'and that is owing to my observation of the world not to personal experience'.

Housman knew that *Last Poems* contained some of his finest verse, but *A Shropshire Lad* retained a special place in his heart. While he grudgingly allowed composers to set poems individually or as part of a song cycle, he steadfastly refused permission for the volume's poems to be reprinted in anthologies. 'Pray who gave Mr. E[dward]. Thomas leave to print two of my inspired lays in his and your *Pocket Book of Poems and Songs*?' he asked Richards in June 1907. 'You must not treat my immortal works as quarries to be used at will by the various hacks whom you may employ to compile anthologies.' He resisted all suggestions for a collected edition of his poems, repeatedly arguing that *A Shropshire Lad* and *Last Poems* were entirely discrete volumes. The only occasion during his lifetime that they were published together was for a 'limited edition de luxe' ('the pompous edition', as he called it) in 1929. Housman agreed to this only 'reluctantly', perhaps bending his hitherto inflexible rule because the two volumes remained separate books within a single slipcase. His argument that the two books were entirely different entities is, however, undermined by our later knowledge that several poems eventually published in the second volume were originally intended for the first, and that the decision to remove five poems from *A Shropshire Lad* and add three others was taken only 'while the book was printing'.

The 'Englishness' of Housman's poetry has been widely recognised. 'If he reminds us of any other poet, it is (now and then) Heine,' the famous critic William Archer noted in an early review of *A Shropshire Lad*; 'yet he is English of the English.' The American poet Louise Imogen Guiney suggested a 'cried kinship' with *Englands Helicon*, the anthology of Elizabethan pastoral poetry published in 1600 and containing works by Shakespeare, Marlowe, Spenser, Drayton, Peele and others. There was, however, a difference, as Archer noted. He detected the influence of the Classics, but went on to suggest that 'The Shropshire of Mr Housman is no Arcadia, no Sicily, still less a courtly pleasaunce peopled with beribboned nymphs and swains. It is as real, and as tragic, as Mr [Thomas] Hardy's Wessex.'

That reality was emphasised by the use of real place-names, unlike those of Hardy, which were largely invented; but the places Housman mentioned were emblematic, sometimes bearing little relation to geographical reality. As Orwell noted, the book is 'full of the charm of buried villages, the nostalgia of place-names, Clunton and Clunbury, Knighton, Ludlow, "on Wenlock Edge", "in summer time on Bredon", thatched roofs and the jingle of smithies, the wild jonquils in the pastures of the "blue remembered hills".' It is much more than that, though. These place-names, however resonant for English readers, would be mostly unfamiliar to foreign ones. One of the earliest American reviewers pinpointed other aspects of Englishness embodied in the poems, noting of Housman's generic Lad, 'Like a true Englishman, he takes his pleasure sadly.' Quoting the first two stanzas of poem XVII, in which the Lad attempts to keep unhappiness in check by the very English expedient of playing football and cricket, the anonymous reviewer went on to add that 'In one of the most tragical lyrics [VIII], the crowning thought of desolation is delightfully English.' This is by way of a joke, since in the poem a man who will not be returning to the family home after murdering his brother reflects that the dinner his mother has prepared for him will have gone cold. It nevertheless points to that strain in English life and letters that is the very reverse of traditional American optimism.

There are always dangers – including those of stereotyping and over-simplification – in attempting to define national traits, but one person who repeatedly did so was the political theorist Sir Ernest Barker (1874–1960), who contrasted what he saw as English values with the kind of nationalism that led to political extremism in mainland Europe. Like Housman, Barker was a classicist from a rural background (in his case in Cheshire, where his father had been an agricultural labourer), and his work and writings were informed by his study of ancient authors. One of the topics addressed in Barker's *National Character and the Factors in Its Formation* (1927) is melancholy. 'A theme or note which is from first to last characteristic of our literature, and a secret of its influence, is one which we may name elegiac,' he writes. 'It is a sadness which is not weakness, and a lamentation which is not unmanly; a melancholy which is mixed with endurance, and a brooding on the passage of time which never becomes despair.' This is precisely the elegiac quality that one finds in Housman's poems, but that quality is also part of an English literary tradition that stretches back across many centuries. Barker quotes the literary scholar W.P. Ker, a colleague of Housman's at University College, London, and one of the three people whose advice he called upon when selecting the contents of *Last Poems*: 'The Anglo-Saxon genius for poetry is best known in the elegies – *The Wanderer*, *The Seafarer*, and others – to which there is nothing corresponding in Germany or Iceland. The English invented for themselves a form of elegy. They seem to have been more readily touched by motives of regret and lamentation than other people.'

In *The Wanderer*, one of the earliest surviving English poems, dating from around the eighth or ninth century, a solitary figure finds himself exiled from his home, cast adrift on an icy sea 'with winter in [his] heart'. Battling through atrocious English weather (frost, snow, wind and hail are all mentioned), he recalls his former life in the warm mead-halls of his beloved lord, whom he has buried after defeat in battle. Thus melancholy and nostalgia are present from the very beginnings of English literature. The notion that the English tendency towards nostalgia is bound up with the loss of empire or loss of power and prestige in the world certainly has some traction, but it overlooks a literary tradition that predates the zenith of imperialism by a millennium. Whatever the root cause, there remains in England a tendency to harp upon past glories rather than looking forward to a promising future, to look back upon a 'land of lost content' rather than suppose that, as that quintessentially American popular standard puts it, 'The Best Is Yet to Come'.

The English are also renowned for their sexual and emotional repression, and were particularly so during the period in which *A*

Shropshire Lad became popular. If in England the traditional landscape is green, lush and productive thanks to all that rain, the emotional terrain is generally thought of as somewhat arid, and Housman himself appeared to embody this perception. His reputation was that of a dry classical scholar, not someone at all likely to have produced anything as deeply felt as *A Shropshire Lad*. The apparent gulf between the lyric poet people met on the pages of *A Shropshire Lad* and *Last Poems* and the man they might, with persistence, meet at his rooms in Trinity College, Cambridge, or indeed be unlucky enough to find themselves placed next to at High Table, seemed both inexplicable and unbridgeable. In fact, at heart Housman was a romantic – though a romantic of a peculiarly doom-laden and tight-lipped English variety: because one is lapidary, it does not mean one has a heart of stone. The cynicism people detected in Housman's work was merely the obverse of the romantic medal, for what are cynics if not disappointed romantics? Furthermore, the repression that seemed to characterise Housman's life and conduct was precisely what produced the poetry and directed the form it took: deep emotion constrained by and contained within very short poems written in strictly observed verse forms.

All these elements contributed to the sense that *A Shropshire Lad* represented something recognisably and cherishably English. The book was published during a period in which what constituted England and Englishness had become a major preoccupation. On the surface, Britain had remained a stable, if very unequal, society during the latter part of Queen Victoria's reign, and its confidence and sense of itself was very much bound up in its empire. Technically, this may have been a British Empire, and many of its servants Scottish, Welsh and Irish, but it was ruled from England and the values it disseminated around the globe were regarded as characteristically 'English'. This was reflected in some of the seminal texts on empire published in the latter half of the nineteenth century. While Charles Dilke called his 1868 book *Greater Britain*, in describing the travels that inspired it, which took him to America, Canada, Australia, New Zealand and India, he wrote: 'I followed England round the world: everywhere I was in English-speaking, or in English-governed lands. If I remarked that the climate, soil, manners of life, that mixture with other peoples had modified the blood, I saw, too, that in essentials the race was always one.' That race too was 'English' rather than 'British'.

Dilke is now chiefly remembered as one of the main players in a sensational Victorian divorce case, but the book he wrote as a young man proved very popular, running rapidly through four impressions and remaining a key imperial text well into the twentieth century. J.R. Seeley's book on imperialism was unequivocally titled *The Expansion of England* and proved even more popular and enduring: published in 1883, it sold around 80,000 copies in its first two years and was still in print at the time of the Suez Crisis in 1956. J.W. Froude's *Oceana* (1886) was subtitled 'England and her Colonies', and in the book he referred to those colonies as 'other Englands'. Like Dilke, Froude had travelled before writing his book and was happy to report that 'Amid the uncertainties which are gathering around us at home [. . .] it is something to have seen with our own eyes that there are other Englands beside the old one, where the race is thriving with all its ancient characteristics.' These ancient characteristics took one back to a time not only before the Acts of Union which united England with Ireland (1801) and Scotland (1707), but even before the Principality of Wales had been subsumed into the Kingdom of England in 1536. Dilke, for example, had written of the global spread of 'Alfred's laws and Chaucer's tongue' to form an imaginary realm he dubbed 'Saxondom'.

In the nineteenth century 'British' values may well have seemed less easy to define than 'English' ones, since they needed to take account of characteristics that were specifically Scottish, Welsh or Irish. Unlike England, those nations were Celtic and had their own languages and customs, though these had to some extent been eroded by centuries of English rule. The separating out of a pure and unalloyed England from the amalgam that was Britain was essentially a nineteenth-century idea – so much so that in 1867 Matthew Arnold could claim that 'in England the Englishman proper is in union of spirit with no one except other Englishmen proper like himself. His Welsh and Irish fellow-citizens are hardly more amalgamated with him now than they were when Wales and Ireland were first conquered.'

In the eighteenth century 'England' and 'Britain' had been more or less interchangeable, as can be seen in two patriotic songs of the period,

'The Roast Beef of Old England' and 'Rule, Britannia!' The words of the former were written by Henry Fielding in 1731 and became a hugely popular ballad when set to music by Richard Leveridge four years later. Fielding laments the current state of the nation and looks back to an age when proper solid English food ensured the country's physical and moral health:

> When mighty Roast Beef was the Englishman's food,
> It ennobled our brains and enriched our blood.
> Our soldiers were brave and our courtiers were good
>> Oh! the Roast Beef of old England,
>> And old English Roast Beef!

'Rule, Britannia!', dating from 1740 with words by James Thomson set to a rousing tune by Thomas Arne, similarly became a popular patriotic song and proved even more enduring. Thomson is best known for *The Seasons* (1730), a cycle of poems about the English countryside, but he was in fact Scottish by birth, having come to London as a young man to make his literary career and remained there for the rest of his short life. Born in 1700, he was of the first generation to grow up in a Scotland united with England, and 'Rule, Britannia!' reflects his interest in forging a new 'British' identity. The song opens with Britain rising from the sea 'at Heaven's command', and while the reference was clearly to Britain's naval supremacy, of vital importance to an island nation, in more general terms the song celebrated a country free from tyranny, its natural beauty kept secure by its stalwart inhabitants:

> Blest isle! With matchless beauty crown'd,
> And many hearts to guard the fair.

These lines owe something to both the aria 'Fairest Isle' in Purcell and Dryden's opera *King Arthur* and the famous speech in Shakespeare's *Richard II*, which hymns 'this scepter'd isle [. . .] This precious stone set in the silver sea' and builds to the climactic paean: 'This blessed plot, this earth, this realm, this England.'

Fielding's vision of a lost society in which 'Our fathers of old were robust, stout, and strong, / And kept open house, with good cheer all day long, / Which made their plump tenants rejoice in this song' came to be known as 'Merry England'. This was an almost prelapsarian world, essentially rural and based around the more cheerful rituals of the church calendar, dancing round maypoles, swilling ale and enjoying a kind of painless feudalism. The term stretches back a long way, but was popularised by William Hazlitt in an essay of that title published in 1819. The denizens of Hazlitt's Merry England were a people who enjoyed cricket, field sports and practical jokes, the open air in summer and the cosy fireside, with a perpetually blazing log, in winter. Their merriness was spontaneous and anarchic, generally reserved for 'high-days and holidays', but also wholesome: 'They are not gay like the French, who are one eternal smile of self-complacency, tortured into affectation, or spun into languid indifference, nor are they voluptuous and immersed in sensual indolence, like the Italians.'

Hazlitt's affectionate caricature mentions Robin Hood and 'Merry Sherwood', but not the Arthurian legends that were taken up as a model of 'Englishness' later in the century. Arthurian knights represented a noble rather than a merry England: chivalrous, virtuous, courageous, their exploits recounted by Sir Thomas Malory in *Le Morte d'Arthur*, published in 1485. The golden age of chivalry was the Middle Ages, but it saw a revival in the reign of Elizabeth I, forming the basis of Edmund Spenser's epic *The Faerie Queene* (1590), an Arthurian allegory in praise of Elizabeth and the knightly virtues of her courtiers. The Elizabethan period was close enough to the medieval period to make its embrace of chivalry seem a plausible 'Indian summer', and any revival there-after seemed unlikely. In the early years of the Industrial Revolution Edmund Burke was able to announce that 'the age of chivalry is gone. That of sophisters, economists, and calculators, has succeeded; and the glory of England is extinguished for ever.' In fact, not only was the glory of England reanimated in the nineteenth century, but a new age of chivalry was ushered in.

This revival of chivalry was a conscious anachronism in which art, literature and fancy dress all played their part. The novels of Sir Walter Scott, the poems of Alfred Tennyson and the paintings of the Pre-Raphaelites all drew upon a romanticised version of the chivalric tradition. England was after all a country that had an armour-clad knight, St George, as its patron saint and featured a 'verray, parfit, gentil knyght' as a pilgrim-narrator in one of its founding literary texts, Chaucer's *Canterbury Tales*. Such figures embodied all the virtues of what became known as a Christian English gentleman, and the public schools which flourished in the nineteenth century aimed to produce generation after generation of this paragon. Cyril Norwood, head-master successively of Bristol Grammar School, Marlborough College and Harrow, would claim that 'The ideal of chivalry which inspired the knighthood of medieval days, the ideal of service to the community which inspired the greatest men who founded schools for their day and for posterity, have been combined in the tradition of English education which holds the field today.' This was the kind of education that produced the country's leaders and the English country gentlemen who would preside over rural society. If country estates were not quite Camelot, they represented a social order in which the lord of the manor exercised a benevolent paternalism, looking after the material and spiritual needs of those who lived and worked on his estate. This resulted in a society that was rigidly stratified but considered just. As Mrs C.F. Alexander succinctly put it in her popular 1848 hymn 'All things bright and beautiful':

> The rich man in his castle,
> The poor man at his gate,
> God made them high and lowly,
> And ordered their estate.

The landowner supposedly kept his side of the social contract out of a sense of duty, which was itself a tithe paid to privilege. As the nineteenth century progressed, this ideal was held up in contrast to the newly rich industrialists who, having missed out on the proper training provided by the public schools, supposedly felt no such obligations towards their workforce.

The consolidation of the concept of Englishness was emphasised not only by the public schools but in such cultural enterprises as the *Oxford English Dictionary*, which began publication in 1884; the *Dictionary of*

National Biography, which first appeared the following year; the National Trust, founded in 1895 to preserve both the landscape and important historic buildings; the National Portrait Gallery, which opened in 1896; and a National Gallery of British Art (now Tate Britain), which opened in 1897. England's long literary tradition had been celebrated in Francis Palgrave's *The Golden Treasury of the Best Songs and Lyrical Poems in the English Language*, which was first published in 1861 and, having run through twenty-three reprints in thirty years, was revised and expanded in 1891. The best of English lyric poetry, in Palgrave's plan, would be disseminated throughout the world: 'wherever the Poets of England are honoured, wherever the dominant language of the world is spoken, it is hoped that they will find fit audience.'

Further education was another way of promoting national identity. University College, London, had introduced the study of English Language and Literature as a degree subject as early as 1828, but it was in 1893 that Oxford University created its own school devoted to these subjects with the intention of reaching out to students who had not received a classical education earlier in life. English Literature, it was argued, 'deepened our sense of the import of nationality by giving the most intense and at the same time most manifold expression of it'. Indeed, early English Literature courses required a working knowledge of English history on the grounds that the study of literature alone was essentially frivolous and undisciplined, 'mere chatter about Shelley'. As with literature, one of the principal concerns of history as taught in universities was how it reflected the character of a society or a nation. Arthur Quiller-Couch, who did much to promote English literature with such anthologies as *The Golden Pomp: A Procession of English Lyrics from Surrey to Shirley* (1895), the first *Oxford Book of English Verse* (1900) and the *Oxford Book of Ballads* (1911), recalled the experience of reading Edward A. Freeman's *History of the Norman Conquest* (1867–76) and J.R. Green's *A Short History of the English People* (1874), 'in which as through parting clouds of darkness we beheld our ancestry, literary as well as political, radiantly legitimised'. The *English Historical Review* was founded in 1886, and in 1900 English history was made a compulsory part of education in secondary schools.

An attempt to spread a proper appreciation of what it meant to be

English throughout the population was one of the motivating forces behind the 'missionary work' carried out by undergraduates in the East End of London. Just as servants of the Empire brought the supposed benefits of English culture and education to the 'natives' of India and Africa, so young men from Oxbridge and the public schools spread their ethos among the urban lower orders. That this represented a kind of cultural takeover-bid was happily acknowledged: 'Colonisation by the well-to-do seems indeed the true solution to the East End question,' read the first annual report of the Oxford House Mission in 1884, 'for the problem is, how to make the masses realise their spiritual and social solidarity with the rest of the capital and the kingdom.' East Enders undoubtedly had their own notions of what constituted Englishness, but cultural cohesiveness was seen by the ruling classes as a way both of uniting the nation and countering the threat of rising socialism.

Despite such missions among the urban masses, the countryside remained the true locus of 'Englishness'. England has always been defined by its landscape. The 'scepter'd isle' of John of Gaunt's speech in *Richard II* is rural rather than urban: another Eden, a 'fortress built by Nature for herself'. The idealised England of this period was characterised by extensive forests in which royalty and the nobility hunted game, dukes lived in exile and outlaws hid. And right at its centre, covering much of the county of Warwickshire, was the huge and ancient Forest of Arden, where Shakespeare grew up, which gave his mother her surname, and which is the nominal setting of *As You Like It*. The English landscape defines English poetry (from William Wordsworth's 'Daffodils' to Edward Thomas's 'Adlestrop'), English painting (Constable and Turner) and English music (Elgar and Vaughan Williams). There are of course other, urban Englands, but the increasingly mythic rural one persists as an idea. Even as late as 1947, in the wake of a war characterised by the destruction of English cities by aerial bombardment, it seems inevitable that the first chapter of a book titled *The Character of England* (edited by Sir Ernest Barker) should consider 'Land and People', as if they were indivisible, and open with the description of a man lying on sheep-cropped downland in high summer. The chapter considers how man fits into this landscape, how he 'has been deeply affected by the character of the small land-mass which time has made and he has called England'. Urban England is acknowledged, but it is seen as a comparatively recent development: 'Towns came late to England and even then, in the Roman Province, not very successfully. In the fifteenth century sophisticated Italians mocked the English gentleman's devotion to his own clods.' The Industrial Revolution brought great change, but even in 1947 there 'have not yet been many generations born in urban surroundings so deep that isolation from nature is almost complete'. The authors continue: 'It is not that the worst towns lack their own startling beauties and a power to awaken the nostalgic devotion of their inhabitants. Yet we are, after all, one with our ancestors; and the inheritance from innumerable generations of lives spent in the closest contact with natural things is still within us. It is noticeable, for instance, that most poetic images still seem to well up from some store of non-urban, non-mechanical impressions, and wholly urban poetry is difficult to conceive.'

Poetry celebrating the modern bustling city had in fact been very much in vogue at the end of the nineteenth century, and after the Georgian interlude it had a revival in the Modernist period, so it was hardly inconceivable in 1947. However, the pastoral 'tradition' of English poetry proved enduring, and the location of *A Shropshire Lad* in a particular if largely imaginary English landscape was a major contribution to the book's popularity and longevity.

Recent debates in Britain about education and immigration have often focused on 'British' or 'English' values, which those on either side of the argument seem hard put to define, preferring merely to flourish the notion like a flag. In 2012 the then Education Secretary, Michael Gove, decided that primary-school pupils should learn poetry by rote, a suggestion that many teachers felt was wholly retrograde and likely to put children off poetry altogether. When the issue was discussed on BBC Television's *Question Time*, a member of the audience asked the panellists to recite a poem they had learned at school and explain how this had been 'useful' in their subsequent careers. The right-wing columnist and controversialist Peter Hitchens was the only panellist prepared to answer the challenge directly. He recited Housman's 'Into my heart an air that kills', and went on to argue that to have such poems in one's head was spiritually enriching: 'I feel very sorry for anyone who hasn't had a chance to learn them. Of *course* people need these things, and what's more they're a *profound* part of being British. If you don't know the literature and the poetry and the music of your own country, then you aren't really fully conversant with its history or its character.'

This particular poem was perhaps an inevitable choice for some-one of Hitchens' generation (he was born in 1951) both to recite and to take as representing part of what it meant to be British. Hitchens is not, however, alone in valuing Housman for his English qualities, as the assessment by Ted Hughes at the head of this chapter testi-fies. Hughes's fellow poet Charles Causley described Housman as a 'peculiarly "English" poet [and] undoubtedly one of our finest lyri-cists'. William Hayes, the Irish physicist who served as president of Housman's Oxford college from 1987 to 2001, suggested that 'the Englishness of Housman's poetry is something which in the century has been approached only by Thomas Hardy and Philip Larkin, both warm admirers of his genius. The long-standing tradition of English poets who have drawn from all that is rich in the English landscape and tradition is recapitulated and carried forward in his poetry.' For the writer and politician Roy Hattersley, '*A Shropshire Lad* is a great statement of English rural life and the nostalgia for our Arcadian past.'

Housman's determination that *A Shropshire Lad* should be both affordable and portable meant that people could take it with them when they set off to defend England and Englishness on those occasions the country came under threat. The book fitted very neatly into the pock-ets of military uniforms in both world wars. When the grandfather of the writer Salley Vickers set off for the trenches in 1916, his wife gave him a copy of *A Shropshire Lad* so that he could, as she put it, carry 'a piece of England' in his breast pocket. She also gave him a cigarette case inscribed with a line from Shakespeare's Sonnet XCVII: 'And thou away, the very birds are mute'. The cigarette case was returned to her after he was killed in action, but not the book. She therefore bought another copy to give to her son, who had been only a few weeks old when his father left for the front. When it was his turn to march away to his own war, Vickers's father gave this copy to his new wife, telling her that if, like his father before him, he failed to return, he wanted her to have the book as a remembrance of them both. He knew most of the poems, and those of Edward Thomas, by heart and so carried them in his head rather than his pocket. This proved essential when, captured shortly before Dunkirk, he entered a German prisoner-of-war camp, where he would spend the rest of the war. To while away the time, inmates gave each other lessons; he taught modern poetry, with a particular emphasis on Housman and Thomas, both of whom kept alive his memories of the English countryside he so loved.

If men such as this felt that they were carrying England in their pockets and in their hearts, what was this England, and how did Housman's poetry come to represent it? Why is it that for many people 'England' has always meant an unspoilt rural landscape rather than the ever-changing urban world in which most English people live? What was the 'England' for which people fought in two world wars? Why were English composers at the beginning of the twentieth century so drawn to traditional folk song, and why did pastoral become the defining idiom, creating a national music that avoided being nationalistic? And why do these poems continue to attract composers, both classical and popular? What was it about this little book of sixty-three poems that appealed to people, and continues all these years later to appeal to people, and how did Housman come to write it?

'Housman Country' is very much more than a tourist-board notion, and in this book I go in search of a landscape that is not merely geographical, but also literary, musical, emotional, even, in the broadest sense, spiritual. In terms of accurate topographical measurements, the real Shropshire is not quite at the heart of England, but it is close. Much the same might be said of *A Shropshire Lad*, which has over the years embodied a notion of England's land and character. Although people have used the book, so rich in allusions to real places, as a kind of guidebook to a specific English region, it could more accurately be described as a gazetteer of the English heart.

II

THE MAN AND HIS BOOK

Some men are better than their books, but my books are
better than their man.

A.E. Housman, 13 September 1933

To anyone taking the air on Hampstead Heath in 1895, he would
have been a familiar figure: a determinedly solitary man in his
mid-thirties, walking energetically, apparently absorbed in his own
thoughts. Slight in build (he had been nicknamed 'Mouse' at school),
neatly and formally dressed, his unusually small feet clad in elastic-
sided boots, he would not have made much impression except for the
fact that he was so often there. Anyone passing him might have taken
him for a clerk, which had until recently been his job, though others
might have detected something faintly military in his bearing.

Hampstead Heath, some 790 acres of common land, was at that
time an expanse of more or less wild English countryside, consisting of
open spaces, woods and ponds, on what was then the northern fringe
of London. It had long been a popular destination for Londoners in
search of fresh air and healthy recreation, and from its highest point it
commanded clear views right across the capital. It had strong poetic
associations: Keats had lived in Hampstead, Coleridge in nearby
Highgate, and the two men had first met while out walking in April
1819, introduced by a mutual friend. Talking non-stop, they had spent
some two hours in each other's company, walking at Coleridge's

'alderman-after dinner pace for near two miles'. When they parted, Keats went a little way before running back and saying: 'Let me carry away the memory, Coleridge, of having pressed your hand!' For his part, Coleridge carried away with him intimations of mortality, remarking to his companion after Keats had gone, 'There is death in that hand.' Amongst many other things, their conversation covered the topic of nightingales, and shortly afterwards, while listening to a bird in his Hampstead garden, Keats wrote his celebrated ode.

The solitary figure walking there some seventy-six years later was also a poet, though he would not have stated this as his occupation and had not yet published a volume of his verse. When he did so the following year, some thought his poems more Classical than Romantic – having relinquished the life of a clerk, A.E. Housman was now earning his livelihood as a professor of Latin – but, like those of Keats, the poems were much concerned with death and the natural world. Housman lived at 17 North Road, Highgate in a house called Byron Cottage, named not after Keats's fellow Romantic but, rather more prosaically, after a governor at a local school. It was about midway between the Heath and Highgate Wood, which had been Housman's favourite haunt until the previous year. Highgate Wood was 70 acres of ancient woodland, a remnant of the vast Forest of Middlesex that covered much of what is now London, as well as parts of Hertfordshire and Essex. The wood had become the property of the Mayor and Commonality and the Citizens of the City of London in 1886, the year Housman had come to live in Highgate. A country boy, Housman had particularly valued the sense one had while walking in this untamed wood of being insulated from the surrounding late-Victorian urban sprawl, and he was not at all pleased when the authorities began tidying it up. In 1894 he wrote a letter to the *Standard* newspaper, which published it on 14 March. Before the wood was acquired for Londoners, he wrote, it was

in a very sad state. So thickly was it overgrown with brushwood, that if you stood in the centre you could not see the linen of the inhabitants of Archway-road hanging to dry in their back gardens. Nor could you see the advertisement for Juggins' stout and porter which surmounts the front of the public house at the south corner of the Wood [. . .] Scarlet flannel petticoats are much worn in Archway-road, and if anyone desires to feast his eyes on these very bright and picturesque objects, so seldom seen in the streets, let him repair to the centre of Highgate Wood.

Trees had also been felled on the north side of the wood, he continued, which meant that people would 'soon be able to look at the railway when they are tired of porter and petticoats'. It appeared, however, that the authorities still had work to do: 'there are a number of new red-brick houses on the east side of the Wood, and I regret to say that I observe no clearing of timber in that direction. Surely, Sir, a man who stands in the centre of the Wood, and knows that there are new red-brick houses to the east of him, will not be happy until he sees them.' Walks screened from railway lines, red-brick villas, scarlet petticoats and adverts for stout were what the correspondent needed in order to write his poetry, in which the contrast between country and urban living was a principal theme.

The letter also suggests Housman's customary mode of discourse, the ironic wit that characterises his correspondence and which he employed most savagely when discussing in print the editorial endeavours of his fellow classicists. Irony was equally a feature of his poetry, sometimes biting, sometimes rueful, the perhaps inevitable strategy of someone who had at an early age seen God's works clearly and found them wanting. It was this that made A.E. Housman seem modern as a poet, even while the verse forms he employed were very traditional. If not a Modernist – not for him the free-verse experiments of T.S. Eliot or Ezra Pound – he was nevertheless, thought Louis MacNeice, the poet 'with whom any history of modern English poetry might very well start'. Indeed, Housman was where MacNeice proposed starting a critical book titled *Modern Poetry*, which the Oxford University Press commissioned him to write in 1937.

Although *A Shropshire Lad* was published in the final decade of the Victorian era, Housman agreed that the book was a chronological anomaly. When asked by A.J.A. Symons for permission to include some of the poems in *A Book of Nineties Verse*, Housman issued through his publisher the customary refusal he gave to anthologists, but mischievously added that Symons 'may be consoled, and also amused, if you tell him that to include me in an anthology of the Nineties would be just as technically correct, and just as essentially inappropriate, as to include Lot in a book on Sodomites'. Janus-like, Housman looked back to the traditional prosody and verse forms of Victorian poetry and forward to a modern world in which irony and stoicism had replaced the long-standing consolations of the Christian faith. In this, as in much else, he resembled Thomas Hardy, another writer who straddled the Victorian and modern ages.

When *A Shropshire Lad* first appeared in 1896 its author was completely unknown outside academic circles. Over a century later, the book and the man are so much of a piece that we find it difficult to separate them one from the other, much as Housman would have liked us to. In addition, we now know a great deal about the author and about what led him to write his poems, so we have to imagine ourselves back to a time when it was the poems alone that caught the reading public's imagination. Housman's original intention had been to publish the volume anonymously under the title *Poems by Terence Hearsay*. It has been suggested that Housman borrowed 'Terence' from the Latin playwright who, brought from North Africa to Rome as a slave, had spent his life in exile from his homeland, a major theme of *A Shropshire Lad*. 'Hearsay' sounds like the surname of a Shakespearean rustic, while also suggesting something unsubstantiated, or even proverbial, perhaps evoking folk memories. Fortunately, the one friend to whom Housman showed the poems before submitting them for publication, his Oxford contemporary A.W. Pollard, suggested changing the title to what now seems the only possible one. The sole traces of Housman's original intention are that 'Terence' is the author to whom a friend complains in the book's penultimate poem, 'Terence, this is stupid stuff', and the person who is told to 'look your last on me' by one of the collection's rural criminals in 'Farewell to barn and stack and tree' (VII). This imaginary author of the poems has otherwise disappeared from the book – if indeed he was ever a real presence there.

Even Housman's name on the paper label pasted on the book's spine would have meant nothing to readers who did not already know the author in his academic guise. No biographical information was pro-vided, as it would be today, and this is exactly as Housman would have wished. In the days before mass communication, professional publicists and the eternal round of literary festivals, the only way most readers met a writer was on the page. Some months after *A Shropshire Lad* was published a bare outline of Housman's life was printed in the *Bookman* magazine's 'New Writers' section, but this focused principally upon his work as a classical scholar. Even when the book began to achieve widespread popularity, Housman deflected any attempts to elicit infor-mation about its author.

1

The Man

'Housman is one of my heroes and always has been,' the American poet John Berryman once said. 'He was a detestable and miserable man. Arrogant, unspeakably lonely, cruel, and so on, but an absolutely marvellous minor poet, I think, and a great scholar.' Berryman had never in fact met Housman, but he was not alone in loving the work at the same time as deploring the character of the man who wrote it. Housman's natural reticence and solitary habits, his apparent failure to form any satisfactory emotional attachment, his devotion to the drier aspects of classical scholarship, and his habit of brusquely rebuffing those who complimented him or asked him about his poetry, have led to descriptions of him as (amongst other things) austere, unapproach-able, aloof, taciturn, arrogant, rude, bitter, morbid, self-pitying, even 'self-loathing'. Those who knew Housman well, however, insisted he could also be clubbable, amusing, and a good conversationalist. The merciless critic who noted down caustic comments as they came to him, with blanks left where names could be filled in when the public occasion arose, was also capable of great kindness and generosity. The scholar whose rooms in Whewell's Court at Trinity struck visitors as self-punishingly uncomfortable and cheerless also relished good food and fine wines and would never miss his college's New Year's Eve feast of oysters and stout. The man who knew that he was not only judged the finest classical scholar of his generation but also a poet whose verses were appreciated by thousands of ordinary readers appeared to have a horror of being praised to his face and fastidiously turned down every academic and other honour offered to him, including in 1929 the Order of Merit, and the post of Poet Laureate the following year.

For all the reports of Housman's moroseness, the wife of his brother Basil remembered a much more light-hearted figure. 'He always seemed to enjoy things and be happy,' she recalled. 'I have known him and Basil laugh until they cried.' This is the Housman who wrote genuinely funny nonsense poetry and boasted that he was responsible for introducing the comic jazz-age fiction of Anita Loos to England. The notion of the supposedly dour and misogynistic Housman enjoying the gold-digging hi-jinks of Lorelei Lee seems unlikely, but he nevertheless insisted: 'I read *Gentlemen Prefer Blondes*, and told my Cambridge friends about it, and before I knew it everyone in the University was reading it, and thereafter the delightful work became popular throughout England.'

Even those who saw Housman regularly could find themselves in two minds about him. A.C. Benson, a fellow member of a small private dining club in Cambridge called The Family, wrote several entries about Housman in his voluminous diaries. In his biography of Housman, Norman Page traces Benson's fluctuating opinions of his colleague, at one moment judged 'very pleasant . . . very friendly and companionable', at another someone who 'sits prim and grim, and casts a chill over the table'. It would seem that Housman's mood was as changeable as the company in which he found himself, and Benson conceded that, although 'shy and formal in manner', he relaxed as he 'warmed up'. Not that Benson much cared for this warmed-up version: 'as he got easier he got *vulgar*'. This appears to be a coded reference to Housman's taste for risqué stories, which the overly fastidious Benson found 'not funny, only abominable'.

Attempts to explain the apparent contradictions in Housman's character began as soon as he was dead. The obituary in *The Times* (to which it is thought Benson at the very least contributed) was more or less constructed around antitheses:

He was a good raconteur, of the pithy and caustic order, and was by no means averse to gossip, nor incurious of the vagaries of human nature. He would sometimes surprise a party by a long quotation, made with rhetorical emphasis and gesture. But on occasions he would be so unapproachable as to diffuse a frost, and shroud himself in impenetrable reserve. He spoke freely of his views and prejudices, which were of an aristocratic and even contemptuous order, but he was most reticent about his experiences.

Housman very seldom betrayed in public any of the passionate emotion which often slips through the fence of his verse, and appeared of all men least tolerant of sentiment. In fact, in his attitude to life, there seemed something baffled and even shrinking, as though he feared criticism and emotion alike more than he relished experience. But he could not be called fastidious so much as impatient of conventions and stupidities. He valued confidence, but held back from intimate relations, and seemed to prefer isolation to giving himself away.

The artist William Rothenstein recognised that 'underneath the dry asperity lay an odd affectionateness'. Rothenstein had long experience of this since Housman never tired of telling him gleefully how much he disliked his portraits of him. Housman's habit of sharp teasing is evidence of this combination of asperity and affection. Teasing is a very English way of showing affection without being too obvious about it, mockery deflecting attention from anything as embarrassing or incriminating as a declaration of fondness, and this was Housman's customary tactic in his correspondence, particularly in letters to those such as Rothenstein and his wife, whom he genuinely liked and counted as friends. Cordiality rather than true intimacy characterised Housman's relationships with such people. Congenial company rather than exchanged confidences was what he apparently sought in a friendship, and, although he could express heartfelt sympathy when people were ill, bereaved, or otherwise in trouble, most of his letters to friends and family tend to be funny at their or his expense.

The author and his publisher

Irony, deployed with varying degrees of gentleness, is also a way of expressing dissatisfaction without (supposedly) causing hurt or offence, and so proved particularly useful to Housman in his dealings with his publisher, of whom he appears to have been genuinely fond but frequently found exasperating – a not uncommon sentiment among authors. However much publishing has traditionally been touted (mostly by publishers themselves) as a gentlemanly trade in which the signing of contracts and payment of royalties are regrettable commercial incursions into the otherwise convivial relationship between editor and author, most writers maintain a sensible distance between themselves and the people responsible for bringing them into print and keeping them there. In Housman's case, these protective boundaries soon dissolved, and on several occasions the customary financial arrangements between author and publisher became reversed.

Of Housman's enduring friendships, the one with Grant Richards is the most fully documented. Richards appears to have kept almost every letter he received from Housman and made these the basis of his 1941 memoir, *Housman 1897–1936*. Although Richards could be obtuse, and was careful to skate around potentially difficult episodes to do with finance and sexuality, his portrait of Housman nevertheless remains one of the best we have, based as it was on a personal and professional relationship lasting almost forty years. It was a relationship that showed Housman to his best advantage: meticulous, funny, patient, generous and loyal.

Housman's very first letter to Richards, who had expressed an interest in taking over the unsold copies of the first edition of *A Shropshire Lad* and issuing a second one, set the tone for all future correspondence. 'I suppose no author is averse to see his works in a second edition, or slow to take advantage of an infatuated publisher,' he wrote, 'and it is impossible not to be touched by the engaging form which your infatuation takes.' He then went on to warn Richards that even if he paid no royalty he would most likely end up out of pocket. Housman would also 'have to ask Kegan Paul if their feelings would be lacerated by the transfer. I do not think very much of them as men of business, but their manager has been nice to me and takes a sentimental interest in the book, like you.' He ended the letter: 'At the present moment I can think of nothing else to damp your ardour.' Housman was clearly pleased that publishers liked his poems, but was careful to employ irony – 'infatuated', 'lacerated', 'sentimental', 'ardour' – in order not to appear *too* pleased or to lay himself open to accusations of taking commercial flattery too seriously.

Having come to terms, Housman wrote that 'after the book is set up I should like to have the sheets to correct, as I don't trust printers or proof-readers in the matter of punctuation'. He was right not to do so, and many of his letters contain wholly justified complaints about misprints, which regularly occurred in new editions of *A Shropshire Lad*. Richards's second edition (1898) was particularly corrupt, and when the publisher proposed a subsequent pocket edition of the book, Housman wrote: 'I should like to correct the proofs and to have them printed as I correct them. Last time some one played games with the punctuation' – games that resulted in forty alterations of punctuation ('30 additions, 8 substitutions, and 2 deletions'), three changes of spelling, some missing letters and the alternate lines of one poem losing their indentation. In spite of Housman's corrections, misprints continued to appear. 'I enclose a copy of our joint work,' he wrote in 1904, sending Richards a marked-up copy of the fifth edition of the poems. 'The results of your collaboration are noted on pages 4, 22, 45, 55, 71, 77, 78, 92, 116.'

Housman was also displeased that, without consulting him, Richards had included this edition in a series titled 'The Smaller Classics'; it was, he said, 'unbecoming that the work of a living writer should appear under such a title', and he took the opportunity to remove it from the imprint two years later. He went on to tell Richards 'how atrociously you behaved in ever including the book in the series, and how glad I am to have the chance of stopping the scandal', but characteristically followed this scolding by expressing the hope that he and Richards might be able to meet up in Paris the following week. What Housman would call 'the atrocious production of 1904' would thereafter be held up as the low point in Richards's publications, although the publisher's editions of Housman's classical works gave further opportunity for 'the usual blunders – numerals wrong, letters upside-down, stops missing, and so on'. Things had not much improved by the time *Last Poems* appeared. In a prefatory note, Housman explained that he was publishing the book 'while I am here to see it through the press and control its spelling and punctuation'; against this in his own copy he wrote 'Vain hope!'

Richards was a man of wide literary sympathies and considerable charm, who shared Housman's enthusiasm for travel, good food and fine wines. The two men often met to lunch or dine in London and made regular gastronomic tours of France together, Housman courageously becoming one of the first people to take frequent advantage of newly introduced and occasionally hazardous commercial aeroplane flights to the Continent. Housman also much enjoyed visiting churches and cathedrals, for architectural rather than religious reasons, but this was an enthusiasm Richards did not share, confessing that he was more likely to remember a good lunch than a noble building. Nevertheless, as far as he was fond of anyone outside his family, Housman was fond of Richards; he even took an interest in the publisher's wife and children, occasionally joining them on holidays and becoming a regular visitor to their succession of homes in the country.

In his trade Richards was a maverick, skilled at both publishing books and publicising them, notably in a column he wrote for the *Times Literary Supplement*. He also hit upon the novel idea of printing in advertisements extracts from unfavourable reviews of books he knew to be controversial, such as Alec Waugh's outspoken public-school novel, *The Loom of Youth* (1917). He published both highbrow and popular books, from George Bernard Shaw and James Joyce to Warwick Deeping and Thomas Burke, the author of *Limehouse Nights* (1916). Alongside commercially successful anthologies and travel guides, his list included books that would become twentieth-century classics, such as Samuel Butler's *The Way of All Flesh* (1902) and Robert Tressell's *The Ragged Trousered Philanthropists* (1914), as well as such representatives of the avant-garde as Osbert and Sacheverell Sitwell and (at the author's expense) Ronald Firbank.

Unfortunately, while Richards took commendable literary risks, he sometimes did so without the wherewithal to support his boldness, and he was first declared bankrupt in 1905. Housman sent a letter of sympathy in which he said he would presumably have to find another publisher for his edition of Juvenal's satires – by which he meant some-one whom he would pay to produce the book. He added that he was content to leave *A Shropshire Lad* where it was, which turned out to be with E. Grant Richards, since Richards relaunched the firm under his wife's name. He was officially 'manager' of the new company, but neither his role nor his financial mismanagement appreciably altered.

By 1908, although still paying off creditors, he took the publishing house back into his own name, and it appeared to prosper, the steadily increasing sales of Housman's royalty-free volume no doubt helping to keep the company stable. By December 1920, however, Richards was once again in difficulties, and Housman wrote him a cheque for £500. (To put this amount in perspective, it represented half the annual salary he was at that time receiving as Kennedy Professor of Latin at Cambridge.) 'I hope this will be some good,' he wrote after explaining that claims upon him from 'other friends' prevented him from lending more: 'I am not losing interest, as I always keep in my current account enough money to flee the country with' – the joke clearly intended to dispel any embarrassment Richards might be feeling and to forestall too fulsome an expression of gratitude. As Housman no doubt realised, the chances of reclaiming this money were slight, and ten months later Richards (clearly unembarrassed) applied for a further loan. Housman gently rejected the appeal, explaining that in addition to the £500 he had already given Richards he had other outstanding loans amounting to £600, half of which he did not expect to get back. 'Naturally, your troubles make me unhappy,' he wrote, 'and I hope you will not increase them by vexing yourself about repaying the £500. I shall never think of it.'

A week later, Housman sent Richards another £300, explaining that one of his loans had just been repaid. This at least helped keep the firm afloat and able to publish *Last Poems*, but Housman had begun to suspect that Richards was not passing on American royalties, and so in January 1924 he arranged for them to be sent to him directly. He was suffi-ciently put out to cease corresponding with Richards personally, only writing letters to the firm. This *froideur* persisted throughout much of the year, and when Housman did again write to Richards directly, on 1 October, about Lovat Fraser's proposed illustrations for *A Shropshire Lad*, he added: 'As matters stand it would cause me embarrassment to stay or dine with you.' A month later relations had thawed sufficiently for Housman to mention the excellence of some sherry Richards had sent him two years before.

The friendship was restored, but in 1926 Richards filed for bankruptcy a second time. The receiver informed Housman that he was due £5 12s 3d for recent sales of his editions of Manilius and Juvenal and for royalties on *Last Poems*. In fact, Housman had received no money for a very long time: in addition to this small sum, he was also owed £1014 11s 8d for sales and royalties going back to 1921. At this point, Housman finally took steps to protect his interests by consulting a solicitor; he also decided that in future he would 'exact' (as he put it) royalties on *A Shropshire Lad*. Even so, he seemed to bear no grudge and the following year he and Richards met up in Paris and spent a happy fortnight 'eating and drinking our way to Dijon'.

When news of Richards's difficulties became public, Housman had been approached by at least one other publisher, but he later said that moving elsewhere would have been a bother. This may have been true, but in spite of considerable provocation Housman remained steadfastly loyal to Richards. As Laurence Housman wrote, although his brother could be very severe about defects of scholarship, he was more forgiving of moral failings: 'Even deflections from rectitude which he would not have tolerated in himself, caused no withdrawal of aid when once it had been proffered; and in a case known to me, conduct which he described as "nefarious" did not alter relations of real personal friendship between him and the offender, though the offence was to himself.'

What have you in your heart?

Richards was clearly one of those few people with whom Housman felt he could relax, even to the point of making sly allusions to such topics as sodomy and *bains de vapeur*. That said, Richards was at pains in his vivid memoir of Housman to refute all hints of possible homosexuality, or anything that 'puts a stigma on Housman's reputation that is entirely unwarranted'. In spite of the language he uses, Richards was a man of the world who had books on his list (by Alec Waugh and Ronald Firbank, for example) in which overt homosexuality, both male and female, provided a principal theme. It is unclear why he should be so vehement, unless he thought that what he called 'a distorted nature discovered through the medium of his poems' would alienate potential readers from Housman's popular and (to his publisher) highly lucrative publications. When he asserted that 'There is no single thing that I observed in my forty years of association with [Housman] that cannot be told openly,' he was either being uncharacteristically naïve or unwittingly providing evidence that even those who believed they knew Housman well were not given access to his most private feelings and beliefs. As Laurence Housman wrote, his brother was 'a shy, proud and reticent character; even to his intimates he was provokingly reserved, finding, I think, a certain pleasure in baffling injudicious curiosity'. This captures Housman well: a genuine reserve that sometimes resulted in rudeness but often manifested itself as a mischievous refusal to be drawn.

Laurence also drew attention to one of the jottings it was Housman's habit to make in books he was reading. In *The Seven Pillars of Wisdom*, T.E. Lawrence had written of himself:

> There was my craving to be liked – so strong and nervous that never could I open myself friendly to another. The terror of failure in an effort so important made me shrink from trying; besides, there was the standard; for intimacy seemed shameful unless the other could make the perfect reply, in the same language, after the same method, for the same reasons.
>
> There was a craving to be famous; and a horror of being known to like being known. Contempt for my passion for distinction made me refuse every offered honour . . .

In his own copy of the book Housman had written in the margin: 'This is me.' It is symptomatic of Housman's oblique methods of self-revelation that he should state what made him the man that he was in such a lapidary form, and not directly but by referring to someone else's self-analysis.

Given the strain such conflicting feelings must have placed on Housman, it is scarcely surprising that Laurence should write of his brother: 'He was not a man of happy disposition.' This is not, however, to say that Housman had rejected happiness as a human ideal or considered it not worth pursuing. In the Introductory Lecture he delivered at University College, London, in October 1892, he had gone so far as to assert: 'Our business here is not to live, but to live happily.' The context for this was Housman's rejection of the social theorist Herbert Spencer's utilitarian concept of education. 'We may seem to be occupied, as Mr Spencer says, in the production, preparation and distribution of commodities,' he continued, 'but our true occupation is to manufacture from the raw material of life the fabric of happiness; and if we are ever to set about our work we must make up our minds to risk something.' Laurence went on to write that in spite of not having a happy disposition, his brother 'extracted from life a good deal of melancholy satisfaction suited to his temperament; and though he smiled at life somewhat wryly, he did manage to smile'.

That wry smile and that melancholy satisfaction were characteristic of both the man and his poetry. It was, however, the apparent differences between the man and the poet that struck many people. His friend Percy Withers referred to aspects of Housman's character that were 'implicit in his poetry' but absolutely 'hidden in his person', while the playwright George Calderon, introduced to Housman by William Rothenstein in around 1901, commented: 'Well, William, so far from believing that man wrote *The Shropshire Lad* [sic] I shouldn't even have thought him capable of reading it!' Rothenstein agreed that Housman 'neither looked nor talked like a poet', and Max Beerbohm memorably likened his appearance to that of 'an absconding cashier'. Rothenstein felt that Housman 'prided himself' on his unpoetic appearance: 'he was grim and dry and seemed to disdain the artist in himself, to be contemptuous of temperament.' Housman clearly did not disdain the artist in himself, but he kept that part of his personality private. In some cases – Oscar Wilde being an obvious example – the man and the writer are all of a piece, but this isn't always the case. W.H. Auden's biographer Edward Mendelson makes a point that is perhaps applicable to many writers, but to Housman in particular: the author of the poetry was someone his friends 'had never met – not the man they joked with over dinner, but the poet who worked alone in a study "more private than a bedroom even", behind a closed door that no one but he was allowed to open'. Housman's door was more firmly closed than most, and for good reason.

That door opened a crack in the poetry in a way it rarely did in the man. The true test of poetry for Housman was not how it stood up to scholarly analysis, but the immediate response it produced in the reader. This response, he notoriously claimed in a lecture given late in his life, was 'more physical than intellectual'. He told his audience that when once asked by an American reader to define poetry, he had 'replied that I could no more define poetry than a terrier can define a rat, but that I thought we both recognized the object by the symptoms it provokes in us'. Poetry, he said, should make one's hair stand on end; it should cause shivers down the spine, a tightening of the throat, tears. This, clearly, is a populist definition, and – to Housman's great satisfaction – it did not please everyone in his audience, which was largely academic. It was particularly striking that this advocacy of an emotional and visible reaction to poetry should be made by someone who appeared, even by the standards of his well-tailored era, rigorously buttoned-up.

Housman did occasionally, and very effectively, let his carefully maintained self-restraint slip. Shortly after his death, one of his students recalled one such occasion in May 1914, 'when the trees in Cambridge were covered in blossom'. Having dissected Horace's ode *Diffugere nives, redeunt iam gramina campis* 'with the usual display of brilliance, wit and sarcasm', Housman ended his class on a wholly unexpected note:

> . . . for the first time in two years he looked up at us, and in a quite different voice said: 'I should like to spend the last few minutes considering this ode simply as poetry.' Our previous experience of Professor Housman would have made us sure that he would regard such a proceeding as beneath contempt. He read the ode aloud with deep emotion, first in Latin and then in an English translation of his own. 'That,' he said hurriedly, almost like a man betraying a secret,

'I regard as the most beautiful poem in ancient literature,' and walked quickly out of the room. A scholar of Trinity (since killed in the War), who walked with me to our next lecture, expressed in undergraduate style our feeling that we had seen something not really meant for us. 'I felt quite uncomfortable,' he said. 'I was afraid the old fellow was going to cry.'

The poem, in other words, had done just what Housman felt poetry ought to do.

On another occasion, two years before his death, Housman was visited in his rooms at Trinity by his brother Laurence. Seeing a photograph of a man hanging over the fireplace, Laurence asked the identity of the sitter. 'In a strangely moved voice he answered, "That was my friend Jackson, the man who had more influence on my life than anyone else."' As with the brief comment on Horace's ode, Housman's voice and manner betrayed a struggle between saying too little and saying too much, something that provides a creative tension in his poems. Laurence went on to remark: 'Only those who knew how impenetrable was my brother's reticence over personal matters, will understand how astonished I was that he should have told me that. Why did he tell me anything more than the name, *unless* he wished me to know?' But what precisely *was* Housman telling his brother? What *was* it that he wished him to know? Even more telling, perhaps, was the fact that the face in the photograph, that of someone who was so important in his brother's life, was one that Laurence had never seen before, or at any rate failed now to recognise. As with his emotions, so with people: Housman liked to keep things compartmentalised.

Housman evidently believed that a writer's work should stand and be judged on its own merits without any reference to the life of the person who wrote it. In his own case, that person was, first and foremost, the leading classical scholar of his generation, and Housman frequently referred to this work as his 'trade', with the suggestion that poetry was a sideline. The notion of the gentleman amateur is distinctly English, with a long tradition of people proving highly skilled at, and often leading the field in, occupations for which they have received no specific training. One thinks of John Vanbrugh, arguably the greatest

English architect of his age, who drew up plans for Castle Howard with no previous experience of technical draughtsmanship; John Constable and J.M.W. Turner, who rose to similar eminence as painters without attending an art school or serving an apprenticeship; the great naturalist, Gilbert White, one in a long line of English clergymen who contributed to the arts and sciences when not writing sermons or taking church services; Gertrude Jekyll, who trained as a painter and turned to horticulture only after her eyesight began to fail, becoming nevertheless the doyenne of Edwardian gardening. A similar strand in English literature was noted by James Sutherland, writing in 1947 in Ernest Barker's *The Character of England*: 'The English poet is rarely a bard or a seer, rarely even a professional poet; his poetry, as often as not, is the product of such leisure hours as fall to the lot of a civil servant, or a parish priest, or a country doctor. This noble English tradition of business in the daytime and poetry at night goes back to Chaucer' – who became the father of English literature while earning his living as a civil administrator and diplomat. Housman saw himself as an amateur poet in both its original meaning of someone who does something out of love for it, and its more usual one of someone who does it for no financial reward, as exemplified by his paying for the first edition of *A Shropshire Lad* and refusing for many years to take a royalty on commercially published editions of the book.

None of this is to suggest that Housman did not take his poetry seriously or indeed have a proper appreciation of its worth. At some private level his poetry was clearly as important to Housman as his scholarly editions of classical writers, but this was not something he wanted to acknowledge publicly: his unexpected display of emotion when reading aloud to his students *Diffugere nives* and his own translation of it, marks a point at which the poet and scholar, the private and public man, met – and almost undid him. While working on the fifth and final volume of his edition of Manilius, he told Percy Withers: 'It ought to be out in a year's time, and then I shall have done what I came on earth to do, and can devote the rest of my days to religious meditation.' As so often, Housman deflects attention from what he is saying, as well as any accusations of sententiousness, with a joke; but the serious point remains. It could be taken to mean that what Housman was put on earth to do was to be a classical scholar, but he had also by this time published his second and, as he hoped, 'Last' volume of poems. When he added 'THE END' to the final page of that book, he meant it, and he wrote almost no poems thereafter.

The many disappointed accounts of what it was like to meet Housman, and attempts by those who did so to reconcile the man and the poet, overlook one essential thing. At the time he was writing *A Shropshire Lad*, Housman was not the prickly old don people encountered at Cambridge during his years of fame, but a comparatively young man in his mid-thirties. The best-known likeness we have of him is a drawing by Francis Dodd dated July 1926, commissioned by St John's College, Oxford, to mark Housman's election as an Honorary Fellow of his *alma mater*. Laurence Housman, who used it as the frontispiece for the posthumously published *More Poems*, described it as 'the best portrait of my brother that has ever been done', but it was drawn more than three decades after the publication of *A Shropshire Lad*. Dressed in a lightweight three-piece suit worn over a wing-collared shirt and tie, and looking more or less at ease, Housman sits on a wooden-framed chair with a rush seat, his hands resting on his thighs. The sketched-in background reveals some ghostly bookcases behind his left shoulder and a sofa piled with more books to his right. His head is turned towards the portraitist, but he is not looking directly at the viewer, and his eyes have a faraway gaze. The bristling eyebrows are still dark, but the hair is grey and parted in the centre into two neat wings, while the moustache is white and luxuriant, curving down around the mouth. This portrait shows Housman as he was at the time: a distinguished Classics don in his late sixties – though Housman himself considered it 'very unlike'. Familiar and often reproduced though the image is (it currently adorns the wrappers of the *Housman Society Journal*), it is no more the face of the man who wrote *A Shropshire Lad* than is the photograph taken by E.O. Hoppé in 1911, which has also been widely reproduced – on the cover of the 1988 Penguin edition of Housman's *Collected Poems and Selected Prose*, for example. In this photograph, of which the subject did not possess a copy and which he claimed was taken merely 'to oblige the artist, as he called himself and perhaps was',

Housman looks considerably older than his fifty-two years. He rests his face upon his left hand, as if in deep and melancholy contemplation, and these features stand out against the sombre background and the dark suit he is wearing. Similarly, the famous descriptions of Housman looking like 'an undertaker's mute' (Richard Middleton) or as if he were 'descended from a long line of maiden aunts' (A.C. Benson: look who's talking) were made when Housman had settled into donnish middle age and are more notable for their wit than their accuracy.

We need to banish these well-known images from our mind when we think of *A Shropshire Lad*, replacing them with the *carte de visite* photograph taken by Henry Van der Weyde in around 1894. The exact date of this photograph has been variously guessed and does not much matter, but Laurence in his memoir *A.E.H.* states that it depicts Housman 'aged 35'. The subject is recognisably the same man as in the later representations, but when we look at it we are usefully reminded that the unhappiness Housman confronts in the poems is that of someone who had not long left his youth behind him. The face, caught almost in profile, is an unexpectedly attractive one, with deep-set eyes and a beautifully straight nose – markedly different from the rather commonplace half-profile he presents to the world in a photograph taken when he was eighteen, before the advent of what he called 'the great and real troubles of my early manhood'. In that portrait he appears unformed, not yet grown into himself – or indeed into the roomy blazer he is wearing. By 1894, however, his face appears notably sensitive, something the full moustache seems designed, but fails entirely, to mask. The ears lie at an unusual backwards angle against the head, away from elegantly narrow sideburns. The hair is immaculate: cut short at the back and sides, parted in the centre, and glossy with pomade. Is it what we now know about Housman's life that makes this *carte* seem like the sort of photograph someone might give to his mother as he set off to fight in a war he did not expect to survive? Or perhaps it is merely the face of a man to whom the worst has already happened, and who has accommodated that worst without it solidifying his features into grim resignation, as in the Hoppé photograph. Whatever the case, there is something deeply moving about this image, something that relates to the poems of *A Shropshire Lad* in a way no other image does. It is also worth noting that when Housman was asked by friends and admirers to send them a copy of his likeness, this was the photograph he always chose, and precisely for the reason that – as far as he could remember – it was taken 'the year when I was beginning to write *A Shropshire Lad*'.

None of the surviving letters from this period mention that Housman was writing poems and assembling them for publication, and those who knew him must have been as surprised as the reading public was when *A Shropshire Lad* appeared as if from nowhere. 'So, Alfred has a heart after all,' one member of the family commented after reading the book. He had indeed, and had secretly lost it to someone who could not respond in kind. It was this, as he privately suggested after the publication of his second volume of poems, that had made him a poet. Whether or not it also contributed to his failing his finals at Oxford and thus derailing the career for which he seemed destined is unproven, but the two events certainly contributed to the 'troubles' of his early manhood. Those troubles also turned him from a skilled writer of occasional and comic verse into one of England's best-loved lyric poets. And it is to them, and to Housman's early years more generally, that we need to look in order to understand how he became the kind of poet – and indeed the kind of man – that he did. It was also his childhood and youth, later recalled as 'the land of lost content', that provided much of the emotional and physical background of *A Shropshire Lad*.

Far in a western brookland
1859–1876

Housman may have struck his later friends and colleagues as a solitary man, but it was not always so. His childhood was spent as part of a large family of seven children, and until their mother fell ill they appear to have had a happy and carefree time at Perry Hall. In 1818 J.N. Brewer's *The Beauties of England and Wales* described Bromsgrove as a 'large, but dirty place, full of shops and of manufacturers of nails, needles, and some sheeting and coarse linen'. By Housman's time, however, Bromsgrove was a reasonably thriving Worcestershire town. Hiring fairs were held in the open-air marketplace just around the corner from Perry Hall; men waited patiently to find work, their prospective employers sometimes in competition with recruiting sergeants who urged the men to join the army instead. Housman would draw upon his memories of both activities when writing *A Shropshire Lad*. He walked past the market every day on his way to the nearby King Edward's School, which he had entered in September 1870. He was a Foundation Scholar, as all the Housman boys would be (at one point bagging five of the twelve scholarships available), in a school where 'all clever boys had to be classics'. This suited young Alfred very well since his interest in the ancient world had already been stimulated by J.E. Bode's *Ballads from Herodotus* (1853), consisting of verse translations of the Greek author, and Lemprière's *Classical Dictionary* (1788), which, as he later put it, 'fell into my hands when I was eight [and] attached my affections to paganism'.

The garden at Perry Hall was almost two acres and largely screened from the house, providing the children with somewhere to pursue their interests free from adult supervision. It had three discrete areas: the ornamental garden, the kitchen garden, and a more or less abandoned area with some old fruit trees in it. Over the years seven chestnut trees had been planted, commemorating the birth of each of Edward and Sarah Jane's children. The garden also contained, running alongside the lawn, the distinctly romantic remnants of the seventeenth-century house that had originally occupied the site: a stretch of red-brick wall with stone-mullioned windows, evoking a former time and other lives now vanished. This house had been replaced by a handsome building with tall Gothic windows, built in 1824 by Housman's paternal great-uncle. Its imposing façade, thickly clad in ivy, gave Perry Hall a four-square appearance, but a range of offices, where Edward none too energetically conducted his solicitor's business, was tacked onto one side. A solid, studded door opened onto a well-lit stone-flagged hall from which a large staircase rose to the floors above. This was in contrast to the back stairs; these served the domestic quarters and were 'dark, twisted and steep, with no window but an opaque square, which drew up a glimmer of light from the kitchen below'. Laurence nevertheless described the house as 'friendly', as indeed it must have seemed, packed as it was with a family of nine, a governess, a nanny and a small retinue of servants.

'Was there ever such an interesting family as we were?' Housman once asked Laurence. 'There were probably many,' Laurence thought; 'but none, I daresay, more interested in itself, when it stood compact and pugnaciously united — seven against the rest of the world. How we loved; how we hated; how we fought, divided, and were reconciled again! How we trained, and educated ourselves; and developed a taste in literature and in the writing of it, in which, until years later, our elders had no part, and with which school-hours had little to do.' As befitted the eldest of the children, Alfred was the undisputed leader, both writing and directing the plays they staged for their parents, and organising literary competitions and other word-games. Some of these games were educational, and Laurence provides an enchanting image of the children, under Alfred's instructions, forming a living orrery on the lawn:

> I was the sun, my brother Basil the earth, Alfred was the moon. My part in the game was to stay where I was and rotate on my own axis; Basil's was to go round me in a wide circle rotating as he went; Alfred, performing the movements of the moon, skipped round him without rotation. And that is how I learned, and have ever since remembered, the primary relations of the sun, the earth, and the moon.

This childhood interest in astronomy eventually led to Housman's principal work as a classical scholar, his edition of Manilius's *Astronomica*. In the Introductory Lecture he delivered at University College, London, in 1892 he would describe astronomy as 'a science which has not only fascinated the profoundest intellects but has also laid a strong hold on the popular imagination', and — perhaps because he lost his religious faith — stars, planets and constellations would also figure in his poetry in astrological aspects derived from the Classics, shaping the fate of men.

Housman had been brought up a devout Christian. Both his parents were the children of clergymen and the household was a conventionally religious one, summoned to the dining room every morning for family prayers before breakfast. The bells of the church of St John the

Baptist, which with its tall steeple rose opposite and above Perry Hall on a small but commanding hill, called the family to morning and evening service every Sunday. It was merely a matter of crossing the road – easier and safer then than now – and climbing a broad flight of steps onto the path that leads through a churchyard ringed with lime trees to the west door. Other bells pealed or tolled throughout the week, marking marriages, baptisms, funerals and events in the church calendar, while the passing hours were marked by the striking of the church clock. The frequent sense in Housman's poetry of the ephemeral nature of life may well have been instilled during a childhood in which life's climacterics and the relentless onward movement of time were regularly and audibly measured out.

It became apparent just how precarious life could be when in 1870 the children's mother fell ill and withdrew from everyday family life to her bedroom. The stability of the Housman family was also being undermined by financial troubles. Perry Hall did not belong to Edward Housman – he was merely a life tenant – but he had nevertheless decided to furnish it in the style he felt appropriate for an English gentleman. In order to do so, he had mortgaged other properties without telling anyone what he was up to. The death of his father early in 1870 and anxiety about money and his wife's health made Edward turn to drink. When alcohol ran out, he would go to the bottom of the garden and throw stones onto the roof of the neighbouring Shoulder of Mutton pub in order to summon fresh supplies.

In the later stages of her illness, Sarah Jane had asked Alfred to pray with her for her recovery. It was presumably this that prompted her to express to her husband the hope that her dying would not cause her eldest son to lose his faith, a wish Edward passed on to Alfred in the letter telling him of her death. Housman did not immediately do so, but within the year had become a Deist, still believing in a Creator but not in one who intervened in human affairs, and he eventually rejected Christianity altogether. His sister Kate recalled that their mother's death 'roused within him an early resentment against nature's relentless ways of destruction', although the children never discussed their loss among themselves. 'Death – that cuts short both joys and sorrows – became an obsession with him, very evident in after life,

44

but there in boyhood,' Kate wrote. Indeed death was the first subject Housman set for his siblings when he started organising the composition of jointly authored poems.

When Sarah Jane died, it was decided that Housman should not return home for the funeral but continue to stay with his godmother Elizabeth Wise at Woodchester. Elizabeth was a long-standing friend of Housman's mother (whose father had been rector at Woodchester), and young Alfred became particularly close both to her elder daughter, Edith, who was some five years older than him, and the family's German governess, Sophie Becker, who would remain a lifelong friend. By the time Alfred returned to Perry Hall, his grieving father had begun drinking even more heavily. An opportunity for Edward to escape everyday reminders of his loss arose in February 1872 when the tenant of the Housman family home, Fockbury House, died. This house belonged jointly to Edward (who had been born there) and his five surviving siblings, all of whom derived income from it being rented out; but Edward was the chief trustee and decided that, rather than finding another tenant, he would move there with his children and let Perry Hall instead. This may have been financially ill-advised, but for the children it offered new excitements of life in the countryside rather than on the edge of a town.

Fockbury House itself, which was just along the road from where Housman had been born, dated back to the seventeenth century, but it had been enlarged and altered over the years, its original half-timbering now a mere remnant among numerous brickwork additions. There had once been a large clock in one of its many gables, and locals still referred to it as 'the Clockus' or Clock House. The property included a large terraced garden and some old farm buildings, but had few of the modern amenities of Perry Hall: there was no gas, no running water, and not as many servants. It was to this house that in July 1873 Edward Housman brought his new bride. Lucy Housman was Edward's first cousin. She had also been Sarah Jane's best friend and had introduced Housman's parents, afterwards acting as bridesmaid at their wedding. At fifty, she was eight years Edward's senior and while he no doubt valued her as someone to relieve a widower's loneliness, another very good reason for marrying her was that she was capable of taking on seven children ranging in age from fourteen to just four years old. Lucy turned out to be far more than merely capable, and almost immediately won the genuine affection of the large brood she had inherited. Housman was soon addressing letters to 'My dear Mamma', and signing himself 'your loving son'.

'Country influences worked strongly in making A.E.H. the man he became,' Kate recorded, and it was at Fockbury that Housman's love of the English countryside was nurtured. It was strengthened by regular visits to Woodchester and his discovery in the attic of his new home of a seventeenth-century herbarium assembled by some ancestors who had lived there. This book taught him about the names and families of plants, leading him in time to become a knowledgeable amateur botanist. Making his way daily to school through the narrow lanes down into Bromsgrove, he could observe native plants, their habitats and flowering seasons. 'Spring Flowers' was another subject Kate remembered her brother setting for family poetry-writing sessions, and many of his own mature poems refer to landscapes, the trees and plants that grow in them, and the changes they undergo as the seasons turn.

Kate described the 'very pretty streams of this brook-girt land', and this, rather than anywhere in Shropshire, is the 'western brookland / That bred me long ago' recalled by Housman in one of the best-known poems in *A Shropshire Lad* (LII). More immediately, probably in 1875, Housman wrote a poem titled 'Summer'. Housman is always associated with the cherry because of the popular poem in which he calls it 'Loveliest of trees', but his favourite tree as a boy was the beech. 'Many years later he told me he was glad he had not been brought up in beech-wood country,' Laurence recalled, 'for, had he been, its beauty would have made him unappreciative of any other kind.' He was nevertheless familiar with beeches because there were several in the garden of Fockbury House, while at Woodchester, he remembered in 1927, 'there used to be a belt of beeches half way up the hill, dividing the downs from the fields and making a piece of scenery which in its way was as beautiful as anything anywhere'. It seems almost inevitable, this being Housman, that he should add: 'and now the greater part of them are down and the whole look of the place changed'. In a different way 'Summer' too embodies the sense of passing time and the inevitability of death that Kate thought characteristic of her brother as a boy: the wind whispers of 'coming Autumn, coming death'. Changing seasons and falling leaves are of course a poetic commonplace, but the mood was one that Housman would make particularly his own. And here it is in a poem he wrote as an adolescent.

> Summer! and after Summer what?
> Ah! happy trees that know it not,
> Would that with us it might be so.
> And yet the broad-flung beechtree heaves
> Through all its slanting layers of leaves
> With something like a sigh.

The continuity between this piece of juvenilia and the work of the mature poet is suggested by the repeated use of the unusual verb (perhaps borrowed from Gray's Elegy) to describe the effect of wind blowing through heavily leafed trees in one of his best loved poems:

> On Wenlock Edge the wood's in trouble;
> His forest fleece the Wrekin heaves . . .

One of Housman's first experiences of longing for a distant home, a principal theme of *A Shropshire Lad*, occurred when, after an outbreak of scarlet fever in the family, he briefly became a boarder at King Edward's School in order to avoid catching the disease. He wrote to his stepmother:

> Yesterday I went into the Churchyard, from which one can see Fockbury quite plainly, especially the window of your room. I was there from 2 o'clock till 3. I wonder if you went into your room between those hours. One can see quite plainly the pine tree, the sycamore & the elm at the top of the field. The house looks much nearer than one would expect, & the distance between the sycamore & the beeches in the orchard seems great, much longer than one thinks when one is at Fockbury.

As Laurence noted, this episode 'has in it the authentic note of the "Shropshire Lad". Even as a boy, separation from home surroundings affected him so much that it pleased him to spend from two to three hours of a winter's afternoon in viewing them from a distance.' Housman's enduring love of trees, most particularly before they shed their leaves, was expressed in a quatrain which he wrote at the same time as the poems of *A Shropshire Lad* and seems to recall the felling of the beeches at Woodchester:

> Give me a land of boughs in leaf,
>   A land of trees that stand;
> Where trees are fallen, there is grief;
>   I love no leafless land.

While exploring their new rural environment, the Housman children frequently visited the homes of local working-class people. These visits were not of a charitable nature, as those of their parents might have been, but entirely and unaffectedly social. It was a curiosity of the English class system that, in rural areas at any rate, the strict divisions that separated adults did not apply to children. Though it would be unthinkable for middle-class parents to mix socially with cottagers and labourers, it was not unusual for their children to spend time in the homes of working-class families, where, more often than not, they were welcomed. Such visits could prove educational as children learned of other worlds and different standards, of hardships but also sometimes of freedom from the sort of constraints that regulated their own lives. 'The depth of feeling of simple villagers and farmhands used sometimes to surprise me,' Laurence recalled, and it seems likely Housman was similarly enlightened. 'Now and then things were told us by our village neighbours of which I have since made literary use,' Laurence continued, and the poems of *A Shropshire Lad* reimagine the experiences of agricultural labourers such as those the Housman children met around Fockbury.

More specifically, Fockbury supplied the 'western horizon' that would haunt Housman as an adult and remind him of 'the happy highways where [he] went' during his childhood (XL). It was a horizon he could see, and which can still be seen, from Broom Hill, a modest knoll the Housman children nicknamed 'Mount Pisgah'. Broom Hill was a short walk from Fockbury House, at the top of the wonderfully named Worms Ash Lane, and Housman and his siblings often climbed it to look out across the Severn Plain to the distant hills beyond. The original Mount Pisgah was what Moses was directed to climb in order to see the Promised Land but, in a twist characteristic of Housman, the Worcestershire Mount Pisgah became in his mind the vantage point from which he looked not on a land full of promise but one saturated in 'lost content'. The view not only extended to the distant Clee Hills of Shropshire, but also took in Bredon Hill in Worcestershire, the location of one of his most famous poems. Mount Pisgah was where the Housman family would go on 22 June 1887 to see the beacons lit for Queen Victoria's Golden Jubilee, a national event commemorated in the very first poem of *A Shropshire Lad*.

At school, meanwhile, Housman was distinguishing himself as a fine classical scholar and the frequent recipient of prizes, winning everything from Mr Case's Prize for Holiday Task and the Government Prize for Freehand Drawing to prizes for English, Greek and Latin poetry. He was not merely good at Classics, but had an interest in the whole of the ancient world. On a visit to the British Museum during a trip to London in 1875, he would report that he 'spent most of [his] time among the Greeks & Romans'. At fifteen, his classical tastes were already formed: he 'did not admire' the Townley Venus, a Roman statue of the goddess naked to the waist, far preferring what he called 'the Farnese Mercury' (more commonly known as the Farnese Hermes), a naked youth sporting little more than a pair of winged sandals. It is altogether characteristic of the young classical scholar that he should ascribe the Roman name of the god to a Roman statue – even if it was the copy of a Greek one – and it is Mercury who would be 'The Merry Guide' in the poem of that name included in *A Shropshire Lad* (XLII). That Christmas, Housman was presented with *Charicles; or Illustrations of the Private Life of Ancient Greece* (a volume that promises rather more than it delivers) as an examination prize for Latin and Greek Grammar, and the following year he received William Smith's recently published *Dictionary of Greek and Roman Antiquities* as the Classical Prize.

The £100 entrance scholarship Housman won to St John's College, Oxford, in 1877 crowned a final year at school garlanded with prizes, including the Senior Wattell Prize, the Head Master's Greek Verse Prize and the Prize for Latin Verse. Housman's taste for writing Greek and Latin poetry was partly inspired by *Sabrinae Corolla in Hortulis Regiae Scholae Salopiensis contexuerunt tres Viri floribus legendis* (1850), which he had been given when he was seventeen. The book is a collection of mostly English verses translated into Latin and Greek by three scholars at Shrewsbury School, and so provides another early association between Housman and Shropshire. The Oxford scholarship was very welcome because the Housman family's finances were becoming increasingly precarious. At Fockbury House Edward was living well beyond his means, and it soon became clear that he would have to return to Perry Hall, which he had meanwhile fraudulently bought and remortgaged. The children could not but be aware of what Kate called the 'increasing restriction of means that fell upon our household', but at eighteen Housman probably knew and understood more than they did what this meant.

When I was young and proud
1877–1881

Given his triumphant school career, Housman seemed destined for further success at Oxford, but in fact his troubles were only just starting. For the first two years all seemed to be going well. He lived within his means, made a close friend of a fellow Classics scholar called A.W. Pollard, and contributed humorous prose and verse to a short-lived university magazine called *Ye Rounde Table* – though he chose 'Tristram', the sad knight, as his *nom de plume*. According to Pollard, who lived on the same stair, Housman was 'generally recognized in the College as exceptionally able', an opinion confirmed when he gained a first in Mods, the exams taken at the end of his second year. At the beginning of Housman's third year, in the autumn of 1879, Pollard moved to rooms in another quad and so the two friends saw rather less of each other. Instead, Housman took up with a science scholar in the same year called Moses Jackson.

Born in Ramsgate in 1858, Moses John Jackson was a brilliant student in a field quite different from Housman's. At the age of seventeen he had matriculated at University College, London, where he was awarded the Neil Arnott Medal in Experimental Physics. After two years at UCL he was offered a scholarship at St John's, arriving in Oxford in 1877. Jackson was also a natural athlete, and was very good looking, but he did not share Housman's interest in the arts. A fellow undergraduate described him as 'a perfect Philistine [. . .] quite unliterary and outspoken in his want of any such interest'. Pollard more kindly described him as 'lively, but not at all witty'. Housman disagreed with these observations, though admittedly he itemised the qualities he saw in Jackson in a reference he later wrote with the intention of getting him a Fellowship at University College, London: 'I believe that if he had been caught young and kept away from chemicals and electric batteries and such things, he might have been made into a classical scholar. Even now, in spite of his education, his knowledge of Liddell and Scott's Greek Lexicon has often filled me with admiring envy. He also, when his blood is up, employs the English language with a vigour and eloquence which is much beyond the generality either of classical scholars or of men of science.'

The tone here, which veers between light mockery and painful sincerity, is characteristic of the letters Housman would write to Jackson over the years. One of the few things the two young men had in common was the companionable habit of taking long walks in the Oxfordshire countryside: '15-mile walks to a good pub to consume old ribs of beef 10" thick, pickled walnuts and a quart of bitter, with a good tub of cream, & rich cheese to finish', as Jackson happily recalled many years later. Pollard felt that Jackson's chief attraction for Housman was his 'simplicity and singleheartedness', qualities that were later ascribed to young men in *A Shropshire Lad*.

At the beginning of their fourth year, in the autumn of 1880, Housman, Pollard and Jackson took rooms together in an old house in St Giles', more or less opposite their college and run by a Miss Patchett. This arrangement may have seemed highly congenial, but according to Pollard it proved fatal to Housman's university career. 'After we had returned from dining in Hall, and had our coffee,' he recalled, 'I mostly retired to work by myself in the lower sitting room, leaving the other two on the first floor.' Whatever these two ill-matched friends did with their evenings, it had nothing to do with their studies. This did not much matter in Jackson's case because he was a natural scholar, 'an absolutely safe first in science in the schools [who] had no need to read much in the evening'. Housman may have seemed similarly gifted, but he had one dangerous flaw: a bumptious disdain for his elders that is characteristic of clever young men. Robert Ewing, the college tutor who had inducted Housman and his fellow freshman, was condemned for mispronouncing a Greek word during a sermon in chapel, after which Housman 'vowed that he would not try to learn anything from such an ignoramus'. Even the great Benjamin Jowett, the university's Regius Professor of Greek, failed to impress Housman, who attended 'a single lecture' from which he 'came away disgusted by the Professor's disregard for the niceties of scholarship'. Part of the trouble was that Housman had already decided that the chief aim of scholarship was to establish correct texts for classical authors. His friend and fellow classicist A.S.F. Gow suggested that philosophy or any 'abstract thought of this kind was distasteful to him, and ancient history he valued less for its own sake than for the light it threw on ancient literature'. Rather than devoting himself to the study of philosophy, Housman had begun work on a commentary on the Roman poet Sextus Propertius. This work would occupy him for many years: when proposing an edition of Propertius to the publisher Macmillan in 1885, he stated that 'There are few authors for whose emendation and explanation so much remains to be done.'

It has often been remarked that Housman's attention to the minutiae of textual emendation – particularly in his five-volume edition of Manilius's *Astronomica* – was the result of a lifetime's emotional self-denial. 'Deliberately he chose the dry-as-dust,' his great admirer and fellow poet W.H. Auden suggested, as if this kind of exacting scholarship was a substitute for the messy business of life. The American critic Edmund Wilson similarly regretted that Housman devoted his time to academic work in which the voice that is heard in *A Shropshire Lad* was more or less silenced – 'that voice which, once sped on its way, so quickly pierced to the hearts and the minds of the whole English-speaking world and which went on vibrating for decades, disburdening hearts with its music that made loss and death and disgrace seem so beautiful, while poor Housman, burdened sorely forever, sat grinding and snarling at his texts'. That the poet and scholar were not in fact two entirely different people is suggested by Gow's observation that 'Propertius had been Housman's first love.' The Latin poet may well have provided the textual scholar with a rich field for 'emendation and explanation', but one can hardly pursue this kind of work without being aware of what the ancient author under examination was attempting to convey. Enoch Powell, who regularly attended Housman's lectures on Latin poets in the early 1930s, noted that it was very clear that 'the marriage of logic with poetic taste in interpreting and correcting a text was not only not unnatural and contradictory but indispensable. The severity of Housman's presentation was the severity not of passion-lessness but of suppressed passion, passion for true poetry and passion for truthfulness.' Unlike Manilius, generally regarded as a third-rate writer whom Housman himself dismissed as 'facile and frivolous [. . .] the brightest facet of whose genius was an eminent aptitude for doing sums in verse', Propertius was a fine elegiac poet of the sort Housman himself would become – and Gow noted that 'Housman's chief love was poetry'. Propertius's poems describe his hopeless infatuation with a woman he calls Cynthia, and it is possible that Housman was becoming aware of the relevance of this archetype to his own burgeoning relationship with Moses Jackson.

Quite how far Housman recognised the nature of his feelings at this stage is unclear. He would in any case have realised that Jackson was entirely heterosexual, so that any hope of reciprocation was remote. Homosexuality was hardly unknown in Oxford, where – until reforms introduced by Jowett in the 1880s, well after Housman had left – Fellows were obliged to remain unmarried and no women were admitted as undergraduates. The exclusion of women meant that Oxford was, as one nineteenth-century alumnus nostalgically recalled, 'a society, a brotherhood, of men living a common life, and having many things in common'; there was, wrote another, a 'close, corporate feeling', characterised by the 'intimate comradeship of men and boys'. Unlike Housman, many young men arrived at the university after several years spent at boarding schools, where in an adolescent all-male atmosphere homosexuality flourished, sometimes in the form of platonic though passionate 'romantic friendships' but elsewhere – mid-Victorian Harrow as described by John Addington Symonds in his memoirs, for example – in the form of fully sexual relationships. The dominance of the Classics in the public-school curriculum undoubtedly fostered an awareness of Greek ideals that did not entirely chime with those of a Christian place of education. As the vice-president of the founding body of Cheltenham College put it at the school's opening ceremony in July 1841: 'Every pious parent must feel that there is great peril in putting into the hands of youth the abominable mythology of the ancients, tending as it does to warp their understandings, and destroy their better feelings. It is painful to think that a classical educa-tion could not be acquired without the use of such works.' At Oxford, Jowett had also introduced reforms to the Greats curriculum, making Plato's dialogues central to the study of Greek: not merely the *Republic*, which might be looked upon as useful philosophical and moral guidance for those whose destiny was to govern the country or the Empire, but also the more problematic *Symposium* and *Phaedrus*, which dealt with love. In his translations of Plato's dialogues (1871–92), Jowett did his best to obfuscate the philosopher's theme of the love between men and boys, treating it metaphorically and drawing parallels with Christian marriage. Others found it inspirational, and Victorian 'Hellenism' often had unmistakable homosexual undertones. Whether or not men went to bed together was beside the point; as many school stories of the period unblushingly demonstrated, a platonic love could be just as overwhelming as one that included a sexual element – as Housman was to find out to his very great cost.

It was at Oxford that, according to his own account, Housman finally lost his faith, becoming 'an atheist at 21'. As with much in Housman's life and work, this statement need not be taken too literally, and there would be little to gain from searching among the biographical minutiae of March 1880 for some anti-Damascene moment. In fact, two years after this apparently decisive statement, he told Kate that he 'went on believing in God till I was twenty-two'. The letters men-tioning religion that survive from his time at Oxford, written to his father and his godmother, are cheerfully irreverent about bishops and preachers, but Housman seems to have attended chapel regularly, as undergraduates were expected to do. None of the sermons he describes would do much to bolster the faith of someone who had 'abandoned Christianity at 13', but Housman's comments upon them were written merely to amuse his correspondents rather than to suggest he was experiencing serious religious doubts. Twenty-one was the traditional age at which people came into their majority, and it is quite likely that Housman was suggesting that losing one's faith was the natural result of becoming a grown-up, that religion was one of the childish things he put away when he became a man. That said, he had certainly got to know Moses Jackson very well by March 1880 and may have already fallen in love with him. When the Shropshire Lad is 'one-and-twenty', a wise man advises him: 'Give crowns and pounds and guineas / But not your heart away' (XIII). Again, one-and-twenty is a symbolic age, one at which, the poem suggests, such advice is of 'no use'. It is only a year later that the Lad can acknowledge, with a resignation born of experience, that the wise man was right: 'And oh, 'tis true, 'tis true'. By the time Housman himself was 'two-and-twenty', he was sharing digs with Jackson and may well have been only too aware that giving his heart away was 'paid with sighs a plenty' and the cause of 'endless rue'. Homosexual feelings were regarded as wholly incompatible with Christian belief in the nineteenth century, and it seems likely that this was what finally put paid to Housman's faith. Jackson's unwitting contribution to this loss is suggested by the letter Housman wrote to Kate about this period of change in his beliefs, because he added: 'and towards the end of that time I did a good deal of praying for certain persons and for myself'.

It was assumed that Housman would have no trouble in repeating his success in Mods when he came to sit Greats in the summer of 1881. While Pollard and Jackson both gained firsts, Housman failed his final examinations entirely. It is possible that the news he received a few days before taking the exams that his father was seriously ill as the result of a stroke affected his performance; but a more likely explanation is that Housman had been distracted from his studies and simply hadn't done enough work. Pollard recalls that when Housman went back to Oxford for his viva, 'the bewilderment of the examiners at finding themselves compelled, as they considered, to refuse even a pass to a man who had obtained a first in Mods, had caused enquiries to be made, which were now passed on to me, as to how it had come about that on some of the papers Housman had hardly attempted to offer any answers'. One of these examiners, H.J. Bidder, had found Housman a recalcitrant and unrewarding student who, when asked to consider the arguments laid out in Plato's *Republic*, would simply outline, at some length, the merits or otherwise of the textual scholars who had edited the work. In one exam, he noted, Housman had remained true to form and 'refused to consider Plato's meaning except so far as it was relevant to the set-tlement of the text'. Housman's answers to those parts of the exam dealing with philosophy, a subject in which he had declined to take any interest and for which he had done no work, were apparently 'so ludi-crously bad as to show that he had not made any effort, and to give the examiners the impression that he was treating that part of the business with contempt'. Bidder's later judgement of Housman was that he was someone 'on whom he had done his best to make an impression – and failed'. The more humiliating failure, however, was Housman's own.

Back at Perry Hall, Housman was greeted with more bad news. Not only was his father's life still in danger, but the prospect of resolving the family's financial problems had been dashed. Displeased by her son's financial legerdemain, Housman's wealthy paternal grandmother had cut both Edward and his children out of her will. Edward had been relying upon this inheritance to get him out of his difficulties: his solic-itor's work barely paid for the upkeep of his family, and if he died or his illness prevented him from returning to work Lucy and the children would be ruined. The small allowance Housman had been receiving from a relative impressed by his results in Mods had been withdrawn, and his scholarship (which had another year to run) was suspended until he obtained his BA. The only thing he could do immediately was to return to Oxford for a term in the autumn in order to obtain his Pass degree. Having done that, he began to study at home for the Civil Service examination, which would be held the following summer. His old headmaster at King Edward's School offered him some part-time teaching, which he gratefully took up in order to earn a little money.

Although living in straitened circumstances, Edward recovered from his stroke and continued to sail through life, cheerfully but ineptly pursuing a number of harebrained schemes – growing and preserving exotic fruits, prospecting for gold in Wales – with the intention of making his fortune. Because he had enormous charm, few people seem to have resented his fecklessness, which put a considerable strain upon everyone but himself. Unable any longer to afford clerical staff for his solicitor's business, he expected his children to take on the work, Clemence in particular becoming an office drudge, while Lucy was obliged to make numerous economies in running the household. As Laurence nicely put it: 'During those years of strain much was secretly done of which my father knew nothing – perhaps preferred not to know, for he had always the gift of taking things more easily than others could; and we would often see him going his own way, showing but little sign of inward disturbance, when the domestic situation was very disturbing indeed.'

Housman certainly did not share his father's infuriating insouciance and appeared sunk into solitary gloom. 'He returned home a stricken and petrified brother, who, from that time, was withdrawn from all of us behind a barrier of reserve which he set up as though to shield himself from either pity or blame,' Kate recalled. 'He met no word of reproach at home, but his own self-reproach was deep and lasting.' Even without the open censure of his siblings, Housman must have realised that his failure was a grave disappointment to them. Kate put it brutally, referring to 'his blamable failure', adding: 'for blamable it was that, knowing the severe difficulties besetting his home, making success for him the one bright spot to which his family could turn with confidence, he allowed his intellectual arrogance to lure him into slackness or negligence instead of making assiduous preparations for his Schools'.

An acknowledgement that Kate was right in suggesting that her brother's outstanding potential had been wrecked by his youthful arrogance is apparent in a poem Housman wrote after he had published *A Shropshire Lad*:

> When summer's end is nighing
>   And skies at evening cloud,
> I muse on change and fortune

And all the feats I vowed
When I was young and proud.

Another poem, written in April 1922, may also commemorate this
academic disaster:

On miry meads in winter
    The football sprang and fell,
May stuck the land with wickets:
    For all the eye could tell
    The world went well.

Yet well, God knows, it went not,
    God knows, it went awry;
For me, one flowery Maytime,
    It went so ill that I
    Designed to die.

It has been proposed that these lines refer directly to Housman's failure
in Greats, which took place that year at the end of May, or to the events
that contributed to his failure. This is certainly plausible, although
in another poem Housman implied that it was 'at four-and-twenty',
which is to say two years after failing his exams, that he thought
'To lay me down and die'. This perhaps merely goes to show that
it is unwise to treat poems as if they were strictly autobiographical.
That said, Kate's recollections suggest that, if not actually suicidal,
Housman became severely depressed in the aftermath of his failure at
Oxford, and it is from this point that he becomes recognisable as the
man who raised a self-protecting shield against the world. The poem
continues:

And if so long I carry
    The lot that season marred,
'Tis that the sons of Adam
    Are not so evil-starred
    As they are hard.

The striking phrase 'The lot that season marred' links this poem both to *'Diffugere Nives'*, Housman's loose translation of the Horatian ode that reduced him to tears – 'But oh whate'er the sky-led seasons mar, / Moon upon moon rebuilds it with her beams' – and the crucial final poem of *A Shropshire Lad*, when he writes of the seeds he has sown that 'some the season mars'. Here, perhaps, is the origin of Housman's strong identification with the 'luckless lads' of that particular poem, and indeed of the entire volume. The world had gone awry for him when he was a young man and never settled back into its proper course – and this is the starting point of his poetry.

Here I lie down in London
1882–1887

Housman had at least learned from his bitter experience, and in July 1882 he passed the Civil Service exam. After he declined the offer of a job in Dublin, his stepmother 'told him he *must* accept the next thing that offered'. Happily that turned out to be a job at the Patent Office, where Moses Jackson was already employed, and so Housman did indeed accept it. He went to London that December, finding lodgings at 15 Northumberland Place in Bayswater, to the north-west of Hyde Park. From there each day he travelled to the Patent Office in Chancery Lane, where he worked as a Higher Division Clerk in the Trade Marks Registry at a meagre annual salary of £100. It was Housman's job to examine applications for new trademarks and compare them with those already received, a daily task that was both tedious and far beneath someone of his accomplishments. His salary was just about adequate to cover his daily expenses providing he was prepared to live frugally. A useful sum of £200 had come to him during the summer when his paternal grandmother's death had released a family legacy over which she had no control, but Housman had made over this bequest to his penurious father. The only money he had, therefore, was what little he had earned as a schoolmaster and the balance of his Oxford scholarship, which after deductions amounted to a few pennies under four pounds, and life in the metropolis on a hundred pounds a year was not easy.

Jackson worked in the same building but in another office as Examiner of Electrical Specifications, a job far superior to that of

Housman in both status and salary. Although, as his supervisor Ralph Griffin recalled, Housman 'did not much love the Civil Servants into whose company he had been pitched', he nevertheless managed to find some he liked in his own department. Griffin had been educated at Cambridge and was not a career civil servant, and he suggested that this might explain why Housman was drawn to him; for himself he described Housman as 'beloved', adding that 'No one could not love him'. Another colleague recalled that Housman's 'most familiar friends were rowing men', which is what Jackson himself had been at Oxford: one of Housman's most valued possessions was a photograph of Jackson posing with his team-mates of the St John's Eight. In particular he spent a good deal of time with Ernest Kingsford and with John Maycock, 'a Thames oarsman and [. . .] *bon vivant*' who wrote light verse and was described as 'his most intimate friend' at the Patent Office. Ten years his senior, Maycock had already been at the Patent Office for fifteen years by the time Housman arrived there. Not a great deal is known about him, apart from the fact that he had a wife called Kate (affection-ately addressed as Kitty) and a son named Henry. It was young Henry of whom Housman reported delightedly in 1885, when the boy was around eight or nine: 'When he goes to heaven, which he regards as a dead certainty, he wants to be *God*, and is keenly mortified to learn that it is not probable he will. However, his aspirations are now turn-ing into another channel: it has come to his knowledge, through the housemaid, that the devil has horns and a tail; and in comparison with these decorations the glories of heaven have lost their attractiveness.' The family shared lodgings in Putney with a friend of Maycock called W.H. Eyre, who was also an active member of the Thames Rowing Club and got to know Housman well.

Housman's friendship with these men was a good deal less compli-cated than the one with Jackson, though Maycock clearly had both a very high regard and a genuine fondness for Housman. The life of a *bon vivant* was well beyond Housman's means, and a good day out for him, Maycock and Eyre would consist of an invigorating walk in rural Surrey followed by a modest dinner at a local inn. The barrier of reserve that Housman had raised back in Bromsgrove, and which he became notori-ous for raising in later life when people attempted to talk to him about his work, was evidently lowered during these walks. Eyre described Housman as 'a most delightful companion, in conversation generally, & particularly in pointing out, what was most charming, & interesting'. Housman, he said, had 'a deep appreciation of the beauties of nature, as regards landscape, & the wild flowers, birds & animals, which one comes across in the course of a long days walk, over fields, & commons & through woods [. . .] He also told us many little anecdotes, which were very amusing, & indeed had a most delightful sense of humour.' Eyre added that Housman was 'very fond of his native country, Salop, & we had many talks about it, as my Mother lived at Shrewsbury, & I had done many walks (not with him) in the fine parts of the county about the Wrekin, Church Stretton & the Clee Hills.' Shropshire was not, of course, Housman's native county, but Eyre was writing, as he noted at the end of this letter, when he was 'aetat 89', recalling events after half a century. It is nevertheless clear that Housman's interest in and affection for Shropshire were already well established, and that Eyre's descriptions of the county were stored away for future literary use.

Despite these essentially hearty new friendships, Moses Jackson remained the principal focus of Housman's etiolated emotional life. In early 1883 the two men decided once more to share accommodation. The third member of the household was Jackson's equally handsome brother Adalbert, who was some seven years his junior and studying Classics at University College, London. When not at the Patent Office, Jackson himself also pursued his studies at UCL, doing further research towards a doctorate in science, which he would obtain later that year. The three young men took lodgings at 82 Talbot Road, a street running across the top of Northumberland Place. Pollard, now working in the Department of Printed Books at the British Museum and living at his family home in Brompton Square, was a member of the same athletic club as Jackson and occasionally visited, but he felt that his friendship with Housman had waned, perhaps because he was an unwelcome reminder of the disastrous end of the Oxford years. The same, however, could be said of Jackson, with whom Housman now spent part of every day in the same household. It is nevertheless telling that although once addressed facetiously in the (grammatically correct vocative) Latin version of his forenames, Pollard subsequently became 'My dear

Pollard', whereas the Jackson brothers were always 'Mo' and 'Add'.

Housman saw little more of his siblings Clemence and Laurence, who were now in London, sharing a home south of the river in Kennington, close to the Arts and Crafts School in which they had both enrolled in order to learn wood engraving and illustration respectively. 'Though he would come dutifully to see us whenever invited,' Laurence recalled, 'he never asked us to his own rooms in return.' They met Moses Jackson only once, at the house of a mutual friend and without Housman being present. Jackson was so surprised to discover that Housman had siblings living in London, neither of whom had ever been mentioned, that he wrote to their father to ask whether some family quarrel of which he was unaware had led to an estrangement. Alarmed, Edward wrote back to ask whether Alfred was leading 'an irregular life' which he wanted kept secret from his siblings. Jackson truthfully reassured Edward that Alfred's life was perfectly blameless, perhaps still unaware that he was himself the object of some highly irregular feelings on Housman's part.

The failure at Oxford may have meant that Housman had no future as a don, but he had been continuing his classical studies in his spare evenings. After a day spent at the Patent Office, he would walk to the British Museum in order to work in the reading room, where he began writing articles on Latin and Greek authors. He also worked here on his proposed edition of Propertius, whose principal theme of unrequited love must have come to seem increasingly painful. As at Oxford, however, the lure of Moses Jackson's company meant that he did not make as much progress as he might have done had he been without distractions. One of the reasons for not inviting people to Talbot Road may have been that Housman did not want witnesses to his deepening attraction to Jackson, but in addition he may not have wanted to share him with anyone – apart, perhaps, from Adalbert. While Adalbert was bathed in the reflected glow of his older brother – and indeed had his own attractions – other people, whether family or old friends such as Pollard, were rigorously kept at a distance from Housman's lodgings.

Adalbert graduated in 1884 and left the household to take up a job as a preparatory-school master outside London. In the autumn of the following year, Housman caused a great deal of alarm by leaving the house in Talbot Road and simply disappearing. Jackson was sufficiently worried to contact Housman's father: 'Whether the worst was feared I do not know,' Laurence wrote. If Housman provided any explanation when he returned a week later, none was ever recorded. The supposition is that Housman had attempted to describe the nature of his feelings to Jackson and that some kind of quarrel had ensued. This, at any rate, is the explanation that Laurence provided and which has – with some caveats – been generally accepted. Housman shortly afterwards moved out of Talbot Road and found new lodgings back in Northumberland Place, at number 39. From there, a month or so later, he moved to Highgate; he would remain there until 1905, when his landlady, Mrs Hunter, moved to Pinner in Middlesex and he went with her. Moses Jackson also left Talbot Road, taking lodgings in Maida Vale; that – for him at any rate – the quarrel had not been fatal is clear from the fact that on weekdays the two men apparently 'met daily at the Patent Office, and as a rule lunched together'. Having been through both public school and Oxford, Jackson cannot have been entirely surprised by the substance of any declaration that Housman may have made, but he may have felt it better to leave such things unsaid. Though he presumably made it clear that there was no question of reciprocation, he seems to have managed to negotiate a way through what must have been a very awkward and embarrassing scene.

Quite how this scene arose or what form it took is impossible now to know, although Housman would later write three poems which appear to have described its outcome. It may be that the presence of Adalbert had prevented Housman from declaring himself earlier, or even that the younger brother had provided some sort of substitute or distraction while living at Talbot Road. Housman was clearly very fond of Adalbert, as two poems he wrote about him make clear. In some letters he wrote to Maude Hawkins, whose *A.E. Housman: Man Behind a Mask* (1958) has been dismissed by the Housman Society as 'The Mills and Boon of Housman biographies', Laurence Housman suggested that his brother and Adalbert may have had some sort of affair. 'I still think there was more *mutual* attraction between [Housman and Moses] than you give credit for,' he wrote. 'But Jackson *shied away* from the full implication, knowing that he could not share it "*in kind*". But (and *this* is what I want you to release [sic: for 'realise'?]): his attraction to the *younger* brother *was* reciprocated.' As evidence of this, Laurence pointed to a poem printed in the posthumous *More Poems*:

> He looked at me with eyes I thought
>   I was not like to find,
> The voice he begged for pence with brought
>   Another man to mind.

This resemblance prompts the speaker to hand the beggar an extravagant half-crown and tell him that any thanks should be given not to him but to this lost friend. That the poem refers to Adalbert seems confirmed by a cancelled final quatrain in which the tramp is given direction for his quest:

> Turn East and over Thames to Kent
>   And come to the sea's brim,
> And find his everlasting tent
>   And touch your cap to him.

It was to the Jacksons' family home in Ramsgate on the east Kent coast that Housman later went to see Adalbert, only to find him away, and Ramsgate is where Adalbert's 'everlasting tent' would be pitched after he died of typhus in his late twenties.

'I doubt whether Moses ever kissed AEH,' Laurence continued: 'but I have no doubt that AJJ *did*.' Quite how Laurence came by this information is unknown: it is almost certain that he never met Adalbert, and Housman seems never to have discussed his private life with his brother. Laurence nevertheless repeated his assertion in a second letter to Hawkins – 'I have *no* doubt whatever that A.E.H. was in a closer and warmer physical relationship with A.J.J. than with his brother Moses' – once again citing the poem already quoted and also indicating the poem that followed it in *More Poems*. This poem, one of the most moving that Housman wrote, is unarguably about Adalbert – it is prefaced with his initials – but, while it laments 'that straight look, that heart of gold, / That grace, that manhood gone', it provides no particular support for Laurence's allegation, which was made in old age, recalling events supposedly taking place over seventy years earlier.

Some have dismissed this story as mere 'wishful thinking' on the part of Laurence, who was himself homosexual, knew both Oscar Wilde and Edward Carpenter, and campaigned modestly for homosexual rights. That said, Laurence's comments seem more than mere speculation: these are direct assertions, with numerous underlinings for emphasis. When Housman moved to his new lodgings in Northumberland Place, he took with him an invitation to Adalbert from the West London Debating Society and one to Moses from the Ealing Rugby Club, poignantly trivial items he kept with him for the rest of his life – though it has been suggested that these objects had merely been used as convenient bookmarks rather than kept as holy relics. Housman was, however, inclined to preserve with great care letters and other written material that meant a great deal to him. It is also the case that he kept two photographs of Adalbert hanging in his rooms alongside those of Moses.

Housman and Adalbert were young men at the time they lived together: the former in his mid-twenties, the latter in his late teens. Even so, the possibility that Housman, knowing he could never have a sexual relationship with Moses, enjoyed one vicariously by sleeping with Moses's brother seems remote from what we know of his character. The truth of the matter will never be known, but Housman's devotion to Moses almost from the moment they met means that any other romantic or erotic relationship would seem unlikely. As Propertius had put it in one of his poems:

My fate is neither to love another nor break with *her*:
  Cynthia was first and Cynthia shall be last.

Joan Thomson, the daughter of J.J. Thomson, Master of Trinity during most of Housman's time at Cambridge, recalled talking to him about love. 'Housman would not tolerate the idea that it was possible for a man truly to love more than one woman in his life; anyone who considered that he had done so had simply never really loved at all.' It is clear from the vehemence with which he expressed this view that Housman was speaking from his own experience of love.

This long and sure-set liking
1888–1894

What is not in doubt is that Moses Jackson had a profound effect on Housman's life and work, though the two men would not meet very often after Jackson joined the Indian Civil Service (ICS) and set off for Karachi in December 1887 to take up an appointment as Principal of the newly founded Dayaram Jethmal Sindh Science College. Jackson's departure for India, and further events in his life over the next four years, were recorded by Housman in the only diaries he is known to have kept, the first of them dated 1888, while Jackson was still at sea. Most of the pages of these pocket appointments diaries appear to have been left blank.* Housman occasionally records the temperature or the date on which wild flowers come into bloom; the only other entries refer to Moses. Not that anyone coming casually across the diaries would know this. Laurence recorded that 'once or twice' Housman used his customary abbreviation of his friend's name, 'Mo', but if so these entries have since vanished, and in every instance Jackson is referred to as 'he' or 'him'. One might surmise that Housman used these pronouns to disguise the identity of the person he was writing about. A more likely and more poignant explanation is that no name was necessary: for Housman there simply was no other 'he' or 'him'.

The first entries in the 1888 diary track Jackson's voyage on the SS *Bokhara*, the ship taking him every day further away: 'Bokhara arrives at Gibraltar', 'Bokhara leaves Naples 4 p.m.', 'Bokhara arrives at Port Said', and so on. At some point Jackson transferred to another ship which, Housman notes on 25 January, 'arrives at Bombay this morning', subsequently adding: '(Midnight of the 24th I learn later)'. Two days later: 'He gets to Karachi at "8 o'clock"', the quotation marks suggesting that Housman got this news from a reliable source, perhaps Adalbert. In July Housman records that one of his colleagues at the Patent Office had received a letter from Jackson, congratulating him

---

*'Appear' because the 1888 diary is the only one to survive intact; of the other three diaries only fourteen detached pages survive, presumably torn from the binding by Laurence Housman.

on being called to the bar, and he notes the form of address: "'My dear Nightingale": "very truly"'. Housman himself did not receive a letter until 19 November, eleven months after Jackson sailed, and he posted a reply on 14 December. Then, on 19 December, 'His grandmother died', suggesting that any connection with Jackson, even one that had just broken, was gratefully seized upon.

The Pettitt's Annual Diary in which Housman made these notes remains in pristine condition, the gilt stamping on its front cover still burnished, its pages crisp. The few notes are all made in Housman's beautiful, neat handwriting. Turning the pages, what strikes one most is that they have almost all been left unmarked, so much so that it seems hardly worth Housman having bought the diary if he had so little to write in it. It is in the later diaries that Housman makes his brief nature notes, but not here. Housman presumably filled his days, but they have gone unrecorded, and the cumulative effect of so many blank pages is desolating. This, one feels, is what his life had come to: a few lines charting Jackson's ever-increasing distance from England; two lunches with Adalbert; the occasional tiny proof of a life continuing elsewhere, which mostly reaches him from other sources; a single letter. In its compressed, uninflected, almost unspoken way, this carefully pre-served and more or less empty ledger of absence is as eloquent as the poems Housman would later write about his friend.

Surviving out of context as individual pages, the other diaries have less impact, but the fragmented story they tell is much the same. The first surviving entry in the diary for 1889 is made on 27 June, when Housman records the temperature, as he does the following day, adding: 'Posted letter to him'. He continues to note the temper-ature and the blooming and fading of flowers, then on 9 July writes: 'Nightingale has not heard from him a long while, but wrote to him about a week ago', which suggests a certain anxiety about communica-tions, as well as a certain rivalry. Jackson returned to England on leave in October, principally in order to marry Rosa Chambers, the young, university-educated and recently widowed daughter of his Maida Vale landlord. Jackson had fallen in love with Rosa almost immediately, but had felt unable to support her on the salary he received from the Patent Office, and it was in order to improve his financial circumstances and so marry her that he had joined the ICS. This had meant leaving Rosa behind in London while he established himself in Karachi. Although Housman met his friend twice during this October leave, he was not — perhaps out of tact — informed of the impending nuptials. 'He was married,' Housman notes on 9 December, though this entry was in fact made retrospectively, for it was only on 7 January the following year, by which time Jackson had taken his bride back with him to Karachi, that Housman noted: 'I heard he was married'. Housman wrote to Jackson two days later, presumably to congratulate him.

Further cause for congratulation came on 2 October 1890: 'His son born' — once again written retrospectively, since news took time to travel all the way from India and it was not until 29 October that Housman noted 'His son's birth in the paper'. A week later Housman records: 'I write to him by this day's mail'. This is the final extant entry for the 1890 diary, and the only surviving entry about Jackson in the diary for 1891 was made eight years later. On the page for Friday 22 May 1891, he has written: '[Sunday 1898, 10.45 p.m., said goodbye.]'. This refers to another of Jackson's home leaves, but it turned out not to be the last time the two men met.

Rosa Jackson would give birth to three more sons. All four boys were sent to England to be educated at a preparatory school at Godalming in Surrey, where the family also acquired a house to which Rosa would return from India for extended periods, settling there on a permanent basis in around 1906. Jackson had asked Housman to be godfather to the youngest boy, Gerald, a duty Housman accepted and took seriously. After leaving Karachi to take up the post of Principal of the Baroda College of Science at the invitation of the princely state's ruler, Maharaja Sayajirao III, Jackson returned to Britain to look at university laboratories with a view to improving similar facilities back in India. He and the maharaja had hoped to detach Baroda College from the University of Bombay, but this proved impossible, and in 1910, still in his early fifties, Jackson retired from the ICS. He returned to England in April and applied for a number of posts there. Housman, by now the highly prestigious Kennedy Professor of Latin at the University of Cambridge, supplied a reference in support of Jackson's application to become Director of Education for the Borough of Bradford, declaring that for thirty years he had 'held his character and intellect in the highest admiration: indeed there is no one to whose example I owe so much'.

Despite Housman's efforts, Jackson was not appointed to this or any other post in Britain and so decided instead to emigrate to Canada and set up as a farmer in British Columbia. Housman clearly regarded this as an odd choice of career for a man in his fifties with no previous experience of agriculture, but with characteristic generosity he offered financial assistance. 'I do not want to make investments on my own account in the wild-cat colony you now inhabit, where you have to put *Angleterre* on your letters to get them to England, but if you happen to want extra capital you might just as well have it from me and prevent it from earning its head off in a current account at a bank.' Although presented as a loan, the money was in fact a gift, which was just as well because Jackson's attempts to become a self-sufficient dairy farmer were more or less doomed from the start. The land he had bought may have seemed very appealing at first glance, heavily wooded and with a fish-filled creek running through it, but creating a farm out of such wildness demanded a great deal of labour. In addition, his family was obliged to live in 'a cramped and primitive wooden house' without electricity or running water. Less than eighteen months after Jackson bought the property, which he named 'Applegarth', a recession drastically reduced the price of milk. A severe drought followed, and a year later the First World War broke out. Jackson's eldest son, Rupert, had been studying medicine at Cambridge, where he occasionally dropped in on Housman at Trinity College, and when war was declared he enlisted with the Royal Army Medical Corps. The other three boys were being home-schooled in Canada while helping out on the farm, but both Hector and Oscar volunteered for the Canadian Expeditionary Force as soon as they came of age, leaving only Housman's seventeen-year-old godson still working the land. With many potential farm labourers now in the forces, keeping the land properly cultivated proved almost impossible and it began reverting to scrub.

During the war Hector occasionally corresponded with Housman and visited him at Cambridge while on leave. The Jackson boys had inherited their father's good looks and Housman approvingly reported that Hector had 'grown up rather a distinguished-looking fellow'. Hector also had a distinguished war, and was awarded the Military Cross. All three serving brothers survived the war, and both Hector and Oscar returned to Canada. Instead of settling back on the family farm, however, they enrolled at the University of British Columbia at Vancouver, where they both studied engineering. Rupert, meanwhile, had married a French woman and settled in County Durham as a general practitioner and consultant surgeon. Hector was killed in a senseless accident in January 1920 when a drunken taxi driver knocked him off his bicycle: he was just twenty-eight. His death and the vain attempts to keep the farm going, particularly after Gerald had gone to UBC to study for a BSc in geology, took its toll on both his parents. Rosa suffered a temporary breakdown, while the anaemia from which Moses had begun suffering turned out to be an early symptom of terminal stomach cancer.

It was Moses Jackson, Housman admitted, who was 'largely responsible' for his second career as a poet. 'I wrote verse at eight or earlier, but very little until I was 35,' he told Maurice Pollet, a professor of English at the Lycée d'Oran in Algeria, who sent him a list of questions about his life and work in 1933. Until around 1886, what Housman chiefly wrote was light verse. Inspired by reading the works of Lewis Carroll and Edward Lear, he had during his boyhood developed both a taste and considerable skill for writing nonsense poetry, and he continued to write comic and occasional verse, parodies and squibs throughout his life, chiefly for the private amusement of friends and relations. A few of these were published, but usually without the author's name attached. The earliest 'serious' poems to be included in the canon of Housman's work were both published in 1881 in an Oxford magazine called *Waifs and Strays*. Both were written while he was an undergraduate 'in his twentieth year' and appeared in the magazine above his initials.

'New Year's Eve' is uncharacteristic both in subject matter and style, being set in church and written in the manner of Swinburne. It is also, by Housman's later standards, very long, running to fourteen four-line stanzas. Although, according to Laurence, Housman had 'ruled out' the poem for republication on the grounds that 'it smacked too much of the Swinburnian style which he had abandoned', these verses became no. XXI of *Additional Poems*. The other poem, 'Parta Quies', is rather more recognisably in Housman's mature style, consisting of two six-line stanzas on the subject of death: its title, taken from Virgil's *Aeneid*, translates as 'rest is won'. Housman chose not to republish the poem during his lifetime, and it first appeared, in a corrupt version and under a different title, as the last item in *More Poems*. In its correct form, it runs:

> Good-night; ensured release,
> Imperishable peace,
>   Have these for yours,
> While sea abides, and land,
> And earth's foundations stand,
>   And heaven endures.
>
> When earth's foundations flee,
> Nor sky nor land nor sea
>   At all is found,
> Content you, let them burn:
> It is not your concern;
>   Sleep on, sleep sound.

The poem may have earned a place in Housman's affections when it transpired that Moses Jackson was able to recite it with remarkable accuracy at the end of his life. Writing from his hospital bed to thank Housman for sending him a copy of *Last Poems*, Jackson wondered if anyone would publish his friend's juvenilia. 'That thing that you published in some aesthetic magazine seems to me, in its disregard of all politeness towards possibilities in the unknown future, seems to me to contain nearly half the philosophy of your two books. You will be surprised at my remembering them so nearly, if I am not quite word-perfect.' He then wrote out the poem from memory, adding: 'It wants the poet to punctuate it'. This was something with which in normal circumstances Housman would have vigorously agreed. Instead, he was deeply moved, writing back: 'I never was more astounded at anything than at your reproducing my contribution to *Waifs and Strays*. I remember you reading it at Miss Patchett's, and how nervous I felt. If I had known you would recollect it 42 years afterwards, my emotions would have been too much for me.'

Even more moving was the fact that, in spite of writing in vague terms about his plans for the future, Jackson evidently suspected that his treatment was proving ineffective: 'I am going on fairly well in this hospital, but will come out of it soon now, well or ill,' he told Housman. Written over several days in a pencilled hand that showed signs of the correspondent's physical weakness, the letter was signed off with 'Goodbye'. The poem may therefore have come into Jackson's mind because he was aware that he would soon be gaining his own 'ensured release', and it is perhaps significant that he had misremembered the title as '*Ave atque vale*', or 'Hail and farewell'. This was one of those Latin tags that had passed into the common currency of English; but Housman would have known, even if Jackson didn't, that it originated in an elegy Catullus wrote bidding farewell to his dead brother. In order to perform funeral rites and pay his respects to his brother's ashes, the poet has had to travel 'through many nations and across many seas' back to Rome from Bithynia, a province in Asia Minor where Catullus was on the staff of the province's governor. Like Housman and Jackson, therefore, Catullus and his brother had been geographically separated when the latter died. Catullus's lament that '*fortuna mihi tete abstulit ipsum / heu miser indigne frater adempte mihi*' ('Fortune has snatched you away, alas, poor brother, unfairly taken from me') is a sentiment that Housman understood all too well, and lamenting the workings of fate was a frequent theme of his poetry.

In his reply to the letter in which Jackson quoted 'Parta Quies', Housman offered Jackson the £500 he was due from Grant Richards for *Last Poems*. Fearful that Jackson would refuse the money, he wrote: 'As I cannot be bothered with investments, this will go to swell my already swollen balance at the bank unless you will relieve me of it. Why not rise superior to the natural disagreeableness of your character and behave nicely for once in a way to a fellow who thinks more of you than anything in the world? You are largely responsible for my writing poetry and you ought to take the consequences.'

Most of the poems Housman wrote directly about Jackson remained unpublished during his lifetime. There were, however, two exceptions: the verse dedication that prefaced the first volume of his edition of

Manilius in 1903 and the 'Epithalamium' he wrote somewhat belatedly to celebrate – if that is the word – Jackson's marriage, which he published in *Last Poems*. These were, in a sense, public poems, though more private aspects of the poet's relationship with his subject were there for anyone who cared to look closely.

The dedicatory poem, though both heartfelt and revealing, prefaced a volume that few people outside the world of classical studies were likely to see. Furthermore it was in Latin. The pre-eminent classical scholar Gilbert Murray thought it the best Latin poem written since antiquity, but this perhaps suggested that one needed to be a classicist of Murray's standing to appreciate it. It would not be published in an English translation until October 1927, when a version by Edmund Wilson appeared in the New York magazine the *Bookman*. It is unclear why Wilson decided to translate the poem, particularly since eleven years later he published an article on Housman that attacked the poet for having failed to mature properly, by which Wilson meant grow out of what he himself regarded as the passing adolescent phase of homosexuality. He instanced Housman's decision to abandon a study of 'Propertius, who wrote about love, for Manilius, who did not even deal with human beings' as a deliberate rejection of creativity for sterility. Whatever he may have thought of Housman's character, Wilson evidently had considerable regard for Housman as a poet, and this may be the reason that he was able to bring himself to translate what amounts to a homosexual love poem. Indeed, he states that it is among the very few examples of Housman's work as a classicist in which 'the voice of the Shropshire Lad comes through'.

The poem is prefaced with Housman's personal dedication:

SODALI MEO

M.I. JACKSON

HARVM LITERARVM CONTEMPTORI

This is a characteristic Housman tease, which translates as 'To my comrade M.J. Jackson, scorner of this scholarship'. The affection displayed in the poem, however, is heartfelt, and it is telling that the verse is written not in the dactylic hexameters employed by Manilius, but in the elegiac couplets favoured by Propertius. It opens with a recollection of the author and his subject walking through the deserted countryside at night, looking up at the stars. This may be intended to refer to walks that Housman enjoyed with Jackson at Oxford, but lovers wandering under the stars is also a poetic tradition of very long standing. In addition, it is an appropriate image to preface a book about astronomy, and Housman goes on to imagine Manilius looking up at the same sky many centuries before and, like any Shropshire lad, becoming mindful of his own mortality and therefore deciding to write his book about the heavens as a stay against time. (The sense that Housman and Manilius, separated by time, were nevertheless looking at the same sky is also reminiscent of the Lad and the Roman witnessing the same wind blowing through the trees in 'On Wenlock Edge the wood's in trouble'.)

Like many ancient texts, the *Astronomica* was lost for centuries, and Housman likens it to a shipwreck, much battered and fragmented, that eventually washes up on 'our strand', a reference to its discovery in 1417 by the Renaissance scholar and humanist Poggio Bracciolini. Housman then writes that he has not (as would be customary) invoked the help of the stars or the gods by dedicating his work as editor to them, but instead selected a human being, a comrade who is mortal, but who will live on as long as the following pages will. He also refers to Jackson having left these shores to follow the stars east, in other words to India, and sends this salutation from the western shore where the poet remains. Housman asks Jackson to accept the poem because in time they will both be dust and the chain of comradeship will be broken. This final image of '*uincla sodalicii*' recalls the last two lines of '*Diffugere Nives*', Housman's translation of Horace's ode (first published in *Quarto* magazine in 1897), in which the chains of Lethe that bound Pirithoüs in the underworld could not be broken even by 'the love of comrades', which is to say Theseus's love of his friend.

Collected in *Last Poems*, the 'Epithalamium' would reach a far wider audience than the dedicatory poem. It was not until five years after the marriage that Housman began drafting it, by which time Jackson had already produced two of the sons the poet wishes upon his friend 'to stay the rot of time'. Unlike the Manilius poem, this one begins conventionally enough with an invocation to Hymen, god of marriage, whom Housman calls 'Urania's son' (Urania being the muse of astronomy and therefore the person to whom the dedicatory poem might have been addressed). Hymen is rather less conventionally summoned both 'to join and part' – to join the groom to his wife, but in doing so to part him from his friends:

> So the groomsman quits your side
> And the bridegroom seeks his bride:
> Friend and comrade yield you o'er
> To her that hardly loves you more.

It is not known who acted as Jackson's groomsman, or best man, but Housman, in his idealisation of the scene, steps up to hand over his friend to Mrs Chambers, who might have been less than flattered at being described as someone who loved her new husband hardly more than the reluctantly yielding Housman did.

The distinctly homophile underpinning of this poem is reinforced by Housman's appropriation of Sappho, a poet who – though little is known about her life – had become associated with female homosexuality, her own name adapted for the adjective 'sapphic' and her birthplace, the island of Lesbos, leading to the coinage of the synonym 'lesbian'. Housman takes some lines of Sappho about the evening star bringing home the sheep to the fold and the child to its mother, and translates and expands them for incorporation in the poem. In the final stanza the poet imagines the marriage bed, which he sees encircled by 'the thoughts of friends' posted to keep the bridal pair from 'nightly harms'.

These poems, along with those Housman wrote which more directly recorded the difficulties of this unequal friendship, are perhaps less important than Jackson's hidden and unwitting status as 'the onlie begetter' of all Housman's poetry. It is generally accepted that it was news of Jackson's illness in 1922 that prompted a hitherto reluctant Housman to begin assembling a second collection of his poetry, revising poems already written and producing new ones. He had additionally proved uncharacteristically anxious to see the book in print in a comparatively short space of time. That Jackson was also 'largely responsible' for the writing of *A Shropshire Lad* was confirmed in a conversation Housman had in March 1925 with A.C. Benson, whose own homosexual life apparently took an even more exiguous form than that of his Cambridge colleague. 'He said that his first poems were caused by a deep personal attachment which had lasted fifteen years and left a deep mark on him,' Benson recorded. 'He said that he had twice felt a loss of vitality in life – at 36 when even his devotion failed – and again lately when he found himself less interested in life.' The reference is clearly to Jackson, whom Housman met in 1880, fifteen years before the literary *annus mirabilis* of 1895, during which Housman wrote the majority of the poems in *A Shropshire Lad*. Housman's comment could be misconstrued to mean that his personal attachment had ended after fifteen years, but it seems more likely that he meant that by the time he was writing the poems the attachment had already lasted fifteen years. That the attachment continued thereafter is evident from other things Housman wrote, though since he turned just thirty-six in March 1895 one has to ask what caused a loss of vitality that same year so debilitating that 'even his devotion [to Jackson] failed'. In the absence of extant letters from this period, we have no way of knowing whether any behaviour on Jackson's part contributed to that failure, but it seems unlikely. It may simply have been that Housman's lassitude was a result of producing so many poems in such a short time – and (so he would claim) against a background of ill health.

It may also be that in writing a corpus of poems inspired by a thwarted passion (including poems not eventually selected for publication in *A Shropshire Lad*) he had to some extent – but only temporarily – exorcised what had been haunting him for fifteen years. He told Maurice Pollet, 'I did not begin to write poetry in earnest until the really emotional part of my life was over,' but a poem Housman drafted in April 1922 suggests otherwise. It opens 'I promise nothing: friends will part' and includes the lines: 'But this unlucky love should last / When answered passions thin to air'. It is always dangerous to read poems biographically, but those which are generally accepted to be about Jackson tend to be about parting, recalling the two friends' mysterious quarrel in the autumn of 1885. That Housman's devotion endured even after passion faded is evident from those of his letters to

Jackson that have come to light. '*Literature as Compensation*,' wrote E.M. Forster in the commonplace book he started keeping in 1921. '"I shall make something out of this some day" must have occurred to many an unhappy man of letters, and to *have* made something is possible – Heine, A.E. Housman, Shakespeare avow it.'

A morbid secretion
1886–1896

The poems of *A Shropshire Lad* were written intermittently over a period of some nine years, though the bulk of them were produced in what Housman described as a period of 'continuous excitement' during the first few months of 1895. Dating individual poems is a hazardous undertaking, largely because in the process of editing his brother's poems and safeguarding his reputation, Laurence Housman mutilated the notebooks in which the poems had been drafted and frequently revised. The principal reason for wanting to date the poems is to establish whether or not there was some kind of scheme to the volume, or to establish relationships between individual poems. It is clear, however, that in the first instance Housman wrote the poems with no particular aim in mind. He told Sir Sydney Cockerell, the long-serving director of the Fitzwilliam Museum in Cambridge, that the poems 'came to him willy-nilly'. When Cockerell asked him 'whether he at once realized their merit', Housman's answer was 'that he had, because they were so unlike anything else that had come to him'. The poems may have bubbled up in his mind as if from nowhere, but Housman was a craftsman and most of them went through several drafts. 'I wrote it thirteen times, and it was more than a twelvemonth before I got it right,' he said of the poem that stands last in *A Shropshire Lad*, and what remains of the notebooks shows that other poems were similarly worked over repeatedly until they satisfied him. As the *Athenaeum* magazine noted of the book: 'It is the sort of easy reading which is hard writing.'

The first of the poems was written in 1886, by which time Housman was living in Highgate. He would later say that all but one of the poems of *A Shropshire Lad* were written at Byron Cottage, and he began drafting these in a notebook in which he had previously jotted down classical references. In an unsigned review of Laurence

Housman's memoir of his brother, Desmond Shawe-Taylor observed that 'Housman is perhaps a unique case of a true poet who produced no poetry in his twenties.' We now know that this is not strictly true, but of the 172 poems eventually included in the canon, fewer than a dozen can be dated to Housman's third decade. One reason for this was that, as Housman wrote in 1892 when applying for the chair of Latin at University College, London, 'During the last ten years the study of the Classics has been the chief occupation of my leisure.' The papers he wrote on Greek and Latin authors had begun appearing in such leading scholarly publications as the *Classical Review* and the *Journal of Philology*, and by 1892 he had published twenty-five of them. It was these that prompted such an impressive array of scholars to provide him with testimonials when he applied for the post at UCL. Housman would later say that UCL had 'picked him out of the gutter, – if I may so describe His Majesty's Patent Office', and it must have been a relief to find a job more suited to his considerable talents. When he opened the new academic year at UCL by delivering his Introductory Lecture to the combined faculties of arts, law and science, he took as his subject the notion that learning and knowledge are valuable for their own sake, but he must also have been aware that after a decade of clerical drudgery, he had at last found a fulfilling means of earning his living.

Terms at UCL consisted of twelve weeks, during which Housman taught for ten hours a week. This left him with weekends and the holidays to walk and think and write poetry, though some of this time was taken up by marking papers and writing the eight or nine lectures he was contracted to deliver each spring. Late in his life, Housman explained how his poetry came to him during his long afternoon walks in Hampstead and Highgate:

> Having drunk a pint of beer at luncheon – beer is a sedative to the brain, and my afternoons are the least intellectual portion of my life – I would go out for a walk of two or three hours. As I went along, thinking of nothing in particular, only looking at things around me and following the progress of the seasons, there would flow into my mind, with sudden and unaccountable emotion, sometimes a line or two of verse, sometimes a whole stanza at once,

accompanied, not preceded, by a vague notion of the poem which they were destined to form part of. Then there would usually be a lull of an hour or so, then perhaps the spring would bubble up again. I say bubble up, because, so far as I could make out, the source of the suggestions thus proffered to the brain was an abyss which I have already had occasion to mention, the pit of the stomach. When I got home I wrote them down, leaving gaps, and hoping that further inspiration might be forthcoming another day. Sometimes it was, if I took my walks in a receptive and expectant frame of mind; but sometimes the poem had to be taken in hand, and completed by the brain, which was apt to be a matter of trouble and anxiety, involving trial and disappointment, and sometimes ending in failure. I happen to remember distinctly the genesis of the piece which stands last in my first volume. Two of the stanzas, I do not say which, came into my head just as they are printed, while I was crossing the corner of Hampstead Heath between Spaniard's Inn and the footpath to Temple Fortune. A third stanza came with a little coaxing after tea. One more was needed, but it did not come: I had to turn to and compose it myself, and that was a laborious business.

In spite of his forbidding reputation, Housman could also be a terrible old tease, and one of his biggest, most successful and most enjoyable teases was the Leslie Stephen Lecture he delivered at Cambridge on 9 May 1933, from which this extract is taken. At some level the lecture is entirely serious, but it was also intended as a playful provocation. Although Housman claimed to have written it unwillingly, allowed it to be published (as was the custom) only grudgingly, and repeatedly asserted that the praise it received was undeserved, the covert pleasure he derived from delivering so contentious a talk in such a distinguished and ordinarily sober lecture series is apparent on almost every page of it. This in itself is wholly characteristic of Housman, much of whose writing is a kind of flirtation with 'truth', a decorous pavane of concealment and revelation. His delight in causing trouble with the lecture became more explicit when he informed Laurence that 'The leader of our doctrinaire teachers of youth is reported to say that it will take more than twelve years to undo the harm I have done in an hour.' That leader, Professor I.A. Richards, was not alone in deploring Housman's deliberately anti-intellectual account of 'The Name and Nature of Poetry', as the lecture was titled.

Housman's principal contention was that 'Poetry is not the thing said but a way of saying it.' He suggested that those who had admired Wordsworth in the nineteenth century did so for the wrong reasons: 'they were most attracted to what may be called his philosophy', while remaining largely deaf to what was far more important, 'that thrilling utterance which pierces the heart and brings tears to the eyes of thousands who care nothing for his opinions and beliefs'. The process by which poetry moves us is mysterious, he thought, appealing to something atavistic in the human psyche. He used an image of the English landscape to illustrate his point. Quoting Milton's line 'Nymphs and shepherds, dance no more', he asked:

> what is it that can draw tears, as I know it can, to the eyes of more readers than one? What in the world is there to cry about? Why have the mere words the physical effect of pathos when the sense of the passage is blithe and gay? I can only say, because they are poetry, and find their way to something in man which is obscure and latent, something older than the present organization of his nature, like the patches of fen which still linger here and there in the drained lands of Cambridge.

Much of the lecture was devoted to the work of other writers, Housman airily dismissing both the Metaphysical and Augustan poets for the likes of the usually despised Isaac Watts. While this infuriated academics in the English faculty, it was what he said about his own work – a subject on which he usually remained silent – that stirred the interest of his admirers. They may not have noticed immediately that, while revealing something of the *processes* of writing poetry, Housman said nothing about its *origins* – except that they apparently lay in the pit of his stomach. As so often with Housman, he proffered information while neatly sidestepping the more interesting and complicated truth about his work. To borrow an image from one of his poems, of all Housman's lads none was more fleet of foot than the author himself.

The substance of what he said, with its carefully adduced supporting detail ('while I was crossing the corner of Hampstead Heath between Spaniard's Inn and the footpath to Temple Fortune'), may indeed have been true, but it is presented so drolly as to deflect any more probing questions about his poetry that may have arisen in his audience's mind.

The experience of writing poetry, Housman told his audience, 'though pleasurable, was generally agitating and exhausting'. It was 'only that you may know what to avoid' that he went on to describe the process. Once again, humour of a particularly dry English kind is used to distract the attention, in this case to steer the audience away from any consideration of what may have been the most revealing thing Housman said about poetry in the whole lecture. It was in this lecture that Housman suggested that the true test of poetry was the physical reaction it provoked in the reader, notably what is technically known as horripilation. 'Experience has taught me,' he said, 'when I am shaving in the morning, to keep a watch over my thoughts, because, if a line of poetry strays into my memory, my skin bristles so that the razor ceases to act.' While the ripples from this joke were presumably spreading through the audience he enumerated other physical sensations, the third of which he could 'only describe by borrowing a phrase from one of Keats's last letters, where he says, speaking of Fanny Brawne, "everything that reminds me of her goes through me like a spear".' This seems, perhaps, an extreme response to a line of poetry, but was Housman in fact talking less about poetry than about what prompted it? Whatever her shortcomings, and these have been argued over since the nineteenth century, there is general agreement that Fanny Brawne was not only the 'one passion' of Keats's life, as his early biographer Lord Houghton phrased it, but was also the inspiration behind many of his best-known poems. Housman too had had one passion in his life, a person who had been 'largely responsible' for the poetry he wrote, and this glancing reference to Brawne seems to be another example of his letting something slip without appearing to, revealing and concealing at the same time.

If members of the audience missed this reference, they may well have nodded to each other knowingly when Professor Housman defined his poetry as an involuntary secretion; not, he suspected, 'a natural secretion, like turpentine in the fir', but 'a morbid secretion, like the pearl in the oyster'. 'Morbid' was certainly a word people associated with the two volumes of poetry Housman had published, in which a kind of overarching existential gloom was luridly augmented with tales of dead soldiers, hanged murderers, youthful suicides and variously doomed lovers. Housman went on to explain that the reason he described his own secretions as morbid was that he had 'seldom written poetry unless [he] was rather out of health'. (He had originally written 'rather out of health or mentally agitated', but deleted the latter perhaps too revealing detail before delivering the lecture.) He had been more explicit about what this ill health was when, three months before delivering the lecture, he told Maurice Pollet that 'a relaxed sore throat' was chiefly responsible for his productivity during what he acknowledged as his 'most prolific period, the first five months of 1895'. Even this malady is vague, however – and possibly strategically vague. Out of health or not, Housman was at the same time apparently downing pints at lunchtime and going for not physically undemanding walks of two or three hours' duration.

Long walks had been a feature of Housman's life since childhood. When the family had moved from Perry Hall to Fockbury, his journey to King Edward's School was one and a half miles, which meant he needed to leave home at seven every morning. This was no great hardship: 'Punctuality, industry, fixed routine, daily walking, love of flowers and trees, woods and hills, all were part of his Fockbury life', his sister Kate wrote, 'and these habits never left him.' Pollard recalled that at Oxford he and Housman 'had from the first taken many long walks together and continued to do so in our third year' (when they sought further exercise by taking up 'elementary lawn tennis'). As we have seen, walks were also a fondly remembered feature of his time at Oxford with Moses Jackson and at the Patent Office with Maycock and Eyre. Although such outings were clearly companionable, Housman's preference was to walk on his own, even while still a schoolboy. 'His sense of some pleasures was acute, and seemed exercised best alone,' Kate remembered. 'It was alone that he liked to tramp to enjoy the sight and smell of the woodlands, or to gaze on a setting sun or a starry sky.' It was just the same when he was a distinguished academic: 'That his daily constitutional should have been solitary is not surprising,' his Trinity friend and colleague A.S.F. Gow observed. 'And when, as often, one met him taking his daily exercise in the country some miles from Cambridge, he walked with a visibly abstracted air and often failed to notice one as he passed.'

The poems he composed while out walking in Hampstead continued slowly to accumulate in his notebooks, but a number of events, both private and public, led to an extraordinary increase in activity during 1895. Up until that point, Housman had drafted nineteen of the sixty-three poems he published in *A Shropshire Lad* (along with a substantial number of poems that would be published in other volumes); but in the course of 1895 he wrote over two-thirds of his first and most famous book, and by the end of the year he had enough poems to make a collection that he felt he might submit to a publisher. When he showed them to Pollard, his friend declared that not only were they worth publishing but that they would still be read in 200 years' time. Macmillan disagreed, and turned the book down, as they had Housman's proposal for an edition of Propertius ten years earlier; but then Pollard introduced Housman to the firm of Kegan Paul, Trench, Trübner & Co., who were very happy to take Housman's money.

2

The Book

As Housman suggested, *A Shropshire Lad* stood apart from the literary period in which it was published. English poetry in the 1890s is associated principally with the so-called Decadents, who took their lead from French literature of the period, notably the Symbolist poets and J.-K. Huysmans' novel *À rebours* (1884), in which the protagonist dedicates his life to art, artifice and the stimulation of the senses. An important influence nearer to home was Walter Pater, the English critic whose *Studies in the History of the Renaissance* (1873) suggested in its 'Conclusion' (withdrawn from the 1877 edition but reinstated in the 1888 one) that readers should aspire to a life dedicated to the sensations of the moment. 'To burn always with this hard gem-like flame, to maintain this ecstasy, is success in life,' Pater declared. 'While all melts under our feet, we may well catch at any exquisite passion, or any contribution to knowledge that seems, by a lifted horizon, to set the spirit free for a moment, or any stirring of the senses, strange dyes, strange flowers, and curious odours, or work of the artist's hands, or the face of one's friend.' One of the leading poets and critics of the period, Arthur Symons, dedicated his first volume of poems 'To Walter Pater in all gratitude and admiration'.

Much of the poetry Symons and his contemporaries wrote extolled exquisite artifice over natural beauty, abandoning the old traditions of English pastoral in order to celebrate the modern urban world. 'I am always charmed to read beautiful poems about nature in the country,' Symons declared in the preface to the revised and enlarged edition of *Silhouettes*, his volume of poems published the same year as *A Shropshire Lad*. 'Only, personally, I prefer the town to the country; and in the town we have to find for ourselves, as best we may, the *décor* which is the town equivalent of the great natural *décor* of the fields and hills. Here it is that artificiality comes in; and if any one sees no beauty in the effects of artificial light, in all the variable, most human, and yet most factitious town landscapes, I can only pity him, and go on my own way.'

When Symons wondered 'why we should write exclusively about the natural blush, if the delicately acquired blush of rouge should have any attraction for us', he was conjuring up a world in which theatre and artifice – both of which had connotations of 'immorality' – were held up for admiration, and his poems celebrate in particular the nightlife of the metropolis with its street lights, its dance theatres and its masquer-ades. This was the world Symons portrayed in his 1895 volume, *London Nights*, which was inspired both by his visits as a critic to music halls and his liaison with a dancer, and had, as he put it, 'no very salutary reputation among the blameless moralists of the press'.

It was a world which found its ideal illustrator in Aubrey Beardsley, who was art editor of the two magazines that became showcases for the Decadent literature of the 1890s: *The Yellow Book*, a literary quar-terly which ran from 1894 to 1897, and *The Savoy*, a monthly which lasted for only eight issues in 1896. The leading figure of the Decadent movement, Oscar Wilde, contributed to neither publication, but a widespread and incorrect report that he had been carrying a copy of *The Yellow Book* when he was led away after his arrest in April 1895 resulted in that magazine's demise two years later. In October 1896, when it became clear *The Savoy* was failing, Grant Richards was asked by a young writer called Hugh Crackanthorpe whether he might step in to save the magazine by becoming its publisher. Richards decided he could not afford to do so, and *A Shropshire Lad* would prove to be a far better investment.

Wilde's trial for homosexual offences, after the collapse of his ill-advised libel action against the Marquess of Queensberry, seemed to confirm the general public's notion that Decadent literature was an endorsement of, or incitement to, immorality. Some writers were already inimical to or distanced from this hitherto dominant literary movement, most significantly those associated with W.E. Henley's *National Observer*, which had congratulated Queensberry and denounced Wilde as 'the High Priest of the Decadents'. Another collection of writers congregated around W.B. Yeats and Ernest Rhys, who had formed the Rhymers' Club in 1890. The fact that these poets held regular meetings at a pub, Ye Olde Cheshire Cheese in Fleet Street, and admitted no women suggests a more robustly masculine grouping than the Decadents, but there was some overlap: Arthur Symons, who had founded *The Savoy*, and two of the leading Decadent poets, Ernest Dowson and Lionel Johnson, were all members of the Club and contributors to the two anthologies of poetry it published in 1892 and 1894. The literary establishment was represented by the distinctly undecadent Alfred Austin, who had been appointed Poet Laureate in January 1896, succeeding Tennyson in the post and providing undistinguished service until his death in 1913, when he was himself succeeded by Robert Bridges. Austin may have been the official laureate, but many people regarded Rudyard Kipling as Britain's true national poet, beating the drum for Empire, and giving a voice to those who had enlisted in the ranks to defend it, in his volumes of *Barrack-Room Ballads*, first collected in 1892. A second series of Kipling's ballads was published the same year as *A Shropshire Lad*, as was Hilaire Belloc's *The Bad Child's Book of Beasts*, containing comic verses not unlike those Housman had occasionally written.

It was against this literary backdrop that *A Shropshire Lad* first appeared and immediately stood out as something wholly original. 'Here is a writer who stands outside all the poetic vogues of today,' wrote 'A.M.' in the *Bookman*. 'He is neither a mystic, nor a symbolist, nor a devotee of ancient forms, nor an interpreter of the ideal significance of the music-halls. But he is a poet. I have seen no book of verses for years that breathes at least more spontaneity, and very few with as much individuality.' A Church of England newspaper called the *Guardian* agreed that it was 'pleasant, after all the books of art-poetry that are now the fashion, to come upon a poet who sings with a natural note,' while Norman Gale noted approvingly in the *Academy* that 'Mr Housman has no more ambition to make his way into a cloud of mysticism than to waste his time and his tune in the music-halls. It is his desire to keep close to flowers and the soil of their parentage.'

It was not just that *A Shropshire Lad* appeared to have blown some invigorating country air into the stuffy metropolitan rooms in which modern poetry self-consciously languished; the book was felt to be unlike anything that had gone before. 'The little volume before us contains, on well-nigh every page, essentially and distinctively new poetry,' wrote Hubert Bland, in an unsigned review in *New Age*. 'The individual voice rings out true and clear. It is not an inspiring voice, perhaps; it speaks not to us of hope in the future, of glory in the past, or of joy in the present. But it says and sings things that have not been sung or said before, and this with a power and directness, and with a heart-penetrating quality for which one may seek in vain through the work of any contemporary lyrist, Mr [W.E.] Henley perhaps excepted.' This was the notice that in the last weeks of his life Housman described as 'the best review I ever saw of my poems'. The overall reaction to the book was summed up by William Rothenstein, who wrote that the appearance of *A Shropshire Lad* in the literary landscape meant that 'people who had sneered at minor poetry were silenced. Here was fine poetry, and a poet taking his place quietly as an immortal, as a great fiddler goes to his seat in the orchestra'.

While some of the book's themes may have seemed familiar from other poetry published at the time, the approach was entirely different. Many 1890s poets wrote in a melancholy vein, but they tended to luxuriate in their affected gloom, whereas Housman was stoical and defiant. As in *A Shropshire Lad*, some of the unhappiness expressed by these poets was caused by doomed or thwarted love or the spectre of early death, but their mood seemed partly to arise from a sense that the century itself was dying, whereas Housman's verse was timeless and universal: 'Its narrow measure spans / Rue for eternity, and sorrow / Not mine, but man's,' as Housman himself put it. In spite of flaunting their 'decadence', a significant number of 1890s writers could be found sooner or later genuflecting or even prostrating themselves at the foot of the cross, whereas Housman rejected Christianity conclusively. The so-called blasphemy of other Decadent poets looks like the result of a schoolboy dare compared with Housman's clear-headed disdain and his pillaging of the scriptures to genuinely subversive effect.

Whatever other influences may have been detected in the book, the prevailing one of France was entirely absent. The book was not only distinctly English but specifically located by its title in the English countryside. Far from celebrating the metropolis, as contemporary poets did, it portrayed London as a place of unhappy exile from the countryside's 'valleys of springs of rivers', its streets thronged with people so 'undone with misery' that they cannot, as friends left behind in Shropshire did, share one's troubles, but only 'look at you and wish you ill' (XLI). There is absolutely nothing glamorous or exciting about London for the country lad who lies alone in his city bed yearning for lost companions and the 'western brookland that bred [him] long ago' (LII).

Another thing that marked out *A Shropshire Lad* as modern was the directness of the language Housman employed and the concision with which he used it, as several reviewers noted. Although some poets in the 1890s adopted a more current and forthright language than had been customary in nineteenth-century verse, others still clogged their poems with 'thee', 'thou', 'thy' and 'thine', 'hath' and 'hast', 'doth' and 'dost', 'sayeth', 'seek'st' and 'ta'en', and so on. Such words are occasionally found in Housman's other poems, but *A Shropshire Lad* is entirely free of such 'poetic' archaisms. It is true that Housman sometimes uses such literary variations as 'ere', 'aye', 'yon', 'tarry' or 'forth', and that less usual archaisms are from time to time judiciously employed to suggest a rural setting, but otherwise the language of the volume is deceptively simple and straightforward. The complexities of the poems are principally to do with tone, which often sets up an uncertainty in the reader about what Housman, beneath what appears to be a delightful artlessness, is really saying.

Anyone opening a book with the title *A Shropshire Lad* might expect it to evoke the life of a single, if emblematic, individual, which is why many commentators have searched for a narrative within the volume. The notion that the book was intended to tell a story surfaced early, Grant Richards describing it in his review of the first edition as 'a biography in verse, in sixty-three short poems, dealing with the loves and sorrows, the dramatic incidents, the daily labours of a Ludlow boy'. That may be broadly true, but later attempts to detail this narrative turn out to be more ingenious than convincing. The fact that Housman moved several poems around within the volume at proof stage has been adduced as evidence of some narrative plan, but if he spent time ordering and reordering the sequence in which the poems finally appeared, he was doing what any poet would when preparing a collection for publication. It is true that in the first poem in the volume, which describes and reflects upon Queen Victoria's Golden Jubilee in 1887, Housman is setting out his poetic stall. The poem is located from the very first line in Shropshire, introduces two themes – soldiering and the death of comrades – that will recur, and adopts a sceptical tone that colours the poet's view of life and fate throughout the volume. Similarly, the two last poems of the book act as a commentary on what has gone before: in the first, the poet is castigated by a bluff friend for the morbid tenor of his verses, while in the second he identifies the intended audience for his poetry, the 'luckless lads' such as himself who have featured throughout the book. It is also true that the poems that come between can be divided (unequally) between those in the first part, which are largely set in rural Shropshire, and those in the second part, in which the poet looks back to this land of lost content from his exile in London, the hinge of the book provided by poem XXXVII, 'As through the wild green hills of Wyre', which is set on a train travelling from the shire to the capital.

The theory that the poems are arranged to portray some kind of personal development, 'a persona who grows and matures with the experiences which the poems record', is more difficult to sustain. It is only possible to claim that 'a progressively tragic view of love is shown in the later Shropshire poems' if one simply ignores those which don't fit the pattern that is being imposed upon them. If Housman, meticulous in all he did, had intended some kind of verse narrative, why did he not enclose it more neatly with one introductory poem and one summarising poem, rather than one of the former and two of the latter? Why does the 'hinge' poem not appear at the midway point, and why was it not part of the volume's original scheme but added only at the very last minute when the rest of the book had already been sent to the printers? One might also seek some explanation for the fact that, although each poem is given a number, some poems – for no reason anyone has explained – have also been given titles. These titles are not spread evenly throughout the book, but occur entirely at random. The clinching argument is that the poems' 'persona' is not in the least consistent: at one moment he is a melancholy twenty-year-old reflecting on the transience of life (as in the second poem, 'Loveliest of trees, the cherry now'), but then instantly changes into a more mature figure who hectors various lads in the voice of a recruiting sergeant (in the third, 'Leave your home behind, lad') or even a scoutmaster urging a slug-a-bed to get out into the fresh air (in the fourth, 'Reveille'). The perspective changes from poem to poem with no detectable pattern, and all attempts to fit the poems into some kind of scheme merely end up looking forced.

A Shropshire Lad is not a poetic Bildungsroman, nor does it provide the sort of narrative that Schubert constructed from Wilhelm Müller's poems in Die schöne Müllerin or Winterreise. Rather, it is a collection of poems loosely bound together by setting, theme and mood, and by the personality of the man who wrote them. 'The Shropshire Lad is an imaginary figure, with something of my temper and view of life,' Housman told an enquirer in 1933, though he was careful to add: 'Very little in the book is biographical.' As is so often the case with Housman, this was true only as far as it went, and part of the attraction of the book, at any rate in its early years, was that readers sensed there must be some sort of story not *in* the poems but *behind* them. In this it resembles another popular work of art of the same period, Edward Elgar's *'Enigma' Variations*, which received its first performance in 1899. Elgar's composition occupies a similar place in the history of English music to that of *A Shropshire Lad* in the history of English poetry, both being works of the nineteenth century that nevertheless mark the beginning of the modern. The *Enigma Variations* are dedicated to 'my friends pictured within', and each of the fourteen variations is a musical portrait of someone Elgar knew, identified in the score by a private nickname, a set of initials, or in one case three asterisks. The work's proper title is *Variations on an Original Theme for Orchestra ('Enigma')*, and it is the 'unplayed theme', as Elgar called it, that gives the piece its name, not the partly hidden identities of the 'friends pictured within' to whom it is dedicated. It is an enigma that remains unsolved. Before the work's first performance, Elgar stated:

> The 'Enigma' I will not explain – its 'dark saying' must be left unguessed, and I warn you that the apparent connection between the Variations and the Theme is often of the slightest texture; further, through and over the whole set another and larger theme 'goes', but is not played [. . .] So the principal Theme never appears, even as in some late dramas – e.g. Maeterlinck's 'L'Intruse' and 'Les sept Princesses' – the chief character is never on stage.

He never did explain it, any more than Housman publicly admitted what lay behind *A Shropshire Lad*, of which it might also be said that the chief character does not appear on stage. This did not prevent people from speculating in both cases. 'It is evident that the "Shropshire Lad" has been hit very hard by a woman,' the poet Richard Le Gallienne declared in one of the book's first reviews. As we now know, he was – to say the least of it – wide of the mark.

While Housman's refusal to allow individual poems from the volume to be reprinted in anthologies – a stricture he did not apply to the contents of *Last Poems* – suggests that he regarded the book as a single entity, this is not at all the same thing as saying that the book forms a consistent narrative. Regardless of the author's wishes, certain poems did take on an individual life beyond the volume, either because they were set to music by composers or because they became popular recital pieces. Housman did his best to prevent the latter fate, refusing permission for any of his poems to be read on the wireless. 'Only the archangel Raphael could recite my poems properly,' he wrote, and archangels seem to have been in short supply at the BBC. 'Auribus', who wrote 'Wireless Notes' for the *Musical Times*, described the Corporation's poetry broadcasts in 1930 as 'often unbearable':

> Some of the gentlemen who practise it are obsessed with the idea that they must use an artificial voice and an artificial intensity of feeling no matter what the character of the words they utter. Every line becomes an oracle. In every line the reciter manages to discover at least one word so heavy with fate that it must needs be voiced with the greatest apprehension. It usually occurs in the last foot. A poetry-speaker will announce in a perfectly natural way that he proposes to give us, say, a bit of Housman. Then, summoning all his courage and lowering his voice about a fifth, he will declaim:

> > Loveliest of trees, the cherry now
> > Is hung with bloom along the bough,

> as if he had just finished murdering Duncan.

The poems of *A Shropshire Lad* may not tell a story, but they are carefully related to each other. The geographical setting announced in the book's title is the most obvious of the ways in which the poems are bound together, although the volume contains several topographical anomalies: 'Bredon Hill' (XXI) is a Worcestershire landmark, while 'The Isle of Portland' (LIX) is a tied island off the coast of Dorset, a very long way from landlocked Shropshire. If the geographical bounds of the poems are a little flexible, Housman Country nevertheless remains distinct and coherent. While *A Shropshire Lad* was not Housman's own title, he clearly thought it a good and appropriate one. The book certainly takes as its principal subject matter the travails of young men either living in or exiled from the English countryside, with place-names borrowed from the real county of Shropshire; but what the title really announces is a theme or mood, rather as Arthur Symons's contemporaneous *London Nights* does, evoking a poetic world rather than anything more specific. Housman's assertion that 'The Shropshire Lad is an imaginary figure, with something of my temper and view of life' supports this view. In fact, Housman first wrote 'an imaginary character', which he presumably altered because 'figure' is less embodied than 'character', suggesting a presiding sensibility rather than an identifiable individual.

The 'Shropshire Lad' in Housman's formulation is essentially the speaker in the poems. He is indeed sometimes a lad, but at other times is an older man who is looking back to his youth, a double perspective that provides additional poignancy, emphasising the unstoppable passage of irrecoverable time. The Lad is also at one moment a friend of the other lads he addresses or writes about, at others an outsider looking on with admiration, affection, envy or fellow-feeling. On only four occasions are these lads allotted names: Fred, Dick, Ned, Maurice. More often they are referred to or addressed as, with varying degrees of warmth, 'lad' or 'lads', 'my lad' or 'my lads', or – simply and most intimately – 'you'. These lads suffer the troubles characteristic of young men of the period: they fall in love with young women who treat them with heartless flirtatiousness, or abandon them for other lovers, or simply die; they enlist in the army and end up 'dead and rotten' on distant battlefields; they get into fights or worse, and end up in gaol or on the gallows; they commit suicide. Such fates make the speaker acutely aware of the fleeting nature of love and life, and this pervasive consciousness of the ephemeral nature of existence is reinforced by the changing seasons. For the speaker, the cycle of birth, death and renewal observed in the natural world that traditionally provides hope – particularly for those with Christian faith – merely reflects the diurnal treadmill on which people trudge round and round until death puts a final stop to what has become a pointless, repetitive exercise. As the taunting blackbird sings in 'When smoke stood up from Ludlow' (VII):

> 'Lie down, lie down, young yeoman;
>   What use to rise and rise?

Rise man a thousand mornings
    Yet down at last he lies . . . '

There will certainly be no bright new dawn of resurrection for those who do at last lie down: no one in these poems rises from the bed of clay. This finality does, however, provide a small consolation because if there is no heaven, then there is no hell either, and the poet is able to reassure those going on that final journey that 'nought's to dread': 'In all the endless road you tread / There's nothing but the night' (LX). The speaker has sympathy with those who, faced with such a grim prospect, take their own lives, but his own philosophy is one of stoical endurance. Dwelling on the inevitability of death, he suggests, only 'lays lads under ground' all the sooner: far better to 'Think no more, lad; laugh, be jolly' (XLIX). This is, perhaps, rather a difficult injunction to obey: it would take a certain amount of willpower simply to endure, let alone rejoice in, the world the poems inhabit.

It was remarked from the very first that *A Shropshire Lad* was, as Hubert Bland put it in a phrase Housman would surely have enjoyed, 'wanting in the note of gladness', and it has been a commonplace ever since that the book is overwhelmingly gloomy. A review in *The Times* of the second edition was headlined 'The Funereal Muse' and, although unwilling to 'reproach [Housman] for preferring – within reason – the tragic side of life as a subject [. . .] to its happier aspect', warned that his 'passion for the society and conversation of Charon will not improve his admirable poetry'. When Ezra Pound published a satirical poem about *A Shropshire Lad* in his *Canzoni* (1911), he reduced 'Mr Housman's Message' to a three-stanza lament which itemised what he saw as the book's essential ingredients: people die before their time, as do birds sitting in hawthorn trees; lads tend to be either hanged or shot; the human plight is a pitiful one; Shropshire is a great deal nicer than London; so, with all this in mind, we should just smile at nature's grim beauty. The poem, which comes with a repeated chorus of the repeated word 'woe', would have been more effective if Pound had imitated the manner as well as the matter of Housman's poetry, but the implied complaint has been repeated by others.

Some even believed Housman was not being altogether serious. An anonymous reviewer in the Philadelphia *Citizen* conceded that the Lad 'moves our compassion by his many woes', but concluded that the whole book was some kind of elaborate joke and that Housman was like the lachrymose Mock-Turtle in *Alice in Wonderland*, of whom the Gryphon says: 'Bless you, he haint got no sorrows. It's only his imagination.' As evidence, the reviewer cited the volume's penultimate poem, 'Terence, this is stupid stuff', without apparently turning the page to discover the book's true envoi. In that final poem Housman adopts the guise of a market gardener who has worked hard to cultivate his flowers, only to find that they do not sell: 'The hue was not the wear'. He nevertheless determines to carry on growing them:

> So up and down I sow them
>   For lads like me to find,
> When I shall lie below them,
>   A dead man out of mind.
>   [. . .]
> And fields will yearly bear them
>   As light-leaved spring comes on,
> And luckless lads will wear them
>   When I am dead and gone.

Housman here identifies the audience for his poems, aware that there are other young men like him who will be familiar with and appreciate what others may decry.

The poems' melancholy has always been part of their appeal, and Housman recognises, as some commentators have not, that there is a difference between sadness and misery. As the popularity of innumerable novels and films repeatedly demonstrates, people enjoy the sadness of others when it is at a safe fictional remove. This may be especially true in England, where 'having a jolly good cry' is often recommended as an enjoyable recreation – perhaps for the very reason that it provides a holiday from the emotional self-denial thought characteristic of the English race. While it is hard to imagine Housman himself giving in to this kind of thing, we have already seen that he could be moved to tears – and he believed that the best poetry always produced such physical reactions.

The imaginary critic who suggests in the volume's penultimate poem that, for a change, the poet might 'pipe a tune to dance to', receives the answer that alcohol rather than poetry is what makes a man merry – at any rate temporarily:

> Oh many a peer of England brews
> Livelier liquor than the Muse,
> And malt does more than Milton can
> To justify God's ways to man.
> Ale, man, ale's the stuff to drink
> For fellows whom it hurts to think:
> Look into the pewter pot
> To see the world as the world's not.
> And faith 'tis pleasant till 'tis past:
> The mischief is that 'twill not last.

The brew the poet provides in his verses, however, is more effective than this temporary remedy because it acts like an inoculation rather than an opiate. He goes on to tell the story of Mithridates, king of Pontus, who protected himself homeopathically from any attempt to poison him by taking regular small amounts of deadly substances. What Housman characteristically fails to add, though no doubt expected his readers to know, is that Mithridates' prophylactic strategy eventually proved his undoing. He may have 'died old', but not as he had wished: defeated and captured by the Romans, he was unable to commit suicide by poison because he had rendered himself immune – a grim irony of the kind Housman particularly relished.

This sort of dark comedy is one of the reasons *A Shropshire Lad* is not the dispiriting read a brief synopsis might suggest. Irony, rather than alcohol or poison, is the remedy Housman himself employed when facing the worst, both in his poetry and in his life, but this has not always been appreciated. The *Citizen* reviewer, for example, tumbled neatly into the trap that Housman had cunningly laid in 'Terence, this is stupid stuff'. The poem appears to be an apologia for what has gone before, in which Terence Hearsay, the supposed author, defends his muse against those who complain that it is too glum. This Terence, however, seems at first quite unlike someone who could have written the book's other poems. He and his critic are depicted as a couple of Shropshire yokels, and there is a suggestion that their conversation is taking place in a pub. The complaints about Terence's poems are couched in an idiom that undermines them: while in essence some of the criticisms seem reasonable, they are exaggeratedly voiced by someone who appears to be both unlettered and drunk.

Housman occasionally uses rhyming couplets elsewhere in the volume, but never to such rollicking effect as in the first two stanzas of this poem, in which the complaint is made and answered. Terence, far from being the sophisticated author of the affecting lyric poems we have just read, is a country bumpkin who likes nothing more than to drink so much that he has to be 'carried half way home' from Ludlow Fair, losing his necktie in the process, and ends up sleeping it off while lying 'in lovely muck', presumably in a roadside ditch somewhere. It has been suggested that Housman used Terence as a distancing device between himself and the poems, creating a country lad who could voice sentiments that perhaps a classical scholar could not; or that by adopting the guise of this Shropshire lad he could make the poems more rurally 'authentic' and hide the inconvenient fact that the author was actually a metropolitan sophisticate. If this was the intention, Housman seems not to have carried it through with much thoroughness or consistency. Indeed, this poem enacts a shift in voice and perspective, from the cheerfully inebriated Shropshire yokel of the second stanza to the (in every sense) more sober and well-read philosopher of the third and fourth stanzas. As William Archer noted: 'Mr Housman writes, for the most part, under the guise of "A Shropshire Lad" – the rustic forefather of his book. But this is evidently a mere mask. Mr Housman is no Shropshire Burns singing at the plough. He is a man of culture. He moves in his rustic garb with no clodhopper's gait, but with the ease of an athlete; and I think he has an Elzevir classic in the pocket of his smock frock.'* The rural clodhopper's gait is apparent only in this single poem, deliberately adopted as a jokey rebuttal of potential critics. Some commentators have been surprised that the author of *A Shropshire Lad* could also have written very funny parodies and squibs, but the two apparently disparate styles of Housman poetry come together in these verses, which were written several months after the majority of the book's other poems.

More representative of the volume's dark humour is the sprightly little poem published as no. XVIII:

Oh, when I was in love with you,
    Then I was clean and brave,
And miles around the wonder grew
    How well did I behave.

But now the fancy passes by,
    And nothing will remain,
And miles around they'll say that I
    Am quite myself again.

The rueful comedy here is very characteristic, while the structure and rhyme scheme make the otherwise surprising conclusion inevitable – and indeed logical. What seems artless, almost a mere ditty (and one that has often been set to music), is in fact tonally sophisticated: the poem appears light-hearted, but this is the kind of lightness that is adopted to conceal deep sorrow, both from others and perhaps from the speaker himself. If not as stirringly plangent as some of the other poems, it nevertheless delivers a powerful little kick.

This literary strategy of surface directness concealing something altogether more complicated, hard truths wrapped in an attractive package of ironic humour, is one Housman used to great effect not only in his poems but also in his lectures and his correspondence. Indeed, he

---

*Elzevir was a Dutch publishing house of the seventeenth and eighteenth centuries renowned for producing pocket editions of classical texts, among them the works of Terence (1635).

uses it so often that it becomes almost reflex, less a deliberate strategy than part of his nature as both a writer and a man. It is here that his tone comes in, often difficult to gauge with any real certainty – which is no doubt just how Housman liked it. The very first poem in *A Shropshire Lad* suggests that Housman's verse may not be quite as transparent and straightforward as it seems. Its account of Queen Victoria's Golden Jubilee lures the unwary reader in with an apparently hearty and patriotic commemoration of the event. The tone of the poem, however, is slippery: what at first seems a Kiplingesque celebration of Shropshire's professional soldiers, and of the Queen and Empire for which they are fighting, turns out on more detailed inspection to be distinctly subversive, undermining the popular sentiment of 'God save the Queen' with a hint of dissent. The faintly blasphemous statement that those who died to save the Queen 'shared the work with God' is reinforced by the lines 'The saviours come not home tonight: / Themselves they could not save'. The use of the word 'saviours', even without an upper-case initial, hints that common soldiers too are doing Christ's work, while the second line is a sly appropriation of the Gospels' account of the Crucifixion, in which the chief priests sarcastically observe: 'He saved others; himself he cannot save.'

'1887' picks out some themes and sets the tone for the entire volume. It immediately locates the book in Shropshire, referring in its opening words to beacons burning 'From Clee to heaven'. Soldiers will appear frequently in the poems that follow, often fondly or wistfully regarded as real or potential 'friends', as they are here. The notion that Shropshire is a county that produces good, honest men, and whose generalised but memorable features include 'skies that knit their heartstrings right' and 'fields that bred them brave', will also run throughout the book. The poem introduces other features such as 'farm', 'town' and 'land', words that will recur in the poems almost as metonyms, standing in as a kind of shorthand for the rural world Housman is evoking. The second poem, 'Loveliest of trees, the cherry now', is one of Housman's best-loved lyrics, three perfect stanzas that announce the book's recurring motif of the evanescence of life. The notion of white blossom and snow mirroring each other and proving at once overwhelming in their effect and wholly ephemeral is repeated in a poem that appears much later in the volume, in which the speaker, now exiled in London, imagines the rural year heedlessly turning without him.

> 'Tis time, I think, by Wenlock town
>   The golden broom should blow;
> The hawthorn sprinkled up and down
>   Should charge the land with snow.

He pictures other, luckier, Shropshire lads and lasses getting out into the spring countryside and pleads:

> O tarnish late on Wenlock Edge,
>   Gold that I never see;
> Lie long, high snowdrifts in the hedge
>   That will not shower on me.

The poignancy here is that the speaker knows full well, as he has already acknowledged in the earlier poem about the cherry, that flowers fade and that his plea that they should linger is a vain one: the gold of the broom is already tarnished and the hawthorn will vanish as quickly as a snowdrift. Knowing that you cannot have something does not necessarily make you stop wanting it, may indeed make that longing all the keener.

The faint echo between poems is something that occurs elsewhere in the book: the contrasting ploughmen in 'When smoke stood up from Ludlow' (VII) and 'Is my team ploughing' (XXVII); the soldiers responding differently to bugle calls in 'The Recruit' (III), 'On the idle hill of summer' (XXXV) and 'The Day of Battle' (LVI); the lovers gathering wild flowers in 'Oh see how thick the goldcup flowers' (V), 'March' (X) and 'The Lent Lily' (XXIX). Other echoes sound between the lad who has 'lost for everlasting / The heart out of his breast' in 'There pass the careless people' (XIV) and the one who asks a friend 'To this lost heart be kind' in 'If truth in hearts that perish' (XXXIII). The speaker in 'Say, lad, have you things to do?' (XXIV) offers much the same to his friend as the more disembodied one does in 'From far, from eve and morning' (XXXII). The wind that blows 'through holt and hanger' and down the centuries in 'On Wenlock Edge the wood's in trouble' (XXXI) is felt in several poems. It blows in, delivering the friend offering his hand and heart in 'From far, from eve and morning'; it blows out of the west land, either 'Warm with the blood of the lads I knew' (XXXVIII) or so cold that it is 'an air that kills' (XL); it accompanies the wing-sandalled messenger of death in 'The Merry Guide' (XLII), and makes nettles perform a *danse macabre* on the graves of those who have killed themselves for love (XVI).

Some of the best-known of the poems are thematically related. The passing of time and the changes this brings link 'Bredon Hill' (XXI) and 'Is my team ploughing' (XXVII). In the first of these poems two lovers enjoying a summer idyll ignore the church bells summoning them to church, thinking they can wait until the bells call them there for their wedding; but winter comes and, instead of the joyful pealing they had imagined, the now solitary young man hears 'the one bell only' tolling for his girl, who has died at Christmas. The following summer the bells continue to peal, an intolerable reminder of the previous year's happiness, and the young man eventually relents: 'I hear you, I will come.' A similarly dark ironic tale is told in 'Is my team ploughing', which takes the form of a conversation between a dead ploughboy and his best friend. The ghost asks about everyday life continuing in his absence, hoping perhaps for evidence that his passing has been marked. Life goes on much the same, the friend replies; but he becomes evasive when the dead lad asks after his girl, for both she and the friend have found solace in the same bed. The changes wrought among lovers by time also provides the theme of 'Along the field as we came by' (XXV), in which the same play is made between the bridal bed and the bed of clay. 'To an Athlete Dying Young' (XIX) salutes a young man who by dying before his time can at least be consoled that he will not be around to see his sporting records surpassed: he is one of those who, like the young men in 'The lads in their hundreds to Ludlow come in for the fair' (XXIII), will 'die in their glory and never be old'.

Elsewhere premature death provides no such consolations. The lad in 'Shot? so quick, so clean an ending?' (XLIV) kills himself in order to avoid disgrace, while the young shepherd who goes 'naked to the hangman' in 'On moonlit heath and lonesome bank' (IX) and the convict who dies in gaol in 'The Isle of Portland' (LIX) meet their deaths utterly alone. That the troubles besetting Housman's lads are nothing new is evident from 'On Wenlock Edge the wood's in trouble' and 'Loitering with a vacant eye' (LI), in which young men learn that the Ancients suffered and endured just as they now do. In the first a lad recognises that the gale blowing through the trees is the same as the one that disturbed them 'When Uricon the city stood', and that a Roman soldier was similarly burdened with untold troubles until death relieved him. The latter poem is set in the Grecian gallery at the British Museum, where a marble statue tells a visiting lad that he too is exiled from his home but that he simply has to endure his lot. Both poems suggest that stoicism is a classical virtue to be emulated.

Another, related way in which the individual poems of *A Shropshire Lad* cohere into a whole is by language, by Housman's repeated use of specific words. These words sound like beats and echoes throughout the book – and indeed beyond, providing additional close links with the poems Housman omitted from this volume but selected for publication in *Last Poems*, and those that appeared posthumously in *More Poems* and *Additional Poems*, some of which were written at the same time. The most frequently recurring word is, of course, 'lad' or 'lads', appearing sixty-six times in sixty-three poems – and many more times in the poems collected in other volumes. While this is only to be expected, the repeated appearance of other words is more telling. 'Friend' and its variants ('friends', 'friendship', 'friendly' and 'friendless'), for example, appear far more often than 'lover' – though the distinction between the two is not always clear. This suggests that the bonds of friendship in Housman Country count for a great deal more than those of conventional romantic love, and it is significant how infrequently the words 'lass', 'girl' and 'girls' appear compared with 'lad' or 'lads': a mere eight times. Housman occasionally refers to someone's 'love' in the sense of a female sweetheart, but these loves tend to betray their lads, and it is not merely the frequency with which certain words occur that is notable, but also the context in which they are found. Hearts and hands – both given and taken – are often mentioned, and looks are cast, but these exchanges tend to be inconclusive or forlorn.

Familiar land, fields, shires and sky are a regular feature of the poems, evoking the rural setting, but they are often, like 'home', 'far', while the many roads that lead to (or more often 'away' from) them tend to be 'long', or even 'endless', and are usually trodden 'alone'. 'Long' is also a regularly occurring measurement of time, generally endured rather than enjoyed, a period in which past pleasures have receded and regrets have accumulated. 'More' is almost invariably preceded by 'no', and 'never' seals off both past and future from the stoically borne present. The volume contains (as Housman puts it in one poem) sighs aplenty, but only two mentions of 'tears', a further hint that stoicism is preferable to giving in to grief. Although the poems sometimes suggest a deceptively sunlit landscape, they also frequently evoke or take place at 'night', and the 'sleep' that awaits lads when the day is done is often permanent, the 'beds' they lie in made of earth, dust or clay. Words connected with death and dying toll throughout the poems, as do ends and endings, while 'ill' is more often than not used to describe luck, how things are faring, or how lads are treated.

As with individual words, so with the book's themes, on which Housman plays a set of variations: love and loss; youth and death; friendship and betrayal; crime and punishment; the passing of time; the military calling; the English landscape; exile from places of past happiness; the country versus the city; the absence of God and the indifference of the natural world to the fate of men. These themes overlap and reinforce each other, providing links between individual poems often separated by several pages. Taken together, they present a view of the world that is both particular and universal. In one way or another the characters in Housman's poems tend to come to grief, but one need not be a Shropshire rustic – or indeed a Classics don – to have felt the pangs of unrequited love, to have experienced that piercing sense of time lost and never to be recovered, or to have been touched by an overwhelming sense of mortality. The Shropshire Lad may rail against fate, but he knows that he can do nothing to prevent it taking its inexorable course.

Another striking and attractive aspect of the book is that it draws on many literary sources. Housman named the principal ones as 'Shakespeare's songs, the Scottish Border ballads, and Heine', but he also drew upon Greek and Latin verse, the Bible, and a wide range of English poets, sometimes marking passages in his own copies of these books as if for future use. Some influences are more general than specific: 'I suppose that my classical training has been of some use in furnishing good models, and making me fastidious, and telling me what to leave out,' Housman told one admirer. Elsewhere individual phrases can be traced to their sources. In 1958 Norman Marlow devoted much of his *A.E. Housman: Scholar and Poet* to this kind of scholarship, and his work has been expanded upon since, notably by Tom Burns Haber in his 1967 critical study, *A.E. Housman*, in a Housman Society publication, *Housman and Heine: A Neglected Relationship* (2011), and more generally by Archie Burnett in his scholarly edition of Housman's poems (1997). Some of these echoes, such as those of George Augustus Simcox's *Poems and Romances* (1869) and Philip Bourke Marston's *Song-Tide* (1888), may have been difficult to detect even when the book was published and now require true dedication to ferret out. Marlow modestly described his own endeavours as 'merely a necessary basis on which a future critic may build', and to that end it is worth briefly considering the influence on Housman of one very familiar and much loved poem.

Like *A Shropshire Lad*, Thomas Gray's 'Elegy written in a Country Churchyard' (1751) is quintessentially English and became very popular in its time, running through some fifty editions during the first fifty years of its publication. Housman owned an 1807 edition of *The Poetical Works of Thomas Gray with an Account of his Life and Writings* and clearly knew the poems well enough to quote or refer to them in his correspondence, even when lying seriously ill in a nursing home. Housman also regarded Gray as an exemplar of literary continence whom he was happy to emulate. In February 1910, in response to one of the frequent enquiries he received about the distant prospect of a second volume of poems, he wrote: 'The other day I had the curiosity to reckon up the complete pieces, printed and unprinted, which I have written since 1896, and they only come to 300 lines, so the next volume appears to be some way off. In barrenness at any rate, I hold a high place among English poets, excelling even Gray.'

Echoes of Gray, though not of his Elegy, have been detected in 'On moonlight heath and lonesome bank' (IX) and 'Into my heart an air that kills' (XL). However, it is hardly a coincidence that for '*Diffugere Nives*', his translation of Horace's ode, Housman should use the metre and rhyme scheme of the Elegy, and the influence of Gray's poem is detectable in both *A Shropshire Lad* and later volumes of Housman's verse. There seem to be at the very least similarities between Gray's ploughmen – 'How jocund did they drive their team afield' – and Housman's: 'And blithe afield to ploughing / Against the morning beam / I strode beside my team' (VII) and 'Is my team ploughing, / That I was used to drive' (XXVII). Similarly, Gray's line 'Where heaves the turf in many a mouldering heap' may have inspired Housman's repeated use of the same verb to describe the workings of nature: 'And overhead the aspen heaves' (XXVI), 'His forest fleece the Wrekin heaves' (XXXI), 'The sigh that heaves the grasses' and 'On acres of the seeded grasses / The changing burnish heaves'. The first line of the epitaph at the end of Gray's poem, 'Here rests his head upon the lap of earth' may well have supplied Housman with the image he uses in the lines about the death of a friend: 'Now to her lap the incestuous earth / The son she bore has ta'en'. Whether or not one agrees that these constitute genuine echoes rather than two English poets using a common literary currency, it can be said more surely that the mood of *A Shropshire Lad* is in direct descent from both the Elegy and Gray's 'Ode on a Distant Prospect of Eton College' (1747). Eton in the latter poem, like Housman's blue remembered hills, is seen from afar, both geographically and in time, and represents a land of lost content where (as Gray imagines it) 'regardless of their doom / The little victims play'.

Possible echoes of and allusions to Matthew Arnold, a poet Housman had long admired, are far more numerous. Writing of their time at Oxford, A.W. Pollard recalled: 'His favourite English poet in these early days was Matthew Arnold, whose "Empedocles on Etna" he recommended to me as containing "all the law and the prophets".' Pollard went on to say that Housman's favourite novelist in his youth was Thomas Hardy, 'and I think Hardy's influence went far deeper than Arnold's'. If so, this was more in mood than anything else, and Housman's later opinion of Hardy, whom he had come to know socially, was expressed very exactly for publication in 1933: 'For Hardy I felt affection, and high admiration for some of his novels and a few of his poems.' More privately, he had told a visitor in 1926 that 'Hardy has surely accomplished what the other novelists could not have done, but he, as a poet, is only "a mere reflection" of the novelist's figure.' In contrast, his admiration for Arnold never wavered. He told the same visitor on a subsequent occasion: 'To tell the truth, I like Matthew Arnold best. While very few people read Arnold's poems, a good many people speak of him and pay their respect for him. Those who cannot take Arnold's humour into consideration are quite out of the question.' There may be a certain amount of fellow-feeling in this last remark, since Housman's own humour has sometimes not been taken into consideration when assessing his poetry. A great many echoes of and allusions to Arnold have been detected in Housman's poetry, notably to 'Empedocles on Etna'. It seems likely that 'Dover Beach' would have appealed to Housman for its evocation of the 'melancholy, long, withdrawing roar' of the Sea of Faith, while the poem's opening appears to reverberate in the first lines of *A Shropshire Lad*'s single coastal poem, 'The Isle of Portland' (LIX). Another of Arnold's poems that might be expected to resonate with Housman, if only for its title, is 'The Buried Life'. Echoes of this poem have been recorded, though not oddly those in the opening four lines of 'Look not in my eyes, for fear' (XV) and the second stanza of 'From far, from eve and morning' (XXXII).

Heine is the most unexpected of those writers whose presence is felt in *A Shropshire Lad*, not least because he stands apart by nationality. Most English people at the time Housman's volume was published would have known Heine's poetry largely in a musical context through Schubert and Schumann's settings, though English translations had been published in America in 1864 and in Britain in 1894. Housman owned a copy of the latter book, Edgar Alfred Bowring's *The Poems of Heine. Complete Translation into the Original Metres with a Sketch of His Life*, and probably knew Arnold's 1865 essay on Heine; but he also owned several volumes of Heine's work in the original German, including the *Buch der Lieder* (1889), *Neue Gedichte* (1876) and an 1885 edition of his collected works. 'Sinner's Rue', published in *Last Poems*, is so closely based on Heine's '*Am Kreuzweg wird begraben*' (*Lyrisches Intermezzo* LXII) that it amounts to an expanded translation, while one of Housman's most touching couplets, 'Homespun collars, homespun hearts, / Wear to rags in foreign parts' borrows both its sentiment and rhythm from Heine's lines 'Deutsche Treue, deutscher Hemde, / Die verschleisst man in der Fremde'. There are echoes of Heine elsewhere among Housman's poems, but the parallels between the two writers are principally structural and thematic. Both used simple verse forms and wrote poems that could easily be understood by ordinary people. Both were inspired to write poetry by disastrous infatuations in their youth. Both dwelt on the changing seasons, evanescence and death.

As to the two other influences Housman himself acknowledged, echoes of twenty-seven of Shakespeare's plays have been traced in his poems, as well as allusions to the *Sonnets* and *Venus and Adonis*, while the rural setting of *A Shropshire Lad* and its stories of doomed lovers clearly owe something to the Border Ballads and English folk poetry in general. The Ballads find their most obvious imitation in both the subject matter and ballad form of 'The True Lover' (LIII), a grisly colloquy between a self-murdered lad and his girl. This poem, which some commentators have dismissed as in poor taste (chiefly for its rather jocular stanza about the bloody results of a slit throat), would not in fact look out of place in Francis James Child's seminal *The English and Scottish Popular Ballads*, which was published in five volumes between 1884 and 1898. The rather different colloquies between the failed seducer and the flirtatious maiden in 'O see how thick the goldcup flowers' (V) and the dead man and his friend in 'Is my team ploughing' (XXVII) also recall these old folk poems. Housman's rural lovers, soldiers and their sweethearts, murderers, suicides and condemned men are all standard features of traditional ballads. In addition, the four-line stanza rhymed *abab* in which the majority of the poems in *A Shropshire Lad* are written is one that was used in many of the Border Ballads.

Echoes of and allusions to works as well known as Gray's Elegy (or indeed Shakespeare, the Bible and the Border Ballads) serve a more important purpose than the admittedly fascinating academic parlour game of hunting them out. They have the effect of making *A Shropshire Lad* seem oddly familiar even at first reading and of establishing it almost at once within a literary canon that readers would subliminally recognise, even if they could not identify the actual sources. An example of this is the use made of the song 'Fear no more the heat o' the sun' from Shakespeare's *Cymbeline*, a poem Housman reckoned along with 'O mistress mine, where are you roaming?' from *Twelfth Night* as 'the very summits of lyrical achievement'. The first two lines of the song, 'Fear no more the heat o' the sun, / Nor the furious winter's rages' are barely recast in 'The Immortal Part' (XLIII): 'Fear the heat o' the sun no more, / Nor the snowing winter wild'. Housman clearly expected his readers to recognise this borrowing, as well as the fairly obvious echo in 'With rue my heart is laden' (LIV), where Shakespeare's couplet from the same song, 'Golden lads and girls all must, / As chimney-sweepers, come to dust' can be heard, both in thought and expression, behind the first stanza. Similarly, one of the reasons that 'Breath's a ware that will not keep' in 'Reveille' (IV) is so arresting is that it strikes an echo from the last line of Feste's song 'O mistress mine' in *Twelfth Night*: 'Youth's a stuff will not endure'.

As well as skilfully adapting or paraphrasing well-known works of literature, Housman coined his own very memorable images and phrases: 'an air that kills', 'blue remembered hills', 'the land of lost content', 'shoulder the sky', 'blood's a rover', 'the idle hill of summer', the 'twelve-winded sky'. As one early reviewer observed: 'In an extraordinary volume, not the least extraordinary feature is the abounding presence of verbal felicity. Arresting phrases are as numerous as sparrows in ivy at night; but not one of them convinces us it has been manufactured, so easily does each fall into its place, so simple are the means by which the novel effect is procured.'

The combined result of familiar echoes and striking new phrases is that *A Shropshire Lad* has itself become one of those books from which people quote or recognise poems or stray lines without necessarily being aware of their origin. The experience of two American readers might stand for many: 'To my knowledge, I'd never intentionally read any A.E. Housman so I was surprised that some of his poems were already familiar to me —"1887" (I) and "When I was one and twenty" (XIII) were both poems I had encountered before, though I couldn't tell you where.' This brought a response from Colorado: 'My dad, who died at age 90 last Dec, loved *A Shropshire Lad* and had a well-worn copy on his bedside table for most of his life. I think Housman is one of those authors that you don't know that you know until someone attributes well-known lines to him.' Those who come to know the poems through reading the book tend to find them roosting immovably in the memory. As one of the book's earliest reviewers put it: 'You may read it in half-an-hour — but there are things in it you will scarce forget in a lifetime.'

3

Lads in Trouble

Early readers of *A Shropshire Lad* would have had no background knowledge about the composition of the poems, or about the events that led to such a concentrated period of writing in 1895. Kate Symons suggested that the death of Edward Housman in November 1894 contributed to this lyric outpouring, partly because of 'the removal of a burden & a distress, for our father had become broken and infirm, though his age was only 63', but also, and crucially, because it revived 'the inevitable poignant memories of youth'. Grant Richards believed that although the death of Housman's father would not have weighed upon him as heavily as that of his mother, 'it could not have fallen lightly on one who was ever strongly affected by the deaths of those he knew, even if they were not closely connected to him'.

A death of someone who was certainly closely connected with Housman, and which undoubtedly affected him deeply, was that of Adalbert Jackson on 12 November 1892. The two poems Housman wrote about him were not included in *A Shropshire Lad*, though they were written at the same period. Adalbert nevertheless became a ghostly presence in the book, because his death was the very first among Housman's close friends and seems likely to have contributed to the recurrent appearance in Housman's poetry of lads who will never grow old. Six weeks before the blow fell, Housman had delivered his Introductory Lecture at UCL, in the course of which he alluded to man's helplessness in the face of the inexorable workings of fate, a helplessness that affects the lives of his Shropshire lads: 'As Sarpedon says to Glaucus in the *Iliad*, a hundred thousand fates stand close to us always, which none can flee and none avoid. The complexity of the universe is infinite, and the days of a man's life are threescore years and ten. One lifetime is not long enough for the task of blocking every cranny through which calamity may enter.'

Calamity befell another young man whom Housman had never met, but whose fate would contribute both directly and indirectly to the poems he was now writing. On 6 August 1895 a nineteen-year-old soldier called Henry Clarkson Maclean committed suicide in a London hotel. Harry Maclean came from an army family living on the Herefordshire–Worcestershire border and was training to be an officer at the Royal Military Academy, Woolwich, in south-east London. His father was Major-General Henry John Maclean, late of the Rifle Brigade, who had served in the Crimean War and taken part in Lord Wolseley's Ashanti Expedition to the Gold Coast in Africa, which effectively won for the British the third Anglo-Ashanti War. The general had four children with his first wife and another four with his second, who was some twenty-seven years his junior. Harry was the eldest of the second clutch, and had one sister and two brothers. In 1895 he had been staying with friends in Oxfordshire and had written to his parents on Saturday 3 August to say that he would be coming home the following Tuesday. His family were therefore puzzled to receive a telegram on that Tuesday sent from Vigo Street in London. The contents of the telegram were not reported, but it was, his father said, 'the first intimation' anyone had that Maclean was in London: 'He had no business in town that the witness was aware of, nor had he any trouble on his mind. He was usually exceedingly cheerful, and there was not the slightest reason to suppose that he contemplated suicide.' Nevertheless, at 5 p.m. that same day he had booked a single room at the Charing Cross Hotel beside the busy London railway station. At around 10 p.m., hotel employees told the inquest, 'a sound was heard like the slamming of a door, but no notice was taken of it.' The sound had in fact been made by 'a service weapon of a large calibre', which Maclean had held to his head and fired once.

It was not until the following morning that a chambermaid found the body. Maclean had considerately left the door to his room unlocked, and he was 'lying on the floor dressed, with the exception of his coat, and with a quantity of blood about his head'. The maid called for help, and Maclean was pronounced dead. 'The body was cold and stiff, and there was a large wound on the forehead, and another on the top of the head, where the bullet had passed through. Near the feet was the revolver.' Propped on the mantelpiece was a letter addressed to 'The Coroner'. It was undated but written on two sheets of the hotel's writing paper. According to the *Malvern News*, before killing himself Maclean 'had carefully destroyed a number of letters and photographs, but several unburned fragments showed traces of a woman's handwriting and it was assumed that the suicide was due to love troubles'. Quite how it was ascertained that the handwriting was that of a woman is unclear, and Maclean's suicide note suggested that this was unlikely to have been the case, unless the letters were from his mother. It may be that the newspaper's reporter was attempting to spare the feelings of a distinguished local family, and the coroner's jury had been equally merciful, bringing in a verdict of suicide while temporarily insane.

Maclean's suicide note had specifically attempted to forestall this conclusion. 'I wish it to be clearly understood,' the cadet had written, 'that I am not what is commonly called "temporarily insane", and that I am putting an end to my life after several weeks of careful deliberation.' The calm and measured tone of the note bears this out:

I do not think that I need to justify my actions to anyone but my Maker, but for the sake of my mother and the few other people who love me I will state the main reasons that have determined me. The first is utter cowardice and despair. There is only one thing in this world that would make me thoroughly happy; that one thing I have no earthly hope of obtaining. The second – which I wish was the only one – is as follows:– I have absolutely ruined my own life; but I thank God that, as yet, so far as I know, I have not morally injured – or 'offended,' as it is called in the Bible – any one else. Now I am quite certain that I could not live another five years without doing so, and for that reason alone, even if the first one did not exist, I should do what I am doing. Of the dreadful blow I am dealing to my mother and the few other people who care for me I am quite aware. It is the one thing that has almost diverted me from my purpose, but, at all events, it is final, and consequently better than a long series of sorrows and disgraces. I hope that they will live to forgive and,

perhaps, to forget me. May God, in His infinite mercy, forgive me
for what I am doing. – H A R R Y   C.   M A C L E A N

It does not take a great deal of reading between these lines to ascertain
what it was that had driven Maclean to this drastic action, and the
timing of his suicide may be significant. Throughout April and May
1895 the newspapers had been very much preoccupied with a series
of trials at the Old Bailey. The first, from 3 to 5 April, was that of the
Marquess of Queensberry for criminal libel. The Marquess had left a
card at Oscar Wilde's club on which he scribbled a message accusing
him of 'posing as a somdomite' [sic]. When Wilde rashly decided to
sue Queensberry, the Marquess rounded up a succession of young men
who would testify that Wilde was not simply a poseur but a practising
homosexual. The trial collapsed and Wilde was arrested on 6 April,
charged with homosexual offences. Wilde's first trial opened on 26
April, but ended on 1 May without the jury having been able to agree
on a verdict. His second trial opened on 22 May and three days later he
was found guilty and sentenced to two years' imprisonment with hard
labour. Although stories of packet boats being filled with men fleeing
to the comparative safety of the Continent in the wake of Wilde's conviction may be exaggerated, the effect of the trial and verdict was both
dramatic and long-lasting. Even homosexual men who had conducted
their private lives discreetly now lived in fear of exposure, blackmail or
arrest, and it was against the background of Wilde's highly publicised
case, in which the 'corruption' of youths by homosexual men was a
constant theme, that Harry Maclean took his own life.

There is in fact no hard evidence to explain why Maclean shot
himself, but Housman clearly thought he knew the reason. It is certainly hard to imagine that 'love troubles' of a heterosexual nature
would have resulted in the language of the carefully written suicide
note Maclean left. Accustomed to seeding his poetry with biblical
allusions and quotations, Housman would have recognised that, in
expressing relief that he had not 'morally injured – or "offended," as
it is called in the Bible – any one else', Maclean was referring the
coroner to the passages in the Gospels of St Matthew and St Mark in
which Christ tells his disciples that to enter the kingdom of Heaven

they should become like children, and warns that 'whoso shall offend one of these little ones who believe in me, it were better for him that a millstone were hanged about his neck, and that he were drowned in the depth of the sea'. The recruitment age in the army was sixteen and it is conceivable that Maclean was worried about 'offending' fellow soldiers younger than himself. Housman might also have recognised something of his own story with Jackson, or the dilemma facing many homosexual men, when Maclean wrote that one reason for killing himself was that there was 'only one thing in the world which would make me thoroughly happy: that one thing, I have no earthly hope of obtaining'.

That Maclean was the direct inspiration for one of the poems in *A Shropshire Lad* is certain, since Housman had tucked into his own copy of the book, beside his poem 'Shot? so quick, so clean an ending?' (XLIV), a report of the inquest published in the *Standard* on 10 August 1895. Written in immediate response to the cadet's suicide, between August and September of that year, the poem also contains lines that more or less paraphrase Maclean's suicide note: 'After long disgrace and scorn', 'Souls undone, undoing others', 'You would not live to wrong your brothers'. Another poem almost certainly inspired by Maclean is 'If it chance your eye offend you', which not only follows XLIV in the published volume but was written immediately after it in Housman's notebook, again in August or September 1895. Furthermore, in the Gospels of both St Matthew and St Mark, Christ's address to the disciples about offending little ones continues with the image Housman uses in this second poem: 'Wherefore if thy hand or thy foot offend thee, cut them off, and cast them from thee'. The faint ghost of Maclean can also be discerned in a draft of 'The Carpenter's Son' (XLVII) written in August 1895, which includes a cancelled couplet derived from the same passage in the Bible:

> Lock your heart and sink the key
> With the millstone in the sea

'Oh who is that young sinner with the handcuffs on his wrists?', written at the same time though not published in Housman's lifetime, was directly inspired by Wilde's prosecution. At the time of his trials, however, Wilde was a portly forty-year-old, and the youthfulness of the poem's sinner suggests that Housman might also have had Maclean in mind.

Many readers would have guessed what the 'ill' was that drove the lad in 'Shot? so quick, so clean an ending?' to kill himself, just as Housman guessed what prompted Harry Maclean's suicide. The vocabulary is very much that of the period used to describe homosexuality, euphemistic but doom-laden: 'disgrace', 'mire', 'undone', 'wrong', 'danger', 'guilt'. What is less clear is Housman's tone. The poem seems straightforward: the sympathetic poet laments the death but also praises the young man for both putting an end to his troubles and avoiding possible transgressions in the future. 'I thought chaps like that shot themselves,' George V, one of England's least imaginative monarchs, is reputed to have said when it was reported that someone he knew was homosexual, and this was an attitude that also prevailed in the 1890s. Housman was not, however, a king but a poet, and a poet who was himself homosexual. Did he really believe that, sad as it was, the cadet had done the right and honourable thing? Or did he believe that he had been unjustly driven to it by 'The laws of God, the laws of man' so vehemently rejected in the poem Housman drafted a few months before both Maclean's suicide and the Wilde trials? In defence of having published some tactful details of the case that gave rise to the Maclean poem, Laurence Housman wrote that 'there may yet be some living whom it will gratify to know that a young life wrecked forty-two years ago left inspiration for another that it was worth the having'. Is he suggesting that Housman was in some way inspired by Maclean's story to put aside any thoughts of ending his own life for similar reasons? If this were the case, then the idea that the poet is straightforwardly praising Maclean for his action seems less likely.

Try reading the poem out loud as though it were written as much in anger as in sorrow – anger not at the cadet's action but at the social and moral forces that led to his death. The danger of doing this is that the tone may become merely sarcastic: what is required is an anger that is rigorously controlled, as Housman's emotions tended to be.

Otherwise, the poem appears to be adopting the accepted values of the day, values that Housman elsewhere rejects. Read straight, the voice of the speaker sounds like that of a conservative schoolmaster or clergyman, and this same voice seems to topple over into parody when it is employed in the poem that follows in the volume:

> If it chance your eye offend you,
>   Pluck it out, lad, and be sound:
> 'Twill hurt, but here are salves to friend you,
>   And many a balsam grows on ground.
>
> And if your hand or foot offend you,
>   Cut it off, lad, and be whole;
> But play the man, stand up and end you,
>   When your sickness is your soul.

One can imagine this forming part of a sermon in the chapel of some particularly dismal public school, but it would be unlike Housman to endorse teachings of the Bible – particularly ones in which metaphor produces absurdity in the suggestion that self-mutilation will make a lad 'sound' and 'whole'. Is the juxtaposition of the commands to cut off a foot and to 'stand up' merely unfortunate and unintended, or is it satirical? As with so much about Housman, the answer is that we simply don't know.

Another poem, 'Her strong enchantments failing', was drafted in 1894, then redrafted at exactly the same time Housman was writing his two poems about Maclean. Housman's original intention was that it would be placed in *A Shropshire Lad* just before the two Maclean poems, as no. XLIII, but for reasons that remain unclear the poem was withdrawn at proof stage.

> Her strong enchantments failing,
>   Her towers of fear in wreck,
> Her limbecks dried of poisons
>   And the knife at her neck.

The Queen of air and darkness
  Begins to shrill and cry,
'O young man, O my slayer,
  To-morrow you shall die.'

O Queen of air and darkness,
  I think 'tis truth you say,
And I shall die to-morrow;
  But you will die to-day.

A young man called Geoffrey Wethered had written to Housman after the poem was published in *Last Poems* apparently to ask its meaning. Housman replied: 'The queen of air and darkness comes from a line of Coventry Patmore's, "the powers of darkness and the air", which in its turn is a reference to "the prince of the power of the air" in Ephesians II 2; and the meaning is Evil.' It has been persuasively argued that the poem is linked to the Maclean poems by the grim theme that in order to kill the evil within, you have to kill yourself. The poem appears to have been open to other interpretations, however. Housman's nephew Clement Symons, who copied it into an autograph book shortly before being killed at Loos, 'believed the poem to depict the vanquishment of cowardice'. This would undoubtedly make sense, in addition to which Housman must have shown Clement the poem, which had not at that point been published, and he would hardly have done so if it were *only* about killing the evil within.

It is, however, what the cases of Maclean and Wilde represented rather than what Housman wrote directly about them that is significant. They suggest the kind of public attitudes towards homosexuality that were prevalent when Housman was writing *A Shropshire Lad*. The poem Housman wrote about the Wilde case angrily and wittily satirises these attitudes, and begins:

Oh who is that young sinner with the handcuffs on his
  wrists?
And what has he been after that they groan and shake
  their fists?

And wherefore is he wearing such a conscience-stricken
    air?
Oh they're taking him to prison for the colour of his hair.

'Tis a shame to human nature, such a head of hair as his;
In the good old time 'twas hanging for the colour that it
    is;
Though hanging isn't bad enough and flaying would be fair
For the nameless and abominable colour of his hair.

It is clear from this where Housman stood on the nature-versus-nurture arguments about what 'caused' homosexuality. The poem also showed, in the last line of its second stanza, a scholarly knowledge of the historical criminalisation of homosexuality: 'the Abominable Crime of Buggery' officially entered English law in a 1533 Act of Parliament, and was subsequently deemed as a crime '*inter christianos non nominandum*' (not to be named among Christians) by Edward Coke in the third volume of his *Institutes of the Lawes of England* (1628). A.S.F. Gow, who was advising Laurence Housman what to publish in *More Poems*, vehemently objected to the suggested inclusion of both this poem and 'Ho, everyone that thirsteth' on the grounds that they revealed rather too much about the author. After a good deal of wrangling, Laurence eventually and very reluctantly agreed to omit the poem, although his own view was that 'we are in a transitional period of public opinion over the H.S. [homosexual] problem, and that in the future it would add to rather than subtract from Alfred's reputation if it were guessed that he had that burden laid upon him by the blind God of Nature.'

It was, however, the Christian God that Housman was inclined to blame, and his belief that religion went hand-in-hand with the law and public attitudes is clear from 'The laws of God, the laws of man', which Housman himself excluded from *A Shropshire Lad*. The fact that he revised the poem for inclusion in *Last Poems* (XII) puts it in a different category from the Wilde poem, of which Laurence wrote in justification for eventually publishing it that, 'though somewhat lacking in literary quality, [it] is so strong an expression of [Housman's] feeling against social injustice that I am sure he would have wished it to be known'. Unlike Laurence, however, Housman was not by nature a social campaigner, and his attitude was altogether more fatalistic. The poem starts out magisterially, with its splendidly defiant and effectively placed rebuttal:

> The laws of God, the laws of man,
> He may keep that will and can;
> Not I . . .

It continues in this vein, with the poet pouring scorn on those who would seek to interfere in his life:

> let God and man decree
> Laws for themselves and not for me;
> And if my ways are not as theirs
> Let them mind their own affairs.
> Their deeds I judge and much condemn,
> Yet when did I make laws for them?

In its final lines the poem shifts in tone from cold anger to vulnerability and defeat:

> And how am I to face the odds
> Of man's bedevilment and God's?
> I, a stranger, and afraid
> In a world I never made.
> They will be master, right or wrong;
> Though both are foolish, both are strong.
> And since, my soul, we cannot fly
> To Saturn nor to Mercury,
> Keep we must, if keep we can,
> These foreign laws of God and man.

The alternative to doing so would be all too vividly demonstrated by the fates of Wilde and Maclean.

It is perhaps hard to imagine Housman 'afraid' of anything, but he may well have been speaking here in the voice of the Shropshire Lad, who in the second stanza of 'Others, I am not the first' (XXX) imagines that:

> More than I, if truth were told,
> Have stood and sweated hot and cold,
> And through their reins in ice and fire
> Fear contended with desire.

Fear contending with desire was a very familiar sensation for homosexual men of the period, and it was almost certainly poems such as these that prompted readers such as Goldsworthy Lowes Dickinson to write to Housman. Dickinson was a close friend of E.M. Forster and the author of such books as *The Greek View of Life*, which was published the same year as *A Shropshire Lad* and earned Housman's admiration. Of *Last Poems*, he told Housman that 'what they say appeals to something very deep in me. And deep calls to deep. It does not follow that surface calls to surface and I am not trying to intrude myself. I wanted to say just this and leave it there.'

That God has much to answer for is evident in another invigoratingly bad-tempered poem in the same volume, in which Housman challenges 'Whatever brute or blackguard made the world'. The poem is ostensibly about that very English subject the weather. It is Maytime, that traditionally hopeful season in which troubles seem often to arrive or weigh heavily upon the poet.

> The chestnut casts his flambeaux, and the flowers
>   Stream from the hawthorn on the wind away,
> The doors clap to, the pane is blind with showers.
>   Pass me the can, lad; there's an end to May.

Cursing English weather is a popular national pastime, but this is no mere case of rain stopping play, preventing the Lad from striding out onto a cricket pitch, 'trying to be glad'. Whereas the cycle of nature is responsible for the evanescence of cherry blossom in the second poem of *A*

Shropshire Lad, the flowers here have been stripped from trees before their time, and the Creator is accused of having arranged this out of sheer spite:

> There's one spoilt spring to scant our mortal lot,
>   One season ruined of our little store.
> May will be fine next year as like as not:
>   Oh ay, but then we shall be twenty-four.

The sheer pettiness of the deity – this 'iniquity on high' – is contrasted with the nobility of humans, who in the final stanza have no alternative but to bear stoically 'The troubles of our proud and angry dust', and 'shoulder the sky' – as, in better, classical times (the Golden Age, indeed), deities did on mankind's behalf. Those who accuse Housman of merely moping should be directed to these poems in which his anger is thrillingly unleashed.

In *A Shropshire Lad*, however, Housman wrote about the wrongs suffered by young men more in sorrow than in anger. These wrongs may be universal, but for some readers they seemed specific. If we can now hear clearly the faint note of suppressed homosexual desire that sounds like a muffled drumbeat throughout the book, it is partly because we know the biographical background to the poems, know what led Housman to write them, know that Moses Jackson was their buried mainspring. Even so, while early readers without access to this information such as Richard Le Gallienne seem surprisingly deaf to those beats, others who were more attuned heard them at the time. These were the 'few young men here and there' for whom Housman said he wrote the poems. Housman also referred to these young men in a poem he drafted at some time between 1895 and 1900. Although he had revised the poem in the spring of 1922 when he was assembling *Last Poems*, there is no evidence he planned to use it to preface that or any other volume. It nevertheless became his apologia when printed by Laurence Housman as the epigraph to *More Poems*, and contains a dedication in the second of its two stanzas:

> This is for all ill-treated fellows
>   Unborn and unbegot,

For them to read when they're in trouble
And I am not.

One of the possible reasons Housman never published the poem during his lifetime is that it had to some extent been made redundant by the final poem in *A Shropshire Lad*, which he had used in the same way (as an envoi rather than, in Laurence's design, as an epigraph) to say much the same thing. Certain readers of that poem would know precisely what Housman meant when he described them as 'luckless lads' and 'lads like me', just as they would be able to identify the ways in which they had been 'ill-treated' and 'in trouble' in the verses prefacing *More Poems*. Geoffrey Wethered had written to Laurence Housman in 1937, presumably explaining in his letter (now lost) what it was about Housman's poems that had particularly moved him. Laurence replied: 'It always pleases me to know that his work had a special appeal to the young. When the appeal is very special, I guess the reason, and am glad that the note of sympathy with trouble got through to them.'

It is no coincidence that Housman himself should refer in a letter to 'the great and real troubles of my early manhood', by which he meant those that gave rise to the poems of *A Shropshire Lad*. 'Trouble' and its variants ('troubles', 'troubled') is another of those words that frequently recur in his poetry, mostly as a catch-all, perhaps, but – as the letter just quoted suggests – also with a more specific meaning. It is unclear in 'In valleys of springs of rivers' (L) what kind of difficulties the lads who 'knew trouble at Knighton' were experiencing, except that there is a suggestion that it was not the kind of trouble that assails people only when they are young: it was a lifelong burden, to be laid down only at death. Similarly, the 'troubles' that afflict the Roman patrolling Wenlock Edge, and have been inherited by the poem's speaker, are relieved only when they and the centurion are 'ashes under Uricon'. Prophylaxis against troubles in 'Terence, this is stupid stuff' is similarly recommended in 'I to my perils of cheat and charmer', published in *More Poems*, in which the poet comes to maturity 'clad in armour':

The thoughts of others
Were light and fleeting,

Of lovers' meeting,
Of luck or fame.
Mine were of trouble,
  And mine were steady;
  So I was ready
When trouble came.

That this trouble is related to those of Housman's early manhood is reinforced by another poem in the volume in which the speaker, as elsewhere, resigns himself to the indifference of other people and the natural world to his sufferings:

The world goes none the lamer,
  For aught that I can see,
Because this cursed trouble
  Has struck my days and me.

The suicidal impulse in early manhood, and the unstated troubles that give rise to it, also surface in the Heine-inspired 'Sinner's Rue'. Here the poet picks the blue 'weed of sorrow' he finds growing at a crossroads, which is where those who killed themselves were traditionally buried. Heine calls this blue flower *die Armesünderblum*, which literally translates as 'the poor sinner's flower': 'sinner's rue' appears to be Housman's own coinage, and not a term otherwise recorded for wild chicory (*Cichorium intybus*).

It seems a herb of healing,
  A balsam and a sign,
Flower of a heart whose trouble
  Must have been worse than mine.

Is the sin that gives the flower its name that of suicide, or is the flower emblematic of some other, unnamed and perhaps unnameable, trouble? The speaker goes on his way determined to continue with his life rather than put an end to it – and he wears the flower on his breast, just as the luckless lads in the final poem of *A Shropshire Lad* will wear the flowers the poet has spent so much time and energy cultivating. If these flowers are not the green carnations Oscar Wilde encouraged young men to sport at the first performance of *Lady Windermere's Fan* in 1892 (and which are too much the product of artifice to grow in Housman Country), then they certainly have a similar emblematic significance.

A Shropshire Lad contains a number of poems that might not strike the average reader as anything out of the ordinary, but would be eagerly and gratefully seized upon by 'luckless lads'. Housman was much amused when the financial expert called in to oversee the restructuring of Richards's publishing house in 1929 described *A Shropshire Lad* as the 'filthiest book I have ever read: all about rogering girls under hedges'. One would be hard pressed to cite any instances of actual rogering in the poems, but many of them describe the kinds of thwarted romances between country lads and lasses that are often found in folk poetry. Other poems, however, describe relationships in which the gender of the beloved remains at best ambiguous. Alongside the hearty companionship of 'true fellows' who are in every sense 'clean' and 'straight', and whose 'heartstrings' are knitted 'right', are friendships characterised by a yearning uncertainty. The glance exchanged between the redcoat and the onlooker in 'The street sounds to the soldiers' tread' (XXII) is no more than that, though charged with an erotic possibility that fizzles out almost as soon as it is ignited, leaving the speaker merely to murmur in the final valedictory line 'Soldier, I wish you well'.

Elsewhere, the look is more lingering:

> Look not in my eyes, for fear
> > They mirror true the sight I see,
> And there you find your face too clear
> > And love it and be lost like me.

The conceit is worthy of Donne or other Metaphysical poets, a school which Housman dismissed in 'The Name and Nature of Poetry' as 'intellectually frivolous'. These four lines are an example of the creative tension mentioned earlier between revelation and concealment, between saying too little and saying too much. A glance gives little time in which to gauge its nature, but a look that is held can be revealing in all kinds of ways. The speaker here, while ostensibly wanting to protect the beloved, is also concerned to protect himself. There is a nod to the traditional notion that the eyes are the mirror of the soul, for the look in the speaker's eyes will 'mirror true' and betray feelings which will indeed become all 'too clear'. In addition the speaker cannot but give himself away when he speaks out: the beloved will see his own image in the speaker's eyes 'And love it and be lost like me'.

The only ambiguity here is that the beloved could, at a stretch, be a woman, but the mirror imagery of the poem would not really work if the two lovers were of a different gender; in addition to which, the poem's second stanza evokes the figure of the 'Grecian lad' Narcissus. There are several versions of the Narcissus legend, but perhaps the best known is found in Ovid's *Metamorphoses*, in which the beautiful youth is loved by the nymph Echo. When he rejects her, he is punished by being made to fall in love instead with his own reflection in a pool. In other versions, Narcissus has male suitors who are similarly repulsed, but most accounts of the legend end with Narcissus trapped by this *amour de l'impossible* and drowning – either accidentally, in an attempt to embrace his own reflection, or deliberately, because he realises that his love is a hopeless mirage. Narcissus had become a popular figure in homosexual literature, partly because of his rejection of Echo for the beautiful youth he finds in the pool (something of a distortion of Ovid's narrative), but also because his story provided a covert way to write about one beautiful youth falling in love with another. The usual suspects line up: the title poem of Edward Carpenter's first volume of poetry, *Narcissus and Other Poems* (1873), is a long, not to say in parts lingering, account of the Greek lad and his 'dream-fed beauty'; André Gide devoted a ten-page pamphlet to the myth, *Le Traité du Narcisse* (1871); Oscar Wilde compares Dorian Gray to Narcissus, and retells the myth from the pool's point of view in 'The Disciple', one of his *Poems in Prose*; while a number of lesser authors wrote poems in which the myth was retold or used as a reference point. In S.S. Saale's 'Sonnet', for instance, a group of grimy urchins sitting on a wall undergo a classical metamorphosis when they 'strip and plunge into the stream below':

Like fragrant ashes from a classic urn,
Flashed into life anew once more we see
Narcissus by the pool . . .

Housman's poem is far more subtle than this kind of thing, although it is possible that he had read Wilde's 'The Disciple', first published in the *Fortnightly Review* in July 1894. Wilde's prose poem ends with the pool speaking and employing a similar image to the one Housman uses in his poem: 'But I loved Narcissus because, as he lay on my banks and looked down at me, in the mirror of his eyes I saw ever my own beauty mirrored.'

Another poem in *A Shropshire Lad* that appears to be as deeply felt as 'Look not in my eyes, for fear' is XXXIII, which opens:

If truth in hearts that perish
  Could move the powers on high,
I think the love I bear you
  Should make you not to die.

These lines echo 'When the lad for longing sighs' (VI), in which a 'Maiden' is told that she 'can heal his ail'; in this case, however, it is the speaker whose love, were it accepted, would make his friend immortal – as indeed being the subject of the poem will give him literary immortality. The friend, however, is inclined to reject the speaker's 'long and sure-set liking', and the poem ends in resignation.

Homosexual readers would also have been alert to the gentle irony of 'The Merry Guide' (XLII), in which the poet encounters an attractive young man clad in little but a feathered cap and winged sandals:

With gay regards of promise
  And sure unslackened stride
And smiles and nothing spoken
  Led on my merry guide.

Like most such young men, this one spells trouble. The teasingly seductive youth refuses to answer the poet's questions about their destination, or even speak at all, merely laughing and beckoning as he lures him to the realm of the dead.

Another classical encounter (LI) is the one that takes place among the antiquities of the British Museum, where the sixteen-year-old Housman decided he preferred the Farnese Mercury (the Merry Guide himself) to the Townley Venus. The Grecian lad the poet finds here is made of marble, but similarly exiled to London from the land of his birth. 'I too survey that endless line / Of men whose thoughts are not as mine,' the poet imagines the statue telling him – thoughts that perhaps cannot be admitted in London, though they may have been acceptable in the land of lost content that was Ancient Greece.

It did not take too much reading between the lines of some of the poems to realise what Housman was saying, and although most public comments about the nature of such poems were either discreet or obtuse, certain people were not prepared to play ball. In his 1932 revue *Words and Music* Noël Coward introduced his wickedly knowing song 'Mad About the Boy', in which three female characters bemoan the fact that they are unrequitedly in love with a film star. 'I know that quite sincerely / Housman really / Wrote *The Shropshire Lad* about the boy,' the schoolgirl declares. Coward had both spotted and cheekily exposed the 'secret' behind the book. Whether Housman ever heard this song is not known, and he might have been appalled as much by the fact that the title of his book was rendered incorrectly as he would have been by its flagrant indiscretion.

Writing about the homosexual undercurrents in the literature of the First World War, the American critic Paul Fussell asked: 'Do the British have a special talent for such passions? An enquirer turning over the names of late nineteenth and early twentieth century literary worthies might be led to think so as he encounters Wilde, Samuel Butler, Edward Fitzgerald, Housman, Hopkins, Symonds, Strachey, Edward Marsh, William Johnson Cory (author of the 'Eton Boating Song'), Hugh Walpole, John Maynard Keynes, E.M. Forster and J.R. Ackerley.'

One could point Fussell to other countries that had a similar homosexual literary tradition, but not perhaps one that flourished in full view as well as having an underground currency. For every volume of privately printed 'Uranian' verse there were many more mainstream volumes that celebrated 'romantic friendships' and the beauty of boys and men. From the public-school novels of the late-Victorian and Edwardian era to the poetry and memoirs that emerged from the trenches, this literature was read and enjoyed by people who would not have thought of it as 'homosexual'. Most readers would have felt the same about *A Shropshire Lad*; but others were grateful to read a book that appeared to allude to their own particular, and more often than not secret and repressed, romantic longings. It is no surprise that Oscar Wilde's friend and champion Robbie Ross learned parts of *A Shropshire Lad* by heart so that he could recite them to the playwright while he was in prison. Housman sent Wilde a copy of his poems when the playwright was released in May 1897, and in July Wilde embarked upon his long poem 'The Ballad of Reading Gaol', which he completed that October. 'I have lately been reading your brother's lovely lyrical poems,' Wilde wrote to Laurence Housman in August, and traces of those poems are discernible in his ballad about a redcoat who is hanged for cutting his wife's throat.

Wilde based the ballad on the case of a fellow prisoner, a soldier hanged in Reading Gaol in July 1896 for precisely the crime described. This is the kind of disaster familiar from such poems as 'The Carpenter's Son', 'The Isle of Portland', 'Farewell to barn and stack and tree', 'The True Lover' and in particular 'On moonlit heath and lonesome bank', with which it shares a similar verse form, though its stanzas are of six rather than four lines. For the most part, the poem is, like *A Shropshire Lad*, written in a direct and modern voice, largely purged of the Decadent and grandiloquent flourishes that characterise much of Wilde's earlier poetry, though whether Housman or two years' hard labour was responsible for this new linguistic austerity is impossible to know. As Housman himself loftily observed, 'Parts of *The Ballad of Reading Gaol* are above Wilde's average' – though he attributed this to his incorrect suspicion that these parts 'were written by Lord Alfred Douglas'.

Like Wilde, E.M. Forster was among those who could 'read' *A Shropshire Lad* rather in the way Housman could 'read' Harry Maclean's suicide note, and it might be thought that he was exactly the kind of young man to whom Housman hoped the book would give pleasure or solace. It seems appropriate that Forster had been introduced to *A Shropshire Lad* by a man with whom he had fallen unrequitedly in love while at university. H.O. Meredith had been educated at Shrewsbury School (which may be where he first encountered Housman's 'local' poems) and had come up to King's College, Cambridge to read Classics, which was also Forster's subject. Aside from being very clever, Meredith was everything that Forster was not: handsome, extrovert, athletic, rebellious and a confirmed atheist. They met during their second year at the university, and Forster fell almost immediately under his spell. Thanks to Meredith's influence, Forster soon abandoned Christianity, and thanks to his sponsorship was elected to the secret *conversazione* society, the Apostles, during his fourth year. The Apostles were distinctly homophile but not necessarily homosexual, and Forster had to be content to have Meredith merely as a loving friend. Only after they had both left Cambridge, towards the end of 1902, did the two men embark on some kind of affair. Quite what form this took is not known, though it proved unsatisfactory, largely perhaps because Meredith was essentially heterosexual – Forster would later base the character of Clive Durham in *Maurice* on him. Whatever the case, it confirmed in Forster something he already suspected. 'I've made two great discoveries,' he wrote in his diary when summing up his life on the last day of 1904: 'the religious about 4 years ago, the other in the winter of 1902'. In both cases – rejecting Christianity and acknowledging his homosexuality – Meredith was the agent, and so it seems additionally appropriate that it was he who introduced Forster to *A Shropshire Lad*.

Although this introduction took place in April 1899, the copy of Housman's book that Forster owned had been given to him in 1900 by another of his Cambridge contemporaries. 'A copy with perfect associations would have overwhelmed me,' Forster confessed, 'perhaps it is well that I never had one. Such as it is, I read it for seven years in an awed, muddled sort of way.' It was when Forster embarked on a solitary walking tour of Shropshire in 1907, 'not yet looking out for its lads', that ideas about Housman's poems coalesced into something slightly less muddled. 'I had a rush of gratitude and love towards the poet who had given me – I didn't know exactly what,' he recalled. This prompted him to write to Housman, but he used the headed paper of the hotel in which he was staying and was 'too delicate' to add his own address. He imagined that any response Housman cared to write would be forwarded to him by the hotel. Housman did not reply.

Forster later recalled that in his letter he had written: 'My obscure admiration has grown with the years.' This admiration was in fact no more obscure than what it was about Housman's poetry that had prompted such gratitude and love, and both became absolutely clear to him when shortly after his walking tour he went to stay with a Classics don called J.M. Phillimore, whom he had met abroad. While discussing Housman's poems, Forster

> ventured to hazard that *A Shropshire Lad* concealed a personal experi-
> ence. Phillimore agreed. Instantly my own conjecture became more
> vivid to me, and I realized that the poet must have fallen in love with
> a man. He happened to accompany my own development from sub-
> conscious to conscious [awareness of his own homosexuality], and
> that is why he is surrounded by an extra emotion [. . .] The football
> and cherry trees, the poplars and glimmering weirs, the red coats,
> the darnel and the beer, the simplicity controlled by a scholarship
> whose strength I took years to appreciate, the home-sickness and
> bed-sickness, the yearning for masculine death – all mingled with
> my own late adolescence and turned inward upon me. To meet the
> poet was not yet a possibility, but I could meet the poems, and as one
> grew stale another would come forward and companion me while
> its predecessor had a wash and brush-up. They seemed inexhaustible
> and the warmth of the writer's heart unquestionable.

Forster would later change his opinion about the warmth generated by Housman's heart, but his love of the poems never wavered. When *Last Poems* was published in 1922, he wrote once again to Housman to express his gratitude. By this time the two men had met at a dinner party in Cambridge, at which G.L. Dickinson had also been present. Forster had the sense not to mention Housman's poetry on this occasion, but after he had read *Last Poems*, he followed Dickinson's lead and sent another letter to the author: 'When I read your other book, it promptly crossed the line that divides a book from a companion,' he wrote, 'and now, after twenty years, I have repeated my luck. I am very grateful indeed to you – glad also that your genius has been recognised, but that is not why I am writing. Indeed, I haven't anything to say at all – only thankfulness from the bottom of my heart and the wish that you may be happy.' It might be thought that (unlike Dickinson) Forster himself had crossed a line in this letter, but although he once again failed to provide a return address, he received a brief but friendly reply in which Housman thanked him for writing, said that he valued what Forster had told him, and that he recalled their meeting. He may also have remembered Forster's earlier letter, for he added: 'perhaps this letter may find you even though you withold [sic] your address'. This would certainly be a characteristic Housman tease, and Forster was pleased enough with this letter to tuck it into his own copy of *Last Poems*.

In 1927 Forster was offered the Clark Lectureship at Trinity College, Cambridge, which involved giving a series of talks on English literature. Housman had been offered the previous year's lectureship but had turned it down on the grounds that 'literary criticism, referring opinions to principles and setting them forth so as to command assent, is a high and rare accomplishment, and quite beyond me'. For some reason, his letter of refusal had been shown to Forster, who copied it in full into his commonplace book. He added a sad little note to say that when he delivered his own lectures, subsequently published as *Aspects of the Novel*, 'Housman came to two and I called on him on the strength of this, but he took no notice.' It is not known when Forster added this note, but his recollection of the Clark Lectureship in the talk he gave to Bloomsbury's long-running Memoir Club, probably in the 1950s, was rather more sanguine. He stated there that Housman 'let it be known, through his circle, that he approved' of those lectures that he had attended. Housman ought to have been flattered by the unattributed reference Forster had made to his poems, as a kind of grace note, in one of the lectures. Forster was talking about moments of intense feeling that stand outside the everyday operation and measurements of time: 'Neither memory nor anticipation is much interested in Father Time, and all dreamers, artists, and lovers are partially delivered from his tyranny; he can kill them, but he cannot secure their attention, and at the very moment of doom, when *the clock collected in the tower its strength and struck*, they may be looking the other way.' The words in italics are taken from 'Eight O'Clock', no. XV of *Last Poems*, as Forster evidently expected his audience to recognise.

Whether or not Housman acknowledged this little nod to him when, after the lecture, the two men dined together in Hall at Trinity is not known, but the conversation appears to have been unusually relaxed. At one point Housman told Forster, 'with a twinkle', that he went to Paris 'to be in unrespectable company'. Encouraged by this apparent confidence, Forster 'ventured to climb the forbidding staircase which led to [Housman's] rooms. They were sported but I dropped a visiting card through the slit.'* Housman appears to have ignored this attempt at further familiarity, perhaps realising that Forster had indeed taken his little joke too seriously.

The following year, Forster published his second collection of short stories, *The Eternal Moment*. One of the stories, 'The Point of It', was partly inspired by 'Hell Gate', an uncharacteristically long and allegorical poem Housman had published in *Last Poems*. Forster sent Housman a copy of the book along with a letter which has not survived, but in which he had written 'somewhat warmly and a little sentimentally', suggesting that the one story 'happens to be as near as I shall ever get to "Hell Gate", and that is why they are coming to you.' Had Forster left it at that, all might have been well, but he went on to write: 'I don't know whether there is such a thing as impersonal affection, but the words best express the feeling I have had towards you, through your poems, for the last thirty years, and I ask you to pardon this expression of it.' This time, Forster recalled, 'I did not conceal my address and I received, all too rapidly, his reply. It was absolutely hateful [. . .] I was so disappointed and hurt that I destroyed it after one rapid perusal.'

Forster was later told that the reason Housman had been so offensive

---

*Rooms in Cambridge were designed with two doors at their entrances. If the outer door was open, visitors were welcome to knock on the inner one; but if the occupant had closed the outer door ('sported the oak'), he was either absent or wished not to be disturbed.

was that he had thought the Clark Lecturer ought to have dined at Trinity more often than he did, and that it had been particularly discourteous of Forster to dine instead with friends at King's College. The civilities of English university life seem arcane to outsiders and it is possible that Housman really had been offended by Forster's disregard for the generally understood rules of college conduct. If so, this seems disagreeably and uncharacteristically petty, particularly in one whose own attention to the usual courtesies of dining in Hall left on occasion something to be desired. There is nothing in Forster's short story that might cause offence, apart from the fact that it isn't very good, allegory being no more Forster's strong suit than it was Housman's. It is true that the protagonist is a civil servant who turns to literature and produces some books that 'whetted the half-educated public, and made it think and feel', but Housman could hardly have thought that Forster had meant anything by this. Forster's own original diagnosis of what had gone wrong, before he was told about the dining solecism, was that 'I had been forcing the pace, I had tried for intimacy too soon, I had presumed, a mere novelist, to parallel myself with a poet. I had made a fool of myself and been snubbed.'

While Forster was surely wrong to suspect that *literary* presumption played any part in this, he was probably right to think that it was his further attempt at intimacy that led to such a brutal rebuff. As his letters frequently show, Housman was not unaverse to praise of his work when it was made on paper rather than to his face; but there remained bounds which could not be overstepped. Housman assured Geoffrey Wethered that 'I value the good opinion of those young men for whom, as you say, my poems were written', while tending to dissuade them from meeting him in person. In reply to the letter Wethered had written to him in 1939, Laurence Housman wrote that his brother's refusal to meet this admirer was wholly characteristic, 'but he liked to be kind to young men, and he nearly always wrote to applicants, even when he refused'. The expression of 'affection', however, even if 'impersonal', presumed too far. 'Mortified as only the cautious can be, I put the man out of my mind,' Forster recalled. 'The poems did not alter, they were still a light in the sky.'

This was generous, and for Forster that light never really went out.

When he wrote a private memoir of Mohammed el Adl, the Egyptian tram conductor with whom he had enjoyed an affair in Alexandria during the First World War, Forster turned to Housman for an epigraph. El Adl had kept in touch with Forster by letter when the novelist returned to England, but had died of tuberculosis in 1922 aged only twenty-three. The memoir is prefaced with the second stanza, unattributed, of 'The rain, it streams on stone and hillock', a poem Housman had written in memory of his brother Herbert and included in *Last Poems*:

> Good-night, my lad, for nought's eternal
>   No league of ours for sure,
> To-morrow I shall miss you less,
> And ache of heart and heaviness
>   Are things that time should cure.

The alterations of punctuation (reproduced here) would have infuriated Housman, but the poignancy of these lines is wholly appropriate to the sad story of Forster's first serious affair, an affair that though brief had a profound effect upon his thinking and outlook. 'It seems to me that to be trusted, and to be trusted across the barriers of income race and class, is the greatest reward a man can ever receive,' he told his friend and confidante Florence Barger. For Forster the affair represented 'such a triumph over nonsense and artificial difficulties: it is a sample of the other triumphs that I am sure come off but of which we hear nothing through the brassy rattle of civilisation so called [. . .] I see beyond my own happiness and intimacy, occasional glimpses of the happiness of 1000s of others whose names I shall never hear, and I know that there is a great unrecorded history.'

Housman would not form part of that history, but he was invoked at the memorial concert held for Forster at King's College a few months after his death in 1970. This included readings of what Forster had written about *A Shropshire Lad* in his diaries and the performance of two songs from Vaughan Williams's *On Wenlock Edge*, 'Bredon Hill' and 'Oh, when I was in love with you'.

4

Buried Lives

It was one thing for young men such as Forster to recognise the homosexual undercurrents running through Housman's poetry, quite another to presume that this gave them special access to the author in person. Housman's disinclination to discuss his personal life with anyone in any detail has inevitably led to a great deal of speculation and argument about what he did or didn't do. There have, for example, been suggestions that his frequent trips abroad, like those of many homosexual Englishmen of the period, satisfied appetites additional to the gastronomic and architectural ones he wrote about in his letters. Much confusion arose over a list of names and prices Housman compiled relating to a stay in Paris, claimed by some as a tariff for young men enjoyed but believed by others to be merely *aide memoire* jottings about restaurants or music halls. There has also been conjecture about someone Housman referred to as 'my gondolier', who was retained to take him round Venice during his visits to the city but, it has been proposed, may also have provided more personal services in the manner of John Addington Symonds's Angelo Fusato. The fact that Housman 'rushed off' in midwinter to attend the gondolier's sickbed is seen by some as proof of a romantic devotion, by others as an act of charity. Suspicion has also been aroused by the mysterious and so far unidentified 'French companion' who sometimes joined Housman on his tours of France. 'I cannot offer you anything of an invitation,' he teasingly warned Grant Richards in anticipation of one such trip, 'for I shall have a friend with me who would not mix with you nor you with him.' Housman had, however, described this friend to Kate as 'a nice young man, not much educated, who regards me as a benefactor', and he would hardly have been so open with her if his benefaction had been in return for sexual favours.

Housman nevertheless seems to have extracted some entertainment from making off-hand remarks that the inquisitive might seize upon. His sly reference in conversation with Forster to the 'unrespectable company' he sought in Paris was matched by his admission to Richards, 'I do know something of [the city's] *bains de vapeur*'. As

Forster commented when reporting Housman's supposed confidence: 'This was offered as a jest, and accepted as such, but so offered that I might make the mistake of accepting it seriously if I chose, which was intriguing.' The same might be said of other 'hints' that Housman evidently enjoyed dropping. It is characteristic, for example, that his letter to Richards about steam baths should continue 'I am flying to Paris (though not necessarily to those haunts of vice)', just as, when he suggested that to include his poems in an anthology of the 1890s would be like including Lot in a book on Sodomites, he should add: 'in saying which I am not saying a word against sodomy, nor implying that intoxication and incest are in any way preferable'. The deliberate ambiguity ('not necessarily', 'not saying a word against') in one who always chose his words carefully is of the same teasing nature as the irony he deployed elsewhere in his correspondence. It is precisely because his customary mode was one of teasing and deflection that Housman is so moving when he lets this mask slip.

The truth is that although we now know a good deal about Housman's emotional life, we still know absolutely nothing about his sex life. W.H. Auden may have been 'pretty sure' that Housman was 'an anal passive', but he based this assertion on nothing more than a hunch and a wish to shock the readers of the *New Yorker*. The Parisian male prostitutes and the affair with the Venetian gondolier, referred to in some books as if established fact, not only have no verifiable substance but have been more or less conclusively proved to be biographical misreadings. One of the poems that Gow vainly attempted to prevent Laurence Housman from publishing is sometimes adduced as evidence that Housman had personal experience of 'stolen waters':

> Ho, everyone that thirsteth
>   And hath the price to give,
> Come to the stolen waters,
>   Drink and your soul shall live.

The concept of stolen waters is taken from the Book of Proverbs: 'Stolen waters are sweet, and bread eaten in secret is pleasant', and the relevant passage is marked in Housman's own Bible. Recommending secret pleasures is not, however, an admission that one has partaken of them oneself. E.M. Forster quoted this poem when reviewing *More Poems* in 1936, and he concluded his notice: 'Perhaps he had a better time than the outsider supposes. Did he ever drink the stolen waters which he recommends so ardently to others? I hope so.' Forster had himself been a slow starter, not having his first sexual encounter until he was thirty-seven, but he had made up for this thereafter and it is perhaps unsurprising that he wanted Housman to have had similar luck. It is, however, one thing to hope that he did, quite another to state that the poem provides evidence that during a trip to Venice in the autumn of 1900 Housman 'tasted some of the pleasures which he had longed for so intensely since childhood'. Had Housman longed for such pleasures since childhood? It would perhaps be 'natural' if he had, but there is no evidence to support this statement.

Modern biography has recognised that a subject's sexual life is a legitimate area of enquiry, and if no trail has been left to follow then it is confidently assumed that there is a 'secret life' to be discovered. We know from the reminiscences of A.C. Benson that Housman enjoyed what were then considered 'off-colour' stories, and that all but one of the letters he wrote to his friend Arthur Platt, Professor of Greek at UCL, were destroyed by the recipient's widow on the grounds that they were 'too Rabelaisian'. A certain number of risqué books were procured for Housman by Grant Richards, and his own library included a collection of volumes on sexual topics, not all of them strictly scholarly. Housman also devoted considerable time to an article he titled 'Praefanda', which addressed the difficulties that occasionally arose in Latin poems on sexual subjects. He wrote it in Latin and submitted it in 1931 to the *Classical Quarterly*, which accepted it and sent him proofs before suddenly getting cold feet. It was subsequently published in *Hermes*, a German magazine of classical studies. 'Praefanda' was one of Housman's serious jokes, in which he applied his exacting scholarship to poems about masturbation, sodomy, fellatio and foreskins (or lack of them). Whether the knowledge of anatomy and sexual mechanics he displayed in the article came from personal experience or merely from reading is impossible to say. We can draw our own inferences from these facts about Housman, but they remain no more than that.

If Housman had a less busy sex life than Forster eventually did, this would not have been as unusual in his own period as it would be today, particularly in the context of university life. Even after dons were allowed to marry, many chose not to, a bachelor's life then being regarded as neither exceptional nor something to arouse suspicion among the prurient. While not necessarily homosexual, universities tended to be homosocial: even after women were admitted as undergraduates, they were corralled within their own colleges, leaving the masculine world of other colleges largely undisturbed. Living within institutions where domestic necessities were provided by servants and companionship by fellow scholars, many men who were not celibate as a result of religious conviction nevertheless found no need for the comforts and consolations traditionally supplied by women and marriage. Bachelorhood had a long tradition within universities and in many cases suited the scholastic temperament, avoiding the kind of obligations and distractions from hard intellectual work that a wife and family might involve. This was the world within which Housman lived in Cambridge for the last twenty-five years of his life.

With regard to Housman's poetry, whether he was sexually repressed or found sexual adventures of which we know nothing is not particularly important. Far more relevant to his work is emotional repression, and of that we have plenty of evidence in his life. Laurence Housman was far from the only person who recorded instances of his brother being caught between the warring urges of concealment and revelation. One of Housman's more unlikely friendships was the one he struck up with Joan Thomson, the young and sympathetic daughter of the Master of Trinity, and during their many conversations he appears to have revealed himself in a way he rarely did to his male friends. The recollections Thomson wrote three years after Housman's death are amongst the most touching and enlightening accounts we have of his character. 'His powers of restraint and self-control were very great,' she recalled, instancing his ability to give up the wine he so much enjoyed for several months because 'some doctor told him that it would be good for his nerves to abstain from alcohol'. This cure was ineffective, 'but the strength of will he must have exerted during a long period was very characteristic of him'.

The exertion of will also controlled Housman's most personal feelings. 'He was capable of emotion terrifying in its strength,' Thomson recalled. 'There were very few outlets for his affection and it was only very rarely possible to catch a glimpse of the man he might have been.' She records Housman enjoying a family Christmas, pulling crackers and reading out the hackneyed rhymes that were included as mottoes, and sitting with a toy animal on his knee while he indulgently watched the hosts' baby grandson at play: 'he looked as if he were then his natural self.' More usual, however, was the solitary figure apparently nursing a private grief. 'His amazing power of self-control must have been necessary indeed to him when the experience came that was the tragedy of his life,' Thomson writes, without saying what that tragedy had been. 'How intensely he had suffered might be guessed by anyone who saw his face as it sometimes appeared at the end of one of his long walks. Perhaps he had recalled some of his own wretchedness as he walked alone and the sadness of his face was as poignant as on the face of a man experiencing the bitterness of sorrow for the first time.' She concluded that Housman was 'ashamed of the strength of his own feeling', which is why he took care to hide and suppress it in the English manner of someone of his background and upbringing.

Housman left a similar impression on his long-standing friend Percy Withers, who wrote in an article published in the *New Statesman* when Housman died: 'The emotions may have run deep in many men, but few can have repressed them so effectually that only intimacy provided a rare and fleeting glimpse.' When in 1940 Withers published his 'Personal Recollections' of Housman in book form, he did so under the title *A Buried Life*. Although he nowhere says so, it seems likely that he borrowed this title from Matthew Arnold. Published in 1852, Arnold's 'The Buried Life' asks whether love can reveal someone's real nature, the 'genuine self' that is otherwise hidden or simply gets lost as we negotiate 'the rush and glare' of daily existence. In its evocation of emotional reticence and repression, this is a very English poem. According to E.M. Forster, writing in 1926, the defects of the English character, so far as the educated classes were concerned, derived from the public schools, whose alumni 'go forth into [the world] with well-developed bodies, fairly developed minds, and undeveloped hearts'. Forster argued that it is these undeveloped hearts, rather than cold ones, that cause Englishmen difficulties: 'For it is not that the Englishman can't feel – it is that he is afraid to feel. He has been taught at his public school that feeling is bad form. He must not express great joy or sorrow, or even open his mouth too wide when he talks – his pipe might fall out if he did. He must bottle up his emotions, or let them out only on a very special occasion.'

As the joke about the pipe suggests, Forster is painting something of a caricature, but the underlying observation is both serious and compelling. He goes on to tell an anecdote about the difference between his own reaction and that of an Indian friend when a holiday they had been enjoying together came to an end: the Indian 'could not express his sorrow too much', whereas Forster, knowing that they would meet again soon, remained sanguine and began to scold his friend for both feeling and showing 'so much emotion upon so slight an occasion'. The Indian remonstrated that emotions could not be measured out 'as if they were potatoes', and when Forster countered that this was 'better than slopping them about like water from a pail', he was told: 'your whole attitude toward emotion is wrong. Emotion has nothing to do with appropriateness. It matters only that it shall be sincere. I happened to feel deeply. I showed it. It doesn't matter whether I ought to have felt deeply or not.' Feeling deeply among late-Victorian and Edwardian Englishmen – and indeed subsequent generations – was not the problem; it was the display of such feelings that was considered more or less taboo. This had become a commonplace when, for example, a local newspaper such as the *Chelmsford Chronicle* reported of the first Armistice Day in 1919: 'It is a strong national trait that we do not carry our hearts on our sleeves, and anything like a display of emotion is, and was, particularly in pre-war days, quite foreign to the British character.' Like the heart not worn on the sleeve, the stiff upper lip that supposedly characterised Englishmen may have become a cliché, but a trembling lip is a real physical symptom that unwillingly betrays deep emotion, whether fear or grief. The popularity of moustaches during this period meant that, behind their bristling defences, lips could, if absolutely necessary, covertly quiver, the failure of nerve this represented remaining largely undetectable.

Percy Withers recorded that on the few occasions he witnessed Housman expressing deep emotion the effect was alarmingly physical. 'The intensity of feeling was shown not by the use of emphatic words or declamatory expressions, but by the physical manifestations of a faltering voice, a flushed face, and an agitation of the frame that gave the impression of a seething force restrained only by the exercise of stern self-discipline, and not always successfully, for a visible tremor would momentarily escape.' It is no coincidence that these physical symptoms are not unlike those that Housman claimed were caused by an encounter with true poetry.

The terror of self-exposure was not restricted to men like Housman who needed to conceal romantic or sexual feelings that were wholly inadmissible. As Arnold wrote in 'The Buried Life':

I knew the mass of men conceal'd
Their thoughts, for fear that if reveal'd
They would by other men be met
With blank indifference, or with blame reproved;
I knew they lived and moved
Trick'd in disguises, alien to the rest
Of men, and alien to themselves . . .

Forster wondered how it was that a nation reputed to be emotionally chilly could nevertheless be pre-eminent in producing poets. 'We can't get fire out of ice. Since literature always rests on national character, there must be in the English nature hidden springs of fire to produce the fire we see.' It was precisely because these springs were hidden that the English were famed for their poetry, according to James Sutherland, writing twenty-one years after Forster in the essay on 'Literature' in Ernest Barker's *The Character of England*. He imagines a foreigner visiting England and asking: 'How is it that this people, apparently so practical, so prosaic, so reticent in expression of their feelings, have produced so much of the world's greatest poetry?'

The answer must surely be that Englishmen, by reason of their defects no less than their virtues, are closer than most peoples to those reservoirs from which poetry springs [. . .] If the Englishman's home is his castle, so to an almost unsociable extent is his mind. Accustomed to respect the intellectual and emotional privacy of his neighbours, he expects a similar forbearance towards himself. More sociable nations put their ideas into a common pool, but the Englishman keeps drawing his up painfully from his own private well for his own private use.

> . . . It may be deep –
> I trust it is – and never dry:
> What matter? if the waters sleep
> In silence and obscurity.

Yet this slow accumulation of experience and thought and feeling, so parsimoniously expended in social intercourse, so rarely tapped and run off in conversation, seems to be peculiarly favourable to the production of poetry. By some strange paradox, what the Englishman cannot bring himself to say even to a friend he tells without inhibition to all the world.

This is what Withers meant when he wrote of those aspects of Housman's character that were 'implicit in his poetry, so hidden in his person'. The critic Brian Reade compared *A Shropshire Lad* to 'a beautiful ruin built over an invisible framework', a framework that Housman was on the whole careful to conceal, and Kate Symons admitted that one of the reasons for her pleasure when *Additional Poems* was published was that 'they tell more of himself and his queer muffled heart than he chose to show'. Sutherland concludes that the paradox of revealing in published poetry what cannot be admitted to friends in private conversation explains why some English poets have been reluctant to discuss their work, instancing (appropriately enough) Thomas Gray in an anecdote related by Matthew Arnold. According to Victor de Bonstetten, a young Swiss whom Gray befriended towards the end of his life, Gray 'would never talk of himself, never would allow me to speak to him of his poetry. If I quoted lines to him, he kept silence like an obstinate child'. As Sutherland notes, this sounds very much like stories told about Housman. It is also possible that one of the reasons Gray *never spoke out* (as Arnold put it) was that, like Housman, he needed to conceal an emotional life that was focused on young men such as Bonstetten.

The widespread difficulty that late-Victorian middle-class men had expressing their feelings is perfectly illustrated by a letter Housman received on his appointment to the Chair of Latin at University College, London. It was written to him by John Maycock, the man described as 'his most intimate friend' at the Patent Office, and demonstrates the bounds within which such intimacy could be expressed. The letter, dated 15 June 1892, was addressed to Housman at Perry Hall, and has often been quoted, but its significance has been overlooked. Housman carefully kept it, in its envelope, until he died, as he did the last letter he received from Moses Jackson. It is by any standards a touching tribute to Housman's character as a young man, but it is the wording Maycock uses in expressing his congratulations and the observation he makes about Housman's friendship with Jackson that provides the more likely explanation for its preservation. 'I am as delighted with your success as though I had got something for myself,' Maycock wrote. 'It is funny to think how I used to chaff you about your work producing no money, and all the time you were working silently on with that strength of purpose which I can admire but can't imitate.' Thus far the letter is of the sort any man might like to receive from a colleague he knew well. It is what Maycock goes on to write, however, that is crucial: 'As a rule English people never allow themselves to say or write what they think about anyone, no matter how much of a pal he may be. Well I am going to let myself loose. I like you better than any man I have ever known.' This declaration evidently stayed with Housman, who three years later, during his period of greatest creativity, wrote a poem that is generally agreed to describe his quarrel with Jackson in 1885, and in which he echoes Maycock's words:

> Because I liked you better
>   Than suits a man to say,

It irked you, and I promised
    I'd throw the thought away.

In an earlier draft the second line read 'Than friends in liking may', which also points to Maycock's letter as a source. The letter continues: 'There is as far as I could ever discover absolutely no flaw in your character as a man, and no one would ever hope for a better friend. I don't say this only on my own account; but I have seen how you can stick to a friend like you have to Jackson. I mean stick to him in the sentimental sense of not forgetting him although he is right out of your reach.' In spite of his ability to let himself loose, as he phrases it, Maycock was very much a product of his period and nationality: the letter is addressed 'Dear Housman' and signed 'Yours faithfully, Maycock'. Had Maycock shared Housman's sexual orientation, one would suspect that the letter was suggesting more than it actually says outright, that Maycock was acknowledging that he knew that Jackson was out of Housman's reach not just geographically but also sexually and emotionally, but this was not the case.

The inability to forget is a theme of 'Because I liked you better', one given a characteristically ironic twist in its final stanza. Housman perhaps thought the poem too revealing, and he did not include it in *A Shropshire Lad*. Jackson would undoubtedly have recognised the poem's scenario, particularly since it continues:

To put the world between us
    We parted stiff and dry:
'Farewell,' you said, 'forget me.'
    'Fare well, I will,' said I.

Jackson had indeed put the world between himself and Housman when he went to live in India. It seems that it was precisely because Housman had apparently cast aside English reticence and told Jackson what he felt for him that the friends had quarrelled and parted. The disparity of feeling between them is subtly indicated in this poem by Housman's precision in the choice of words: the friend's purely conventional

'Farewell' is returned to its constituent parts and its original and more potent benediction in the speaker's almost imperceptibly altered echo, 'Fare well'.

The tension in 'Because I liked you better' between what is felt and what is said is wholly characteristic of Housman's best poems. By choosing to write poetry that is both conventional in its form (requiring scansion and rhyme) and very brief in its extent, Housman contains the emotions with which his speakers are struggling within a tight framework, and by doing so makes them all the more powerfully felt. In many cases the very form of his poetry enacts their subject: the repression and containment of difficult or troubling feelings. Unsurprisingly, this is most apparent in the poems Housman wrote that appear to recall his quarrel with Jackson. 'Because I liked you better' continues:

> If e'er, where clover whitens
>   The dead man's knoll, you pass,
> And no tall flower to meet you
>   Starts in the trefoiled grass,
>
> Halt by the headstone shading
>   The heart you have not stirred,
> And say the lad that loved you
>   Was one that kept his word.

The promise has been kept because the speaker's heart is beyond stirring, and his ability to remember has been extinguished by death. As in 'Oh, when I was in love with you', the poem is directed by the form and patterns of the verse to a conclusion that is both neat and unexpectedly logical.

Within these bounds, the poem is also a good deal less simple and straightforward than it first appears. For example, the ironic ending is reinforced by the reference to clover, one of the plants whose blooming Housman noted in the pocket diaries in which he also recorded events in Jackson's life. The entry for 28 June 1889 reads:

Temp. 80
Posted letter to him
Elder fading mostly
Vetch, clover, cheesecake, hemlock, in bloom.

As someone keenly interested in plants, Housman would almost certainly have been aware of the traditions and beliefs surrounding clover. It was once planted on graves because its vitality made it a symbol of resurrection, in addition to which its three leaves were a symbol of the Trinity. (The 'trefoiled grass' in the poem refers not to bird's-foot trefoil, but to clover, for which the botanical Latin name is *Trifolium*.) Housman also mentions clover growing on a grave in *A Shropshire Lad*: in 'Along the field as we came by' (XXVI) the speaker predicts a time 'When I shall sleep with clover clad, / And she beside another lad.' More pertinent to the Jackson poem, however, are clover's secular associations: it was a symbol of 'true, yearning love' in the Middle Ages, and in the language of flowers 'the White Clover carries a promise ("*I shall remain faithful*")'.

Another poem in which two friends, who we can assume are Housman and Jackson, part in that stiff and dry English manner opens:

> Shake hands, we shall never be friends; give over:
>   I only vex you the more I try.
> All's wrong that ever I've done or said,
> And nought to help it in this dull head:
>   Shake hands, goodnight, goodbye.

The awkwardness of the scene is beautifully captured in the halting lines, particularly the first, which has an extra foot and disrupts the scansion by reversing the more rhythmic word order of 'we never shall be friends'. This poem was drafted at the same time as 'Because I liked you better', revised in 1895 and then again in 1922, when Housman was preparing *Last Poems*, only to be discarded once more, presumably for the same reason. Both poems imagine future circumstances in which the friend who has rejected the speaker calls him once more to mind:

> But if you come to a road where danger
>   Or guilt or anguish or shame's to share,
> Be good to the lad who loves you true
> And the soul that was born to die for you,
>   And whistle and I'll be there.

Roads, usually long and deserted ones along which people make their solitary way, are a frequent feature of Housman's poetry. This one is more metaphorical than most, but imagines the sort of extreme conditions that might lead the friend to recall the speaker's existence. Danger is fairly straightforward, but guilt, anguish and shame might well suggest the kind of things to which homosexual men were exposed in the late-Victorian period. 'Shame', in particular, was a code word in homosexual writing at this time. In Lord Alfred Douglas's infamous poem, 'Two Loves', for example, two youths appear to the poet in a dream. When asked his name, the pallid youth replies 'Love', only to be rebuked by the other youth, who sings of 'pretty maids'. 'He lieth, for his name is Shame,' this second youth declares. The pale youth sighs and replies: 'Have thy will, / I am the love that dare not speak its name.' The poem was published in December 1894 – alongside a second poem 'In Praise of Shame' – in *The Chameleon*, an obscure undergraduate magazine, but it reached a wider and appalled public the following April and May when parts of it were read out and discussed during the cross-examination of Oscar Wilde at the Old Bailey. Whether or not Housman was aware of this particular meaning of 'shame' is impossible to say, but the attention he appears to have paid to the Wilde trials suggests that he may have been.

The apparently rather maudlin appeal by the true-hearted speaker to treat him well is turned round in the last line of Housman's poem, in which he offers to come running at any summons to protect his friend, rather as the disembodied speaker in 'From far, from eve and morning' (XXXII) blows in to offer his hand and receive confidences. This final line echoes the refrain of a Robert Burns poem of 1793, 'Oh Whistle, an' I'll come to ye, my lad', and it can hardly be a coincidence that in Burns's poem a young woman is encouraging a lover while warning him to keep their relationship a secret.

The third, and most successful, poem about the parting from Jackson consists of a mere four lines:

> He would not stay for me; and who can wonder?
>   He would not stay for me to stand and gaze.
> I shook his hand and tore my heart in sunder
>   And went with half my life about my ways.

The relaxed quality of the first two lines does nothing to prepare us for the desolating terseness of the third line, or the fatalistic resignation of the last one. Readers with some knowledge of the Classics would have recognised the allusion to the story in Plato's *Symposium* about the origins of the human race, in which creatures split in two by Zeus spent their lives searching for their lost 'other half'. If humans were lucky enough to find this missing half, they would form indissoluble bonds and be extremely happy. Housman's poem suggests that the speaker, having imagined that he had found that lost portion, is now condemned to go out into the world again permanently maimed.

Equally moving are three short poems derived from Sappho that Housman wrote about Jackson. The first of these to be published was the last to be written, in 1922 while Housman was assembling *Last Poems*, where it appeared as no. XXVI. As he admitted, Housman took this Ancient Greek fragment and turned it into an English ballad, both in its structure and its language.

> The half-moon westers low, my love,
>   And the wind brings up the rain;
> And wide apart we lie, my love,
>   And seas between us twain.
>
> I know not if it rains, my love,
>   In the land where you do lie;
> And oh, how sound you sleep, my love,
>   You know no more than I.

The lovers are in different lands, but there is a suggestion here, not apparent in the other versions, that they are tenuously bound together because neither knows whether or not it is raining in the far country – but this is only because the distant lover is sleeping soundly rather than lying awake like the speaker. The ballad-like form of the poem, with its repetition of the tag 'my love' at the end of every other line, will lead most readers to imagine it concerns a man and a woman. This is the version Housman chose to publish; but the earlier versions are more direct and more powerful. In both of them the speaker is alone, thinking of a lover in a distant land, as Housman may have lain awake thinking of Jackson, who was in India at the time the poems were written. 'The weeping Pleiads wester' is the more obviously mournful, with its repeat of 'weeping' and 'sighs'; but it is the other poem that, in its hard-won restraint and its acknowledgement of unequal affections, is the more moving:

> The rainy Pleiads wester,
>   Orion plunges prone,
> The stroke of midnight ceases,
>   And I lie down alone.
>
> The rainy Pleiads wester
>   And seek beyond the sea
> The head that I will dream of,
>   And 'twill not dream of me.

This poem is related to Jackson by the fact that the 'Epithalamium' Housman wrote for him was drafted on its verso, by the shared source of Sappho, and by the sense of friends or lovers separated by geography.

The tension between expressed and unexpressed feelings in many of the poems is also apparent in the correspondence between Housman and Jackson that has so far been published. These letters display the awkwardness arising from a disparity of feeling that Housman uses to such effect in the poems. Housman sent Jackson a copy of *Last Poems* on the day it was published, with a long and jocularly boastful letter in which the combination of his natural modesty and the urge to impress his friend makes for uneasy reading. The joke Housman made in respect of the proposed Braille edition of the book gets its first airing here. 'The cheerful and exhilarating tone of my verse is so notorious that I feel sure it will do you more good than the doctors,' he wrote; but he goes on to add a second reason for sending Jackson the poems: 'you do not know, and there are no means of driving the knowledge into your thick head, what a bloody good poet I am'. Housman nevertheless has a very good go at convincing Jackson by sending evidence of the esteem in which he is held. 'In order to intimidate you and repress your insolence,' he continues, 'I am enclosing the review and the leader which the *Times* devoted to the subject.' He went on to tell Jackson that the first edition of *A Shropshire Lad* he had sent him was 'now worth £8 or more if you have kept it at all clean', and that the average annual sale of the book was now over 3000. Of the new book he wrote: 'It is now 11 o'clock in the morning, and I hear that the Cambridge shops are all sold out.' He concluded this catalogue by writing, in one of those instances when sharp teasing and painful sincerity warred for supremacy: 'Please to realise therefore, with fear and respect, that I am an eminent bloke; though I would much rather have followed you round the world and blacked your boots.' He then swiftly passed on to more general news from England, and ended the letter on a curiously formal note: 'My very kind regards to Mrs Jackson.'

Jackson had gone into hospital a few days after receiving this letter and did not have it to hand when he replied from his bed there. He declined to take seriously what he called, with some justification, Housman's 'extraordinary exhibition about blacking boots!' 'My most presentable boots are brown,' he wrote, 'requiring no blacking, Larry old chap. At home I wear boots of canvas & rubber composition, known as snagproof, as your choice is for an absolute sinecure.'* Jackson may have lived abroad for thirty-three years, but he was still very much a product of his English era and upbringing, able to deflect any potentially embarrassing displays of feeling by turning them into a joke. It may be that this response provoked Housman to declare more directly in the letter already quoted that he was 'a fellow who thinks more of you than anything in the world'. This declaration too was hedged about

---

*'Larry' may have been a boy who blacked boots for Miss Patchett's lodgers.

with jokey insults about the 'natural disagreeableness' of Jackson's character, though it might be said that Housman's devotion was made all the more forceful since it was expressed in counterpoint to, and in spite of, Jackson's supposed failings.

These letters not only provide poignant evidence of the gulf between Housman's feeling for Jackson and Jackson's for Housman; they also painfully acknowledge and exemplify what Housman in 'If truth in hearts that perish' (XXXIII) had called 'This long and sure-set liking, / This boundless will to please'. He may well have had that poem in mind when he wrote these letters to his seriously ill friend, since it continues: '– Oh, you should live for ever / If there were help in these.' In January 1923, over a quarter of a century after he wrote these lines, Housman sent a letter to Pollard giving news of Jackson's death at the age of sixty-four. With a lapidary poignancy characteristic of his best poems, he declared: 'Now I can die myself: I could not have borne to leave him behind me in a world where anything might happen to him.' He would in fact live for another thirteen years.

5

Last Poems, Last Years

A Shropshire Lad had become so popular during the First World War that in the summer of 1918 Richards proposed a new edition of 5000 copies, even though the cover price would have to be increased to 1s 6d 'owing to the cost of labour and material'. On being informed of this, Housman (referring to increased wages on the home front) replied: 'The working classes at any rate can well afford 1/6, though I don't know if 5000 will want to.' In the event the book sold over three times that number of copies during the last year of the war. Perhaps encouraged by these sales, Housman took a rather more sanguine view of the prospects of his keenly anticipated second volume of poems and suggested a first print run of 10,000 copies. Richards, having consulted booksellers, decided to print only 4000 copies, which he judged enough 'to make as certain as I could that everyone who was sufficiently intelligent could get a copy on the day of publication'.

The publication of *Last Poems* on 19 October 1922 turned out to be a major literary event, attracting widespread coverage in the press. As Housman had boasted, the book was not merely reviewed in *The Times*, but in the same issue became the subject of an editorial headed 'Ave Atque Vale', acknowledging Housman's declared intention in the volume's prefatory note that these would indeed be the last poems he would publish. The following week, a cartoon by Bert Thomas appeared in *Punch*, depicting an uncharacteristically jolly Housman, dressed in a ploughman's smock and hob-nailed boots and piping on a flute, dancing his way into the Temple of the Muse, where he is greeted by a laurel-wreathed figure exclaiming: 'Oh, Alfred, we have missed you! My lad! My Shropshire Lad!' The reading public had certainly missed Housman and Richards's caution proved unnecessary: not only was the book already reprinting on the day of publication, but by the end of the year, a mere ten weeks later, Richards had been obliged to print a further 17,000 copies.

As *The Times* had, most critics took Housman at his word (while hoping that they might be wrong), and so used reviews to pronounce judgement on what they now considered his complete oeuvre of just over 100 poems. *Last Poems* was generally and rightly regarded as all of a piece with *A Shropshire Lad*. *The Times* called the new book 'a continuation' of the earlier one, while J.C. Squire in his *London Mercury* described the poems as '"extra numbers" to the *Shropshire Lad*, as good as the old'. The *TLS* review appeared under the headline 'The "Shropshire Lad" again', and as a contented Edmund Gosse observed: 'We wanted, not another *Shropshire Lad*, but more of the old one, and that is what we have got.' Gosse was among several critics who felt that if anything these new poems were technically even better than those in the first volume. Looking back, he suggested that there were 'one or two' poems in *A Shropshire Lad* in which 'the tune wavered on the instrument': 'In the new volume, I cannot discover any fault of this kind, the mastery of technique having become complete, the music impeccable.' 'In almost each of the forty-one poems in this book,' wrote Amabel Clough-Ellis in the *Spectator*, Housman 'has achieved that complete fusion of rhythm, sound and sense which characterise a perfect work of art', while the *Bookman* described *Last*

Poems as 'a collection of lyrics so singular and exquisite that almost the only adequate way to recommend them to readers would be to quote shamelessly from every page'.

Housman had this time made proper arrangements to have his book published in the United States, by Henry Holt & Co., which had that same year published the 'Authorised Edition' of *A Shropshire Lad*. The book appeared in November and received reviews equal in their enthusiasm to those in England. Lee Wilson Dodd in the *Literary Review* suggested that the poet could now be referred to simply as 'Housman', 'for he belongs to the immortals'. He commended Housman's small output, particularly when compared with the productivity of other well-known writers: 'Mr [H.G.] Wells, for example, has written a library, while Housman has composed a few lines of verse. Yet it is probable that a hundred or so words by Housman will be remembered, treasured (though never by many), long after the million or so words by Mr Wells have been forgotten.' The suggestion that Housman appealed only to the discerning few was at odds with what Amabel Clough-Ellis had claimed. For her, Housman was 'that rare being, a poet with a public. Indeed, his one chance of being misjudged may be that he is too popular.' Clearly, even Housman's sales could not match those of America's most popular poet, Ella Wheeler Wilcox, whose *Poems of Passion* (1883) sold 60,000 copies in two years. The widespread pirating of *A Shropshire Lad* in America nevertheless suggested that publishers at any rate thought that Housman would be treasured by the many. The result of Housman's disinclination to prevent pirated editions, wrote the American collector Carl J. Weber, was 'a large number of American printings, and the creation of an immense audience for Housman'.

Furthermore, since Housman took no steps to prevent it, as he did in England, his poems reached a new audience when they were widely anthologised in America. When Weber donated his entire collection of Housman material to the Colby College Library in Maine in 1946, he also 'examined twenty-five American anthologies covering the poetry of Housman's period, in the thought that editorial selections among the *Shropshire* [*Lad*] poems might give some indication of their popularity with American readers.' He found that 'Reveille' had appeared in eighteen of the twenty-five anthologies, 'With rue my heart is laden' in sixteen, 'Loveliest of trees, the cherry now' and 'To an Athlete Dying Young' in thirteen, 'When I was one-and-twenty' in eleven, 'Is my team ploughing' and 'Think no more, lad; laugh, be jolly' in nine, and 'Bredon Hill' in seven. Well over a third of the poems had been anthologised, in addition to which thirteen of them had been published by Housman's fervent American admirer Witter Bynner in *McClure's Magazine*, of which he was poetry editor and which at the time had a 'huge and important circulation'.

As in England, literary young men claimed to have many of the poems by heart. 'When I was a student at Yale, I read and memorised considerable portions of *A Shropshire Lad*,' recalled Stephen Vincent Benét. Carl Van Doren similarly claimed that 'Most of the Shropshire lyrics [. . .] I knew by heart.' The fact that *Last Poems* appeared in America at the same time, and from the same publisher, as the authorised edition of *A Shropshire Lad* helped consolidate Housman's reputation there. Neilson Abeel, editor of Princeton's *Nassau Literary Review* (founded 1842), wrote that to him and his classmates of 1922 'Housman came as a discovery. Soon we knew all the poems of *A Shropshire Lad*, and quotations from them became part of our everyday speech.' The British writer Beverley Nichols recalled meeting a manufacturer of suspenders in Providence, Rhode Island, who produced from his pocket a first edition of *A Shropshire Lad*, the poems of which he knew by heart and proceeded to declaim. 'I have seldom heard poetry recited so beautifully,' Nichols reported.

Housman would have been pleased that ordinary readers such as Nichols's businessman had read his poems and learned them by heart. He was less pleased by an encounter in 1927 with a rather more illustrious American admirer of his work. 'I had a visit not long ago from Clarence Darrow, the great American barrister for defending murderers,' he told his brother Basil. 'He had only a few days in England, but he could not return home without seeing me, because he had so often used my poems to rescue his clients from the electric chair.' Of all Darrow's cases the most notorious was that of Nathan Leopold and Richard Loeb, two wealthy young men from prominent Chicago families who in 1924 stood trial for the apparently motiveless abduction and murder of a fourteen-year-old schoolboy called Bobby Franks. The case against the pair was overwhelming and the only thing a defending lawyer could do was to argue that the death penalty should not be imposed. To this end, Loeb's family contacted the most famous lawyer in the country.

Darrow was both a passionate opponent of the death penalty and a keen reader of poetry, and when it came to defending these two apparently indefensible young men, he turned to Housman, many of whose poems he reportedly knew by heart. His closing argument at the hearing in Cook County on 22 August 1924 was long, impassioned and somewhat rambling, lasting in all some twelve hours. Part of Darrow's ploy was to keep emphasising the youth of the defendants, whom he frequently referred to as 'boys' and on nine occasions as 'lads'. In two instances Shropshire Lads were also invoked. He suggested that Leopold and Loeb might be any parents' sons, and to this end quoted the whole of 'The Culprit' from *Last Poems* to suggest that the defendants were 'victims'. 'I remember a little poem that gives the soliloquy of a boy about to be hanged,' Darrow said, 'a soliloquy such as these boys might make.' In the poem the condemned lad imagines the moment of his conception, at which his father was not considering how his son might turn out, and the moment of his birth, at which his mother is simply glad to have borne a son. At the point of execution, however, the lad is alone:

> Oh let no man remember
>   The soul that God forgot,
> But fetch the county kerchief
>   And noose me in the knot,
>   And I will rot.

For effect, Darrow had altered the words 'county kerchief' to 'County Sheriff', this being the title of the region's highest law-enforcement officer.

Towards the end of his closing statement, Darrow turned once again to Housman, using 'When hollow fires burn out to black' from *A Shropshire Lad* to suggest the bleak future that faced Leopold and Loeb whatever sentence was passed: 'I care not, Your Honor, whether the march begins at the gallows or when the gates of Joliet [Penitentiary] close upon them, there is nothing but the night, and that is little for any human being to expect. But there are others to be considered. Here are these two families, who have led honest lives, who will bear the name that they bear, and future generations must carry it on.'

Darrow's heartfelt rhetoric won the day and the judge sentenced Leopold and Loeb to life imprisonment for the murder plus ninety-nine years for the kidnapping. Housman's only recorded reaction to the trial itself was that 'Leopold and Loeb owe their life sentence partly to me'. Darrow had given him a copy of his speech, 'in which, sure enough, two of my poems are misquoted'. The second violation of the text was presumably unintentional: Darrow had rendered the second line of 'When hollow fires burn out to black' as 'And lights are fluttering low', rather than 'guttering low'.

True to his word, Housman published no more poems after the appearance of his second volume. He did, however, publish an edition of Lucan's *Bellum Civile* in 1926 and the fifth and final volume of Manilius's *Astronomica* in 1930 – both at his own expense. He also continued to contribute the occasional pungent review to the *Classical Review* and the *Classical Quarterly*, in which his savagery and wit showed no signs of diminution. Of the French scholar W. Morel's *Fragmenta Poetarum Latinorum*, for example, he wrote in 1928: 'I should have written less harshly if Mr Morel had not taken measures to secure favourable reviews from his own countrymen. By duly disparaging Baehrens (in bad Latin) on his first page, and by ritual homage to Leo and Cichorius and other acceptable names, he has done his best to create a friendly atmosphere and obtain commendation irrespective of desert; and he must not be surprised if smoke ascending from domestic altars draws in a current of cold air from abroad' – an air that kills, perhaps. Housman found compositors of classical texts no more competent than those employed by Richards to set up his poetry, asserting of H.J. Izaac's edition of Martial in 1931 that: 'The printers have indulged immoderately in their favourite sport of dropping letters on the floor and then leaving them to lie there or else putting them back in wrong places'.

His most substantial piece of writing from his last years, however much he may have disparaged it, was the Leslie Stephen Lecture on 'The Name and Nature of Poetry'. The lecture had cost him a great deal to write, partly because by 1933 his health was in serious decline. Housman was rightly proud of his strong constitution, and the worst thing about increasing age was the limit it put on his daily walk. 'In the course of this year I have grown older, which shows itself in my walking powers,' he complained to Kate at the end of 1932, when he was just three months short of his seventy-third birthday. 'After five or six miles, though I do not get tired, my legs tend to act sluggishly. My heart, according to the doctor, is going on all right.' This optimism proved unfounded, however, and the following June, a month after delivering the Leslie Stephen Lecture, he wrote to Laurence: 'I suppose I ought to warn you that I am not in rude health. On the pretext that my heart was all over the place, after walking too much, I suppose, in the hot weather, the doctor sent me to bed for a week in a nursing home, where the heart must have disappointed him bitterly, for it behaved with the utmost decorum.' From what he wrote to a friend about his heart 'now behaving with monotonous correctness', it seems the problem was some kind of arrhythmia.

What worried Housman more was his psychological state: 'My real trouble, which I have often had before, is nervous depression and causeless apprehensions, aggravated by the fact that I am going to move into new rooms [in Trinity] next term.' These depressions, he said, tended to last three months, and could no longer be alleviated by physical activity: 'In previous visitations of this nervous trouble I have been physically strong and able to take good long walks,' he complained during an unusually hot spell in July; 'but at present, though my heart appears to be all right again, I am feeble, partly no doubt because of this weather.' While on his customary summer holiday in France he was struck down with a 'violently painful inflammation of the throat' which resulted not in an outpouring of poetry but in a bout of influenza that left him further enfeebled. Although he recovered to some extent, partly thanks to a tonic 'known among doctors as "honeymoon mixture"', he was still complaining the following spring that he had not returned to his former good health. It was the further diminution of his ability to walk long distances that most preyed on him, because it robbed him of something that 'all his life had given that quiet companionship of nature which suited him best'. 'The doctor does not want me to take walks of much more than a mile,' he told Laurence, 'and I myself am not inclined to do much more than twice that amount. I still go up my 44 steps [to his rooms on his Trinity staircase] two at a time, but that is in hopes of dropping dead at the top.'

By the summer of 1935 he was telling Richards: 'The continuation of my life beyond May 1933 was a regrettable mistake' – though continue it did for another ten months. A three-week holiday in France and Switzerland in August and September got off to a bad start when he banged his head while entering a taxi, the resulting wound requiring stitches. 'Do not expect bulletins,' he wrote home to Kate; 'death or grave illness will be duly notified to you by the Head Porter at Trinity.' He returned to England in an aeroplane fighting headwinds ('The machine was not particularly unsteady, except in taking off and in landing'), and wearing a skullcap to cover the part of his head that had been shaved in order to stitch his scalp. 'I do not expect to go abroad again,' he told Kate, and although he was pronounced 'very well' by the doctor he consulted on his return, a few weeks later he endured another spell in the Evelyn Nursing Home in Trumpington Road with 'breathlessness, weakness, and the dropsical swelling of the ankles and knees'. He would remain there for over three weeks, though he insisted upon summoning a taxi to take him back to college to deliver his twice-weekly lectures.

In order to thwart his hope of dropping dead while ascending to his rooms in Whewell's Court, arrangements had been made for him to move into a set of ground-floor rooms in Trinity's Great Court, 'with a bathroom which dazzles the beholder and is equipped with every imaginable luxury, including a thermostat'. He was still troubled by sleeplessness, largely caused by the difficulties he was experiencing with his breathing but partially relieved by bromide washed down with champagne – 'but I wake up early and worry'. Quite what was worrying Housman is not known: his breathing problems were in fact Cheyne-Stokes respiration, often a symptom of heart failure, but from everything he wrote it seems that approaching death was not something that greatly concerned him.

He was unwell enough to check himself back into the Evelyn for Christmas, and reported: 'The other night they gave me heroin instead of my usual soporific, and I learnt what it is to be totally deprived of intellect.' Smacked out or not, he was sufficiently alert to refuse permission for the National Federation of Women's Institutes to reprint his poem 'Fancy's Knell' in their magazine. He returned to Trinity in mid-January, 'but with no strength for anything beyond my actual work', and continued to lecture and to correspond, but by 22 March was back in the Evelyn once more. He rallied in order to rebuke a persistent and tiresome American admirer, Houston Martin, who wanted him to read a study he had written of him. 'I hope that if you can restrain your indecent ardour for a little I shall be properly dead and your proposed work will not be by its nature unbecoming,' Housman wrote. 'But the hope is not more than a hope, for my family are tough and long-lived, unless they take to drink.' He told Martin that he did not forbid him from quoting from his letters, but added: 'I think you should ask yourself whether you are literary enough for your job. You say that I may think it "indignant and presumptious" for an American to write such a book before an English one has appeared. By *presumptious* you mean *presumptuous*, and what you mean by *indignant* I have no idea.'

Housman returned to Trinity on 21 April, and two days later delivered his first lecture of the new term. It would also be his last lecture, and J.J. Thomson, who attended it, recalled, 'He was terribly ill and must have had an invincible determination to lecture in such a state.' He returned to the nursing home on 25 April, writing a brief note to Kate to inform her. It would be the last letter he wrote, and it ended with the one-word postscript: 'Ugh!'

Kate's son Jerry Symons went to view the body in the nursing home's chapel, where it was laid out beneath a purple and gold silk pall. As he reported: 'There was a great composure and firmness of expression, and the look on the face was that of a man who had met the storms of life and faced and fought them. I cannot call it serene, it still held what I can only call a proud challenge – "I am captain of my soul and master of my fate; do your worst; I scorn you." Indeed, his features in death were a mirror to all he had suffered from life, and of his attitude to it – it was the face of an autocrat and an aristocrat facing a silly mob and defying it.'

III

ENGLISH LANDSCAPE

The graver sides of life, the deaths, the partings, the
yearnings for love, have their deepest expression in the heart
of the fields.

E.M. Forster, *Howards End*

Little Brampton in Shropshire is not much more than a few farm
buildings spread out around a crossroads in the Clun Valley. It
barely even counts as a hamlet, but standing to one side of the junction itself is an unexpectedly grand fingerpost, erected in 1800 by the
2nd Lord Clive. Set into a low stone wall on a stepped square plinth,
it consists of a banded and domed limestone pillar with four cast-iron
arms into which the following place-names are cut so that the sky can
be seen beyond them: Bᶳ CASTLE, LUDLOW, Cᴺ GUNFORD and
CLUNN.

This part of Shropshire is true Housman Country: the ancient
market town of Ludlow stands at its very heart, while Clungunford
and Clun are saluted in a prefatory quatrain to the fiftieth poem of *A
Shropshire Lad* as being among 'the quietest places / Under the sun'. The
direction pillar, as it is more properly called, was moved slightly to its
present position during a road improvement scheme in 1929, around
the time such popular books as H.V. Morton's *In Search of England* were
encouraging people to explore the countryside in motor cars. Even
so, the junction at Little Brampton is of two small B roads rather than

major highways, and some 120 years on from when Housman wrote his poem the countryside around Clungunford and Clun is still remarkably quiet. It is possible to take a day-long walk in the Clun Valley on a fine October day, passing through Sowdley Wood (which contains large numbers of Housman's favourite beech trees) and along the many footpaths and bridleways that cross the fields, without encountering more than a couple of other people. The view is of gentle hills divided by old hedges into small fields in which large and ancient trees act as way-guides. There are substantial woods, but also numerous small coppices, spinneys and thickets, while sunken and green lanes and narrow little bridges over the River Clun and its tributaries suggest generations of people travelling the country on foot. Although forestry work is carried out in the larger areas of woodland, the landscape still conforms to Housman's ideal of 'a land of boughs in leaf / A land of trees that stand'.

There is no record of Housman ever having visited this particular area, but it is impossible to walk in it without his poetry beating in one's mind. While he undoubtedly put Shropshire on the map for many readers, he often acknowledged that he did not in fact know the county at all well. 'I know Ludlow and Wenlock, but some of my topographical details – Hughley, Abdon under Clee, – are sometimes quite wrong,' he wrote in 1933. Laurence Housman visited Shropshire a few months after his brother's book had been published, and reported back that Hughley Church, of which Housman had written 'The vane on Hughley steeple / Veers bright, a far-known sign', not only had no steeple but could hardly be 'a far-known sign' since it was buried in a valley. Furthermore, Housman had written that on the north side of the church 'slayers of themselves' lay in 'steeple-shadowed slumber'; in fact, Laurence reported, this part of the churchyard was the final resting place of 'respectable churchwardens and wives of Vicars, all in neatly tended graves'. Housman admitted that he had caught a glimpse of the church during a visit he paid to Shropshire 'to gain local colour', as he mischievously put it, after the bulk of the poems had been written. 'I ascertained by looking down from Wenlock Edge that Hughley Church could not have much of a steeple,' he told Laurence. 'But as I had already composed the poem and could not invent another name that sounded so nice, I could only deplore that the church at Hughley should follow the bad example of the Church at Brou, which persists in standing on a plain after Matthew Arnold had said [in his poem of that name] that it stands among mountains.' Other place-names, Housman admitted, were chosen for euphony rather than for any particular associations.

These names are nevertheless scattered throughout *A Shropshire Lad* like fingerposts, apparently placing poems in precise locations: Ludlow, Shrewsbury, Knighton, Hughley, Buildwas, Clunton, Clunbury, Clungunford and Clun; Clee, the Wrekin, Wenlock Edge, Wyre and the Welsh Marches; the rivers Severn, Teme, Corve and Ony.* No wonder William Archer, reviewing the book, was able to declare, 'Shropshire no longer lacks its poet'; while Michael Peele, who reproduced a great deal of earlier poetry about the county in his 1923 volume *Shropshire in Poem and Legend*, acknowledged that 'In [Housman] the county at last has a poet worthy of its loveliness.' Housman's notion that his book would be set in the county he had looked at from afar during his childhood was not there from the beginning, however, and in early drafts of the poems some of the place-names were taken from elsewhere: not only was Wenlock in ''Tis time, I think, by Wenlock town' (XXXIX) originally 'Stourbridge', at the time a small town in Worcestershire but now part of Birmingham's metropolitan sprawl, but the broom in the same poem was originally urged to 'tarnish slow on Kinver Edge', which is on the Worcestershire–Staffordshire border. Similarly, in 'The Welsh Marches' (XXVIII) the Severn originally ran down to Bewdley, again in Worcestershire, rather than to Shropshire's Buildwas.

Western Horizons

Housman's reasons for choosing Shropshire as the ostensible setting for his book may have been personal, but the county had long been

---

*As Housman might have noted: 'Pronounced Onny' – and indeed this is how it is more usually spelled. It is unclear where Housman found this variation. The small town of Onibury (with a single rather than a double 'n', but still pronounced with a short 'o') derives its name from the river.

renowned for its landscape and history. It is geologically rich and geo-graphically diverse, with its dramatic hills rearing up from wide plains, its ancient (though now patchwork) forests of Wyre and Clun, the River Severn more or less bisecting the county, and the River Teme running along its south-west border. The past here, as in much of England, is both palpable and curiously layered, so that the ghosts of other, earlier lives tread beside you as you walk in it. Shropshire is criss-crossed with ancient paths, fortifications and tracks, dotted with ancient buildings or their remains, and boasts parish churches still in use which date back to the Norman Conquest, when William I more or less handed over the county to his cousin Roger de Montgomery, whom he made Earl of Shrewsbury. Making your way on foot up onto Panpunton Hill above Knighton, you tread a steep path that runs alongside Offa's Dyke, the defensive barrier against the Welsh constructed by a king of Mercia in the eighth century and still visible. At Clun the towering remains of an eleventh-century border fortress rise on a mound at the edge of the town. The nave and chancel of St Swithun's Church at Clunbury date from the Norman period, and the misericords beneath the seats of the choir stalls in St Laurence's Church in Ludlow were carved in 1447. The Lancashire-born topographical writer Joseph Nightingale, who wrote the article on Shropshire for John Britton's monumental twenty-seven-volume survey of *Beauties of England and Wales* (1801–16), declared: 'Of the beauties of England, perhaps no other county con-tains a more interesting share than the one now under consideration. It possesses every variety of natural charm: the bold and lofty moun-tain; the woody and secluded valley; the fertile and widely cultured plain; the majestic river, and the sequestered lake. It is no less rich in the remains of ancient times, which awaken a thousand enthusiastic reflections, by engaging us in the contemplation of the memorable events of our history.'

Shropshire, then, already carried numerous romantic and historical associations when Housman wrote about it, and its apparent mystery was partly the result of it being comparatively unknown and unvis-ited, far removed from such large cities as London, Birmingham or Manchester. This isolation would begin to change at around the time Housman published his book, when Church Stretton attracted the attention of property speculators who wanted to develop the small town of around 1000 inhabitants into a spa comparable with Cheltenham or Malvern. The town was beautifully situated among what had become known as 'The English Highlands' or 'Little Switzerland' – sobriquets that were something of an exaggeration, since ranges in the Lake District and the Pennines are far loftier. Looking out of your window as you pass through this area on the road or railway line that both run along the valley, you see The Long Mynd to the west and The Lawley, Caer Caradoc and Ragleth Hill to the east. These are certainly dramatic, but they are given an intimate, human scale by the gentler and greener folds of land amongst which they rise and, as a Victorian guidebook stated, do 'not offer any very arduous task to the ordinary mountaineer'. Indeed, although the hills had a 'reputation for being somewhat dangerous at times in consequence of fogs and the precipitous character of the passes', they tended to attract energetic walkers rather than people equipped with ropes and crampons.

Hitherto, the attractions of the area were deemed to appeal 'principally to the geologist', although anyone interested in Britain's ancient history would find plenty to explore, since Church Stretton is situated on Watling Street and the surrounding area is rich in ancient camps and earthworks, while The Port Way, which stretches the length of The Long Mynd, is an ancient track supposedly used by Neolithic traders. The town itself was also well known for its mineral water: the Church Stretton Aerated Water Company was founded in 1881 as 'sole lessees of the Long Mynd Spring, the purest water in England'. This small local enterprise was soon overtaken by the Stretton Hills Mineral Water Company, which opened a factory beside the Cwm Dale Spring on the town's outskirts in 1883. The combination of mineral water and clean air was touted as successful in 'the treatment of neurasthenia, for the baneful effects of influenza, for sleeplessness, for delicate children, for convalescence after illness, for anaemia and general debility, for some forms of gout and rheumatism, for chronic bronchitis, for catarrh, for weak digestion, sluggishness of the liver, obesity and for the most elderly and semi-invalid people'. Developers began promoting Church Stretton as a health resort and building villas to attract summer visitors. A 'Hydropathic Hotel' was opened, but although railway connections had improved significantly when the line between Hereford and Shrewsbury became part of a main line connecting Wales and the north of England (which also meant that the journey there from London took only four and a half hours), the ambitious plans of the developers were unfulfilled, and this part of Shropshire remained largely unspoilt.

Making the steep and rough ascent from Carding Mill Valley alongside a small stream, you reach The Port Way via Dr Mott's Road, which is in reality an old path which a local physician paid to have improved in the mid-nineteenth century in order to be able to visit the more remotely situated of his rural patients. A track branching up and off The Port Way, with expanses of heather and bracken growing out of an almost black peaty soil to either side, leads to Pole Bank, which at 1696 feet above sea level is the highest point on The Long Mynd. From here, in every direction, you can see far beyond the immediate and neighbouring hills to such distant ranges as the Malverns and the Brecon Beacons. If you manage to hit that lucky moment when the tourist season has ended but the autumn weather is still holding fine, it is possible to find yourself as solitary as Housman liked to be on his own long walks. The land stretches away across this beautifully stark moorland plateau in all directions and the wind snatches at your Ordnance Survey map as you try to identify the coloured counties and innumerable landmarks that surround you. A distant vehicle might be making its way along the metalled but still treacherous Burway, and among clumps of bright yellow gorse small groups of sheep may be cropping the sparse and springy turf, but otherwise you are exhilaratingly alone in this vast expanse of hill and sky. To find yourself up here, so far removed from your fellow humans, so small and insignificant as the heavens and earth wheel around you, is both thrilling and sobering. You get a sense of how unyielding and inhospitable this ancient landscape would be in the depths of winter, with the colour leached out of the sky and not even a flicker of the sharp October sun that now intermittently flashes out from behind the clouds. This is the chill and brooding hillscape Housman writes about in his poem about the approach of the last fair of the year at Church Stretton:

In midnights of November,
    When Dead Man's Fair is nigh,
And danger in the valley,
    And anger in the sky,

Around the huddling homesteads
    The leafless timber roars,
And the dead call the dying
    And finger at the doors.

This traditional fair got its name from the number of people who perished while attempting to fumble their drunken way home across these forbidding hills, with their deep valleys and ravines, in the dark nights of winter.

'Nature meant me for a geographer,' Housman once wrote, but much of the topographical knowledge he possessed about Shropshire was derived not from personal observation but from what he had been told about the county while out walking with W.H. Eyre during his Patent Office days. Describing Shropshire in 1934 to his young American admirer Houston Martin, Housman referred to 'the southern half of the county, to which I have confined myself', and this is the region that Eyre had walked and knew well. It is also notable that this southern part of Shropshire is largely rural, an England that seemed then, and seems now, unchanging. It was a very different picture if one travelled north-east from the sheep-scattered uplands of the South Shropshire Hills to Ironbridge Gorge, which is often referred to as the crucible of the Industrial Revolution. It was here that fossil fuels mined in nearby Coalbrookdale fired the furnaces in which iron ore was smelted. Now a UNESCO World Heritage Site and a 'major visitor attraction', the region was not recommended to the Victorian tourist: 'The greater part of the district between Coalbrook Dale and Wellington [some six miles to the north] is occupied by furnaces, forges, collieries, and brick-yards, brilliant enough at night-time, but black, dirty, and dusty in the day,' an 1870 guidebook warned. 'An additional feature of dreariness is caused by the dismantled colliery-stacks and engine-houses.' This, both geographically and spiritually, is a long way from the 'smooth green miles of turf' that characterise Housman Country to the south.

The kind of local knowledge that Housman gained from Eyre was supplemented with details he found in *Murray's Handbook for Shropshire and Cheshire* (1879). It is here that he came upon what he called the 'traditional' quatrain (described in the guide as 'a popular doggerel') that prefaces 'In valleys of springs of rivers' (L). He wrote marginal notes in his own copy of the book, and perhaps the most striking example of the way this guide inspired his poetry is in the clear derivation of the famous concluding lines of 'On Wenlock Edge the wood's in trouble' (XXXI): 'To-day the Roman and his troubles / Are ashes under Uricon' more or less paraphrases the guidebook's reference to 'the Saxon and English Wrekin, in which the name of Vr-ikon, "City of Iconium", whose ashes smoulder beneath its slopes, is virtually enshrined'. It was also from this guidebook that Housman got information about the Dead Man's Fair at Church Stretton and the name Hell Gate (given to one of the entrances to some ancient British earthworks on the Wrekin), which he borrowed for the title of the long allegorical poem that so struck E.M. Forster.

To the authors of *Murray's Handbook* Shropshire seemed ideally representative of English life and landscape. 'There is so much variety in Salop that it may be considered an epitome of England,' they wrote. This variety could best be appreciated from the summit of the Wrekin, which although rising a mere 1320 feet above sea level,

is conspicuous far and wide, and forms an unmistakeable landmark in every phase of Shropshire scenery [. . .] The view is remarkable, beautiful, embracing the whole of Shropshire, the ranges of Church Stretton, the Longmynd, and the Stiper Stones, the Welsh mountains, in which the Breiddens, the Berwyns, and in the far distance Snowdon, are conspicuous, the hills of N.E. Cheshire and Derbyshire, the heights of Cannock Chase, the Clent and Rowley Hills, Titterstone Clee and the Malverns, while within the radius is a wonderful panorama of Black country and Shropshire hedgerows – towns, villages, churches, ironworks, mansions, rivers, and railways.

Housman, however, was not looking out across Shropshire from within the county; he was instead viewing its distant hills from the Worcestershire of his youth. The direction of his gaze is altogether different, and direction is all-important as far as the poems are concerned.

Housman may have told Maurice Pollet that he had a 'sentimental feeling for Shropshire because its hills were our western horizon', but he was perhaps more accurate when he told Houston Martin: 'Shropshire was our western horizon, which made me feel romantic about it.' There is only a word's difference, but Housman's romanticism rarely sank to sentimentalism. Kate Symons recorded that one of the pleasures of her brother's early years 'was to reach some point where he could see extensive views': 'Mount Pisgah' provided the ideal vantage point for him 'to gaze on the sunset lands of Shropshire'. For someone of Housman's temperament, a western horizon had more affecting associations than an eastern one, for it is indeed where the sun sets and the day dies amid regrets for time lost and things done badly or not at all. The contrast between this and the more hopeful eastern horizon, from which the sun rises and each new day seems charged with possibilities, is made clear in one of the earliest of Housman's mature poems, which was written between 1886 and 1890 but remained unpublished during his lifetime:

How clear, how lovely bright,
How beautiful to sight
    Those beams of morning play,
How heaven laughs out with glee
Where, like a bird set free,
Up from the eastern sea
    Soars the delightful day.

To-day I shall be strong,
No more shall yield to wrong,
    Shall squander life no more;
Days lost, I know not how,
I shall retrieve them now;
Now I shall keep the vow
    I never kept before.

—Ensanguining the skies
How heavily it dies
    Into the west away;
Past touch and sight and sound,
Not further to be found,
How hopeless under ground
    Falls the remorseful day.

If there is sentimentality here, it is deliberate and strategically placed in the first stanza, which bubbles with an optimism proved false by the stock images Housman employs. We somehow know that the self-reforming zeal of the second stanza will last no longer than the life of a mayfly, and the poem's final lines beautifully embody and perform the dying fall of eternal disappointment: hopes and resolutions sink irretrievably with the sun beyond the horizon. The stoical Housman can withstand this, but he does not recommend it to others, and in the very first of his *Last Poems* warns:

Comrade, look not on the west:
'Twill have the heart out of your breast;
'Twill take your thoughts and sink them far,
Leagues beyond the sunset bar.

The first poem of *A Shropshire Lad* that Housman wrote (XL) is also about something lost and out of reach, both geographically and emotionally. Whether or not he was aware of the fact, Shropshire is the coldest of all the English counties, and this makes the first two lines of this poem all the more effective, combining the meteorological and emotional into one unforgettable image:

Into my heart an air that kills
    From yon far country blows . . .

Air traditionally gives life, but this air, blowing in from an irrecoverable past, *kills*, stopping the heart of both the poet and the reader. The terrain of the poem is seen from such a distance that only vague

landmarks are visible: hills, farms, spires, highways – no human figures. 'The past is a foreign country,' L.P. Hartley famously observed:
here it is all too recognisably English, a place for which one yearns in
vain. Nostalgia has become debased in recent years through too much
careless handling, transformed into a kind of comfort blanket for
adults in which they can wrap themselves against the chill winds of the
present. No such cosy consolations are found on Housman's horizon:
true nostalgia is deadly. The land across which the poet is looking is at
first barely recognisable: 'What are those blue remembered hills,' the
poet asks, 'What spires, what farms are those?' The moment when this
landscape comes into focus and can be identified is precisely the same
moment that it is gone for ever:

> That is the land of lost content,
>   I see it shining plain,
> The happy highways where I went
>   And cannot come again.

That is what true nostalgia comes down to: you may be able to recognise past happiness, but you cannot regain it.

Though apparently placed in no particularly significant position in
the sequence of lyrics that make up *A Shropshire Lad*, this poem stands as
the triangulation point from which Housman Country can be surveyed
and mapped out. The preferred view of Housman Country is indeed
from a distance, both in time and geography – and distance distorts.
It is when the Lad is furthest away from his country, looking back at it
from exile in London, that he finds it most appealing, and this reflects
the nostalgia not only of Housman himself, obliged to abandon the
rural scenes of his youth in order to earn a living in the capital, but of
a large swathe of the English population.

The Town Built Ill

When the Shropshire Lad set out on his train journey 'through the
wild green hills of Wyre' to London (XXXVII), he was following
a pattern that had become familiar by 1896. A series of agricultural

depressions during the second half of the nineteenth century had led to a huge population shift from the countryside to the large cities. One of the causes of these depressions was the repeal of the Corn Laws in 1846. Introduced at the beginning of the nineteenth century, the Corn Laws imposed tariffs on imported cereals with the intention of keeping prices artificially high and so giving British landowners an advantage in the domestic market. Arguments over the Corn Laws set the countryside against the city. Landowners were keen to maximise profits by keeping the price of corn high, but this meant that the price of bread went up. Industrialists needed to keep wages low, but if the price of bread went up, then wages had to increase as well in order to keep the workforce fed. As landowners had feared, once the Corn Laws were repealed, Britain was gradually flooded with imported grain, grown more cheaply on larger landmasses such as North America and Russia than at home, and now easily transported thanks to developments in steam navigation.

In addition to falling prices, English weather played its part, with a run of particularly poor summers between 1875 and 1882 wrecking the corn harvests. Britain's reliance on imported grain had risen from a tiny 2 percent in the 1830s to a huge 45 percent in the 1880s, and by the middle of the latter decade, land used to grow corn in Britain had shrunk by over one million acres. People began leaving the land partly because of the continuing depression, but also because the increasing mechanisation of farming made large numbers of them redundant, and city jobs that did not rely so heavily upon the vagaries of the English climate promised more security. During the second half of the nineteenth century the agricultural workforce shrank by almost a half, and by the beginning of the twentieth century 77 percent of the population of England and Wales lived in towns and cities, leaving a mere 23 percent in rural districts.

Statistical facts do not, however, accurately reflect how people feel. Britain may have become the world's first urban industrial society, but for many of its inhabitants in 1896 'England' still meant a tranquil pastoral landscape of small villages, ancient parish churches, picturesquely thatched cottages and teams of horses ploughing the fields. This dream of England has proved highly resilient, remaining part of the nation's iconography long after the last working horses were put out to pasture. Many of those who had left their often dilapidated and insanitary cottages behind them when they went in search of better pay and prospects found themselves crammed into urban slums and tenements. Gazing out of their dismal city dwellings onto cheerless back yards, the new urban population might well have felt a pang for the rural lives they had left behind them. However squalid and impoverished these lives might have been, people did at least have access to fresh air among fields and woods. Walter Southgate in *That's the Way It Was*, a classic autobiography of urban working-class life at the turn of the twentieth century, recalled that 'If a tuft of grass appeared in the crevices of stones and clinker' in his family's sunless East End back yard, his mother 'would tend it as if it was a lily [. . .] It reminded her, she said, "of the country".'

Whatever the newly urbanised working-class population may have felt about the rural life they had abandoned, middle-class writers and social reformers began holding up the English countryside as a source of aesthetic and moral ideals. The contrast between a simple, innocent pastoral world and a sophisticated and corrupt urban one had been common literary currency in Europe for many centuries, stretching back to the Ancient Greeks. A countryside in which shepherds and goatherds stood around decoratively among their flocks, piping merrily or discussing the gods and muses, clearly bore little relation to the agricultural realities of Greece in the third century BC, which was when Theocritus wrote his *Idylls*, and the Pastoral mode from the very start described a wholly idealised landscape. The word 'idyll' has nothing to do with the English word 'ideal', but is derived from the Greek word for a short poem. It says much for the widespread notion that the perfect life was a pastoral one, however, that a word first used to describe a poem of rural life based on Theocritus's model would be adopted to describe any period or situation characterised by absolute contentment.

The contrast between urban and rural life in England was neatly summed up and Christianised by the eighteenth-century poet William Cowper, who declared: 'God made the country, and man made the town', rather as if that settled the matter. For Cowper the English countryside, to which he had retreated after suffering a breakdown, represented a peaceful and serene refuge from the thrusting life of the city: it was where a man could enjoy the therapeutic benefits of being close to, and in harmony with, nature. The deleterious effects of urban life became a national issue a century later, during the 1880s and 1890s, when anxieties arose about the physical and moral effects poverty and overcrowding in large industrial cities were having on the English race. The fact that Britain was the world's first industrialised society may have brought economic benefits to the country as a whole, but the teeming slums of major cities showed all too vividly the human consequences of such advances. Writer-philosophers such as John Ruskin and William Morris inveighed against the dehumanising aspects of industrialisation, and novelists such as Charles Dickens, with his grimly delineated accounts of life among the urban poor, left his readers with indelible images of squalor and criminality. Almost as striking, though they provided charts and statistics rather than thrilling plots, were such sociological studies as Henry Mayhew's *London Labour and the London Poor*, based on interviews with working people and published in four volumes between 1851 and 1861.

By the 1880s there was widespread alarm at the seemingly unstoppable decline into crime and degradation in the poorer quarters of the capital. An inquiry conducted by the Social Democratic Federation in 1885 concluded that some 25 percent of the population of London lived in extreme poverty. The businessman and philanthropist Charles Booth suspected that these figures were an exaggeration and in 1887 embarked on his own sociological survey, eventually publishing the results in seventeen volumes as *Life and Labour of the People in London* (1902–03). His findings suggested that in fact one-third of Londoners were living in some degree of poverty, and his research was illustrated by maps in which individual streets were colour-coded from yellow for 'Upper-middle and Upper classes. Wealthy' to black for 'Lowest class. Vicious, semi-criminal'. Those areas showing large amounts of black were portrayed in such books as Arthur Morrison's *Tales of Mean Streets* (1894) and *A Child of the Jago* (1896), two classics of what came to be known as 'slum fiction'. These stories suggested that life for the London poor had changed little from that endured by Dickens's Oliver Twist some sixty years earlier – except that there was no happy ending.

The principal reason the English race needed to be kept fit and healthy was in order to differentiate it from the 'inferior' races it ruled in the British Empire, and medical examinations undergone by recruits for the Boer War suggested that those poor specimens of it packed into urban slums and rookeries were no longer fit for purpose. The notion that people in the first city of Empire (London) might be living in conditions not dissimilar to those of the native poor in the second city of Empire (Calcutta) was highly disturbing. It was evident that the rural classes were in every way far more healthy than their city counterparts, and this supported the rather more fanciful belief that the English countryside was the true repository of old English values. Something of this is apparent in E.M. Forster's *Howards End* (1910), a novel much concerned with England and Englishness, and much influenced by Housman. Leonard Bast, the young clerk befriended by Margaret and Helen Schlegel, though not a slum-dweller, is the physically and spiritually degraded result of the population shifts of the nineteenth century. 'One guessed him as the third generation, grandson of the shepherd or ploughboy whom civilization had sucked into the town,' Forster writes; 'as one of the thousands who have lost the life of the body and failed to reach the life of the spirit. Hints of robustness survived in him, more than a hint of primitive good looks, and Margaret, noting the spine that might have been straight, and the chest that might have been broadened, wondered whether it paid to give up the glory of the animal for a tail coat and a couple of ideas.'

The encroachment of the modern, with its ills as well as its benefits, was more apparent in towns and cities than in the countryside. Even so, as the nineteenth century drew on there was a concern that the English landscape itself was under threat. The Commons Preservation Society was founded in 1865 and the following year tore up the railings that had been erected around Berkhamsted Common by a local aristocrat attempting to enclose it within his own private estate. Legal proceedings were then taken to ensure that the common was retained for local people, and two of the CPS's leading members went on to found the National Trust in 1895. The Trust acquired its first threatened building the following year, but it was always intended that the organisation should protect open spaces: it created its first nature reserve, Wicken Fen in Cambridgeshire, in 1899, and acquired its first archaeological site, the Neolithic White Barrow on Salisbury Plain, in 1909. Nevertheless, in spite of the arrival of the railways, modern architecture and infrastructure had far less impact in rural areas, and when people spoke of England's 'unchanging landscape' they were not altogether exaggerating.

Traditionally there had also, until the population shifts of the later nineteenth century, been little change or movement among rural people, whose ancestors were often laid out generation after generation in the same parish churchyard. Working the land was felt (mainly by those who didn't do it) to be far more representative of the 'real' England than working in a factory. The pace of rural life was thought to be more in tune with English values than the bustle of the city, the daily round and the changing seasons that characterised the English scene more perceptible amongst fields than in bustling urban streets. In the countryside the squire still stood at the apex of local society, occupying the 'Big House', with his staff, tenants and workers taking up fixed and appropriate positions in the hierarchy beneath him. It was not only an unchanging landscape that could be found in rural areas, but unchanging values. The countryside represented stability and continuity, the cities rupture and flux. None of this stood up to much scrutiny, of course, but nations tend to define themselves less by statistical facts than by received ideas that have a symbolic rather than a literal truth.

These ideas were not merely sociological but cultural, reflected as much in the literature and music of the period as in population studies. In his 1890 novel *The Tragic Muse*, for example, Henry James provided an almost mystical notion of what rural England meant, none the less powerful for being written by an expatriate American. The novel's protagonist is visiting his benefactor, who lives in a country town dominated by its ancient abbey and surrounded by sweet-smelling hayfields. It is a place where

> the tide of time broke with a ripple too faint to be a warning. But there was another admonition that was almost equally sure to descend upon his spirit in a summer hour, in a stroll about the grand

abbey; to sink into it as the light lingered on the rough red walls and the local accent of the children sounded soft in the churchyard. It was simply the sense of England – a sort of apprehended revelation of his country. The dim annals of the place appeared to be in the air (foundations bafflingly early, a great monastic life, Wars of the Roses, with battles and blood in the streets, and then the long quietude of the respectable centuries, all cornfields and magistrates and vicars), and these things were connected with an emotion that arose from the green country, the rich land so infinitely lived in, and laid on him a hand that was too ghostly to press and yet somehow too urgent to be light. It produced a throb that he could not have spoken of, it was so deep, and that was half imagination and half responsibility.

This 'sense of England' was fully established in the literary culture by the time *A Shropshire Lad* was published, and Housman's book enacted the unwilling move from a rural life to an urban one, and the sense of loss that this entailed. This is where the perspective mentioned earlier comes in, the notion that Shropshire seems more idyllic when the Lad looks back on it from his London exile than when he was there among his doomed and unhappy fellows.

A similar perspective is found in another very English poet, John Masefield, in such poems as 'London Town', first published in 1903 and collected in his *Ballads and Poems* of 1910. Masefield is a poet popularly associated with seafaring, but his roots were deep in the Herefordshire and Worcestershire countryside around Ledbury, where he had been born in 1878. 'For some years, like many children, I lived in Paradise, or, rather, like a specially lucky child in two Paradises linked together by a country of exceeding beauty and strangeness,' he wrote in his childhood memoir *Grace before Ploughing*. These two linked paradises were Ledbury and Bredon Hill: 'For some blissful years I knew them both as only a child can know a country.'

The trouble with Paradise is that you are likely to be cast out of it and, after time spent at sea, Masefield returned to England to become a clerk in London, from where, like the Shropshire Lad, he looked back longingly towards the rural life he had left behind. This is a landscape very similar to Housman's. 'London Town' recognises the capital's allure in a way Housman's poems never do, but it is nevertheless a town the poet is 'glad to leave behind':

> Then hey for croft and hop-yard, and hill, and field, and
>   pond,
> With Bredon Hill before me and Malvern Hill beyond,
> The hawthorn white i'the hedgerow, and all the spring's
>   attire
> In the comely land of Teme and Lugg, and Clent, and
>   Clee, and Wyre.

This celebration of 'all the land from Ludlow town to Bredon church's spire' (an area that more or less encompasses the eastern aspect of Housman Country) is evidently strongly influenced by *A Shropshire Lad*: there is even a reference to 'mill and forge and fold', which virtually repeats the second line of 'The lads in their hundreds to Ludlow come in for the fair' (XXIII).* The poem's tone, however, is entirely different, its rhythms unequivocally cheerful. The countryside here is still within reach and is suffused with wholly happy memories. Masefield's is a poem of celebration rather than regret, of life rather than death.

By contrast, Housman the Latinist would have been familiar with the tag '*Et in arcadia ego*', first alluded to in Virgil's *Eclogues*, and with the notion that it is Death who is warning 'I, too, am in Arcadia'. This presence is felt throughout *A Shropshire Lad*, where even the flowering of plants and trees acts less as a herald of new life than as a *memento mori*. As William Archer observed in his 1898 review of the book:

> Never was there less of a 'pastoral' poet, in the artificial, Italian-Elizabethan sense of the word. The Shropshire of Mr Housman is

---

*Housman's influence upon Masefield has not, perhaps, been much explored. 'I had a very great admiration for his poems,' Masefield wrote on Housman's death. That this admiration was of long standing may be seen from such poems as 'On Malvern Hill' (published in *Salt-Water Ballads*, 1902), which in its title, prosody, vocabulary and theme (that of 'the wind's riot' evoking the ghosts of long-dead Romans) is more or less a recapitulation of 'On Wenlock Edge the wood's in trouble'.

no Arcadia, no Sicily, still less a courtly pleasaunce peopled with beribboned nymphs and swains. It is as real, and as tragic, as the Wessex of Mr [Thomas] Hardy. The genius, or rather the spirit, of the two writers is not dissimilar. Both have the same rapturous realisation, the same bitter resentment, of life. To both Nature is an exquisitely seductive, inexorably malign enchantress. 'Life's Ironies' might be the common title of Mr Hardy's long series of novels and Mr Housman's little book of verse. And both have the same taste for clothing life's ironies in the bucolic attire of an English county.

Archer has borrowed this suggested collective title from Hardy's 1894 volume of short stories, *Life's Little Ironies*, and it is possible that Housman may have borrowed Archer's notion of Nature the enchantress for a poem he wrote in April 1922 and published in *Last Poems*. It seems more than coincidental that Housman, who had read and commented on Archer's review in advance of publication, mildly suggesting to his publisher that it 'may create some sort of demand' among readers, should have written a poem about 'nature, heartless, witless nature' that begins:

> Tell me not here, it needs not saying,
>   What tune the enchantress plays . . .

There are indeed similarities between Hardy and Housman in the matter, though rarely in the manner, of their writing. Max Beerbohm asked:

> How compare either of these grim two?
>   Each has an equal knack,
> Hardy supplies the pill that's blue,
>   Housman the draught that's black.

Both men acquired a knowledge of the countryside in childhood when walking considerable distances to their respective schools, and both came to see nature as something that bewitches humans but is not to be trusted. There is one crucial difference, however. For Hardy, nature remained entirely indifferent to the sufferings of humans, resulting in what Philip Larkin (who would know) called the poet's 'temperamental sunlessness'. The term might equally well be applied to Housman, but although 'heartless, witless nature' may be indifferent to the assorted ills of Shropshire lads, it also provides a kind of solace not to be found in the urban environment:

> In my own shire, if I was sad,
> Homely comforters I had:
> The earth, because my heart was sore,
> Sorrowed for the son she bore;
> And standing hills, long to remain,
> Shared their short-lived comrade's pain.

This comfort drawn from nature has nothing whatever to do with traditional notions of renewal and rebirth, however; indeed, it is precisely because the year is dying with the turning seasons that it chimes with the speaker's mood:

> And bound for the same bourn as I,
> On every road I wandered by,
> Trod beside me, close and dear,
> The beautiful and death-struck year . . .

This 'comradeship' is contrasted with the genuine and much more distressing indifference of the speaker's city-dwelling fellow men, those identified in poem XIV as 'the careless people' who pass the solitary figure by: 'careless' in the sense of carefree, because they do not share his anxieties; but also culpably so because they do not even notice someone in distress.

Such indifference was presumably less upsetting for Housman himself when he went walking on Hampstead Heath in order to think out his poems. Few writers want to be approachable when they are at work, and accounts of Housman's distracted or preoccupied air when encountered during his solitary walks suggest that this kind of 'loneliness' was both self-imposed and necessary to his poetry. Hampstead Heath may not have been the western brookland of Housman's childhood, but in the 1890s, before the constant background hum of motorised traffic, it provided the poet with a means of thinking himself back into that lost landscape. It was not merely that the physical exercise of walking was conducive to writing poetry, it was that these walks took the poet across a hilly terrain, through woods and around ponds that approximated the rural world he was reimagining in his poems. The Heath was not merely conveniently close to Byron Cottage, it provided an environment far wilder than, say, Hyde Park, which would have been the nearest large open space in which to go walking had Housman remained living in Bayswater. Hampstead Heath was on the fringes of London rather than in the centre and was not hemmed in by buildings or thronged with the office workers and nurses wheeling prams who frequented Hyde Park's more manicured topography. Even in London, Housman's kind of walking had more in common with the Romantic poets' engagement with landscape than with leisurely strolls in fashionable parks, where stopping to talk to other people was part of the experience.

Hark, the Empty Highways Crying

If the Augustan poets saluted the impress of man upon the landscape – the houses he built, the gardens he laid out – then the Romantics re-embraced an untamed England in their objective to become closer to nature. The best way of doing this was by encountering it on foot. Long walks had been part of English rural life for centuries: for many people who could afford neither horse nor cart nor other form of transport, walking was the only means of getting from one place to another. Walking as a recreation, however, started to become popular in the early nineteenth century. Before that, most tourists travelled by coach or carriage, rattling from one 'sight' to another and seeing large tracts of the countryside only in passing. The Romantic poets were pioneers in recreational walking. As well as bringing them closer to nature, walking represented that other Romantic aspiration: freedom. Samuel Taylor Coleridge, who like his friends William and Dorothy Wordsworth covered great distances when out walking, wrote of the sense of liberation felt by those who set out on foot: 'every man his own path-maker – skip & jump – where rushes grew, a man may go'. The Wordsworths had moved to Alfoxden in Somerset in 1797 specifically to be near Coleridge, who lived a three-mile walk away in Nether Stowey. Companionable rambles in the Quantock Hills were part of the daily routine, with Wordsworth and Coleridge discussing political and literary matters, while Dorothy quietly took in the landscape, the weather, the trees and plants in order to write about them in her journal, which she began keeping in January 1798. In December 1799 the Wordsworths moved to Grasmere in the Lake District, some twenty-five miles south from where they had been born in Cockermouth, and here, the following May, Dorothy began writing another set of journals. Walking remained a feature of their life together, and had a considerable influence on Wordsworth's poetry, from 'Tintern Abbey' to *The Prelude*, some of which absorbed and refracted Dorothy's journals. As well as daily rambles, there were longer excursions, such as the nine-day one through the Lake District undertaken by Coleridge in August 1802.

Coleridge was as good a talker as he was a walker, and the two habits were for him closely related. One of the places he did both was Shropshire. In 1798 he took charge of a Unitarian congregation in Shrewsbury, with a view to becoming its minister. The previous incumbent had failed to identify Coleridge when he went to meet the coach, and was explaining this to the congregation when a man he had seen engaged in energetic conversation with his fellow-passengers arrived and 'dissipated all doubts [as to his identity] by beginning to talk. He did not cease while he staid; nor has he since, that I know of.' The reporter is William Hazlitt, whose family had moved to the Shropshire market town of Wem the year before. The nineteen-year-old Hazlitt 'rose one morning before daylight to walk ten miles in the mud' to Shrewsbury to hear Coleridge preach, and was suitably impressed. Hazlitt's father had also been a Unitarian minister and it was the custom for ministers to visit each other when in the area, so the following week Coleridge came to Wem to dine off a leg of Welsh mutton and turnips. The next morning, he set off back to Shrewsbury. 'I accompanied him six miles on the road,' Hazlitt recalled. 'It was a fine morning in the middle of winter, and he talked the whole way.' Coleridge spoke of philosophy and politics and walked in much the same way as he talked: 'I observed that he continually crossed me on the way by shifting from one side of the foot-path to the other. This struck me as an odd movement; but I did not at that time connect it with any instability of purpose or involuntary change of principle, as I have done since. He seemed unable to keep on in a strait line.' Hazlitt, perhaps understandably, would later write that he, like Housman, preferred walking on his own and in silence: 'I can enjoy society in a room; but out of doors nature is company enough for me,' he wrote in his essay 'On Going a Journey' (1822). 'I cannot see the wit of walking and talking at the same time.'

Hazlitt had been invited by Coleridge to visit him in Somerset and it seemed only appropriate that most of his 150-mile journey to Nether Stowey was accomplished on foot: through Shrewsbury, Worcester, Upton-upon-Severn, Tewkesbury, Gloucester, Bristol and Bridgwater. This seems a huge distance, but such walks were not uncommon at the time. While in 1773 Samuel Johnson and James Boswell made their tour of Western Isles by carriage, boat and on horseback, the Romantics accomplished similar tours mostly on foot. A six-week trip around Scotland undertaken by Coleridge and the Wordsworths in the summer of 1803 may officially have been made in a jaunting car, a rather more elegant version of a pony cart, but the roads were often so bad that they had to get down and walk much of the way. After the party broke up, Coleridge went off on his own, setting out for Edinburgh from Tarbet: by the time he had reached Perth he calculated that he had walked 263 miles in eight days, despite suffering from atonic gout and being prescribed carminative bitters in order to rid himself of 'truly poisonous, & body-&-soul-benumming Flatulence and Inflation'. Uncertain health seemed no obstacle to such excursions, and when John Keats and his friend Charles Brown went on a tour of northern England, Scotland and Ireland in 1818 they covered over 600 miles in forty-four days, mostly on foot – a circumstance that some have argued hastened the poet's death just three years later. The Romantic attitude to walking was summed up by Hazlitt: 'Give me the clear blue sky over my head, and the green turf beneath my feet, a winding road before me, and a three hours' march to dinner – and then to thinking!'

Exploring the countryside on foot became increasingly popular during the nineteenth century, with guidebooks including suggestions for lengthy walks as part of a tourist's experience. The *Murray's Handbook* that Housman used when checking local details recommended 'Pedestrian Tours' of between eleven and twenty miles. As the nineteenth century progressed and more and more people found themselves pent up in industrial towns and cities, recreational walks in the countryside became increasingly popular, either undertaken informally or in organised groups. Detailed maps for those who wanted to ensure they did not get lost on country rambles had slowly become available from the turn of the eighteenth and nineteenth centuries. The first Ordnance Survey map (covering Kent and part of Essex) had been published on 1 January 1801, but the subsequent mapping of the whole country would not be complete until 1870. These early maps were not very portable: the first one was made up of 'four massive rectangular sheets, each one around thirty inches wide and twenty inches high'. They were also expensive: the map for Devon covered eight sheets and cost six guineas, the equivalent of 'forty days' wages for a craftsman in the building trade.' By 1870, however, the price had dropped to 2s 6d, bringing maps within the financial reach of many more people. The familiar Revised New Edition of one-inch-to-the-mile OS maps was published between 1896 (the year *A Shropshire Lad* was published) and 1904, a period that coincided with the rise of hiking as a popular pastime.

It was also during this period that poetry, its *fin-de-siècle* flirtation with the metropolitan life snuffed out with the century, re-embraced the countryside. A man like Housman who composed his poems while striding energetically across the land was in marked contrast to the traditional late-Victorian image of the poet, languishing picturesquely, and preferably consumptively, in a city garret – or indeed Gilbert and Sullivan's Wildean aesthete in *Patience*, who recommended that you merely 'walk down Piccadilly / With a poppy or a lily / In your medieval hand'. Robert Louis Stevenson's *Songs of Travel and Other Verses* was published the same year as *A Shropshire Lad* and similarly stood apart from 1890s metropolitan greenery-yallery, celebrating life on the open road and a different kind of bohemianism from the one found at the Café Royal. If Housman's poems are poems of exile from 'the happy highways' of his rural childhood, Stevenson's were written at an even more remote distance from home, in the South Seas, and are similarly infused with yearning for the countryside of his youth. It seems hardly coincidental that when Stevenson died in 1894, Housman should write a poem about him, incorporating lines from Stevenson's own 'Requiem' and published above an obituary in *The Academy* magazine. The first poem in Stevenson's *Songs of Travel* was 'The Vagabond':

> Give to me the life I love,
>   Let the lave go by me,
> Give the jolly heaven above
>   And the byway nigh me.
> Bed in the bush with stars to see,
>   Bread I dip in the river —
> There's the life for a man like me,
>   There's the life for ever.

Literary vagabondage was taken to the limit by W.H. Davies, who in 1893, at the age of twenty-two, left his Welsh home for America, where he spent six years travelling round the country both on foot and by leaping on and off freight trains. To earn his keep he begged or did casual work, and he often slept rough. His travels came to an end when he was involved in an accident: he missed his footing while trying to jump on a train, as a result of which his right leg had to be amputated at the knee. He returned to Britain and ended up in London, drinking heavily and living in doss-houses, from which he set off tramping the countryside on his wooden leg as an itinerant pedlar. The title poem of his first volume of poetry, *The Soul's Destroyer*, published in 1905, describes the poet waking up with a crashing hangover,

> With limbs all sore from falling here and there
> To drink the various ales the Borough kept
> From London Bridge to Newington, and streets

> Adjoining, alleys, lanes obscure from them,
> Then thought of home and of the purer life,
> Of Nature's air, and having room to breathe,
> A sunny sky, green field, and water's sound . . .

This vision of nature inspires him to set out from London to walk back to Wales:

> All day walked I, and that same night, I scorned
> The shelter of a house, lay peaceful down
> Beneath the glorious stars [. . .]
> Such joy a hundred times a day was mine
> To see at every bend of the road the face
> Of Nature different. And oft I sat
> To hear the lark from his first twitter pass
> To greater things as he soared nearer heaven;
> Or to the throstle, singing nearer home . . .

Davies is clearly an extreme case, and this poem is as much about the destructive nature of alcohol as it is about the contrast between the streets of London and life on the open road. It was not, however, merely indigence that made him declare in his *Autobiography of a Super-Tramp* (1908): 'I would rather take a free country walk, leaving the roads for the less trodden paths of the hills and lanes, than ride in a yacht or coach.' The freedom he felt as a walker is the same as Coleridge's: 'every man his own path-maker'.

Davies may have walked partly from financial necessity, but in the early years of the twentieth century walking and poetry had once again become associated in the way they had been for the Romantics. ''Tis spring; come out to ramble / The hilly brakes around', Housman urged in 'The Lent Lily' (XXIX), one of several poems in which the pleasures of country expeditions are recommended. The reveille in Housman's poem of that name (IV) is not a military one: it is a call to those who waste their time lying late in bed to get up and out into the countryside.

Up, lad, up, 'tis late for lying:
   Hear the drums of morning play;
Hark, the empty highways crying
   'Who'll beyond the hills away?'

It is not merely that walking in the countryside is good for the health
and spirits; Housman reminds the lad that life is too short to idle away:

Clay lies still, but blood's a rover;
   Breath's a ware that will not keep.
Up, lad: when the journey's over
   There'll be time enough to sleep.

A renewed popular association of poetry and walking was partly a
reaction against the Decadent poets of the 1890s. The novelist Penelope
Fitzgerald, writing in 1977 about the generation who became young
men in the 1900s, described the early years of the twentieth century
as 'a time of great popular writers'. The public 'enjoyed, without
perceiving any subtleties, the stories of Hardy, Conrad and Kipling.
Furthermore, they read poetry. The "pocket anthology" fitted into a
Norfolk jacket and could be taken out on long weekend walks; it had
fine thin pages and a piece of ribbon attached as a bookmarker. *The
Golden Treasury* (1891 edition) was the right size for this, so too was *A
Shropshire Lad.*'

Palgrave's *Golden Treasury* was itself conceived while walking. The
book's compiler, Francis Turner Palgrave, had become a friend of
Tennyson and in 1860 had accompanied the poet on a walking tour
of Cornwall in search of places associated with King Arthur as background material for *Idylls of the King*. It was 'while traversing the wild
scenery of Treryn Dinas', an Iron Age cliff-fort on a Cornish prom-
ontory, that Palgrave suggested the idea of an anthology to Tennyson,
hoping that the poet would become its co-editor. In the event, Palgrave
received only encouragement and occasional advice from Tennyson,
who found Palgrave's devotion rather tiresome. Unaware of this, he
dedicated his anthology to Tennyson, and what many readers saw as
the imprimatur of the Poet Laureate undoubtedly helped the book

become widely popular. In his preface to the first edition, Palgrave wrote: 'Poetry gives treasures "more golden than gold", leading us in higher and healthier ways than those of the world, and interpreting to us the lessons of Nature.' The title page carries an engraving of a naked shepherd boy sitting on a rock beneath a tree on which a warbling bird perches; he is playing on a pipe and a dog is lying at his feet. Also on the ground are some pan pipes, apparently discarded, and this along with the fact that the boy has human rather than goat's feet suggests an English Arcadia rather than a classical one. Indeed, the very first poem in the book is Thomas Nashe's 'Spring' from his play *Summers Last Will and Testament* (1592), in which 'shepherds pipe all day' in the daisy-spangled English fields while 'the pretty birds do sing'. Anyone who doubted that the mainstream of English poetry – at any rate as it was perceived in 1891 – was a pastoral one need only leaf through this anthology.

Although consisting of nearly 400 pages, *The Golden Treasury* was deliberately designed to be both affordable (originally retailing at 4s 6d) and portable, 'a small octavo of a very pretty shape and size and type' bound in gold-stamped green cloth. Another inexpensive book to slip into the jacket pocket was E.V. Lucas's *The Open Road: A Little Book for Wayfarers*, first published by Grant Richards in 1899 and in its thirty-third edition by 1923. It had been specially devised for the literary-minded rambler, and is the book that in *Howards End* Leonard Bast recommends to the Schlegels after he has spent a whole night walking in the countryside, setting out from Wimbledon for the North Downs. Bast was just the sort of reader Lucas had in mind when compiling the book, which, he wrote, 'aims at nothing but providing companionship on the road for city-dwellers who make holiday. It has no claims to completeness of any kind: it is just a garland of good or enkindling poetry and prose fitted to urge folk into the open air, and, once there, to keep them glad they came – to slip easily from the pocket beneath a tree or amongst the heather, and provide lazy reading for the time of rest, and perhaps a phrase or two for the feet to step to and the mind to brood on when the rest is over.'

The endpapers depict two highly stylised English landscapes, one illuminated by the sun, the other by the moon, through which the broad open road of the title winds, and they were designed by William Hyde, whom Grant Richards employed to illustrate an edition of *A Shropshire Lad* in 1908. The first section of the anthology is titled 'The Farewell to Winter and the Town' and opens with Edward FitzGerald's 'The Meadows in Spring'. Lucas was one of those anthologists who fell foul of Housman, who affected to be 'speechless with surprise and indignation' when he discovered that some of his poems had been included in *The Open Road*.

A similar volume to Lucas's was Alfred H. Hyatt's *The Footpath Way: An Anthology for those who travel by Countryside* (1906). 'This little selection is intended for those who, in search of quiet, and having slipped the volume into the pocket, desire to refresh the mind while resting beside "the footpath way",' Hyatt wrote in his introduction. 'Most of the poems and passages chosen to fill these pages throb with the true joy of the open air, each in its turn suggesting some happy country thought or painting some pastoral scene.' Hyatt believed that even a bicyclist would miss out on much of what Nature has to offer – 'she flies before the scorching cycle like a frightened bird' – and that the only true way to appreciate the countryside was on foot. 'Man was a born pedestrian,' he writes, 'and it is only at walking pace, an easy loitering pace too, that Nature can really be got to talk.' Like Lucas's anthology, this one admits a few Americans such as Walt Whitman and Washington Irving, but is essentially promoting the discovery of the English landscape.

Perhaps the most literary of all ramblers was Edward Thomas, who had been a lover of the countryside from his earliest years. He began his career as a prolific writer of prose, much of which he considered hack-work undertaken simply in order to feed his family. He nevertheless became one of the most prominent and popular celebrants of the English countryside in such books as *The Heart of England* (1906), *The South Country* (1909), *The Icknield Way* (1913) and *In Pursuit of Spring* (1914). He did not start writing poetry until 1914, and although he is counted amongst the war poets (he was killed at Arras on Easter Monday in 1917), all his poems were written before he went to the Western Front. Many of them are about the English landscapes he explored on foot, notebook in hand, taking his 'credo' from Richard

Jefferies, the nineteenth-century nature writer whose biography he wrote in 1909: 'Let us get out of these indoor narrow modern days, whose twelve hours somehow have become shortened, into the sunlight and the pure wind.' Getting outdoors and into the countryside was also the impulse behind Thomas's popular anthology *The Pocket Book of Songs for the Open Air* (1907). 'I have gathered into it much of the finest English poetry,' he wrote in the volume's introduction, 'and that, at its best, can hardly avoid the open air.' The very first poem in the anthology, printed without the poet's permission and to his considerable annoyance, was Housman's 'Reveille'.

Two Pilgrims in Housman Country

Many writers make a particular landscape their own when they write about it, and readers often like the idea of visiting places they feel they know from books. Local tourist offices are only too happy to exploit such connections by enticing people to 'Wordsworth Country', 'Brontë Country' or 'Hardy's Wessex'. Among the events organised in 2009 to mark the 150th anniversary of Housman's birth was 'A walk in Housman Country', which was in fact restricted to the area around Clun. The difference between this 'Housman Country' and other landscapes associated with writers – or indeed painters ('Constable Country') or composers ('Elgar Country') – is that the man after whom it is named never lived or worked there. Whereas writers such as Wordsworth, Hardy and the Brontës were describing in their stories, novels and poems real places that they knew intimately, when in 1926 Housman donated the manuscript of *A Shropshire Lad* to the library at Trinity College, he observed that 'it reposes in the appropriate company of Milton's *Lycidas*', a pastoral elegy in which an idealised Theocritan 'Cambridge' bears little relation to the real university town.

Answering Laurence's complaints about the inaccuracy of 'Hughley Steeple', Housman had said that he 'did not apprehend that the faithful would be making pilgrimages to these holy places'. As the volume grew in popularity, however, those who had come to love the poems naturally wanted to visit the places that had 'inspired' them, and many carried with them pocket editions of the book. Norman Nicholson, a genuinely local English poet of a later generation, much of whose work was inspired by the village of Millom in Cumbria, where he spent most of his life, once remarked: 'You might as well use *A Shropshire Lad* as a guide to [Shropshire] as use Rossetti's "Blessed Damozel" as a guide to heaven.' Others disagreed. Edmund Gosse wrote that Housman 'never describes' the countryside in which his poems are set, 'but he indicates its character in a way which exceeds the impression made by any topographical survey, however accurate. I have wandered on "the high-hilled plains", needing no guide but one little olive-coloured book of verses.' Stephen Tallents, who as public relations officer for the General Post Office in the 1930s would be responsible for commissioning many well-known documentary films about England and the English, had visited Housman Country while awaiting the results of the Civil Service exams in 1908. He had recently been studying at the University of Grenoble, where he had become a particular friend of a French girl, and on his return to England he sent her a silk scarf and a copy of *A Shropshire Lad*, 'with a plea that she should make "Loveliest of trees, the cherry now" a part of her English studies'. He then set out on a solitary walking tour beginning at the English Bridge in Shrewsbury. 'The *Shropshire Lad* had brought me to Shrewsbury,' he recalled. 'It was delightful to walk through the woods of Wenlock Edge, with the forest fleece of the Wrekin to the north behind me, and Clee and Cleobury away to the east; delightful, too, to be woken up in Ludlow on a Monday morning by the church bells truly playing *The Conquering Hero comes*.'

Two of the most distinguished literary pilgrims to Housman Country during this early period, both of them clutching their copies of *A Shropshire Lad*, were Willa Cather in July 1902 and E.M. Forster in April 1907. Cather, who was thirty-two when *A Shropshire Lad* was published, had been born in Virginia, but moved at the age of ten to Nebraska, which would provide the setting for her best-known novels. It would be difficult to imagine a landscape more different from the treeless American prairies than the dramatic limestone escarpment of Wenlock Edge or 'the wild green hills of Wyre' that were the settings for Housman's poems, but Cather was immediately captivated by this wholly other world. '*Do* I know a Shropshire Lad?' she wrote in 1903, the year in which she published her first and only volume of poetry. 'Do I? Isn't the internal evidence of my own poetry all against me? Why I've been Housman's bond slave, mentally, since his volume first appeared some six years ago.' Armed with this volume, Cather not only made a pilgrimage to Shropshire during a European trip in the summer of 1902 but even tracked down the author in Pinner. She was accompanied by a young friend called Isabelle McClung, in whose house she lived while working on magazines in Pittsburgh. 'As soon as I got to England, I went straight to Shropshire,' she reported (not quite accurately: the two women had in fact spent five days in Chester, before they 'coached fifty miles to Shrewsbury'). 'When we got into Shropshire we threw away our guide books and have blindly followed the trail of the Shropshire Lad and he has led us beside still waters and in green pastures.' They went 'to all the places – Shrewsbury, Ludlow, Knighton, and the rivers "Ony and Teme and Clun".' In Shrewsbury they

saw how

    'High the vanes of Shrewsbury gleam
    Islanded in Severn stream,
    The bridges, from the steepled crest,
    Cross the water east and west.'

We sat for two sunsets on the very spot where he must have done it and watched the red steeples in the clear green water which flows almost imperceptibly. And what do you think was going on in the wide meadows on the other shore? Why boys were playing *foot-ball*!

    'Is football playing
    Along the river shore?'

Well I guess yes. And we went to Shrewsbury jail. You remember

    'They hang us now in Shrewsbury jail;
    The whistles blow forlorn

And trains all night groan on the rail
To lads that die at morn.'

Of *course* they do, for the jail, which is the most grewsome [sic] building the hand of man ever made, is on a naked hill right over the switch yard and station, so you see 'forlorn' was not put there [just] to rhyme with morn.

Travelling on to Ludlow, they 'heard the bells of Ludlow play "The Conquering Hero Comes" of a Monday', just as Housman recorded in 'The Recruit' – 'and even now they are calling to farm and lane and mill,' she reported, referring to another line of that poem. They particularly admired Ludlow Castle, 'one of the most perfect Norman-Elizabethan compounds in England and the least visited [. . .] Isn't it nice that Sir Philip Sidney grew up and first wrote in Ludlow castle when his father held the Welsh borders here for Elizabeth? We have read those two singing Shropshire lads until our eyes are blinded and our reason distraught.' Cather was inspired to write a poem about the red field poppies that grew on the castle's turrets; the influence of Housman is clear, not least in the archaic use of 'mind' for 'remember':

I'll mind the flowers of pleasure,
Of short-lived youth and sleep
That drank the sunny weather
A-top of Ludlow keep.

'We are going to bicycle to *Wenlock Edge* this afternoon,' she reported, '"Oh tarnish late on Wenlock edge" etc. I'll not quit Shropshire till I know every name he uses. They are just making hay now, too, and I think I might almost find Maurice behind the mow somewhere' – Maurice being the murdered brother in 'Farewell to barn and stack and tree' (VIII). They may not have come across any corpses, but they did find a bookseller who delighted them when he said: 'You must not carry these books; I will send them up to your hotel by my lad.' Cather felt that 'Somehow it makes it all the greater to have it all *true*' – and she would have been disappointed to discover that far from sitting on the banks of the Severn at Shrewsbury 'on the very spot' that she had found, Housman had cribbed such details from *Murray's Handbook* – possibly the very guidebook she had cast aside in favour of *A Shropshire Lad*.

The one thing the two women had not been able to find in Shropshire was any trace of the man himself: 'Of him not a legend, not a button or feather or mark. Nobody had ever heard of him or seen his book. There was a copy in the Shrewsbury public library, but the leaves were uncut.' Undaunted, Cather 'battered on the doors of his publishers until they gave me his address', and she and her companion, now accompanied by another friend, Dorothy Canfield (who had come over from Paris, where she had been studying), decided to pay Housman a visit. They trundled out along the Metropolitan Railway line to Pinner, where they found their hero in 'an awful suburb in quite the most horrible boarding-house ever explored'. This was 1 Yarborough Villas, which was indeed an unlovely semi-detached house built in the 1850s.

Housman turned out to be as dingy as his surroundings, and he had clearly made no effort to make himself presentable for his lady visitors. 'He is the most gaunt and gray and embittered individual I know,' Cather reported. 'He is an instructor in Latin in the University of London, but I believe the position pays next to nothing. The poor man's shoes and cuffs and the state of the carpet in his little hole of a study gave me a fit of dark depression.' Cather had been looking forward to spending the afternoon with the man who in her opinion was 'making about the only English verse that will last, the only verse of this decade I mean', but any attempts to discuss that verse were, as was customary, deftly brushed aside. It was fortunate for Housman that Miss Canfield had studied Classics, which allowed him to steer the conversation 'in safe and impersonal channels'. The fact that this opportunity had been wasted, the afternoon spent discussing 'other things than Mr Housman's verses', so upset Cather that she apparently burst into tears as soon as she left the house.

To her great annoyance, a fanciful version of her unlikely encounter with her favourite poet was concocted by Ford Madox Ford and published in his 1932 autobiography *Return to Yesterday*. According to Ford, Cather was president of the Pittsburgh Shropshire Lad Club and had led a delegation of ladies to visit Housman in Cambridge, where she presented him with a golden wreath. The publication of this fantasy led to Cather being 'besieged by demands to "tell what I know about Housman" [. . .] a heavy price to pay for a very brief acquaintance', and in April 1947 she decided to write a detailed article refuting Ford's fantasy and describing what had really happened. Just over a fortnight after she wrote to Dorothy Canfield asking for her recollections, however, she died suddenly and the article was never written.

Cather, though she became a writer of place in her novels, was not the most obvious of Housman fans. The principal relationships in her life were all with other women, but she was well aware of the appeal of *A Shropshire Lad* for a certain category of young men. 'Several rather mushy boys (young men they were, apparently) have sent rather horrid manuscripts on Houseman [sic] to me,' she complained to Canfield shortly before her death. 'Why do all these Willie boys sigh for him so, and claim him for their own? The word "lad" seems to hypnotize them.'* One young man who, if not mushy, was by his own admission certainly something of a muff, was E.M. Forster, whose own pilgrimage to Housman Country was made five years after Cather's. By the time the twenty-eight-year-old Forster set off for Shropshire, he had already made similar explorations of other parts of rural England, most notably in September 1904 when he had gone walking in Wiltshire. It was here that he came across Figsbury Rings, the Iron Age hill fort, and talked to a lame shepherd lad, a landscape and an encounter that would inspire his personal favourite amongst his novels, *The Longest Journey* (1907). For Forster the ancient Wiltshire landscape was 'charged with emotion', and the same might be said of his experience of Shropshire. It is significant that he embarked on his tour of the county immediately after taking a walking holiday with a small group of friends that included H.O. Meredith, the former lover who had introduced him to *A Shropshire Lad*. In addition, he had recently become smitten by a seventeen-year-old Indian called Syed Ross Masood, who had been sent to him to be coached in Latin while waiting to go up to Oxford.

---

*Somewhat confusingly, since 'Willie' was her own pet name for herself, Cather used this term to denote effeminate or homosexual youths, of whom she disapproved.

Masood was an immensely glamorous, boisterous and self-dramatising young man, very free with oriental endearments but entirely hetero-sexual. (He is clearly the 'Indian friend' mentioned by Forster in his 'Notes on the English Character'.)

Forster was still very much under Masood's spell when he made his tour of Shropshire. Like Cather, he began his pilgrimage in Shrewsbury, which he found 'Unspoilt and alive: a city with vigour still adjusted to its beautiful frame. Poetry – or luck – in every inch of it. Gloriously piled on a curve of the Severn, wh. two fine bridges traverse – the English and the Welsh, and against which laps the Quarry, with a magnificent avenue of limes.' These were the two bridges referred to in the first stanza of 'The Welsh Marches' (XXVIII), which Cather had quoted.

Forster was writing up his journey during his stay at the sixteenth-century timber-framed Angel Hotel in Ludlow, 'sitting in the great bow window which commanded the sloping street'. The weather had been far from perfect:

Wet walk from Wellington over Wrekin, which was foul with orange peel & bottles. No view: but plumes of trains pushing through the mist [. . .] Ate sandwiches walking. Buildwas Abbey is transitional: nave & crossing arches perfect. In a field of intense green by the Severn. Much Wenlock I hadn't time to see, since I lingered over cider at the 'Rock House' [. . .] Train after a tunnel got out on Wenlock Edge. 'Hughley Steeple' below, & to right the Wrekin as an inflation. So did I see it yesterday from Uricon. Ludlow seems something special: a tower at crossing of the Chester colour and many old houses. Feel very happy.

His diary entry ends: 'Want to write to A.E. Housman.' – and the resulting letter was the one the poet failed to answer.

Like Cather, Forster enjoyed identifying places mentioned in *A Shropshire Lad* (he had also walked to Clun), and he too was inspired to write a poem – 'Ludlow', dated April 1907 – in which Housman's influence is clear. Indeed, the few poems Forster wrote in his twenties all show the influence of Housman in their rhythms, rhyme schemes, vocabulary and subject matter. 'Ludlow' naturally includes echoes of Housman, having been written during the Shropshire tour, but two years later Forster wrote 'Incurious at a window', which reads like a more boldly homoerotic recension of 'The street sounds to the soldier's tread' (XXII). Housman Country would also be incorporated in Forster's novels, notably *Howards End*, published three years after his visit. Part of the novel is set in Oniton, a border town in what Mr Wilcox calls 'the wrong part of Shropshire', where he owns a house he has bought for no apparent reason and does not much like. In the 1960s Forster's friend William Plomer asked about the origins of Oniton, which (like the real Onibury) takes its name from the River Onny. 'How lovely to be asked whether Oniton is any where,' Forster replied.

> No one but you has asked, and those chapters in the book have always given me a particular feeling.
> It is *Clun*. I can't be sure of the date from my diary, but my map shows that I walked there, over Clun Forest, from Newto[w]n (Montgomery), and walked the next day to Ludlow. I was alone, except for the dubious company of A.E. Houseman [sic]. There are breaths from him in those chapters, the best I think being at the end of ch. 29.

The walk from Clun would have taken him through Onibury, and the final paragraph of Chapter 9 of *Howards End* is indeed replete with borrowings from *A Shropshire Lad*:

> Day and night the river flows down into England, day after day the sun retreats into the Welsh mountains, and the tower chimes, 'See the Conquering Hero'. But the Wilcoxes have no part in the place, nor in any place. It is not their names that recur in the parish register. It is not their ghosts that sigh among the alders at evening. They have swept into the valley and swept out of it, leaving a little dust and a little money.

Margaret Schlegel, who loves Oniton and the Wilcoxes' house there, eventually settles at Howards End, the house that Mrs Wilcox intended to leave to her. Howards End is in Hertfordshire, at the edge of London's northward suburban sprawl, rather than in the rural fastness of Shropshire, but it is removed enough from the urbanised village of Hilton still to embody the English countryside. Sitting within 'the peculiar sadness of a rural interior', Margaret is prompted to some thoughts about the countryside clearly influenced by Forster's reading of *A Shropshire Lad*:

> . . . the graver sides of life, the deaths, the partings, the yearnings for love, have their deepest expression in the heart of the fields. All was not sadness. The sun was shining without. The thrush sang his two syllables on the budding guelder-rose. Some children were playing uproariously in heaps of golden straw. It was the presence of sadness at all that surprised Margaret, and ended by giving her a feeling of completeness. In these English farms, if anywhere, one might see life steadily and see it whole, group in one vision its transi-toriness and its eternal youth, connect – connect without bitterness until all men are brothers.

Forster also claimed that he made his 'favourite characters' quote Housman's poetry. Both the Emersons do so in *A Room with a View*, which he was writing at the time he toured Shropshire and which would be published the following year, dedicated to Meredith. George Emerson is just the sort of troubled young man whom Housman hoped would appreciate his poems. His doting father, who is clearly Forster's favourite character in the novel, is puzzled by George's unhappiness, which seems to have no discernible cause. 'How can he be unhappy when he is strong and alive?' Mr Emerson asks during their holiday in Florence. 'What more is one to give him? And think how he has been brought up – free from all the superstition and ignorance that lead men to hate one another in the name of God. With such an education as that, I thought he was bound to grow up happy.' The absence of any be-lief in God, as Housman knew, did not necessarily make a man any happier: 'I only know what is wrong with him,' Mr Emerson tells Lucy Honeychurch, 'not why it is.' When Lucy, 'expecting some harrowing tale', asks about the nature of George's difficulty, Mr Emerson replies:

'The old trouble; things won't fit [. . .] The things of the universe. It is quite true. They don't,' and then goes on 'in an ordinary voice, so that [Lucy] scarcely realized he was quoting poetry', to recite the first stanza of 'From far, from eve and morning' (XXXII). 'We know that we come from the winds and that we shall return to them,' continues Mr Emerson. 'But why should this make us unhappy?' Forster does not identify the poem or its author, but he evidently expected his readers to know it and to be aware of its plea (not quoted) to 'Take my hand quick and tell me, / What have you in your heart', a snatched moment of intimacy in the face of life's transience. In essence, this is what Mr Emerson wants Lucy to do for his son.

For George himself, life is ruled by fate, as in Housman's poems: 'Everything is fate. We are flung together by Fate, drawn apart by Fate – flung together, drawn apart. The twelve winds blow us – we settle nothing –'. The winds of Housman's poem that blew the Emersons into Lucy's company in Italy later blow them to Summer Street, the village in Surrey where she lives at a house called Windy Corner. They also blow in Mr Beebe, the clergyman whom Lucy originally met in Tunbridge Wells then re-encountered in Florence, and who now takes charge of the parish. A hint that Mr Beebe is not quite the sympathetic character he at first seems occurs when he drops in on the Emersons in their new house to find books lying around waiting to be shelved. '"A Shropshire Lad". Never heard of it,' he declares complacently. Neither has he heard of the famously iconoclastic *The Way of All Flesh*, whose author, Samuel Butler, provided Forster with a partial model for Mr Emerson. Both Butler and Housman feature in a list of names Forster noted in his diary on the last day of 1907, the year he made his Shropshire pilgrimage and completed *A Room with a View*. What these unannotated names have in common is that they were those of artists and writers Forster knew, or suspected, to be homosexual, all of whom are acknowledged or unacknowledged presences in a novel which, although it has a heterosexual romance at its core, contains a distinct subtext aimed at the kind of readers who recognised something of their own troubles in *A Shropshire Lad*.

A Georgian England

The English countryside would become central to a new poetic movement promoted by Edward Marsh in his five anthologies of *Georgian
Poetry*, which appeared between 1912 and 1922. The Georgian Poets
were not a group as such, and had no poetic manifesto, but they
wrote a new kind of poetry, casting off the fustian and decadence of
late-Victorian verse in order to write about the contemporary world
in language that was robust and straightforward. Marsh had solicited a
contribution from Housman for the first volume, but had been politely
turned down, partly because Housman felt that he would have been
as out of place in a Georgian anthology as in an 1890s one. 'I do not
really belong to the "new era",' he wrote, 'and none even of my few
unpublished poems have been written in the last two years.' Many of
the Georgian Poets celebrated the English countryside, a theme echoed
by D.H. Lawrence, himself a contributor, when he declared: 'we are
awake again, our lungs are full of new air, our eyes of morning'. The
first volume of *Georgian Poetry* (which was published in the last weeks
of December 1912, going through thirteen editions and selling some
15,000 copies in its first year) was prefaced by a quotation from Lord
Dunsany in which he stated that among the attributes of being a poet
was 'to know nature as botanists know a flower', and it included
Lawrence's 'Snap-dragon' and Wilfrid Wilson Gibson's 'Geraniums'
amongst its botanical specimens. Gibson also spends summer days
and nights out in the fields in 'The Hare', while W.H. Davies imagines
passing 'the livelong day / With Nature' among grazing sheep in a
'flowery, green, bird-singing land', Edmund Beale Sargant gets lost
in 'The Cuckoo Wood', and Walter de la Mare's Traveller discovers a
mysteriously empty house in a forest in 'The Listeners'.

De la Mare's haunting poem (unlike most of those selected by
Marsh) would become a hugely popular anthology piece, but it was
Rupert Brooke's 'The Old Vicarage, Grantchester' that George Orwell
would later identify as 'the star poem of 1913', the year in which most
people bought and read *Georgian Poetry 1911–12*. It is also the poem that
shows most clearly the influence of Housman, whom Brooke had six
years earlier declared 'the only proper poet in England'. Brooke had

admired Housman ever since his schooldays at Rugby, where at the end of his final term in 1905, in a paper on modern poetry delivered to the Eranos literary society, he introduced his audience to *A Shropshire Lad*. When he went up to King's College, Cambridge, the following year he forged a close friendship with the future politician Hugh Dalton, largely based on their mutual admiration for Swinburne and *A Shropshire Lad*, which they often read aloud to each other. Housman himself was then still teaching at University College, London, and by the time he came to Cambridge, Brooke had left, although he was working on the dissertation that would see him elected a Fellow of King's in 1913. In 1911 Brooke had entered a competition run by the *Westminster Gazette* for 'the best new and original letters to a live poet'. He had been in Munich when he read in a newspaper of Housman's election as Kennedy Professor of Latin at Cambridge, and he sent two poems, both in verse. The first, 'A Letter to a Live Poet', won the competition, and though sometimes claimed to be about Housman seems to have nothing to do with him; it was instead, according to Brooke's biographer Christopher Hassall, written 'with Lascelles Abercrombie in mind'. His second submission was titled 'A Letter to a Shropshire Lad (Apropos, more or less, of a recent appointment)'. Housman was in Paris when this impertinent piece of work was published in the newspaper, and it is not known if he ever saw it. The poem shows Brooke's thoroughgoing knowledge of Housman's work, parodying or lifting and adapting lines from a large number of the poems, which was something Brooke occasionally did in his personal correspondence. It even opened with a version of the traditional lines with which Housman had prefaced 'In valleys of springs of rivers':

> Emmanuel, and Magdalene,
>   And St Catharine's, and St John's,
> Are the dreariest places,
>   And full of dons.

The poem then sets out to lament that a poet should end up an academic, a fate, he suggests, almost as bad as that of the Woolwich cadet:

Latin? so slow, so dull an end, lad?
   Oh, that was noble, that was strong!
For you'd a better wit to friend, lad,
   Than many a man who's sung his song.

And so on, for another ten stanzas, few of which would have passed Housman's stern editorial eye.

A rather better salute to Housman is 'The Chilterns', a poem Brooke wrote in the same year as 'The Old Vicarage, Grantchester'. Its stanza form was perhaps chosen in honour of the one used by Housman for his own doomed hilltop romance. Brooke's poem is far cruder than Housman's 'Bredon Hill', both in its language and its sentiment, its cynicism of a far coarser order; but it occasionally seems to aspire towards the Housmanesque, as in these lines:

But the years, that take the best away,
   Give something in the end;
And better friend than love have they,
   For none to mar or mend,
   That have themselves to friend.

In other stanzas Brooke associates clover with death and refers to 'darkening shires', and these, along with the use of the word 'friend' as a verb, and indeed the whole atmosphere of the poem, show his debt to *A Shropshire Lad*. A critic writing of Brooke in 1919 seemed to align him with Housman, although the older poet is not mentioned by name: 'He was obsessed by the modern melancholy. Fired by that love of English life and English scenery which is the hall-mark of the public school and University man, bubbling over with delight in life and love and sweet companionship, he could nevertheless rarely escape, even for an hour, from the depressing conviction of the transient quality of all beauty and all human enjoyment, even indeed of love itself.'

In his Rugby lecture, Brooke had caught the sharp tang of *A Shropshire Lad* well by recommending it should be read 'on an autumn morning when there is a brave nip of frost in the air and the year is sliding quietly toward death'. A slightly sharper Housman-like tang might have prevented 'The Old Vicarage, Grantchester' becoming a soft target for Brooke's detractors. It earns its place in Housman Country, however, as both a poem of exile (written, as its subtitle states, in the Café des Westens in Berlin, and opening with Brooke imagining the lilac blooming outside his room back in England) and as a poem of place. Brooke's England, though located some 135 miles due east of Ludlow, is very much like Housman's Shropshire. It is a place 'Where men with Splendid Hearts may go', men who are close cousins of those Lads of the Fifty-third, raised under 'skies that knit their heartstrings right', the lads in their hundreds who are 'handsome of heart', those 'hearts of gold' left behind in Shropshire after the poet has moved to London, the 'kind . . . single-hearted' lads now lying in the churchyard at Hughley. Like 'The country for easy livers, / The quietest under the sun' found around Ony and Teme and Clun, there is 'peace and holy quiet' at Grantchester as well as 'a slumberous stream' that appears to be a tributary of the one that lulls the lad lying 'On the idle hill of summer' in Shropshire. In short, Housman's western brookland is spiritually not very far from this eastern Brookeland, a clearly identifiable land of lost content about which the exile asks:

> Say, is there Beauty yet to find?
> And Certainty? And Quiet kind?
> Deep meadows yet, for to forget
> The lies, the truths, and pain?

The roll-call of towns and villages surrounding Cambridge is even more thorough than Housman's Shropshire gazetteer, and the poem was dismissed by the dyspeptic Orwell as 'nothing but an enormous gush of "country" sentiment, a sort of accumulated vomit from a stomach stuffed with place-names'. Orwell does, however, concede that, while the poem is 'something worse than worthless' as a piece of literature, 'as an illustration of what the thinking middle-class young of that period *felt* it is a valuable document'.

In the same essay, published in 1940, Orwell made much the same point about *A Shropshire Lad*, for which he retained a grudging admiration but now found of more sociological than literary interest. Brooke, on the other hand, never lost his enthusiasm for Housman's work, and even seems to come well out of his encounters with the man. In February 1913 he went to Cambridge to stay with Edward Marsh's father, who was Master of Downing College. Brooke was undergoing the latest in a series of emotional crises and, having attended a dinner in honour of Charles Lamb, had sat up most of the night writing to his erstwhile lover Ka Cox, who was in Germany. He was not therefore at his best when Housman came to dinner the following evening and afterwards watched him and the Master play billiards. Brooke was 'exhausted with nagging trouble and lack of sleep, and at dinner could hardly focus his attention on Housman, the one man whom he had longed for so many years to meet', writes Hassall. 'Numb, stupid with heartache, he listened to Housman's gentle encouragement of his verses, and for a moment, if for a moment only, he may have forgotten that he was helpless to give Ka the love she needed.' One of the reasons for this helplessness was a young art student called Phyllis Gardner, who had more or less fallen in love with Brooke at first sight when they happened to be on the same train from London to Cambridge in November 1911. In September 1912 Brooke had paid his first visit to her family home at Tadworth in Surrey, where in her attic studio Gardner attempted to draw the young poet. Sitting on a cushion, Brooke 'took out of his pocket a little book he had brought up with him from downstairs – A.E. Housman's poems – and read a few things to me', Gardner recalled. Distracted either by Housman or by her burgeoning feelings for her subject, Gardner seemed unable to get the drawings right,

> and at last I got rather cross over it, and then had an interval during which I did not try to draw, but listened to him reading poems. He read 'The quietest places under the sun', till the tears stood in my eyes: his voice was such an exquisite instrument, and his feeling for the poetry so exact: I have never heard anyone read as he read. He read 'When I was one-and-twenty', and 'Are the horses ploughing' [sic], and a lot of other things. And then I tried again at the drawing, but with not much better success.

She had little more success in her relationship with Brooke, who was at the time entangled with several other women.

It was Brooke who had proposed the idea for the *Georgian Poetry* anthologies to Marsh, and he was as keen as anyone to get out into the open air. He did this in pony caravans with a group of friends satirically dubbed by Virginia Woolf 'the Neo-pagans'. Neo-paganism was an idealistic and in the end impracticable blend of politics, personal relationships and the simple life. Taking their ideas from the homosexual sandal-wearing sage of Sheffield, Edward Carpenter, the progressive tenets of Bedales, an independent co-educational boarding school founded in 1893, Cambridge Fabianism, and the university's 'secret society', the Apostles, the Neo-pagans were idealistic and muddled in about equal measure. Liberated young men and women threw off the outmoded patriarchal values of the nineteenth century along with most of their clothes (nude bathing featured prominently among their outdoor activities) in the mistaken belief that a cheerful and chaste comradeship between the sexes would be the result. The tensions that naturally arose when young people went off on high-minded camping holidays together, unchaperoned but sworn to continence, could have been predicted, and several Neo-pagans, including Brooke himself, suffered breakdowns of varying degrees of seriousness. Brooke's close friend Jacques Raverat, apparently driven to the brink of madness by sexual frustration, recuperated by going to France in the care of his father and a hypnotherapist, where he 'lay nude in the sun, read Housman, Henley and Meredith, and let [the therapist] operate on his subconscious'.

Brooke left England in May 1913, partly to escape from his increasingly tangled love affairs, and did not return until June the following year. 'The South Seas are a Paradise,' he wrote from Fiji. 'But I prefer England.' He announced that on his return he would embark on a walk he punningly dubbed 'a Poet's Round': 'One starts from Charing X, in a south-easterly direction, and calls on De La Mare at Anerley, on S.W. to find [W.H.] Davies at Sevenoaks, a day's march to Belloc at Kingsland, then up to Wibson [i.e. Wilfrid Gibson] on the borders of Gloucestershire, back by (Stratford), RUGBY [where his mother lived], and the Chilterns, where Masefield and Chesterton dwell. Wouldn't it give one a queer idea of England!'

In the event, he only visited Gibson, one of a group of poets who had congregated around the village of Dymock on the Gloucestershire–Herefordshire border, which would give them not a queer but a compelling 'idea of England'. Gibson, Lascelles Abercrombie, John Drinkwater, Edward Thomas and the American interloper Robert Frost became known as the Dymock Poets, and for them the local landscape, like Housman's Shropshire, grew into an emblem of rural Englishness, celebrated in the poems they published in their journal, *New Numbers*. 'Here in our quiet country village they lived,' wrote the Rev. J.E. Gethyn-Jones, former vicar of the parish, in *Dymock Down the Ages* (1951). 'They walked these lanes, these fields, these woods. They sought the first primrose on Hazards bank, the early daffodil in the coppice at Elmbridge by the Leadon stream, and, daintiest of all, the frail bluebell among the Ryton firs.' They were in fact doing just what Housman did when he noted down the first appearance of wild flowers in his pocket diaries, and what he recommended to others in *A Shropshire Lad*: seeking out daffodils and 'palms' (pussy-willow or catkins) in 'March' (X); primroses, daffodils and windflowers in 'The Lent Lily' (XXIX); and 'bluebells in the azured wood' in 'In my own shire, if I was sad' (XLI). Brooke described Abercrombie's cottage as 'the most beautiful you can imagine: black-beamed & rose-covered. And a porch where one drinks great mugs of cider, & looks at fields of poppies in the corn. A life that makes London a very foolish affair.'

Brooke wrote this in a letter on 6 July 1914. Within a month Britain would be at war with Germany, and the small scarlet field poppy, hitherto associated with the peaceful English countryside, would become a symbol of death and destruction on the battlefields of the Western Front.

IV

ENGLISH MUSIC

Nowhere in the English thesaurus is there verse more apt for music.

Ernest Newman, 1922

During the Second World War, the composer E.J. Moeran spent much of his time in Kington, a small market town in the north-west corner of Herefordshire close to the Welsh border. Like Housman, several of whose poems he had set between 1916 and 1932, Moeran was a keen walker, often to be seen striding out in a pin-striped suit worn over an open-collared shirt, a pipe clenched between his teeth. The son of a clergyman, he had been brought up on the Norfolk coast at Bacton, but his parents had moved to Kington in 1937. They lived at Gravel Hill, an Italianate villa on the edge of the town found for them by their elder son, Graham, a vicar in nearby Leominster. Moeran's mother immediately set about converting a small studio at the side of the house into a study in the hope of persuading Moeran, whose life had always been unsettled, to move in. Moeran was very much a composer of place who, again like Housman, found long walks an aid to composition. His music had been inspired not only by the Norfolk Fens, but also by Kerry in Ireland, where his family had its roots, and he had collected and arranged folk songs from both places as well as from Suffolk. Having settled into Gravel Hill, he praised Kington's 'wonderful air', pronouncing the town 'the healthiest place in Britain', and enjoyed walks on Hergest Ridge on the western fringe of the town or longer excursions over the border into Radnorshire.

Although Moeran is often thought of as an East Anglian or Irish composer, it was during his Kington period that he wrote some of his best-known works, notably the *Rhapsody for Piano and Orchestra* (1942–3) and the *Sinfonietta* (1944), which he described as 'a symphony of the Welsh Marches'. The middle movement of the *Sinfonietta* came to him while standing on Rhos Fawr, the bare summit of Radnor Forest, and should, he said, be 'played at a brisk walking pace'. He also began work on the *Cello Concerto* (1945) and the *Cello Sonata* (1947), both written for Peers Coetmore, who shared his love of walking and whom he married at Kington church in the summer of 1945. His friend Lionel Hill recalled a trip to Rhos Fawr: 'He took us out beyond Radnor by train, and thence by bus to a spot from which we climbed up and up, seemingly above the world, until the ground flattened out to give us superb views for miles around in all directions. I remember Jack pointing and saying, "Over there is Elgar country, and there, Housman country."'

Elgar Country and Housman Country are linked both geographically, by the River Severn, and spiritually, by a sense of place and a certain melancholy. Louis MacNeice's pronouncement that Housman was the person 'with whom any history of modern English poetry might very well start' echoes the widespread idea that the first performance of Elgar's *Enigma Variations* at St James's Hall in London on 19 June 1899 is where any history of modern English music might start. Although Elgar never set Housman, many other composers did, and as a result the poet became – very unwillingly – a key figure in what came to be known as the English Musical Renaissance. 'I am tempted to think that Housman did a tremendous service to English composers when he wrote those wayward, passionate, disturbing lyrics,' wrote the music critic Stephen Williams in 1938, reviewing a concert of English songs which included settings of poems from *A Shropshire Lad* by Arthur Somervell, Ralph Vaughan Williams, George Butterworth, John Ireland and Ivor Gurney. This was not, to say the least of it, Housman's intention in publishing the volume – 'I wish they would not call me a *singer*,' he complained of its first reviewers. 'One fellow actually said *minstrel*!' – and it is perhaps as well that he was safely dead when Williams's article appeared. Similar things had, however, been written during his lifetime. When *Last Poems* appeared in 1922, England's foremost music critic, Ernest Newman, somewhat tactlessly observed that while 'all but about half a dozen' of the sixty-three lyrics in *A Shropshire Lad* had 'cried out for music: of the forty-one in *Last Poems*, hardly more than half a dozen are first-rate material for the composer'. If Housman ever read this, it must have been with mixed feelings: outrage that Newman appeared to regard providing material for composers as the principal job of a poet, but quiet satisfaction that the new volume seemed less likely to succeed in this task.

Newman may have been right, for although *Last Poems* inspired many fine songs, composers continued to turn first to *A Shropshire Lad*. Housman's poems became among the most frequently set of all English verse during the twentieth century: a catalogue of *Musical Settings of Late Victorian and Modern British Literature* compiled in 1976 listed nearly 400 published settings: only Walter de la Mare had more. Contemporary classical composers continue to set Housman's poems, but the most active period was between 1904 and 1940, for which the catalogue listed 176 individual vocal settings by forty-seven composers. Further research carried out by Kevin Robert Whittingham for a 2008 thesis on 'A Shropshire Lad in British Music Since 1940' showed that there were in fact 236 settings by fifty-eight composers during this period, though some 24 percent of them had remained unpublished. The best known, the ones that have stayed in the concert repertoire and have been frequently recorded, date from the two decades immediately before and after the First World War.

While Housman regularly gave composers permission to set his words – and by charging no fee inadvertently encouraged them – he carefully avoided listening to the results. His apparent lack of interest in classical music is well documented. 'He cared little for paintings, nothing for music,' Percy Withers observed at the outset of a well-known anecdote:

Since he had so often and so unaccountably allowed his verses to be set to music, and had never as I knew experienced the results, it occurred to me that he might like to hear gramophone records of

Vaughan Williams' settings sung by Gervase Elwes. I was oblivious of the effect until two of them had been played, and then turning in my chair I beheld a face wrought and flushed with torment, a figure tense and bolt upright as though in an extremity of controlling pain or anger, or both. To invite comment or question was too like bearding the lion in its den, so I ignored the subject and asked mildly if there was anything else he would like. A pause. There was a visible struggle for self-possession, a slow relaxation of posture, and then a naïve admission that people talked a good deal about Beethoven's Fifth Symphony: had we got a record? I turned it on, and watched. The Sphinx-like countenance suggested anything and everything but pleasure, though there was an expression of contentment during the slow movement, and faintest praise of it, and it alone, at the close.

An explanation of this indifference or hostility to music was provided by Housman's young friend Joan Thomson. 'Good critical taste was so essential to Housman that it was difficult to persuade him to say whether he liked a piece of music he had just heard if he had not known it before,' she recalled. 'He would declare that he did not know enough of music to be sure of his judgement, and he could not bear the idea of admiring anything unworthy.' This allowed Housman to avoid passing comment on any settings sent to him: 'I am sorry that my knowledge of music does not permit me to express or form a competent judgement of it,' he told one composer.

In fact, Housman knew a great deal more about classical music than he pretended. When William White, in a detailed article on 'A.E. Housman and Music' in *Music and Letters* in 1943, asserted that 'Housman had little interest in music, rarely (if ever) attended concerts, even disliked listening to music', Kate Symons responded:

Considering the evidence that exists of A.E.H.'s marked indifference to music in after life, it is no wonder that Professor White wished to know whether it had been inherent from his earliest years. It had not. Writing as a sister, one of the few living persons who can know anything about my brother's boyhood, I should like to tell Professor White, and anyone else interested in the question, that in boyhood music attracted my brother in so marked a degree that it came as a surprise on survivors of his family to read, after his death, reminiscences from later-day friends which appeared to show in A.E.H. ignorance of music, or even antipathy. To us the incidents of these reminiscences suggest either a pose, concealing a hidden attachment, or that the early attachment had really died away. Either is possible through the suppressions that my brother practised – to his lasting loss.

(Whether or not it was conscious or merely coincidental, it is worth noting parenthetically that the language used here – 'hidden attachment', 'suppressions' – would seem to relate Housman's feelings about music to his feelings about Moses Jackson.) Kate went on to recall that the Housmans were a musical family: their stepmother played the piano and both she and their father belonged to the Bromsgrove Philharmonic Society, 'bringing oratorio and other music better than our glees into our drawing-room practisings'. Housman had studied the piano in his youth, buying sheet music and attempting to master 'pieces that pleased him most', but he gave up when he recognised he had no particular aptitude for it. He nevertheless attended concerts and 'enjoyed Beethoven, Mozart and Mendelssohn at home'. He also 'had a pleasant singing-voice – baritone – and it took his fancy to learn to accompany and sing, solo, an absurd comic song of the Bab Ballad type. He was in request to sing this song at little parties in other houses than ours, and I have heard that he sang it sometimes in London in the days of his sad pilgrimage. This was looked on as a great joke, for it was incongruous with his usual reserved bearing.'

A taste for the 'Bab Ballads' of W.S. Gilbert would fit with Housman's love of nonsense rhymes, and in later life his musical tastes were largely limited to the songs of the music halls. His pretence to know nothing of music is, however, exploded by the recent discovery of a letter to Arthur Somervell, who in 1904 was one of the very first composers to set poems from *A Shropshire Lad*. Since most applications to set his words to music came through his publisher, Housman was inclined to let Grant Richards reply on his behalf, only rarely entering into direct correspondence with composers. This was perhaps as well. Like some of the composers who came after him, Somervell not only set Housman's words but occasionally adapted them, and while it seems unlikely that he sought permission to do so, he evidently had the temerity to write to Housman complaining about the use of the word 'rotten' to describe dead soldiers in 'On the idle hill of summer' (XXXV), which he set as the sixth song in his *A Shropshire Lad* cycle. Housman was not pleased.

My dear Sir,

I returned from abroad a few days ago and found your letter here.

As to what I have written, I resemble Pontius Pilate and Mr Chamberlain; and my opinion of the propriety of the word has not been altered by the death of one of my brothers in the war. I am however disposed to agree with you as to the difficulty of sitting down to the piano and warbling out 'rotten'. But I am not willing that poetry should make any concessions to music, at any rate to modern European music, which I regard (I am afraid you will think this another hard saying) as unsuitable for union with words. Europeans, in order to enjoy the sensual luxury of harmony, employ the diatonic scale, whose intervals have no resemblance to the modulations of human speech, which is the interpreter of human emotion; and consequently European music can only express emotion in the vaguest manner, and when wedded to words, which express emotion with precision, it becomes, strictly speaking, nonsensical. I am just returned from Constantinople where I have been listening to a good deal of Asiatic music: I think it ugly, but it is not unsuitable for union with words, because it is very chromatic and its range is hardly more than half an octave.

In expressing these opinions to you I must naturally do so with the diffidence which you are good enough to say you feel in taking exception to my verse.

I am yours very truly

A.E. Housman

The style is characteristic, notably in the deadly use of the word 'warbling' and the apparently polite but in fact heavily ironic last paragraph. What is more remarkable, however, is that Housman, who claimed to have no knowledge of music, is nevertheless capable of writing about the technical differences between European and Eastern music, and between the diatonic and chromatic scales.

If Housman thought European music unsuitable for the setting of words, and greatly disliked the results, it seems odd that he gave so many composers permission to use his poetry. By the time he died in 1936, some seventy-five individual songs and twenty-nine song cycles had been composed setting poems from *A Shropshire Lad* – as well as other songs and cycles setting verses from *Last Poems*. Most of the individual songs were for the usual 'art song' combination of voice and piano, though there were also settings for voice, piano and string quartet and men's, women's and mixed choruses. In addition, Housman's correspondence contains a substantial number of letters giving permission for settings that either never materialised or have since disappeared. Housman occasionally provided explanations why he allowed the wholesale ransacking of his poetry by composers, but he was not consistent and was often flippant. In 1906, for example, giving H. Balfour Gardiner permission to publish his setting of 'The Recruit', he told Richards: 'I always give my consent to all composers, in the hope of becoming immortal somehow.' Richards felt that it was rather the other way round and referred to composers who 'helped themselves to fame and popularity' by plundering *A Shropshire Lad*.

Richards did, however, concede that this large number of settings by English composers contributed to the increased sales of the volume. Indeed, while Housman's remark may have been intended ironically, it is fair to say that some degree of the immortality he achieved was indeed due to the musical settings of his poems, which brought them to a whole new audience beyond that of the poetry-reading public. Housman gave Percy Withers a different reason for invariably granting composers permission to set his words: the results 'mattered nothing; words sung ceased to be poetry, and were not estimated as poetry'. A few weeks before his death, giving permission for an unlikely and apparently unfulfilled plan to set 'Hell Gate', Housman cheerfully supposed that 'the orchestra will *drown* out the words'. He similarly imagined that broadcasting song recitals based on his poems would achieve poor results: 'I don't allow the wireless people to recite my poems,' he reminded Richards in 1927, when radio technology was still comparatively crude, 'but as I allow the poems to be sung to music there is no reason why the songs should not be broadcast. I daresay the music is spoilt; but that is the composer's look out; and the words are mostly inaudible.' If audiences could not make out the words, Housman was not going to help them, and he would not allow composers to print his verses in concert programmes.

Land Without Music

Reluctant as Housman was to be taken up so readily by English composers, he had inadvertently provided them with something they had long been seeking. As Newman put it: 'Never before had an English poet produced so many poems that had all the qualities requisite to poetry that is to be set to music – concision and intensity of tone, the utmost simplicity of language, freedom both from involution of structure and from simile, and a general build that was virtually that of musical form.' There was, however, a more important reason that Housman proved so popular with composers. The publication of *A Shropshire Lad* coincided with a widespread movement to re-energise English music and forge a new national style.

Throughout the nineteenth century English music had been dominated by foreign composers and foreign performers. The classical concert repertoire was largely made up of the works of the established composers of Germany, Austria, France and Italy, while a survey of London's principal orchestras carried out in 1866 discovered that of 419 instrumentalists only 253 were British, and that many of these had been obliged to go abroad for their musical training. The Royal Academy of Music had been founded in 1822, but only a tiny proportion of professional musicians had trained there: no more than 17 percent of those surveyed. Even many of the instruments English musicians played and the sheet music from which they read were manufactured or published abroad, mostly in Germany. Britain's favourite 'English' composers were in fact both German: Handel did not settle in London until the age of twenty-eight, after being educated in his native land and working for six years in Italy, while a century later Mendelssohn, although similarly adopted by the English, remained a German subject, based and principally employed in the country of his birth. Both composers excelled at the oratorio, a form that dominated Victorian English music-making, largely thanks to a proliferation of choral societies in the nineteenth century, and Mendelssohn's hugely popular *Elijah* (1846) had provided a useful model for English-language choral works.

English opera barely existed during the Victorian period, partly because the grand romantic emotions characteristic of such stage works were simply considered un-English. As one historian put it: 'It has more than once been suggested that the reason why opera never developed here as it did in Italy is to be found in our individual attitude to music in general. For the Italian, it is thought, music is a direct expression of emotion; hence with him drama naturally issues in song. For the Englishman music is something loftier than this, so that he is not so easily inclined to subordinate it to the theatre.'

It would certainly be difficult to envisage an English *La Traviata*, *Carmen* or *La Bohème* at this period. Similarly, art songs such as the German *Lied* or French *chanson* had no real English equivalent at this time: instead English composers churned out drawing-room ballads, which were hugely popular but largely sentimental in both their music and lyrics. It was only in churches that an English musical tradition remained unbroken from the days of Byrd and Tallis, though it was considerably diluted during the nineteenth century. Much of the music performed at England's foremost triennial music festivals – the Three Choirs (founded in 1724, which took place by rotation at Gloucester, Worcester and Hereford), Birmingham (1768), Norfolk & Norwich (1824), Leeds (1858) and the London Handel Festival (1859) – was religious. 'Loftier' than Italian song this may have been, but as one historian observed in 1947, 'The choral festivals have been responsible for quantities of rubbish by [English] composers now mercifully forgotten.'

In spite of the appearance of new choral pieces, the works of Handel, Haydn and Mendelssohn remained a mainstay of these festivals until the 1880s. It was in that decade that the works of J.S. Bach were rediscovered and widely performed, but more importantly it saw renewed interest in Henry Purcell. Although Purcell had died in 1695, aged just thirty-six, he was seen by many people as the last genuinely great English composer until the arrival on the musical scene of Elgar 240 years later. The founding in 1876 of a Purcell Society belatedly acknowledged his importance, and resulted in his works entering the repertoire once more. A particular significance of Purcell was that he set English words, and in *Dido and Aeneas* (1688) composed the last truly English opera of any lasting significance until Benjamin Britten's *Peter Grimes* in 1945.

Housman was not alone in professing to have little time for classical music. England's musical reputation abroad during the nineteenth and early twentieth centuries was summed up in the title of Oscar Schmitz's notorious 1904 book *Das Land ohne Musik*. England, Schmitz declared, was 'the only cultured nation without its own music (except street music)' – this being the kind of music Housman himself claimed most to enjoy. By the time Schmitz published his opinion, things had in fact changed considerably, but this dim view of English musical culture had been expressed much earlier – in 1871, and by an Englishman. The Rev. H.R. Haweis was an extraordinary figure. The son of a clergyman, he was born with a club foot, and a disease of the hip during childhood restricted his growth to under five feet tall. He nevertheless became a skilled fiddle player and went up to Trinity College, Cambridge, where he founded a quartet society, began contributing to newspapers and periodicals, and studied the manufacture of violins. After graduating, he travelled to the Continent for his health and ended up fighting alongside Garibaldi. Having celebrated the unification of Italy, he returned to England and entered holy orders, becoming a priest in London's East End, where both oratorios and orchestral music were performed at the cultural evenings he organised for his working-class parishioners. He soon gained a reputation as a popular preacher, even when he embraced spiritualism, a creed he did not find incompatible with the tenets of the Church of England. Thomas Hardy left an unkind account of Haweis having difficulty climbing into a pulpit to deliver a sermon on Cain and Abel (in which he made excuses for the former): 'His black hair, black beard, hollow cheeks and black gown made him look like one of the skeletons in the Church of the Capuchins, Rome.' Haweis declined to believe in the doctrine of eternal damnation, and, although married, took one of his parishioners as a mistress and had an illegitimate child with her. He was a well-known lecturer who undertook extensive tours both in Britain and abroad, a leading Wagnerite, an editor of *Cassell's Family Magazine*, contributed an article on bell-ringing to the *Encyclopaedia Britannica*, and wrote several books on musical and religious topics.

The most popular of his publications – going through sixteen editions in its first thirty years – was *Music and Morals* (1871). In this book he complained that England was not only lacking in proper religious feeling, but also in the appreciation of all the arts, most notably music. Much as Schmitz would conclude over thirty years later, Haweis decided that 'the English are not a Musical People [. . .] England is not a musical country'. English composers, he suggested, were far too influenced by European music. They did not write for English audiences, and English audiences far preferred drawing-room ballads and music-hall songs to serious music. This deplorable state of affairs would not change 'until music is felt here [in England], as it is felt in Germany, to be a kind of necessity – to be a thing without which the heart pines and the emotions wither – a need, as of light, and air, and fire'. His solution was to forge a national music:

> We must not be content with foreign models, but we must aim at forming a real national school, with a tone and temper as expressive of, and as appropriate to England, as French music is to France, Italian to Italy, and German to Germany [. . .] When we have a national school of music, and not before, we shall have high popular standards, and the music of the people will be as real an instrument of civilization in its way, and as happily under the control of public opinion, as the Press, the Parliament, or any other of our great national institutions.

Haweis's book was published at a time when many people were echoing his complaints and attempting to do something about it. The Education Act of 1870 had made provision for the teaching of music in elementary schools, while the National Training School for Music (NTSM) was founded by public subscription and with royal patronage in 1876, with

Arthur Sullivan – 'the only English composer we have', as *The Orchestra* magazine bluntly put it – as its first principal. The school was to be part of the cultural complex built on land in South Kensington bought with the proceeds of the Great Exhibition of 1851. The aim of the NTSM, according to its charter, was 'To establish for the United Kingdom such a School of Music as already exists in many of the principal Continental countries, – a School which shall take rank with the Conservatories of Milan, Paris, Vienna, Leipsic, Brussels, and Berlin, – a School which shall do for the musical youth of Great Britain what those Schools are doing for the talented youth of Italy, Austria, France, Germany, and Belgium.' This the Royal Academy of Music had signally failed to do: while it had some success training people to teach, the music critic who carried out the 1866 survey of London orchestras stated that he could 'not remember one great instrumental player the Academy has turned out during the last 25 years'.

The NTSM was established precisely to address the failings of the RAM, but itself foundered after only six years, partly because Sullivan was a reluctant and lacklustre principal. Like the RAM, the School failed to attract orchestral instrumentalists, or (as was the original intention) enough people applying for scholarships. It had also attracted less funding than had been planned for, and so few objections were raised when the scholarship scheme was abandoned and the places filled by those who could afford the fees. These students unfortunately tended to regard music as a drawing-room accomplishment rather than a profession, and the examining board concluded that the standards of teaching were similarly unambitious. When these criticisms were ascribed to his *laissez-faire* directorship, Sullivan argued that 'when a principal had exercised due care in the choice of his staff and in the organization of work of a Music School it was not for the best interests of the school that he should be constantly fretting the teachers by undue interference in the details of the instruction given to the pupils'. He nevertheless resigned in 1882, and was succeeded by John Stainer, the organist at St Paul's Cathedral who would go on to compose *The Crucifixion* and other popular oratorios. Under Stainer's direction the School staggered on for a few months until it was subsumed into the Royal College of Music.

The original plan had been to merge the NTSM and the RAM,

but the latter institution was opposed to this idea. Instead proposals for a Royal College of Music, led by the Prince of Wales and actively supported by other members of the royal family, were put forward at the end of 1881. The person behind this scheme was George Grove, editor of *Grove's Dictionary of Music and Musicians*, which appeared in four volumes between 1878 and 1889. International in scope, the dictionary nevertheless did much to promote English music, with Purcell allotted a longer article than Bach. Although Grove was not a professional musician, he was appointed the RCM's first director when it opened in 1883, remaining in the post for eleven years. His staff included Charles Villiers Stanford, Hubert Parry and Walter Parratt, and his aim, in which he largely succeeded, was to produce 'more and better music in England, more and better English music'.

The question remained: What kind of English music should English composers produce? The answer, it turned out, was pastoral music celebrating the English landscape. In many cases this landscape would be a real one, with pieces named after specific geographical locations; elsewhere the music would portray a more generic or idealised landscape of the sort Housman depicted in *A Shropshire Lad*. At a fundraising meeting for the RCM held in December 1881, the newly created Duke of Albany (otherwise Prince Leopold, the Queen's youngest son) had declared that England had been the first great musical nation of Europe. In support of this unfashionable notion, he drew the audience's attention to the well-known medieval song 'Sumer is icumen in', 'one of the choice musical treasures of the British Museum, [which] is now accepted by the most learned antiquaries of England and Germany [. . .] as the work of a monk of Reading in Berkshire in or about the year 1226'. 'This tiny glee,' he went on, 'which is the germ of modern music, the direct and absolute progenitor of the Oratorios of Handel, the Symphonies of Beethoven, the Operas of Wagner, is a purely English creation, dealing with English sights and sounds – the cuckoo, the blooming meadow, the budding copse, the buck, the doe, the cattle, the sheep and lambs, of the pastures of Berkshire'.

'Sumer is icumen in' is in fact a very sophisticated little song in the form of a six-part 'rota', a kind of English part-song, in which each voice comes in at precise, overlapping intervals. Musical scholars have come to different conclusions since 1881; although the exact date and authorship is unknown, the words of the song are in a robust Wessex dialect of the sort local people would have recognised. That the authorship could once have been confidently ascribed to a monk in Berkshire goes to show that the countryside it described was generically English rather than characteristic of a specific region. The two-note song of the cuckoo has always been regarded as the traditional herald of the English summer, while references to seeds growing, meadows blowing, and sheep and cows calling after their young are equally timeless and regionally unspecific. This was the English landscape that many of the leading figures in the English Musical Renaissance would turn to for inspiration – and many of them would be graduates of the Royal College of Music. Amongst those who studied composition at the RCM, Ralph Vaughan Williams, Ivor Gurney, Arthur Somervell, John Ireland, E.J. Moeran, Ernest Farrar and George Butterworth all set Housman's poems in the early years of the twentieth century.

The Tunes of Old England

Composers were not only inspired by the English landscape, but also by the kind of music that had for centuries been made by ordinary people in rural areas. English folk song may not have had quite so ancient a lineage as 'Sumer is icumen in', but it was nevertheless handed down generation by generation and had its roots in the English countryside. In the search for a new kind of English music many composers began exploring these old traditional songs, which had long been neglected by the musical establishment. Anticipating both Haweis and Schmitz, Carl Engel, a London-based German musicologist who specialised in music and nationality, noted in *An Introduction to the Study of National Music* (1866) that 'Although the rural population of England appear to sing less than those of most other European countries, it may nevertheless be supposed that they also, especially in districts somewhat remote from any large towns, must still preserve songs and dance tunes of their own inherited from their forefathers.'

What virtually no one had done was to make collections of these English songs and dances as had been done in both Wales and Scotland, though in the same year that Engel's book appeared John Hullah, Professor of Vocal Music at King's College, London, had published *The Song Book: Words and Tunes from the Best Poets and Musicians.* Hullah's selection was inclusively British rather than narrowly English. 'In the bringing together of the Songs of Great Britain and Ireland,' he wrote in his preface,

> an opportunity will be afforded both for confirming a just impression in respect to them, and also for removing a false one; – by showing, on the one hand, that, as a body, they will not suffer by comparison with those of any other nation – perhaps, even, with those of all other nations put together, – on the other, that the *English*, as well as the Scottish, the Welsh, and the Irish, *have national melodies* – a truth which, old and irrefragable as it may be to those who have looked into the matter, will be altogether new to, and require confirmation with, those who have not.

These were '*National* songs – songs which, through their truth to nature, their felicity of expression, and the operation of time, have sunk "deeper than did ever plummet sound" into the hearts of the people among whom they have sprung up and circulated'.

English songs occupy the first and largest of the book's five sections, with 114 songs compared with 80 from Scotland, 50 from Ireland and a mere 14 from Wales; but although Hullah's selection includes a few genuine folk songs such as 'The Miller of Dee' and 'The Lincolnshire Poacher', these sit beside 'Rule, Britannia', 'The Roast Beef of Old England', and songs from the plays of Shakespeare, *The Beggar's Opera*, and such now forgotten eighteenth-century operas as William Shield and William Pearce's *Hartford-Bridge, or, The Skirts of the Camp*. Hullah had drawn heavily on William Chappell's *Popular Music of the Olden Times* (1855–9), much of which was similarly taken from printed and authored sources. These songs may have become 'traditional', but they were evidently not what Engel meant by 'national songs'.

A few years later, in a series of articles written for the *Musical Times* and collected as *The Literature of National Music* (1879), Engel returned to his theme. There are surely, he wrote,

English musicians in London and in the large provincial towns who might achieve good results if they would spend their autumnal holidays in some rural district of the country, associate with the villagers, and listen to their songs. What change can be more desirable for a professional man, who in the greater parts of his engagements moves in the fashionable circles of society, and is compelled to inhale the impure air of the concert-room – what could be more beneficial to him than an occasional abode among the peasantry in a village, where the pure and invigorating air, and the beautiful scenery, invite to rambles in the fields and woods, and chase away those morbid feelings and crazy notions which very likely have taken possession of the drawing-room musician?

When Engel published his book there was in fact one very small collection of genuine English folk songs, the Rev. John Broadwood's *Old English Songs as now sung by the Peasantry of the Weald of Surrey and Sussex*, published privately in 1847. The importance of Broadwood, whose book contained only sixteen items and was not widely distributed, is that he noted down the songs he heard with great accuracy. His work was carried on by his niece Lucy Broadwood, who with H.F. Birch Reynardson published in 1889 an expanded edition of her uncle's book as *Sussex Songs*. That same year saw the publication of the Rev. Sabine Baring-Gould's collection of *Songs and Ballads of the West*, collected in Devon and Cornwall and subtitled 'A Collection Made from the Mouths of the People'. Unfortunately Baring-Gould occasionally found what came out of the mouths of the people indelicate if not actually indecent, and his important work in collecting folk songs was somewhat compromised by his insistence upon rewriting offending lyrics to make them suitable for a middle-class Victorian audience.

Other collections included Frank Kidson's *Traditional Tunes* (1891), collected in Yorkshire and southern Scotland, and Lucy Broadwood and J.A. Fuller-Maitland's *English County Songs* (1893), covering most areas of England. The seriousness with which folk music was being taken by the end of the century can be judged from the fact that when the English Folk-Song Society was established in June 1898, it included among its vice-presidents both Parry and Stanford, as well as Stainer and the principal of the RAM, Alexander Mackenzie. The 'primary object' of the EFSS was 'the collection and preservation of Folk-songs, Ballads, and Tunes, and the publication of such of these as may be advisable'. At its inaugural meeting the following February (attended, amongst others, by Elgar, who formally proposed the adoption of the committee's first report), Parry gave an address that echoed Engel in its notion that the collecting and study of folk music was a thoroughly salubrious occupation for the jaded denizens of metropolitan drawing rooms. Unlike Baring-Gould, Parry found 'nothing in folk-music common or unclean', nothing to resemble the sort of songs that diverted the populace – and indeed Housman – in the music halls of the period. Folk music was, however, under threat in the same way that the English countryside was. 'The modern popular song reminds me of the outer circumference of our terribly overgrown towns,' Parry told the assembled guests,

> where the jerry-builder holds sway, and where one sees all around the tawdriness of sham jewellery and shoddy clothes, the dregs of stale fish, and pawn shops, set off by the flaming gin-palaces at the corners of the streets. All these things suggest to one's mind the boundless regions of sham. It is for the people who live in these unhealthy regions, people who have the most false ideals, who are always scrambling for subsistence, who think that the commonest rowdyism is the highest expression of human emotion; for them popular music is made, and it is made, with a commercial object, of snippets of musical slang. This is what will drive out folk-music if we do not save it. The old folk-music is among the purest products of the human mind. It grew in the hearts of the people before they devoted themselves assiduously to the making of quick returns. In the old days they produced music because it pleased them to make it, and because what they made pleased them mightily, and that is the only way in which good music is ever made.

Folk music, Parry concluded, was 'characteristic of the race – of the quiet reticence of our country districts – of the contented and patient and courageous folk, always ready to meet what chance shall bring with a cheery heart'. In all but cheery hearts, this race bears comparison with the one that inhabited Housman's imaginary Shropshire in a book that additionally embraces the popular notion that quiet country places are more appealing than noisy, populous cities. It was in these cities that the English race was seen to be degenerating to a point that it was unfit to be sent out to police the Empire. Parry's speech asserted not only that folk song provided a pure and unpolluted cultural source for the regeneration of national music, but that this regeneration was as much a national enterprise as building and maintaining the Empire.

One person not apparently in attendance that evening was Cecil Sharp, who would nevertheless become the most important figure in the English folk-music movement. Born in 1859, Sharp had shown considerable musical ability at school, but had studied mathematics at Cambridge, after which he went to Australia to work first in banking and then as a lawyer, eventually becoming assistant to the Chief Justice of South Australia. In 1886 he contracted typhoid and returned to England to recuperate; he would suffer from ill health in various forms throughout his life and once gave instructions that any announcement of his death should read 'after a long illness most *im*patiently borne'. He had also continued to pursue his musical interests in Australia, becoming director of the Adelaide String Quartet Club in 1883, and his original intention upon returning to England was to remain there and find employment as a professional musician. When these hopes foundered, he resumed his life back in Australia, eventually giving up his job in the justice department to become co-director of the Adelaide College of Music. After quarrelling with the other director, he returned to England in 1892 to write and to teach music.

Sharp's interest in folk song was prompted by an encounter with a group of Morris men on a snowy Boxing Day in 1899. He was staying with his mother-in-law at Headington, near Oxford, and was looking out of a window onto the drive when 'a strange procession appeared: eight men in white decorated with ribbons, with pads of small latten bells strapped to their shins, carrying coloured handkerchiefs; accompanying them was a concertina-player and a man dressed as a "Fool"'. The men formed two lines and when the concertina player 'struck up an invigorating tune, the like of which Cecil Sharp had never heard before', they started their leaping dance. That tune was 'Laudnum Bunches', and was followed by three others: 'Cease your funning' (from *The Beggar's Opera*), 'Blue-eyed Stranger' and 'Rigs o' Marlow'. Sharp had been unwell but he entirely forgot his illness as he listened to and then questioned the men. The concertina player was a young man called William Kimber, from whom Sharp noted down five tunes the following day, and many others later on.

Sharp was at that time teaching music in a preparatory school. As in the wider musical world, German influence was marked in musical education, and Sharp decided that the music he had heard at Headington, which consisted of 'good, strong, simple melodies which were essentially English in character', should be taught in schools. In 1902 he compiled and published *A Book of British Songs for Home and School*, and while its contents were taken from printed sources, notably Chappell's *Popular Music of the Olden Times*, it included a number of folk songs. This was no mere antiquarianism; as with Parry, for Sharp folk music was bound up with notions of Englishness and national regeneration. 'Our system of education is, at present, too cosmopolitan,' he wrote in 1907; 'it is calculated to produce citizens of the world rather than Englishmen. And it is Englishmen, English citizens, that we want. How can this be remedied? By taking care, I would suggest, that every child born to English parents is, in its earliest days, placed in possession of all those things which are the distinctive products of its race.' These included the English language ('the mother tongue'); 'the folk tales, legends and proverbs, which are peculiar to the English; the national sports, pastimes, and dances, also'. And of course folk songs: 'English folk songs for English children, not German, French, or even Scottish or Irish'. These songs were

> simple ditties which have sprung like wild flowers from the very hearts of our countrymen, and which are as redolent of the English race as its language. If every English child be placed in possession of all these products, he will know and understand his country and his countrymen far better than he does at present; and knowing and understanding them he will love them the more, realize that he is united to them by the subtle bond of blood and kinship, and become, in the highest sense of the word, a true patriot.

The idea that the nation could be bound together and reinvigorated by old country songs and dances would persist into the First World War, where folk songs often featured in concerts for the troops. The theatre producer Lena Ashwell's book *Modern Troubadours* (1922) provided 'A Record of the Concerts at the Front' that she had organised. 'When Miss Carrie Tubb and Miss Phyllis Lett were in France in September 1916 with the Westminster Singers, they all agreed that the taste of the soldier audiences was extraordinarily good,' she reported. 'They loved the old folk-songs.' Troops were even taught folk dance, presumably following Sharp's suggestion that this kind of recreation led to 'the quickening of the national spirit'. According to Ashwell,

> At one point there was quite a big vogue in France for the country dances, folk dances, morris and sword dances. All this work was started by Miss [D.C.] Dakin[g], and there were a number of teachers in different Bases who undertook to teach these dances to the men. Some of them were wildly enthusiastic, and thoroughly enjoyed the dances; of course, some of the men were 'bored to tears'. There were weekly demonstrations in many of the huts, but the dancing was especially used in convalescent camps [. . .] I heard delightful stories of the band playing on the sands of Trouville, while the convalescents danced themselves back to health.

One soldier was even reported by Sharp's associate Maud Karpeles to have joined in and completed the dance 'with an amputated toe in a new boot'.

The demand was such that the English Folk Dance Society eventually sent out fifteen teachers to the front. During demonstrations 'Everyone crowded round; no one laughed; someone said "That's the stuff to give 'em".' As one historian put it: 'The spiritual essence of the England for which these men had fought and suffered was thus instilled in order to restore them to health. Thaumaturgy had its place alongside surgery in the shambles of the Somme – evocative enough for what folk-music had come to stand for, and of the power with which it was invested.' Karpeles conceded that 'not many of the men joined the [English Folk Dance] Society after they had been demobilized', but if folk dancing hadn't actually won the war, it was nevertheless celebrated along with the Allied victory. During the elaborate Peace Day celebrations in July 1919, the society organised an event in Hyde Park at which one thousand people performed folk dances, accompanied by the band of the Fourth Royal Fusiliers.

The folk music that had kept the troops on their toes had been collected and preserved by a group of enthusiasts, headed by Cecil Sharp. In the late summer of 1903 Sharp had gone to stay with the Rev. Charles Marson, whom he had met in Adelaide but who was now vicar of Hambridge in Somerset. He was accompanied by Mattie Kay, a young woman with a fine voice and perfect diction whom he had met in Lancashire and more or less adopted, encouraging her to undergo proper musical training. While taking tea in the vicarage garden, Sharp overheard someone singing to himself as he mowed the lawn. Upon making enquiries, Sharp discovered that the song was 'The Seeds of Love' and that the singing gardener was called – most appropriately – John England. Sharp took down the song, harmonised the tune, and that same evening he and Mattie Kay performed it at a choir supper. The song was a familiar one, but as a member of the audience put it, this was the first time that it 'had been put into evening dress'.

There would later be criticism that this kind of arrangement of folk song for performance in the concert hall took a rural working-class tradition and traduced it, sprucing it up for consumption by middle-class metropolitan audiences. There is no doubt that it is a very different experience listening to the recording Vaughan Williams made in around 1908 of an Essex countrywoman singing 'Bushes and Briars' unaccompanied and listening to the tenor Robert Tear singing the song in the composer's arrangement with a spare piano accompaniment. Had it not been for people like Sharp and Vaughan Williams, however, it is quite possible that such songs would have been lost for ever. Vaughan Williams had been aware of traditional tunes since childhood, when he first heard 'The Cherry-Tree Carol'. This song perhaps dates back as far as the fifteenth century and was included in *Christmas Carols, Old and New* (1871), edited by John Stainer and the hymnologist Henry Ramsden Bramley. The words, in their many variants, were also included in Child's *The English and Scottish Popular Ballads*, which became a major source of folk-song lyrics. In 1893, when he was twenty-one, Vaughan Williams discovered 'Dives and Lazarus', dating back to the mid-sixteenth century, which Lucy Broadwood and J.A.F. Maitland had included in their *English County Songs*. 'I had that sense of recognition,' he later recalled, '– "here's something which I have known all my life – only I didn't know it!"' In 1903 he was invited to a parish tea at Ingrave in Essex, where he had been told that some of the elderly villagers might be able to sing old songs for him. He was introduced to a labourer called Charles Pottipher, who agreed to perform for him in private. Like Sharp, who went on to note down further Somerset folk songs, publishing 130 of them in five parts between 1904 and 1919, Vaughan Williams would be inspired by Pottipher's rendition of 'Bushes and Briars' to begin collecting folk songs, eventually taking down more than 800 in Essex, Sussex and Norfolk.

Sharp himself also travelled farther afield and collected some 1500 tunes in four short years. Some of these were published in book form, but many others appeared in the *Journal of the Folk-Song Society*, which was founded in 1899. By the time he died in 1924, Sharp had collected around 3000 tunes from twenty-seven English counties, as well as another 1700 tunes of English origin in the Appalachians during extended trips to America during the First World War.

The old songs of unschooled country people seem at first sight an unlikely starting point for a wholesale national musical renaissance. It was felt, however, that because folk songs had been handed down orally, generation after generation, and in rural regions remote from the musical fashions that swept through the major cities and national academies, they had an unimpeachable authenticity. This was the music of the people, reaching far back into England's past, kept alive in English villages, and unsullied by the Continental tastes and influences that had been embraced by the metropolitan musical establishment. In addition, many of the tunes, even when sung in the unaccompanied quavering voices of the elderly, were both highly sophisticated and extremely beautiful. As Vaughan Williams put it, writing of Sharp's *Folk Songs from Somerset* (1904–19):

Such a wealth of beauty as this volume, containing, to mention only a few, 'High Germany', 'The False Bride', 'Searching for Lambs' and 'The Crystal Spring', was something we had never dreamed of. And where did it all come from? It was not a bit like Purcell or [Thomas] Arne or Sterndale Bennett.* Nor apparently could we trace it to watered-down reminiscences of Schubert or Mendelssohn. It must therefore be indigenous [. . .] Sharp believed, and we believe, that there, in the fastness of rural England, was the well-spring of English music; tunes of classical beauty which vied with all the most beautiful melody in the world, and traceable to no source other than the minds of unlettered country men, who unknown to the squire and the parson were singing their own songs, and, as Hubert Parry says, 'liked what they made and made what they liked'.

Vaughan Williams's reference to the unwitting squire and parson suggests a further appeal that folk music held for him and composers such as Gustav Holst: as committed socialists, they were delighted to embrace and promote a working-class musical tradition.

Composers made both simple and complex arrangements of folk songs, putting them into evening dress for solo singers or choral groups. Vaughan Williams himself began arranging folk songs at around the time the first settings of Housman's poems appeared. He arranged 'Bushes and Briars' in 1903 and five other songs from Essex the following year, publishing a collection of fifteen *Folk Songs from the Eastern Counties* in 1908. He would go on to publish some 260 arrangements of English folk songs, carols and dances, along with another thirty-one arrangements of Scottish, Irish, Welsh and Continental ones. It is no coincidence that two other composers known for their settings of Housman – E.J. Moeran and George Butterworth – also collected and arranged English folk songs.

The greater influence of folk song in the classical world was upon orchestral writing. Elgar had already established himself by the time

---

*William Sterndale Bennett (1816–75) was an English composer, conductor, pianist and teacher, admired by both Mendelssohn and Robert Schumann, and was in succession Professor of Music at Cambridge and Principal of the Royal Academy of Music.

Sharp began collecting, and despite his attendance at the first meeting of the EFSS thereafter paid little attention to folk tunes, although the theme for his *Introduction and Allegro for String Orchestra* (1905) was based on a song he had overheard while staying in Wales. Younger composers, however, drew upon folk song to provide the basis for orchestral and other works: Vaughan Williams's *In the Fen Country* (1904), *Rhapsody No. 1* (1906), *Six Studies in English Folk Song* (1926), *Five Variants on Dives and Lazarus* (1939) and the opera *Hugh the Drover* (1924); Gustav Holst's *Songs of the West* (1906), *A Somerset Rhapsody* (1907), *Phantasy Quartet on British Folksongs* (1916) and *At the Boar's Head* (1925); Frederick Delius's *Brigg Fair* (1908); George Butterworth's *Two English Idylls* (1911) and *The Banks of Green Willow* (1913); Percy Grainger's *Green Bushes: Passacaglia on an English Folksong* (1906) and *Lincolnshire Posy* (1937); E.J. Moeran's *Rhapsody No. 2* (1924).

It may also be no coincidence that in the years before the First World War there was a vogue for setting to music poems that celebrated country walking. Engel's suggestion that composers should set off into the English countryside in search of folk music in remote hamlets and villages had been taken seriously, and this kind of field research often involved tramping across large tracts of rural England in order to hear elderly country folk perform songs or play tunes. Between 1901 and 1904 Vaughan Williams wrote a cycle of nine *Songs of Travel* setting poems from Robert Louis Stevenson's volume of the same title, describing life on the open road of the kind recommended by Edward Thomas and E.V. Lucas. Vaughan Williams's cycle opens with 'The Vagabond' and ends with 'I have trodden the upward and the downward slope', and in between there is a celebration of sleeping under the stars, roadside fires, birdsong, sunsets and infinite shining heavens. Ernest Farrar's *Vagabond Songs* (1911) comprises settings of Arthur Symons's 'The Wanderer's Song' ('Give me a long white road, and the grey wide path of the sea, / And the wind's will and the bird's will, and the heartache still in me'), D.G. Rossetti's 'Silent Noon', in which two lovers lie hidden in grass on a languid English summer's day, and Stevenson's 'The Roadside Fire', which Vaughan Williams had also set in his *Songs of Travel*. In 1912 came John Ireland's *Songs of a Wayfarer*, eclectically setting poems by William Blake, Shakespeare, Rossetti, Ernest Dowson and

James Villa Blake (1842–1925), a Unitarian minister from Chicago who is chiefly known in Britain because Ireland went on to set further poems by him about woodland, birdsong and shepherd boys. Like the cycles by Vaughan Williams and Farrar, *Songs of a Wayfarer* embraces life on the road beside streams, along footpaths and over stiles.

Severnside

Edward Elgar had emerged as the beacon of the English Musical Renaissance and was already closely associated with the landscape in which he lived and wrote. Elgar's music would come to represent two kinds of Englishness: mass flag-waving and solitary introspection. His most popular work remains 'Land of Hope and Glory', a patriotic song for which words were written by Housman's Cambridge colleague A.C. Benson to fit music taken from the *Pomp and Circumstance March No. 1* (1901). Sung with varying degrees of competence and rowdiness at the Last Night of the Proms, Conservative Party conferences and assorted sporting events, the rousing chorus has become an alternative national anthem. The suggestion that the tune could be the basis of a song was made by Edward VII, but Elgar was dismayed by the result. Such works as *The Banner of St George* (1897), the *Coronation Ode* (1902), the *Crown of India Suite* (1912) and *The Spirit of England* (1916) nevertheless suggested a composer who was highly skilled at evoking imperial self-confidence, and in 1916 *The Times* would comment that 'Since the war began Elgar, more than ever before, has been regarded by the British people as their musical laureate.' More genuinely characteristic of Elgar's work, however, are pieces that are meditative and melancholy – such as parts of the *Enigma Variations*, the *Introduction and Allegro for Strings*, and the concertos for violin (1910) and cello (1919). Elgar may have written an overture inspired by and named after Froissart, the historian of chivalry from whom Shakespeare borrowed many details for his history plays, but it should be remembered that it was Froissart who first noted that the English take their pleasures sadly – an observation that, as we have seen, was used in an early review of *A Shropshire Lad*. Elgar himself summed up the contradictory elements of his work when he wrote in his sixties: 'I am still at heart the dreamy child who used to be found in the reeds by Severn side with a sheet of paper trying to fix the sounds and longing for something very great.'

The lands around the River Severn are strongly identified not only with both Elgar and Housman but with the English Musical Renaissance more generally. Rising in the Cambrian Mountains of mid-Wales, the river flows through the English counties of Shropshire, Worcestershire and Gloucestershire, eventually discharging into the Bristol Channel. Gloucestershire in particular was a county in which a number of English composers were born or spent time: Hubert Parry's family were the squires of Highnam Court, just outside Gloucester; Vaughan Williams was born in the Cotswold village of Down Ampney, the name of which he gave to the tune he composed for the hymn 'Come Down, O Love Divine'; Gustav Holst and C.W. Orr were born in Cheltenham, Herbert Howells in Lydney and Ivor Gurney in Gloucester; Gerald Finzi spent a formative period during the 1920s living at Painswick, where he wrote his *Severn Rhapsody* (1924). All of them except Parry and Holst would set poems from *A Shropshire Lad*.

Like that of Housman's poetry, the 'Englishness' of Elgar's music was seen to be closely bound up with a very particular and localised English landscape. A 'biographical sketch' of Elgar in the *Musical Times* in October 1900 begins by imagining a 'quiet stroll' on the Malvern Hills, 'greatly enhanced by the companionship of one who habitually thinks his thoughts and draws his inspirations from these elevated surroundings'. And it is not only Elgar's surroundings that are elevated in the article. The composer had always been regarded as an outsider. He was Roman Catholic, his father had been a shopkeeper and his mother the daughter of a farm labourer, and he was largely self-taught, attending neither the Royal Academy of Music nor the Royal College of Music. These sorts of things mattered to the snobbish Victorian musical establishment, but now that Elgar had achieved such eminence (he would be knighted in 1904 and in 1911 became the first musician to be appointed to the Order of Merit) things looked rather different. The principal career of Elgar's father was skilfully glossed over in the article; instead William Elgar had been 'an assistant in the music-publishing house of Messrs. Coventry and Hollier, then in Dean Street, Soho' before starting 'a music-selling business of his own' – though he was 'much more of a musician than a business man'. The lowly agricultural working-class origins of Elgar's mother were similarly enhanced when she was described as 'descended from a fine old yeoman stock of Weston, Herefordshire, and therefore intensely English'.

Intense Englishness, with its reach back into the distant past, now mattered in music. The article was even prefaced with the opening lines of William Langland's fourteenth-century allegorical poem, *Piers Plowman*, in which a narrator called Will falls asleep on the Malvern Hills and sees, in a dream-vision, the eponymous agricultural labourer offer to show a group of pilgrims the way to Truth just as soon as he has finished ploughing his half-acre of land. The first standard edition of the poem had appeared in 1886, edited by W.W. Skeat, who described Will as 'worthy to be honoured by all who prize highly the English character and our own land'. Skeat does not attach a great deal of importance to the Malvern Hills setting of the poem, since much of the narrative is in fact set among the streets and taverns of London (and is the direct inspiration for Elgar's *Cockaigne* overture of 1901); but he also quotes Henry Hart Milman, who in his *History of Latin Christianity* (1854–5) noted that although Will has spent some years in the capital, 'his home, his heart is among the poor rural population of central Mercian England' – people like Elgar's maternal family and the hapless agricultural labourers of Housman's poetry.

The Malvern Hills did not merely 'present the earliest classic ground of English poetry'. As the article goes on to observe, the spectacular view from Elgar's recently built house on a hillside in Malvern Wells 'begins and ends with two cities so long associated with the Three Choirs Festivals – Worcester on the left, Gloucester on the right. Between these extremes, through which the Severn flows its tranquil course, lies the vale of Evesham, where Muzio Clementi, "the father of modern pianoforte-playing," had his cottage and where he died.* The venerable Abbey of Tewkesbury comes within the range of vision, and, on a clear day, even the historic battle-field of Edge Hill, although forty miles distant.' The author has already pointed out 'the site of a

---

*Although of Italian birth, Clementi was brought to England at the age of thirteen under the patronage of Peter Beckford (cousin of the more notorious William) and subsequently made his life there as a composer, performer and first director of the Philharmonic Society. He is buried in Westminster Abbey.

Roman encampment [. . .] traditionally associated with Caractacus', by which he in fact means the British Camp, where according to legend the first-century British king made his last stand against the Roman invaders – an episode Elgar had made the subject of an 1889 cantata. In short, the article locates Elgar not simply in an English landscape but amidst the places of English history: musical, ecclesiastical and military.

In the inaugural lecture he delivered at the University of Birmingham, where he became the first Chair of Music in 1905, Elgar rejected the popular notion that 'certain boisterous, heavy, strenuous choral works have represented the height of English music and represent the English spirit'. He felt that young composers should instead 'draw their inspiration more from their own country, from their own literature – and, in spite of what many would say – from their own climate. Only by drawing from any real English inspiration shall we ever arrive at having an English *art*.' Elgar himself drew on all these aspects of England, but it was the English landscape that had the greatest influence on him. He explored much of it by bicycle, sometimes travelling fifty miles in a day, and frequently claimed that the countryside could be heard in his works. While rehearsing the second movement of his *Symphony No. 1*, he told the orchestra: 'Don't play it like that: play it like – like something you hear down by the river,' and claimed that he could not conduct his own music 'without finding that his mind slipped back to summer days on the Malvern Hills, to *Birchwood* or to the drowsy peace of Longdon Marsh'. Birchwood was the rented cottage where he spent summer weekends between 1898 and 1903, while Longdon Marsh is another western brookland of streams and willows, this one near Upton-upon-Severn with views of the Malverns. The latter is where Elgar spent time composing his 1903 oratorio *The Apostles*: 'In Longdon Marsh' is written on the score.

Even when exiled from what he called 'that sweet borderland where I have made my home', he continued to take his inspiration from it: the *Cello Concerto* was largely written in Sussex, but Elgar told a friend that he should not be surprised if, when out walking on the Malvern Hills, he should hear the concerto's main theme: 'it's only me – don't be frightened'. Someone who heard Elgar's music all too loudly when walking on the Malverns was E.J. Moeran, who while staying in Ledbury, struggling to write his *Second Symphony*, claimed that Elgar had 'cursed' the surrounding landscape for other composers.

In 1929 Elgar moved into his final home, on Rainbow Hill in Worcester, where he wrote his *Severn Suite* for brass band and the final *Pomp and Circumstance* march, the idea for which he originally sketched on an Ordnance Survey map of Gloucestershire while out motoring. When he was dying Elgar requested that he should be buried near Powick, where he had once been conductor of the lunatic asylum's staff band and which stands at the confluence of the Severn and the Teme, two of the rivers that flow through *A Shropshire Lad*. 'It is certain that no one was ever more involved with the very spirit and essence of his own country,' Elgar's daughter Carice recalled.

> It was in his very bones – Worcestershire was everything to him, the very look of spring coming, the cottages, the gardens, the fields and fruit orchards were different to his mind in Worcestershire from anywhere else. He loved England and would delight in seeing places new to him and get their atmosphere and understand the feeling of other parts of England – but Worcestershire remained supreme. From walking, driving and bicycling there was very little of the county he did not know, and his memory for every village however remote, and every lane however twisty and bewildering, was extraordinary. He had a wonderful gift of sense of locality and a wonderful memory.

The Singing Lad

The influential music critic Edwin Evans felt that *A Shropshire Lad* offered English composers what the poetry of Verlaine had recently offered the French. It was, he wrote in 1918, a volume 'in which the truly lyrical qualities of the English language are reflected as they have seldom been, if ever, in our time. Within the same number of years, or less, from their publication, the poems of Verlaine, in which the essential lyrical qualities of the French language have the same prominence, had supplied the foundation of a veritable library of French song which threatens in course of time to become as formidable as that which owes its existence to the poetry of Heinrich Heine.'

He went on to suggest that English composers had been 'slow to discern' the qualities of Housman's poetry, and in this he and his colleague and rival, Ernest Newman, were for once in agreement. At this stage, Newman felt that composers had not yet taken full advantage of what Housman offered: 'Mr. Housman's book of poems, – now a quarter of a century old, – is so purely English a thing that it is a pity our English composers have not found a real musical equivalent of it. Had we a [Hugo] Wolf among us, it would not have been a mere poem or two here and there from the collection that he would have set. He would have felt that here was something peculiarly English from first to last; and he would have set virtually the whole of the sixty-three poems, doing for Mr. Housman what Wolf did for Mörike, for Goethe, for Eichendorff, and others.'

By the time the two critics were writing, English composers had in fact begun to set Housman's poems, though often without particular distinction. The earliest evidence of permission being sought to set a poem from *A Shropshire Lad* is a letter Housman wrote to Grant Richards in June 1903. 'I have no objection to Mr Ettrick setting the verse to music,' he told his publisher, 'but I have not extracted fees from other people who have set other pieces, so I don't want to begin now.' There is no trace of any Housman settings by Henry Havelock Ettrick, a composer who appears similarly to have vanished into oblivion, leaving behind a handful of published songs. The letter makes it clear that Ettrick was not the first composer to have approached Housman, but it is not until 1904 that a setting is known to have been completed. 'When I was one-and-twenty', for voice and piano, was published that year by the baritone Michael Maybrick under his customary pseudonym of Stephen Adams. Maybrick was a popular performer of his own songs, most of them with words by Frederic Weatherby, the author of 'Danny Boy' and 'Roses Are Blooming in Picardy'. Many of the songs the two men composed are about seafaring, but perhaps their most famous song is 'The Holy City', a perennially popular and highly glutinous religious piece. There is presumably someone around who owns a copy of Adams's Housman setting, but no copy exists in the files of its publisher, Boosey & Hawkes.

Arthur Somervell's *A Shropshire Lad* cycle of ten songs, dating from the same year, not only survives but was an immediate success, has been frequently recorded, and is regularly performed over a century after it was first published. The first known performance of the piece was given on 3 February 1905 by the well-known baritone Harry Plunket Greene at the Aeolian Hall, where it was paired with five of Vaughan Williams's *Songs of Travel*. Situated in London's Bond Street, the hall had become a leading venue for chamber-music recitals, and several of the musical compositions based on Housman's poems received their premieres there. The *Musical Times* judged the *Shropshire Lad* settings 'amongst the best Dr Somervell has written', adding that 'the work so pleased that Mr Plunket Greene announces that he will repeat the Cycle on March 9 in the same hall'. Somervell may have gritted his teeth and set the line 'Lovely lads and dead and rotten' unaltered in 'On the idle hill of summer', but he took considerable liberties in set-ting other poems, omitting three of the five verses of 'There pass the careless people', repeating the first verse after the second in 'Think no more, lad; laugh, be jolly', and emphatically repeating the final line of 'The lads in their hundreds to Ludlow come in for the fair'.

Somervell had already written a song cycle derived from Tennyson's 1855 monodrama *Maud*, condensing the poet's long narrative into thir-teen songs. The story there was ready-made, and it has been asserted that Somervell created a similar narrative for *A Shropshire Lad*: it 'would seem to relate memorable incidents in the career of a lad who starts life in a village and ultimately becomes a soldier', explained the critic in the *Musical Times*, which is about as far as one can go. As with the book itself, however, there have been later and unwise attempts to construct a rather more detailed narrative: 'In No. 1 ("Loveliest of trees") the hero, aged twenty, marvels at the beauty of spring and feels the stir-rings of romance.' There is in fact nothing in the poem (II) to suggest such stirrings: on the contrary, springtime blossom makes the 'hero' acutely aware of mortality and the passing of time. 'Already in No 2, though a year or two later ("When I was one-and-twenty"), he rues having given away his heart, a theme pursued and deepened in No 3

("There pass the careless people"), possibly because (as is implied by Housman in "Bredon Hill", No 4) there has been a guilty outcome and the girlfriend has died in childbirth.' Housman implies no such thing in 'Bredon Hill', and such fabrications merely serve to undermine an interesting thesis, which, however, further falls apart in an attempt to make the remaining songs outline a military career that ends with the hero 'at the point of death in some foreign field' (apparently represented by 'Into my heart an air that kills'), with 'The lads in their hundreds' awkwardly providing some kind of coda. In fact Somervell's arrangement merely follows Housman's own order for the first eight songs, then places two poems out of sequence for the last two.

Somervell's settings sound much more of the nineteenth century than the pre-war cycles by Vaughan Williams and Butterworth. In particular, the swaggering march of 'The street sounds to the soldiers' tread' seems more appropriate to Kipling than to Housman, sheer heartiness eradicating any ambiguity in the glance exchanged by the soldier and the onlooker. Similarly, there seems an insufficient shift of tone between the first and second verses of 'When I was one-and-twenty': the tune slows down towards the end but does not quite lose its jauntiness, particularly in the seemingly irrepressible piano accompaniment. When *The Times* praised Somervell's 'broad and manly treatment' of the poems, these were presumably the songs it had particularly in mind.

A more convincing melancholy steals in with Somervell's setting of the pared-down 'There pass the careless people', and the change of mood in 'In summertime on Bredon' is beautifully managed, with the pealing bells of the accompaniment dying out for the verse in which the speaker's love goes to church alone for her funeral, then coming back again in the final verse as a heedless and intolerable reminder of lost happiness. The mere suggestion of a drum in the piano part of 'On the idle hill of summer', becoming more obvious and strident when the idler joins the colours in the final verse, is a far more delicate evocation of the military life than that of 'The street sounds to the soldiers' tread', while the sad and lovely tune Somervell writes for 'White in the moon the long road lies' contrasts well with the rollicking drinking song that is 'Think no more lad'. Somervell's most ingenious idea was to have the tune used for the cycle's first song, 'Loveliest of trees', return on the piano for 'Into my heart an air that kills', the voice at first floating on it on a single repeated high note but then descending to follow the accompaniment at the moment the Lad recognises that the land he is looking at is one of lost content. This is both effective and affecting and sets us up for the final song, 'The lads in their hundreds', one of the very best settings of Housman's poem, with its appropriate shift from major to minor at the point the singer wishes he could get to know the assembled young men.

On the whole, Somervell got the musical afterlife of *A Shropshire Lad* off to a very good start, and the years before the outbreak of the First World War saw several more settings by both well-known and now forgotten composers. Those who set individual songs for voice and piano include the pianist and stage-musical composer Dalhousie Young ('Bredon Hill', 1905); H. Balfour Gardiner ('The Recruit' in 1906 and 'When I was one-and-twenty' as the second of his *Two Lyrics* of 1908); Ivor Gurney ('On your midnight pallet lying', 1907); Frances Weir ('With rue my heart is laden' under the sentimental title 'Where Roses Fade', 1911); Graham Peel ('Soldier I wish you well' from 'The street sounds to the soldiers' tread' and 'In summertime on Bredon', both 1911); Peter Warlock (''Tis time, I think, by Wenlock town' as 'Remembered Spring' and 'Loveliest of trees, the cherry' as 'The Cherry Tree', both around 1913 and now lost); Frank Lambert, best remembered for such popular Victorian ballads as 'God's Garden' ('The street sounds to the soldiers' tread', 1914); and Arthur Bliss (''Tis time, I think, by Wenlock town', published somewhat confusingly as 'Wenlock Edge' in 1914, and 'When I was one-and-twenty', composed the same year but not published until 1924). Of these, Peel's 'In summertime on Bredon' is the most enduring, its immediate popularity further boosted when it was recorded by Gervase Elwes in 1916.

More significantly, *A Shropshire Lad* was also used as the basis for further song cycles, including Graham Peel's *Four Songs of a Shropshire Lad* (1910), Hugh Priestley-Smith's *From the West Country* (consisting of five songs, 1913), and Alfred Redgrave-Cripps' *Five Shropshire Lad Songs* (1914). In effect, most of these were simply collections of songs, but both Vaughan Williams and Butterworth produced cycles similar to those constructed by Schubert and Schumann from poems by Müller and Heine. Vaughan Williams's *On Wenlock Edge*, for tenor, piano and string quartet, was first performed at the Aeolian Hall on 15 November 1909 by its dedicatee, Gervase Elwes, the pianist Frederick Kiddle and the Schwiller Quartet. It remains, along with Butterworth's two cycles, the best known of all Housman settings and would reach a new and wider audience when a gramophone recording was released in March 1917, with the same singer and pianist but with the London String Quartet replacing the Schwiller.

Elwes was noted for 'his policy of encouraging the young English composers of merit' and had already performed a version of 'Is my team ploughing' for voice and piano at the Aeolian Hall in January 1909, when it was described in *The Times* as 'a miniature tragedy of the utmost force and originality'. For the November concert he was unwell, and decided not to sing the other songs in the programme in order to save his voice for Vaughan Williams's cycle. The performance nevertheless impressed the critic of *The Times*, who – although he unfortunately attributed the words of the songs to Laurence Housman – wrote that all six songs were 'remarkable for accurate accentuation of the words and for genuinely deep expression, with an appropriately rustic flavour about the themes'.

Somervell's settings of Housman, good as they are, seem rather Victorian and staid when placed alongside Vaughan Williams's dramatic and richly coloured ones. This is partly the result of the forces Vaughan Williams employed, but also of the three months the composer had spent in Paris being taught by Ravel and coming under the influence of French impressionism. The drama of the cycle is apparent from the first song, 'On Wenlock Edge', which opens with the agitated strings imitating the threshing of storm-blown trees. The second song, 'From far, from eve and morning', introduces tranquillity; the voice hovers above slow piano chords and gentle runs, and the introduction of the strings is held off until the second verse. This is followed by a highly dramatic, not to say overwrought 'Is my team ploughing?' and a charmingly jaunty 'Oh when I was in love with you', before we come to the cycle's showpiece, 'Bredon Hill'. The cycle ends with 'Clun', in which the rippling notes of the piano suggest the poem's 'valleys of springs of rivers', and in which singers invariably mispronounce 'Ony'.*

The strengths and weaknesses of the cycle are most clearly displayed in its two most dramatic songs. In 'Bredon Hill', Vaughan Williams takes full advantage of having a chamber ensemble at his disposal rather than just a piano. In a slow instrumental introduction the strings and piano evoke the still summer's day in which the two lovers lie on a hilltop surveying the surrounding countryside and listening to skylarks singing far above them, before the piano drifts off to create the sound of the pealing bells. When the voice is introduced, it pursues its own line, floating dreamily on top of the music which does not so much accompany it as form a continuing atmospheric backdrop. In the third and fourth verses, which Vaughan Williams runs together, the bells become more insistent as they summon the lovers to church, and a sense of foreboding is suggested by the strings, which had created the summer idyll, falling silent. They return with chilly, long-drawn-out notes suggestive of the ominous 'snows at Christmas' in the fifth verse, and a plucked string joins the piano to imitate the single tolling bell that sounds throughout the sixth verse describing the funeral of the dead girl. For the final verse, the music returns (as the poem does) to the opening line and once again evokes a tranquil summer's day, but 'noisy bells' crash in on the piano, making the steeples not so much 'hum' as positively judder; agitated strings meanwhile suggest the worked-up state their pealing now provokes in the singer, who eventually cries out 'Oh, noisy bells, be dumb' before reluctantly answering their summons. The bells die away and the untroubled summer's day returns, though now overlaid with defeat as the singer repeats the last half of the poem's final line: 'I will come'. The song amounts to an entire monodrama and it is unusually long, lasting between around six and three-quarter and eight and a half minutes, depending on the performers. (Compare this with settings of the same poem by other composers, which last between two and three-quarter and four and three-quarter minutes.) The influence of Ravel, particularly 'La vallée

---

*Of the nine recordings I have, only Peter Pears and Anthony Rolfe-Johnson get it right.

des cloches' from his *Miroirs* (1905), is very apparent here, while at the same time the music seems quintessentially 'English', its evocation of lovers lying at peace in the English countryside recalling the composer's much simpler but extraordinarily beautiful setting for voice and piano of Rossetti's 'Silent Noon' (1904).

'Is my team ploughing?' has become something of a showpiece for singers because it requires them to use two voices: a quiet, ghostly one for the dead lad and a more hearty one for his living friend. This is the setting that particularly outraged Housman when he learned that Vaughan Williams had 'mutilated' the poem by cutting the second and third verses. 'I wonder how would he like me to cut two bars out of his music,' he grumbled. When told of Housman's objection, Vaughan Williams tartly replied: 'the composer has a perfect right artistically to set any portion of a poem he chooses provided he does not actually alter the sense [. . .] I also feel that a poet should be grateful to any one who fails to perpetuate such lines as:

> The goal stands up, the keeper
> Stands up to keep the goal.'

Vaughan Williams also repeated the 'Yes, lad' in the first line of the final verse, a repetition that adds to the inappropriate hysteria of the entire setting. Ernest Newman, who was not an admirer of the cycle, found this song particularly unsatisfactory. Vaughan Williams, he wrote, 'falsifies the very essence of the poem by exaggerating the contrast between the dead man and the living. He turns the poem into a sort of long-distance telephone conversation, in which one voice sounds very thin and the other aggressively robust. The two are never in the same focus, as Butterworth makes them, and as they undoubtedly ought to be.' He felt that Vaughan Williams had gone for melodrama, when what was needed was pathos: 'Dr. Vaughan Williams's setting flies in the very face of all that is most delicate, most artistic, most human in the poem. What is the use of the poet softening the final blow as he does if Dr. Vaughan Williams is to deal it afresh at the dead man with a sledge-hammer?' Newman even agreed with Housman that Vaughan Williams's cutting of the text was damaging, because omitting the two verses 'destroys the poet's effect of the gradual, almost casual, transition from the ghost's questions about the common things of life to the questions about his sweetheart'. Newman's criticisms are harsh but not unfair, and Vaughan Williams's setting of 'Is my team ploughing' justifies Housman's frequent complaints that musical settings did violence to his poems.

On Wenlock Edge nevertheless did much to establish Vaughan Williams as a leading composer, and it rightly remains hugely popular, unlike his later version of the piece for tenor and orchestra, which he claimed to prefer, but which at the time of writing exists in only two recordings, whereas the original version is available in fifteen. The Housman settings also prepared the way for *The Lark Ascending*, one of the great works of twentieth-century English pastoral. It is not always remembered that this 1921 'Romance for violin and orchestra', which frequently tops polls of the nation's favourite piece of classical music, was not the composer's first evocation of a lark soaring above the English countryside: he had already achieved this in his setting of 'Bredon Hill'.

George Butterworth: England's Loss

The two Housman song cycles composed by George Butterworth have been recorded almost as often as Vaughan Williams's *On Wenlock Edge*, and they receive many more live performances – partly because they require just a singer and a piano. Of all Housman settings, Butterworth's remain perhaps the best loved. The reasons for this are not entirely musical, although their apparent folk-song-like simplicity and the sense that they are 'purely' English has endeared them to many audiences. As Vaughan Williams wrote of Butterworth: 'he could no more help composing in his own national idiom than he could help speaking in his own mother tongue.' Butterworth was himself one of those lads who would die in their glory and never grow old, and his death on the Somme in 1916 is generally acknowledged as the greatest loss that English music suffered in the First World War. In addition, Butterworth's name would always be associated with Housman's because, of the few completed works he left behind, three were derived from *A Shropshire Lad*: the two cycles, *Six Songs from 'A Shropshire Lad'* and *Bredon Hill and Other Songs*, both composed between 1909 and 1911, and the orchestral rhapsody *A Shropshire Lad*, which received its premiere in 1913.

Born in London in 1885 into a wealthy middle-class family, Butterworth was brought up in York and educated at Eton. Although he had played the organ and written hymn tunes at his Yorkshire prep school, and had received musical tuition during the holidays, it was at Eton that he started writing music in earnest. He developed his talent further when he went up to Trinity College, Oxford, ostensibly to read Greats. He soon became involved in the musical life of the university, attending the many concerts on offer, performing on his own instrument, the piano, singing in choral works and doing some conducting: he would be elected president of the University Musical Club in his second year. It was while he was at Oxford that Butterworth was introduced to Vaughan Williams, who would become one of his closest friends. A lecture there by Cecil Sharp on the folk songs he had collected in Somerset, chaired by Lucy Broadwood, stimulated Butterworth's own interest in folk music, and he joined the English Folk-Song Society in 1906 while still an undergraduate. In September of that year he travelled to Herefordshire with an Eton and Oxford contemporary three years his senior called Francis ('Timmy') Jekyll in order to collect his first folk songs in the picturesque village of Weobley, famed for its many timber-framed buildings. Timmy was the nephew of Gertrude Jekyll, doyenne of the English gardening style pioneered by William Robinson in *The Wild Garden* (1870), which had argued for a more natural and less formal style of gardening than the geometrical bedding schemes so popular during the Victorian period. Like her nephew, Gertrude Jekyll had been a collector, travelling widely in search of plants rather than songs. The plants she favoured were often selected and developed from species long familiar in the cottage gardens of the rural poor. The use to which she put these plants in her designs was a good deal more sophisticated than that of agricultural labourers, and her approach was not unlike that of composers who developed and adapted the folk songs they had collected in remote villages.

Sometimes accompanied by Timmy Jekyll, sometimes by Vaughan

Williams or Sharp, but more often on his own, Butterworth would become a leading collector of folk songs and Morris tunes. In 1907 alone he noted down well over one hundred tunes and songs, not only from Herefordshire, but also from Sussex, Oxfordshire, Yorkshire, Buckinghamshire and Shropshire. Perhaps because he was devoting more time to his studies, he was slightly less assiduous in his collecting the following year, but nevertheless left Oxford that summer with only a third-class degree. This conveniently meant that a career in the law, towards which his father had hoped to steer him, was out of the question. He worked for a while as a music critic on *The Times* and contributed articles to *Grove's Dictionary of Music and Musicians*, but in 1909 went to teach at a public school, Radley College in Oxfordshire, where he was valued as much for his sporting prowess as he was for founding the school's choral society.

He left the job after a year to enrol at the Royal College of Music, where he studied the organ and the piano as well as harmony, counterpoint and composition. By this time he had written a *Duo for Two Pianofortes: Rhapsody on English Folk Tunes*, which was premiered at Eton in June 1910 but subsequently destroyed or lost. Butterworth may have found the RCM unsatisfactory, leaving after only a year, but it was during his time there that he wrote the *Two English Idylls*, which were based on folk songs he had collected in Sussex in the spring and summer of 1907, and which remain among his best-known works.

After leaving the RCM, Butterworth dedicated much of his time to the English Folk-Song Society. He not only continued to collect songs and tunes, publishing some of them in the *Journal of the Folk-Song Society*, but learned Morris dancing and gave numerous public demonstrations of the art as a member of the first men's 'side' (or team) of the English Folk Dance Society. The society was founded in 1912, with Lady Mary Lygon (the unnamed subject of the thirteenth portrait in Elgar's *Enigma Variations*) as its first president. Its aim was to promote traditional dance in much the same way as the English Folk-Song Society promoted traditional song. Butterworth spent April 1912 bicycling round Oxfordshire noting down the steps and tunes of Morris dances from the old people he met in pubs or visited at their cottages or in the workhouse, and he would collaborate with Sharp on several publications about traditional dance. Thanks to the many demonstrations undertaken by Butterworth and others, Morris dancing ceased to be regarded as 'a pastime for cranks', and became absorbed into mainstream culture; it featured for example in the Oxford University Dramatic Society's production of Thomas Dekker's *The Shoemaker's Holiday* in 1913, where the audience demanded encores from the dancers, and in Harley Granville-Barker's production of *A Midsummer Night's Dream* at the Savoy Theatre in 1914, where folk tunes ousted Mendelssohn's incidental music.

Alongside his musicological work, Butterworth was working on his own closely allied compositions. Chief of these was his *Folk Songs from Sussex*, arrangements for voice and piano of eleven songs he and Jekyll had collected during their travels in that county, which were published in 1912. 'It has often been my privilege to hear him improvise harmonies to the folk-tunes which he had collected,' Vaughan Williams wrote, 'bringing out in them a beauty and character which I had not realised when simply looking at them. This was not merely a case of "clever harmonisation"; it meant that the inspiration which led to the original inception of these melodies and that which lay at the root of George's art were one and the same, and that in harmonising folk-tunes or using them in his compositions, he was simply carrying out a process of evolution of which these primitive melodies and his own art are different stages.'

These folk-song arrangements were made between 1906 and 1909, and may in some way be seen as preparing the ground for the two *Shropshire Lad* cycles that Butterworth began working on in the latter year – although he had composed a setting of 'When I was one-and-twenty' as early as June 1905, when he was himself still nineteen but already felt that he could improve on Somervell's version. Butterworth owned a copy of the 32mo edition of Housman's book, which would have been handy to slip into a pocket when he went on his walking tours to collect folk music.

The pencilled notes that Butterworth made in this copy suggest that at one point he envisaged a narrative cycle of fourteen songs, beginning with 'Reveille' and its command to wake in the early morning and get out into the countryside. This would have been followed by a new setting of 'When I was one-and-twenty', establishing both the age and mood of the protagonist, whose lovelorn unhappiness would be further emphasised in 'When the lad for longing sighs', with thoughts of suicide being provided by 'Oh fair enough are sky and plain' and the other Narcissus poem, 'Look not in my eyes, for fear'. The mood shifts in the next proposed setting, 'Think no more, lad', advice which apparently leads the protagonist, in 'The Recruit', to enlist – though this decision may not be entirely a happy one, since the next poem is 'Into my heart an air that kills'. This is followed by 'Is my team ploughing?', suggesting that the protagonist has died, and it has been argued that for the remaining poems in Butterworth's proposed sequence, 'the emphasis shifts to his friend left behind'. He perhaps recalls 'The lads in their hundreds', amongst whom his friend, one of the 'lightfoot lads' in 'With rue my heart is laden', was numbered, since these are the next two settings. These are followed by the other ploughboy poem, 'When smoke stood up from Ludlow', with its own intimations of mortality, and the sequence would end with 'The New Mistress' and 'On the idle hill of summer'.

Like the proposed narrative of Somervell's cycle, this one doesn't entirely work, not least because the last two poems suggest entirely different reasons for enlisting: in the first the lad determines to join the colours after an argument with his lover, who rejects him; in the second he is attracted by the romance of soldiers marching while he lies dreaming on a hillside. It seems likely that the difficulty of creating such a narrative was the reason Butterworth abandoned this scheme and instead, after further sifting during which he added and rejected poems, eventually composed two groups of songs that are related merely by mood. Nine of the songs, which had not at that point been allocated to their two groupings, were performed at Oxford's University Musical Club in May 1911, sung by the baritone J. Campbell McInnes, with Butterworth himself at the piano.

It is perhaps unsurprising that of all the settings of Housman's words, Butterworth's are most closely allied to folk song. The tune he eventually used for 'When I was one-and-twenty' is marked on the score 'Traditional', but the apparently simple and pared-down quality of his music throughout his two cycles recalls the kind of tunes he had himself collected. The folk-song element also takes his songs away from the drawing-room ballad style of Balfour Gardiner, Graham Peel and the less successful settings of Somervell. It might even be said that Butterworth takes *A Shropshire Lad* out of the drawing room altogether and back into the open air where it belongs. It is not, however, that Butterworth is striding out across the English countryside with boy-scout heartiness: instead there is a sense that he, like Housman's Lad, is accompanied on his walks by 'the beautiful and death-struck year'. This is not because we know that Butterworth was as doomed as the Shropshire lads of his source material – he could not, after all, have foreseen his fate when he wrote the songs; rather, it is that he more than any other composer captures Housman's particular sensibility.

Some of what people who knew Butterworth have written about him suggests he may have shared aspects of Housman's temperament. Outwardly, he was a rather hearty figure, usually seen with a pipe in his mouth, every inch the straightforward product of public school and Oxford. Although he had something of the traditional Yorkshireman's habit of plain speaking, he was in other ways reticent: 'reserved' was often used to describe his manner. His friend R.O. Morris, a musician who would become a professor at the RCM, wrote: 'Under a somewhat gruff and imperturbable exterior there lay an ironic and fastidious temperament that could only be satisfied with the best, and directed upon itself a criticism far more searching than it would ever level at another.' It was for this reason that Butterworth went through all his compositions before going to France, destroying any that did not satisfy him. Morris continued: 'Only those who knew him intimately could guess at the searchings of the heart, the struggles and developments and reaction, that were taking place under that outward serenity.' There has also been speculation about Butterworth's sexuality, with no con-clusive evidence one way or the other. He was thirty-one when he died but no women outside his family seem to have featured significantly in his life, his friendships being almost entirely with men; this would not, however, have seemed particularly unusual or 'suspicious' at the period. Was he simply a man's man, hiding nothing at all behind that thick moustache, or did he, like Housman, have some secret sorrow that fed into his work? The pianist Graham Johnson, who has often performed settings of *A Shropshire Lad*, has written that the homosexual subtext of Housman's book during the author's lifetime 'seems only to have struck those who were "in the know" – Butterworth among composers, for example, but seemingly not Vaughan Williams'. The strain of melancholy in Butterworth's music certainly seems at odds with the rather bluff figure that emerges from recollections of the composer, and it is telling that Butterworth thought Somervell's Housman settings 'much too flippant for the words'.

Butterworth had been at the annual Stratford-upon-Avon Summer School of Folk Songs and Folk Dance when war was declared. Stratford had become a locus of Englishness, 'a quiet little heaven where it was always May, with the nightingales shaking silver in the dark trees at night', in the memory of the travel writer H.V. Morton, and precisely the kind of place you might expect to find people being taught traditional folk dance. It was not simply that Stratford was the birthplace of England's national writer, but it was where the actor-manager Frank Benson held his annual Shakespeare Festival, of which Vaughan Williams was musical director. Morton continued:

> I remember [Benson] waving his arms at me in a storeroom hung with hams that he used as an office, and telling me, as I sat worshipping him from a sugar crate, that only through Stratford, the common meeting-place of the English-speaking world, could we heal the pains of Industrialism and make England happy again. We were to make the whole world happy, apparently, by teaching it to morris-dance and to sing folk-songs and to go to the Memorial Theatre. With the splendid faith of Youth we pilgrims believed that England could be made 'merrie' again by hand-looms and young women in Liberty gowns who played the harpsichord. Then, I seem to remember, shortly after that war was declared.

Butterworth enlisted on 1 September and was shot dead by a sniper in the early hours of 5 August 1916, a war hero whose men had named a communication trench after him, and who had been mentioned in dispatches and twice recommended for the Military Cross all within the same month. The second recommendation resulted in the award of the medal on the night he died. He was buried where he fell, but his grave was subsequently lost and his name inscribed instead on the Memorial to the Missing of the Somme at Thiepval.

Butterworth's apparent affinity with Housman's poetry makes his settings the most poignant of them all. Even 'Think no more, lad' recognises in the music of the second verse (as Somervell, for example, does not) that the reason the lad is being encouraged to drink is in order to forget his mortality. That mortality is evident from the very opening of Butterworth's first cycle, the descending notes on the piano in 'Loveliest of trees' suggesting that the cherry's beauty is evanescent and its blossom will inevitably fall. Descending chords are similarly used to accompany the voice of the dead lad in the last song of the cycle, 'Is my team ploughing?' Whereas the final verse of Vaughan Williams's setting, in which the friend admits his betrayal, verges on the hysterical, in Butterworth's setting it is merely desperately sad, with the falling chords that represent the dead ploughboy played once more on the piano after the singer has sung his last phrase, 'Never ask me whose'. In between these two songs are a properly rueful 'When I was one-and-twenty' and a sorrowing 'Look not in my eyes'; the aforementioned 'Think no more, lad'; and the most moving of all settings of 'The lads in their hundreds', the gently rocking piano accompaniment of which continues for several bars after the final words – as effective in its less emphatic way as Somervell's repeat of the final line. 'Is my team ploughing?' provides a perfect end to the sequence, as Butterworth must have realised after hearing the song performed: he originally ended the cycle with 'Think no more, lad', but changed his mind when he came to publish the work.

Butterworth's *Six Songs*, which received their premiere at the Aeolian Hall in June 1911, sung by Campbell McInnes with Hamilton Harty at the piano, are less about creating drama than about evoking a mood of loss and regret, and although they are sometimes performed and often recorded with *Bredon Hill*, it is this first cycle that steals into the heart in the way Housman's best poems do. *Bredon Hill* nevertheless shares the earlier cycle's sense of romantic apprehension, of a beautiful but haunted English landscape in which the almost imperceptible passing of time will bring unwelcome change. Butterworth never set 'Into my heart an air that kills', but all his songs suggest a land of lost content. Particularly effective in the second cycle are the two hilltop poems: 'Bredon Hill', with its mere suggestion of the pealing and tolling of bells; and 'On the idle hill of summer', in which the music, evocative of a drowsy afternoon in the English countryside, persists unchanged through the third verse describing the dead lying abandoned on the battlefields, a device that implies that (as Housman would put it) nature, heartless, witless nature, is indeed indifferent to the fate of men and neither cares nor knows.

Butterworth's other work derived from *A Shropshire Lad* was his 'Orchestral Rhapsody' of that title, which received its premiere at the Leeds Music Festival on 2 October 1913 and which he described as 'in the nature of an orchestral epilogue' to his two song cycles. Butterworth had originally called the composition an 'Orchestral Prelude' and given it the title *The Land of Lost Content*, which he subsequently changed to *The Cherry Tree*, chiefly because its main theme was derived from his setting of 'Loveliest of trees, the cherry now' – although it also, to touching effect, quotes the first line of his setting of 'With rue my heart is laden' on a solo flute just as the piece dies away. In a letter to Herbert Thompson, the music critic of the *Yorkshire Post* who was writing programme notes for the concert, Butterworth explained that 'the title has no other significance, & has no more concern with the cherry trees than with beetles (I wish I could suggest a better one). If it has any "meaning" at all, it is more in the nature of a meditation of the exiled Shropshire Lad [. . .] Please explain that it is not a description of orchards – I'm sorry to be so misleading.' After toying with other titles, Butterworth decided on 'A "Shropshire Lad" Rhapsody, for Full Orchestra', adding: 'be careful of the inverted commas' – advice that was ignored when the piece was published the following year as *A Shropshire Lad: Rhapsody for Full Orchestra*. Ever since there has been some confusion as to the correct name of the work, which has been performed and recorded under several variations of this title.

The piece attracted widespread praise, E.J. Dent stating that Butterworth now stood beside Vaughan Williams, whom he had hitherto regarded as 'our one really great composer'. It rapidly became part of the concert repertoire and in March 1914 was heard alongside

Butterworth's lively third folk-song idyll, *The Banks of Green Willow*, at the latter work's London premiere. These orchestral works established Butterworth as one of the leading English pastoralists, and the *Rhapsody* in particular was a regular feature in concert programmes during the latter years of the war and immediately after it, played in memory of its composer and more widely as a lament for the almost prelapsarian England that existed before the cataclysm.

There were other losses to music in the war, including Ernest Farrar and Willie B. Manson. Farrar had taught both Frank Bridge and Gerald Finzi at the Royal College of Music, and was killed in September 1918 at the age of thirty-three, having spent only two days in action. Like Butterworth, he was careful to destroy any compositions that did not satisfy him before setting off for the front, but among pieces that survive are his *Three Part Songs* for mixed chorus, setting 'Oh when I was in love with you', 'When I was one-and-twenty' and 'Think no more, lad; laugh, be jolly', and his three-movement orchestral suite, *English Pastoral Impressions*. The first movement of the suite, 'Spring Morning', quotes 'Sumer is icumen in' and introduces bells; these prepare the way for the second movement, which is titled 'Bredon Hill'. This movement does not follow the poem but reflects its mood in the manner of Vaughan Williams (to whom the suite is dedicated), with an evocation of a still summer's afternoon, distantly pealing bells, and a lark soaring on a solo violin. It has been suggested that the third movement, 'Over the Hills and Far Away', may also owe something to Housman, its drums and a horn imitating a bugle call inspired by 'On the idle hill of summer'. These, however, introduce a lively folk tune on the woodwind that seems distinctly unmilitary, nearer in mood to *The Banks of Green Willow* than to Butterworth's Rhapsody.

Manson, who had been born in New Zealand, studied composition at the Royal Academy of Music, where he won several prizes and was appointed a sub-professor of harmony and composition. His *Three Poems from 'A Shropshire Lad'* ('Think no more, lad', 'When I came last to Ludlow' and 'Loveliest of Trees') were written around 1915, when he was eighteen or nineteen, but not published until 1920. He enlisted as a private in the London Scottish Regiment in January 1916 and was killed six months later on the first day on the Somme, which was also his twentieth birthday. His body was never found and his name joined Butterworth's on the Memorial to the Missing at Thiepval.

E.J. Moeran, who as a keen motorcyclist had enlisted as a dispatch rider, was rather luckier, though the head wound he received in 1917 necessitated the insertion of a metal plate in his skull and was the cause – some said – of his unstable behaviour during the remainder of his life. He composed *Four Songs from 'A Shropshire Lad'* after joining up but before he had been sent to the front, and the manuscript is inscribed 'Midsummer 1916'; the four songs are 'Westward on the high-hilled plains', 'On the Road to Ludlow' (setting 'When last I came to Ludlow'), 'This time of year a twelvemonth past' and 'Far in a western brookland'. Moeran had composed only one song before this collection, and would go on to set other poets, but he often came back to Housman.

The war period produced one other Housman song cycle, H.S. Goodhart-Rendel's mis-titled *Four Songs from 'The Shropshire Lad'* (1917), and a handful of individual songs, most notably Janet Hamilton's 'By Wenlock Town' and 'With rue my heart is laden', the first of which became the best known of her four settings of Housman's poems because it was recorded by Gervase Elwes; Ivor Gurney's 'On Wenlock Edge' (1917), which has more or less vanished from the repertoire, and 'The Cherry Tree' (1918), which he later revised as 'Loveliest of trees', the second song in his cycle *The Western Playland*; and John Ireland's first Housman setting, the last three stanzas of 'March', published under the title 'The Heart's Desire' (1917).

Interlude
1918: A Shropshire Lad Spat

Up until 1918 thirty-three of the sixty-three poems in *A Shropshire Lad* had been set to music, the most popular choices being 'When I was one-and-twenty', 'Think no more, lad; laugh, be jolly', 'Loveliest of trees, the cherry' and 'Bredon Hill'. These would remain among the most frequently set of the poems, but not everyone approved of composers' efforts to capture Housman's words in music. It was during the last year of the war that this became the focus of a public spat between

Ernest Newman and Edwin Evans about the Englishness of English music.

The championing of English music had gathered momentum in the years leading up to the outbreak of war. The Society of British Composers had been founded in 1905 to promote and organise publication and performances of British music, and although it would not survive the war, being wound up in 1918, a series of concerts arranged by Balfour Gardiner at the Queen's Hall between March 1912 and March 1913 did much to gain English music a proper audience. The programmes were packed with works by Holst, Vaughan Williams, Parry, Arnold Bax, Granville Bantock, Roger Quilter and Cyril Scott, and according to Percy Grainger 'altered the way the composers thought about themselves and the way the musical public thought about English music'. On one occasion, E.J. Moeran, unable to get a ticket for a performance of a Bach Passion in St Paul's Cathedral, went instead, and without great enthusiasm, to a Queen's Hall concert of contemporary British music. Having unexpectedly enjoyed it, he attended other similar concerts, hearing at one Vaughan Williams's *Norfolk Rhapsody*, which seemed to him 'to breathe the very spirit of the English countryside'. This in turn prompted him to buy Cecil Sharp's *Folk Songs from Somerset* and embark on his own search for folk songs in his native Norfolk.

The whole issue of nationality and music had become more acute when Britain found itself at war with Germany. There was an ill-advised move to outlaw modern German and Austrian music, but although planned performances of Wagner and Richard Strauss at the Henry Wood Promenade Concerts were cancelled in August 1914, it was quickly realised that musical life in Britain would simply grind to a halt if this policy were pursued. A good deal of patriotic music was written to order during the war. Elgar's *Carillon* for orchestra and reciter, with words by the Belgian poet Émile Cammaerts about the German invasion of his country, was first performed in London in December 1914 and then toured the country, proving very popular. His more substantial *The Spirit of England* set words by Laurence Binyon, including 'For the Fallen', for orchestra, soprano and tenor soloists and chorus. It was first performed in its entirety in October 1917, although two of the three settings were premiered the year before. Parry's *The*

Chivalry of the Sea for orchestra and mixed chorus, setting words by the Poet Laureate, Robert Bridges, was written for a concert given in December 1916 to commemorate the Battle of Jutland. His setting of William Blake's 'Jerusalem', which rapidly became another alternative national anthem, had been written earlier that same year for the Fight for Right Movement at the request of Bridges, and was intended to promote morale on the home front. Bridges had suggested that if Parry were unavailable, Butterworth should be approached, which would no doubt have resulted in something very different indeed. Like Butterworth, a large number of the younger composers were otherwise occupied on various fronts, and what music they managed to write while on active service was mostly performed and published after the war had ended.

It was against this backdrop that Newman and Evans had their exchange of views about the setting of English poetry with particular reference to *A Shropshire Lad*. Before the war, Newman had famously argued that there was no such thing as 'national' music and had entered a debate on the subject with Cecil Sharp in the *English Review* in 1912. This, however, was not the same as saying that there was no such thing as 'English' music, or indeed 'English' poetry, of which Newman thought *A Shropshire Lad* a pre-eminent example. 'Surprise was recently expressed in another quarter,' he wrote in his 1918 article,

> that I – I of all people – should be either so impudent or so illogical as to speak of any music or poetry being 'English', after my horrible record in the matter of the 'nationalist' theory. The surprise could not have been greater or more pained had the late Dr. Crippen, after his domestic experiments with poison, burst into song on the subject of the happiness of married life. I am sure there is nothing consciously impudent in my speaking of 'A Shropshire Lad' being English, and asking for an English musical setting of it; and I hope there is nothing illogical in my doing so.

Newman felt that his critics had failed to differentiate between 'English' music and 'national' music: 'A "national" movement in art or literature is never a national movement in the sense that it either emanates from the whole nation or appeals to the whole nation. It emanates from a number of people of a certain way of thinking, who concentrate on this, for a time, to the exclusion of other ways of thinking which, though of no particular interest to them, are of the greatest interest to other people of the same nationality.'

He went on to insist that Housman's poems were 'English' rather than 'national': 'These poems are English, in the sense that only in England, perhaps only in Shropshire, would a lad look out upon the world with such eyes, and find such words in which to express himself; but the poems are not national, because English people of other heredities and in other environments would see life from quite another angle, and express what they saw in quite other ways.'

Newman maintained that very little 'great English art' had been made out of the musical settings of *A Shropshire Lad*. In particular, he felt that Vaughan Williams's *On Wenlock Edge* had been absurdly overpraised. Evans disagreed – as indeed he disagreed with everything Newman wrote about what constituted English music – feeling that it was not merely in language that Housman and Vaughan Williams were 'English'. The 'sentiment' shown in both the poems and the music also reflected the nation:

> it varies, of course, from one poem to the next. But there are pervading characteristics, notably a certain ingenuousness that is in harmony with our national character, and a melancholy, devoid of weakness, such as one can associate with a climate which, though conducive to depression, has helped to mould a robust race by developing its powers of resistance. There is, in fact, something paradoxical, and not to be found elsewhere, in our ability to use the greyest of tints without making them an expression of weakness. The ingenuousness referred to [. . .] is the quality most admired by those foreigners who really understand us, but no foreigner could express it. The critical realism of the Latins, and the crocodile sentiment of the Germans, stand equally in the way. It takes an Englishman to express it without either the excessive, hollow sentimentality of the German or the latent scepticism of the Latin.

This kind of chauvinism is perhaps understandable, expressed as it was while the country was at war. Evans was, however, making a musical point too. Part of Vaughan Williams's success was that the 'musical sentiment' of *On Wenlock Edge* was 'as sincere and as unsophisticated as that of the poems themselves. Nowhere is it marred by the self-indulgence of excess, and nowhere does it show signs of being studied or self-conscious. It is fresh and spontaneous and therefore convincing. Wherein it resides is a psychological rather than a technical question, and it would be a sin to dissect it. It expresses, as it were, in the colouring of his own climate, the clean faith of the healthy young Englishman.'

Spontaneity and artlessness, untainted by Continental self-indulgence and self-consciousness, were the true marks of the English character – and we are not that far away from Hazlitt's dissection of that character in his 'Merry England' article published almost exactly a century before. Not that Evans is entirely against foreign exuberance (particularly among Britain's allies), and he goes on to characterise contemporary music much as Housman would define poetry in his Leslie Stephen Lecture some fifteen years later:

> There is in modern music much that makes its emotional appeal more directly through the senses, and less through the intelligence, than was the rule when the great rhetorical forms of the sonata and the symphony were at their zenith. Perhaps the most complete illustration of this is furnished by the introduction to the second tableau of Stravinsky's 'Le Sacre du Printemps'. Contrary to academic opinion this is not a lapse from high estate, but a return to the natural functions of music, and a reassertion of its independence, which had become compromised by purely intellectual considerations [. . .] Although not in the direct stream of this tendency, 'On Wenlock Edge' derives some of its power from a similarly direct appeal that, for want of a better word, one may designate as physical.

In other words, Vaughan Williams's music makes the same direct appeal that Housman's poetry does.

Ivor Gurney: Composing for England

It was not only Edwin Evans who thought *On Wenlock Edge* a fine example of the Englishness of English music. Ivor Gurney went to a performance of the piece in May 1920 and afterwards wrote on his programme: 'Purely English words retranslated and reinforced by almost purely English music – the product of a great mind not always working at the full of its power, but there continually and clearly apparent. The French mannerisms must be forgotten in the strong Englishness of the prevailing mood – in the unmistakable spirit of the time of creation. England is the spring of emotion, the centre of power, and the pictures of her, the breath of her earth and growing things are continually felt through the lovely sound.'

Of all the composers who set Housman's words, none was more obsessed by the idea of England and Englishness than Gurney. The second of the four children of a tailor, he was born in Gloucester in 1890. His background was modest and, to judge by their surviving letters, his parents' education had been rudimentary. When his mother and father took Gurney to be christened, they had omitted to provide godparents, so the officiating vicar and his young curate were obliged to step in. This was a piece of extraordinary luck, since the curate, Alfred Cheesman, was a cultivated and well-read young man with a fondness for boys, and young Ivor soon became his protégé. It was Cheesman who introduced Gurney to poetry and who suggested that he should apply to join the cathedral choir at the age of ten, which meant that he would also be able to attend the adjoining King's School on a scholarship.

Gurney subsequently became an articled pupil of the cathedral organist, Herbert Brewer, who was also a composer and a leading figure in the Three Choirs Festival. As a chorister and a King's schoolboy, Gurney had been taken into the heart of Gloucester's ancient history, and the palpable presence of the past accompanied him as he explored the surrounding streets: 'Yet walking Gloucester History seems / A living thing and an intense', he wrote in a poem of 1927. His father came from Maisemore, a small village upriver along the Severn, and every Sunday evening, weather permitting, would walk there to visit his mother, often taking his children with him on a round journey of some eight miles. In this way Gurney got to know the countryside as well as he already knew the city. As he grew older, he would go walking on his own or with friends such as F.W. ('Will') Harvey, a budding poet two years his senior who lived at Minsterworth, a Severnside village a few miles to the west of Gloucester, and Herbert Howells, another of Brewer's pupils, who lived some nineteen miles downriver at Lydney.

Gurney was introduced to the poetry of Housman at the age of seventeen, when Alfred Cheesman gave him a copy of *A Shropshire Lad*. He must have been struck by Housman's use of place-names, since these would become a notable feature of his own poetry; the difference was that Gurney knew intimately all the places he mentioned in his poems. But these names would similarly conjure up a lost world, particularly when, like the Shropshire Lad, Gurney was exiled from his western homeland in London, was looking out across the ruined landscapes of France and Belgium while serving as a private in the First World War, or was confined to an institution in the unlovely environs of Dartford in Kent. Within months of receiving *A Shropshire Lad*, Gurney had set his first Housman poem, 'On your midnight pallet lying', which has a distinctly, not to say rather too obvious, military piano accompaniment, but is nonetheless a considerable accomplishment for a seventeen-year-old. The following year, in May 1908, he asked permission to set 'Loveliest of trees, the cherry now' and 'Is my team ploughing'. Housman, amused by the correspondent's address, told Grant Richards: 'Mr I.B. Gurney (who resides in Gloucester Cathedral along with St Peter and Almighty God) must not print the words of my poems in full on concert-programmes (a course which I am sure his fellow-lodgers would disapprove of); but he is quite welcome to set them to music.'

It would be some years before this happened. In the meantime, it was Gloucester's turn in 1910 to host the Three Choirs Festival, during which Gurney and Howells attended the first performance of Vaughan Williams's *Fantasia on a Theme by Thomas Tallis*. The piece may have had a mixed critical reception, but for Gurney it was a revelation, and the two young men were so excited that they couldn't sleep afterwards and spent the rest of the night pacing the streets. They felt, they said, that 'something of great importance had happened in English music'.

The following year Gurney won an open scholarship to the Royal College of Music. 'Why does he bother?' Brewer complained. 'He can get all he wants here.' This proved prescient because, although Gurney clearly benefited from his time at the RCM, Gloucestershire would always be the mainspring of both his music and his poetry. He enjoyed exploring the London streets and the River Thames, but never seemed at home in the capital. 'For one thing the boy was wearing a thick, dark blue Severn pilot's coat, more suggestive of an out-of-door life than the composition lesson with Sir Charles Stanford for which (by the manuscript tucked under his arm) he was clearly bound,' a friend recalled. Gurney was already suffering from the nervous and digestive problems that would plague his life, and when in 1913 he experienced some sort of breakdown he was sent back to Gloucestershire to recuperate. Rather than stay with his parents, whose fraught relationship made their home less than restful, he was sent to Framinlode, on the banks of the Severn, to stay with a lock-keeper whose family he had known for several years. Part of his convalescence took the form of helping the lock-keeper load barges, mend boats, fish for eels and make hay, and his health eventually improved sufficiently for him to return to London and complete his studies. He continued to miss Gloucestershire. Lodging in Fulham, he recalled Barrow Hill, which rises a short distance from Framinlode: 'lovely in itself, though tiny and probably not above 200 feet high', it nevertheless gave

> a view of the Forest of Dean, hills on the West, the whole broad Severn on the SW, Gloucestershire to the Southern Border to the S. And the whole line of Cotswolds on the S, SE and E. Likewise the Malverns on the North! Oh, what a place! Blue river and golden sand, and the blue-black hills — in fine weather of course.
>
> London is worse than ever to bear after that.

Stanford, meanwhile, was doing his best to teach the young man composition. Although he numbered Vaughan Williams, Holst, John Ireland, Frank Bridge, Ernest Farrar and Arthur Bliss among his pupils, he said of Gurney: 'Potentially he is the most gifted man that ever came into my care. But he is *the least teachable.*' Gurney wrote some settings of Elizabethan poets, and although they would not be published as a cycle, he referred to them collectively as 'the Elizas'. 'I have done 5 of the most delightful and beautiful songs you ever cast your beaming eyes upon,' he told Will Harvey with characteristic ebullience. 'They are all Elizabethan – the words – and blister my kidneys, bisurate my magnesia if the music is not as English, as joyful as tender as any lyric of all that noble host.' He would frequently talk of 'the special Glory of English music', and clearly saw himself as finding a place in that tradition.

In spite of being very far from A1 in the army's fitness grading, Gurney attempted to enlist in the first month of the war, 'driven' to it, he later claimed, by the 'appeals and scorn' of an older woman friend. He was rejected because of his poor eyesight, but tried again in early 1915, by which time recruiting sergeants had become less fussy. He was accepted into the Reserve Battalion of the Gloucesters and began training at Northampton and Chelmsford, where, since some country recruits could not tell left from right, soldiers were issued with two bands to tie round their legs, one of hay and the other of straw, so that the drilling sergeant could call out 'hay' and 'straw' instead. As for many other soldiers, it was some comfort for Gurney to belong to his own county's regiment, but even in Essex he felt homesick for the western landscape he so loved. 'I suppose you are in Glostershire,' he wrote enviously to Herbert Howells, 'and soon will see apple blossom and the pear trees "praising God with sweetest looks". Sometimes my heart aches for Framinlode and my little leaky boat; my gun and the ever changing Severn, now so full in Flood.' Returning to Colchester after five days' leave in September, he reported that 'the beauty of my own county astounded and enchanted me more than ever [. . .] Gloster's delicate colours, long views and sea breezes are the whole breadth of England away. That soil bore me and must ever draw my dreams and for ever be home to me.'

He found little opportunity to write any music while serving in the army. 'When I can lie quite still in joy by the side of some stream or in a meadow for an hour or more, then music will come easily and well,' he wrote in October 1915 when embarkation for France was in prospect. 'Not till then.' In the meantime, he set about writing his own 'ballad of the Cotswolds, after Belloc's "South Country"', which echoes Housman:

> When I am old and cannot bide
> The grimy townships more,
> When dreams and images will not
> Assuage my longing sore,
> I'll shake their mire from my quick feet
> And shut an alien door
>
> And get me home to the dear West
> Where men drive ploughing teams . . .

Gurney's battalion was eventually posted to France in May 1916. He had spent his pre-embarkation leave bicycling round Gloucestershire, storing up images of familiar country scenes to sustain him in the future.

Conditions at the front made composing music not merely difficult but well-nigh impossible. Unable to perform the task himself, he encouraged Herbert Howells, who was prevented by ill health from joining up, to write music celebrating the English landscape. Learning that Howells intended to dedicate his 1916 Piano Quartet 'To Chosen Hill and Ivor Gurney who knows it', he wrote: 'If you could write a Quartett [sic] inspired by Chosen, I can only conjecture how Framinlode would move you did you know it as I know it to be – the most magical and fascinating of places. Then Crickley Hill, a magnificent conception. Cranham, especially Portway; little Minsterworth, Redmarley, the noble Malvern road. Someday perhaps . . . ' For the most part, all Gurney could do at the front was to store up his impressions for later use: 'This autumnal morning stirs in me all those thoughts which shall someday crystallize into the "English Preludes",' he wrote to his friend and patron Marion Scott. Meanwhile, he continued to encourage Howells: 'I wait for the Violin Sonata clear fairly simple with the romantic slow movement singing of Western things. Show us Tintern and sunset across the Malvern and Welsh Hills. Make us see the one evening star among the trees.' His own plan was to turn his attention to poetry instead, although this was intended as a temporary measure: 'once in England and once with a healthy mind, I shall for ever chuck the Muse of Verse (if she was ever mine to chuck) and grind hard at Music.'

Gurney would in fact become as well known a poet as he is a composer. One of his most frequently anthologised war poems was written after news reached him in August 1916 that Will Harvey had failed to return from a patrol and was presumed dead. 'Here I am beside a French canal,' Gurney wrote, 'watching the day, and remembering with an ache what Glostershire is in such a season as September, and with whom I usually spent the best of it.' His poem written in memory of Harvey recalls those lost pre-war summers:

> He's gone, and all our plans
>   Are useless indeed.
> We'll walk no more on Cotswold
>   Where the sheep feed
>   Quietly and take no heed.
>
> His body, that was so quick,
>   Is not as you
> Knew it on Severn river
>   Under the blue
>   Driving our small boat through.

In the poem's final stanza, the quick body is compared with the image Gurney now has in his mind of Harvey's corpse, but this touching elegy proved premature. Harvey had in fact been captured and taken to a prisoner-of-war camp, where he would remain, safe but yearning for Gloucestershire, for the rest of the war.

The country names Gurney so often repeated in his letters also fill his first volume of poems, *Severn and Somme* (1917). Its title embodies the contrasts between what he often referred to as his 'Western' homeland (as in the title of his second Housman song cycle, *The Western Playland*) and the Western Front. 'A burning love for Gloucester, Severn, and

Cotswold shines through almost every poem of Mr Gurney's, and it is expressed with the force and simplicity natural to so genuine a passion,' wrote the reviewer in the *Times Literary Supplement*. 'The beautiful Cotswold names chime sweetly through the book like a bloom on the fragrant freshness of the verse.' Much the same had been said of *A Shropshire Lad*, but Gurney chose place-names because they meant something to him personally rather than evoking by their sound an emblematic landscape. 'I find a store of poetry, an accumulation of pictures – dead leaves, Minsterworth Orchards, Cranham, Crickley and Framinlode reach,' he had written while still in England. 'They do not merely mean intensely to me; they are me.' Far from choosing place-names for their euphony, as Housman did, he chose them despite their lack of it: 'You are right about Crickley Hill not sounding well,' he wrote to Marion Scott, who had queried the use of the name in the last line of a poem. 'Believe me, the view makes up for it, and I wrote from the viewpoint rather than the name.' Perhaps he was right; the reviewer in the *TLS* singled out the line as an example of the love of Gloucestershire he or she so admired in the poems. It was perhaps inevitable that, referring to Will Harvey, whose first volume of poems had recently appeared under the title *A Gloucestershire Lad at Home and Abroad*, and through him back to Housman, the review of the book in the *Sunday Times* should appear under the headline: 'Another Gloucestershire Lad'.

In spite of the conditions in which he found himself at the front, Gurney had not in fact abandoned music altogether, and managed to draft some songs. 'By a Bierside', setting words by John Masefield, was 'written whilst lying on a damp sandbag in a disused trench mortar emplacement'. He also wrote 'In Flanders', setting words by Will Harvey that chimed with his own feelings for England:

> I'm homesick for my hills again –
> My hills again!
> To see above the Severn plain,
> Unscabbarded against the sky,
> The blue high blade of Cotswold lie;
> The giant clouds go royally

> By jagged Malvern with a train
> Of shadows.

'Do you know, standing off from my song, I can now see that the very spirit of my country is quick in the song,' he wrote to Marion Scott. 'Gloster itself shines and speaks in it. It is as if, on the long night work, some kind of spirit of home visited me, when I think of it. And the end of the song is exactly like the "high blue blade" [sic] fading away to distant Bredon just above Evesham.'

The Malverns were not the only blue hills Gurney had in mind on the Western Front. 'I wonder whether at last I might try Housman's *Shropshire Lad*?' he wrote in April 1917 from a hospital in Rouen, where he was recuperating from a bullet wound he had received in his right arm during an attack on Good Friday. He had not brought his copy of the book with him and asked Scott to send him another one, along with some musical manuscript paper. Having re-read the poems, he reported 'once again I feel rather incapable of setting them', which suggests that his earlier plan to set 'Loveliest of trees, the cherry now' and 'Is my team ploughing' had been abandoned. 'Such precise and measured verses are too easy to set,' he felt, 'do not give the scope that R. Bridges songs offer one.' Nevertheless, back in the line some six weeks later he reported: 'In my head is "On Wenlock Edge" waiting to be written.' The opportunity to do so came in September when Gurney was gassed at St Julien and sent back to Britain to be treated at a hospital near Edinburgh.

Discharged in October, Gurney was sent on a signalling course at a military camp in Northumberland, from where he wrote to Jack Haines, a Gloucestershire solicitor, minor poet and amateur botanist to whom he had been introduced either by Cheesman or Harvey, asking for the 6d edition of *A Shropshire Lad*. (Having lost several volumes at the front, he had returned for safe keeping the copy that Marion Scott had sent him in France.) 'Well, here comes Housman's Song,' he announced on Christmas Eve, but his setting of 'On Wenlock Edge' for voice and piano was not published during his lifetime, nor was it revised for either of his Housman song cycles. He continued to be plagued by illness, at first put down to the after-effects of gas, but there was evidently something more seriously wrong with him. In May 1918 he was sent to a hospital specialising in treating the effects of war trauma, but by now he feared that he was going mad. He wrote Marion Scott a farewell letter before setting out to drown himself in the canal, but in the event lacked the resolve, and after several more months of medical treatment was discharged from the army as medically unfit for further service. The official diagnosis was 'deferred shell-shock', and Gurney's future looked very uncertain: but at least he was finally going back to Gloucestershire.

He returned to the Royal College of Music in January 1919 to take up his scholarship, which had been left open for him, and to study composition under Vaughan Williams. Although his friends and family were worried by his unpredictable behaviour, he was writing a great deal of music, including a *Gloucestershire Rhapsody*, which would remain unperformed until 2010, and a setting of 'Is my team ploughing', which would be included in his second Housman cycle, *The Western Playland*. Back in Gloucestershire he was reunited with Will Harvey, and began to collaborate on an unrealised *Gloucestershire Lad* song cycle, of which only 'Walking Song' was completed to add to 'In Flanders'. In the second half of the year he composed some forty songs as well as several instrumental pieces, and this frenetic creative activity continued through 1920, matched by his erratic wandering around the countryside, walking from place to place and sometimes covering huge distances (London to Gloucester, for example), sleeping in the open, and earning a little money by labouring on farms or singing folk songs in wayside pubs. He always carried with him his notebooks, in which he wrote down snatches of music and poetry.

Given the chaos into which Gurney's life was descending, it is astonishing that between September and December 1919 he managed to complete the first of his Housman cycles, *Ludlow and Teme*. Inspired by Vaughan Williams's *On Wenlock Edge*, Gurney had set seven poems for male voice (baritone), string quartet and piano. The cycle starts with a beautiful setting of 'When smoke stood up from Ludlow', followed by a dreamlike 'Far in a western brookland', the words of which would have increasing potency for the composer, a sprightly ''Tis time, I think, by Wenlock town' and a rather rambling setting of 'The lads in their hundreds' under the title 'Ludlow Fair'. 'On the idle hill of summer' recaptures the mood of the second song, evoking a summer idyll that is interrupted by the strident call of the military before the piano and strings return us to the hillside. 'When I was one-and-twenty' is accompanied by a charmingly tripping tune that only falters right at the end, and the cycle ends with a somewhat melodramatic 'The Lent Lily'. It was performed by Steuart Wilson, the Philharmonic Quartet and Gurney himself on piano in March 1920 at a 'Gloucestershire Evening' organised by Marion Scott at her London house. Wilson was the dedicatee of Vaughan Williams's *Four Hymns* (1914), and he would become the leading interpreter of the composer's *On Wenlock Edge* after Gervase Elwes was killed in an accident at a railway station in Boston in 1921. He also benefited after the war from a fund set up by George Butterworth's father which allowed him to spend time studying singing in France, and he gave further performances of *Ludlow and Teme* in 1920.

Later that year Gurney completed his second Housman cycle, which he had been working at on and off since 1908. *The Western Playland (and of Sorrow)*, to give its full if rather clumsy title, was scored once again for baritone, string quartet and piano and comprised 'Reveille', 'Loveliest of Trees', 'With rue my heart is laden', 'Twice a week the winter thorough', 'Along the field as we came by', 'Is my team ploughing', 'Into my heart an air that kills' and 'March'. It received its premiere at the Royal College of Music in November 1920 and is generally agreed to be less successful than *Ludlow and Teme*, which is far more often recorded and performed. In particular, the setting of 'Is my team ploughing' seems not to differentiate either in the vocal line or the accompaniment between the two speakers, and the instrumental coda at the end of the cycle has been criticised as both unnecessary and directionless. Part of the problem was that Gurney had carried out major revisions when the cycle had already been accepted for publication. The differences between the manuscript and the published version have been described as mostly irreconcilable, but a new performing edition of the piece was produced in 2013 and appropriately received its premiere at the Ludlow English Song Weekend that year.

Strenuous attempts had been made to find Gurney employment in order to introduce some stability into his rapidly unravelling life, but his mental state had deteriorated to such an extent that in September 1922 he was sent to a convalescent home for neurasthenics near Bristol. His problems turned out to be far worse than neurasthenia (a rather vague medical term that now included shell shock): he was in fact suffering from some form of paranoid schizophrenia and was shortly transferred to Barnwood House, a private asylum on the outskirts of Gloucester. Vaughan Williams generously guaranteed £100 towards the cost of his care and other friends and admirers raised funds, but his condition appeared to be worsening rather than improving and on 21 December he was taken to the London Mental Hospital at Dartford. Incarceration in an institution far from his beloved Gloucester was a particularly cruel fate for a man whose entire life and work were bound up with the English landscape across which he had spent so much time freely tramping. In this, as in much else, he felt a natural affinity with Edward Thomas, whom he never met but knew about through their mutual friend Jack Haines. Thomas had regularly walked the same part of the country as Gurney when he was living at Dymock and was, Gurney thought, 'English at the core', which counted for a great deal. Gurney's great admiration for Thomas's poems led him to set at least nineteen of them – six as *Lights Out*, for voice and piano, composed between 1918 and 1926, jointly dedicated 'To Minsterworth' and 'to the 2/5th Gloucesters', and his only completed song cycle apart from the two based on Housman. He also set a great many poems by Thomas's Dymock neighbour W.W. Gibson and other Georgian Poets such as Rupert Brooke, W.H. Davies, Walter de la Mare and Robert Graves. In a memorial edition of *Music & Letters* Vaughan Williams wrote that Gurney was composing his songs at a time when the Georgian Poets 'had just rediscovered England and the language that fitted the shy beauty of their own country. Gurney has found the exact musical equivalent both in sentiment and in cadence to this poetry.'

The empathy Gurney felt for Thomas was increased when he learned that the poet had suffered from severe bouts of depression. He believed that Thomas 'had the same sickness of mind I have – the impossibility of serenity for any but the shortest space'. One of those who visited Gurney in Dartford was Thomas's widow, Helen, who on one occasion took along her husband's 'well-used ordnance maps of Gloucester':

This proved to have been a sort of inspiration, for Ivor Gurney at once spread them out on his bed and he and I spent the whole time I was there tracing with our fingers the lanes and byeways and villages of which he knew every step and over which Edward had walked. He spent the hour in re-visiting his beloved home, in spotting a village or a track, a hill or a wood and seeing it all in his mind's eye, a mental vision sharper and more actual for his heightened intensity. He trod, in a way we who were sane could not emulate, the lanes and fields he knew and loved so well, his guide being his finger tracing the way on the map. It was most deeply moving, and I knew that I had hit on an idea that gave him more pleasure than anything else I could have thought of. For he had Edward as his companion in this strange perambulation and he was utterly happy.

Gurney continued intermittently to write poetry and work at his music, and he published his two Housman cycles in 1923 and 1926 respectively. He would remain at Dartford until he died of tuberculosis in 1937.

Between the Acts

Gurney's two cycles were part of a new upsurge in *A Shropshire Lad*'s musical afterlife during the 1920s and 1930s. Between the two world wars some 100 settings were made of poems from Housman's volume, either as individual songs or as parts of song cycles – and this does not take into account the songs that began to appear after 1922 when composers turned their attention to *Last Poems*. Like those composed before and during the First World War, these songs vary in quality, and the majority of them have failed to keep a place in the repertoire. Of those that have, the most significant are settings by E.J. Moeran, John Ireland, Vaughan Williams and C.W. Orr, although mention should be made of two individual songs by Cecil Armstrong Gibbs (1899–1960) and Muriel Herbert (1897–1984). Gibbs, whose family wealth derived from the manufacture of the well-known toothpaste and other toiletries, was a child prodigy who was supposedly able to improvise tunes on the piano before he learned to speak and whose first song was composed at the age of five. Although he wrote choral and stage music, he remains best known for his songs, in particular those setting the poems of his friend Walter de la Mare. His one setting of Housman, 'When I was one-and-twenty' for voice and piano, dates from 1921, when Gibbs himself was twenty-two, and its beautiful, wistful tune more than holds its own among the much better known settings from this period. Women composers of the early twentieth century were even more likely than their male counterparts to slip from history, but Muriel Herbert is among those who have been rediscovered in recent years. Born in Sheffield and brought up in Liverpool, she won a scholarship to the Royal College of Music in 1917 and studied composition there with Stanford. Her most active period as a composer was the 1920s, before her marriage in 1928 and the subsequent birth of her two children, the younger of whom became a well-known biographer and critic under her married name of Claire Tomalin. Herbert's setting of 'Loveliest of trees' for voice and piano is very much of its period but, with its subtly descending accompaniment suggesting falling blossom, is nonetheless touching and effective and deserves a place in the repertoire.

After demobilisation E.J. Moeran had returned to the Royal College of Music to take up his studies and began collecting folk songs once more, publishing them in the *Journal of the English Folk-Song Society*. His arrangements for voice and piano of some of the songs he had collected were published as *Six Folksongs from Norfolk* in 1924 and *Six Suffolk Folksongs* in 1931. Before heading for East Anglia, however, he had returned to Shropshire with his second Housman cycle, *Ludlow Town* for baritone and piano, written in 1920 and first performed at the Wigmore Hall in December 1924, the year they were published. The cycle consists of 'When smoke stood up from Ludlow', 'Say, lad, have you things to do?', 'Farewell to barn and stack and tree' and 'The lads in their hundreds', and deserves to be better known than it is. Moeran tended to choose the more rural and locally specific of Housman's poems to set – though he wrote most of the songs before he went to live just over the Shropshire border at Kington, and composed ''Tis time I think, by Wenlock Town' (1925) while travelling on a train between London and Westbury in Wiltshire. The English countryside always attracted him, however, and was the inspiration of much of his music, and it was no doubt Housman's generic landscape that drew him to these poems as much as their mood. Perhaps because his own life was distinctly troubled, Moeran is finely attuned to the melancholy of the poems, which he often brings out in the questioning piano part of his settings. He revised his earlier setting of 'Far in a western brookland' in 1925, and in 1931 set 'Loveliest of trees, the cherry now' and the first two of three versions of 'Oh fair enough are sky and plain'. This last song was one that seemed to preoccupy him. Although he professed to think the final version, completed in 1934, the best, he did not destroy earlier ones and when the song was published in 1957, seven years after his death, it was in the first and simplest version – though all three have now been recorded. Having spent so much time on this poem about a lad standing on 'the cressy brink' of a river and imagining himself drowning, it is a grim irony of the kind Housman would have appreciated that it was water that finally claimed Moeran. Having descended into alcoholism, and fearing that he would go mad and be sent to an asylum, he retired to Kenmare in County Kerry, where in December 1950 he suffered a stroke while standing on the pier and died when he fell into the water.

Moeran's tutor at the Royal College of Music, John Ireland, was born in Cheshire in what he called 'a pleasant country place'. He too was inspired by landscape, particularly by two of the places in which he lived, Sussex and the Channel Islands. The former is evoked in both his piano piece *Amberley Wild Brooks* (1921) and *A Downland Suite* (1936), the latter in *An Island Spell* (part of his *Decorations* for solo piano, 1912–13) and *Sarnia: An Island Sequence* (also for piano, 1940–1). The writer Jocelyn Brooke, whose opinion Ireland said he rated higher than that of any music critic, tried to suggest the particular quality of the composer's music, drawing a parallel with Housman. Recalling the anxious summer of 1939, in which war became inevitable, Brooke wrote: 'In the verse of Yeats or Housman, in certain passages of Delius or John Ireland, I would detect the same quality: a kind of remote, nostalgic awareness of some legendary past.' Like Housman, Ireland seemed to speak directly to Brooke:

Ireland's music has the quality of a personal communication which, if one happens to be, so to speak, on the right 'wavelength', seems to be addressed to oneself alone [. . .] much of his music corresponds almost uncannily with certain moods and emotions which one recognizes as part of one's own experience, associated in the main with the English countryside and with the tutelary genius of a particular place: the sense of

> old, forgotten far-off things
>   And battles long ago.

For Brooke, this music evoked 'a country of the mind to which I find myself returning, with a recurrent nostalgia, over and over again'.

There was, however, another aspect of Housman's poetry that particularly drew Ireland to it. Whether or not Vaughan Williams or any of the other composers of the period recognised a homosexual subtext in Housman's poetry is open to question, but Ireland was certainly 'in the know', and indeed 'on the right wavelength', as Brooke put it. When choosing titles for their songs, most composers used those supplied by Housman where they existed, or – as was more often the case – the first lines of the poems, either in full ('Far in a western brookland', 'With rue my heart is laden') or in a shortened form ('Loveliest of trees', 'The lads in their hundreds'). In almost every instance, Ireland chose his own titles, and in doing so made the poems reflect his own emotional difficulties. His early setting of 'March', for example, dispensed with Housman's two opening stanzas about astrology and animals, starting straight in with 'The boys are up the woods with day / To fetch the daffodils away', and took its title, 'The Heart's Desire', from the poem's final verse.

Boys and the heart's troubling desires were something of a preoccupation for Ireland, and both his Housman cycles were dedicated to a former chorister at St Luke's Church in Sydney Street, Chelsea, where he was organist and choirmaster from 1904 to 1926. The diminutive son of a local picture-framer, Arthur George Miller joined the St Luke's choir during the First World War, when he was about ten, and remained a close friend of Ireland for many years. During the 1920s he was the dedicatee of several of the composer's most intensely felt works, including the two Housman cycles, *The Land of Lost Content* and *We'll to the Woods No More*. He is also presumed to be the unacknowledged inspiration behind other compositions. *Two Songs*, for example, written in early 1920, set poems by Philip Sidney and Aldous Huxley, the first of which ('My true-love hath my heart, and I have his, / By just exchange one for the other given') suggests mutual love, while the latter ('Thick-flowered is the trellis / That hides our joys') suggests secrecy. Both are set simply for 'voice and piano', but one can safely assume that Ireland intended them to be sung by a male singer, which is the current practice. A few months later Ireland began work on *The Land of Lost Content*, also for voice and piano and written for Gervase Elwes, in which he set six of Housman's poems. It starts conventionally enough with 'The Lent Lily', which is similar in subject matter to 'The Heart's Desire'. From boys and girls gathering flowers in springtime, we move on to 'Ladslove', a distinctly Uranian title which emphasises the homosexual nature of 'Look not in my eyes'. 'Goal and Wicket' depicts a lad in 'Twice a week the winter thorough' playing sports in an attempt to keep sorrow at bay. The reason for his sorrow may be explained by the next song, which sets 'If truth in hearts that perish' as 'The Vain Desire'. Further vain desires are apparent in 'The Encounter', a title which focuses our attention on the glance exchanged between the poet and the redcoat in 'The street sounds to the soldiers' tread'. The cycle ends with an 'Epilogue' in which there are further exchanges of looks between lads in a setting of 'You smile upon your friend to-day'.

The cycle seems related both to the *Two Songs* and to other compositions from this period. *On a Birthday Morning* for solo piano bore the dedication 'Pro amicitia' (for friendship), and the birthday it was celebrating was that of Miller, who became seventeen on 22 February 1922, a date which is added to the score. Miller's subsequent birthdays would be similarly commemorated, as were outings the pair made in Ireland's car to Dorset, Somerset and Wiltshire, visiting historical sites. The setting of Christina Rossetti's 'When I am dead, my dearest', for example, is dedicated 'To A.G.M.: Cerne Abbas, June 1925', while the tardy completion of *Three Songs* (Emily Brontë's 'Love and Friendship', the anonymous 'Friendship in Misfortune' and D.G. Rossetti's 'The One Hope') in July 1926 meant that it had to be retrospectively dedicated 'for February 22, 1926', which was Miller's twenty-first birthday. Ireland's second Housman cycle, *We'll to the Woods No More* (written 1926–7), was dedicated 'To Arthur: in memory of the darkest days'. This darkness seems to have been connected with an unexpected change in Ireland's emotional life. In October 1926 he left St Luke's and two months later married a seventeen-year-old pianist thirty years his junior called Dorothy Phillips, with Miller acting as witness. Miller himself married the following year, though he and Ireland remained close. Ireland's marriage, perhaps predictably, proved short-lived and was probably unconsummated; the couple divorced in September 1928.

It was against this background that Ireland wrote his second Housman cycle, which sets the epigraph and 'When I would muse in boyhood' from *Last Poems*, while a third movement for piano only titled 'Spring will not wait' is prefaced with a quotation from ''Tis time I think by Wenlock town', a poem Ireland had previously set as 'Hawthorn Time' (1919). This is a cycle of yearning regret, signalled by the first lines of the first song: 'We'll to the wood no more, / The laurels all are cut'. Ireland's setting of this poem, which was derived from what Housman called 'an old French nursery rhyme', is particularly impassioned and despairing. The second song recalls similar 'wild green woods', where the speaker spent his boyhood dreaming of finding 'friends to die for'. These friends are found and prove 'hearts I lost my own to', a line that recalls the Sidney poem Ireland had set in *Two Songs*, but without its sense of happy reciprocation: in Housman's poem the friends go abroad and die, as Moses Jackson would do. The third movement also alludes to the recollection of happier times in the English countryside, now irretrievably lost. It begins rather more optimistically than the two songs, but gradually becomes increasingly sombre and towards the end quotes from the music that accompanied the repeated 'no more' in the first song. The cycle is both true to the mood of Housman and appears to reflect Ireland's own circumstances.

Ireland's personal life continued to be complicated. By the time his marriage was dissolved he had met Helen Perkin, another young pianist, the same age as his former wife. He appears to have been almost as infatuated with her as he had been with Arthur Miller, a troubled shift in devotion reflected in his *Songs Sacred and Profane*, written between 1929 and 1931. Whether or not Ireland had planned to propose to Perkin or whether he had been warned off marriage by his earlier venture into matrimony is unclear, but he was deeply upset when she married someone else in 1934, and from this time composed works in which his appreciation of boys became even less guarded. His original intention had been to call the central movement of the contemporaneous *Sarnia* 'Boyslove' (it was inspired by, and dedicated to, the ten-year-old son of the proprietor of a hotel in Guernsey where Ireland was a resident, and was eventually published as 'In a May morning'), while his 1943 *Fantasy Sonata* for clarinet and piano is subtitled 'Ode to Giton', a reference to the sixteen-year-old lover of the narrator in Petronius's *Satyricon*.

He had returned to Housman for inspiration for the first of his *Three Pastels* of 1941 for solo piano, 'A Grecian Lad', which was prefaced with lines from 'Look not in my eyes, for fear'. Housman, who had refused Ireland permission to print the whole of 'Into my heart an air that kills' at the head of the score of *The Land of Lost Content*, was no longer around to object, and one wonders what he would have made of this appropriation, especially given that the other two *Pastels* were archly titled 'The Boy Bishop' and 'Puck's Birthday'.

While it seems clear what it was about Housman's poetry that so appealed to the tortured and repressed John Ireland, Charles Wilfred Orr was an obsessive of a different order. He wrote only thirty-five songs (and little else), twenty-four of which set poems from *A Shropshire Lad* and *Last Poems*. Like Gurney, he was a Gloucestershire lad, born in Cheltenham in 1893, the son of a captain in the Indian army who had died of tuberculosis shortly before his son's birth. Orr suffered from poor health, which interrupted his education (he left school at fifteen) and kept him from serving abroad in the First World War, despite his having gained a commission in the Coldstream Guards. Encouraged by Frederick Delius, whom he had boldly approached in a Lyons Corner House after a concert, he enrolled at the Guildhall School of Music in 1917 to study composition, but he found his tutor's lack of appreciation of contemporary music stifling and left in 1919 to spend a summer studying counterpoint with E.J. Dent. Through Delius he met Philip Heseltine (otherwise the composer Peter Warlock), who introduced him to musical circles in London and arranged for the publication of his earliest songs.

Orr's first encounter with Housman was when he heard Graham Peel's 'In summertime on Bredon'. He bought a 1914 edition of *A Shropshire Lad*, which he kept all his life: 'I carried [it] about with me everywhere, learning almost all of the poems by heart, and hoping against hope that one day I might be able to set some of them in a way that Wolf or Schubert might have approved'. Like Willa Cather and E.M. Forster before him, he made a tour of Shropshire, photographing the places named in the poems. He even managed to slip into one of Housman's lectures at Cambridge, though the two men never met. Orr made his first Housman setting, 'When the lad for longing sighs', in 1921, and in 1923 published *Two Songs from 'A Shropshire Lad'* ('Loveliest of Trees' and ''Tis Time, I Think, by Wenlock Town'). He followed these with nine further individual settings, five of which were collected in 1927 as *Five Songs from 'A Shropshire Lad'*. His *Cycle of Songs from 'A Shropshire Lad'* (1934) set seven poems and was followed by *Three Songs from 'A Shropshire Lad'* in 1940, and individual settings of 'The lads in their hundreds to Ludlow come in for the fair', 'The Isle of Portland', 'Soldier from the wars returning' and 'In valleys green and still'.

When Orr could not find a British publisher for his settings he had the idea of getting them published in Germany or Austria. He therefore applied for permission to have the poems translated into German, a written request across the corner of which Housman wrote 'Refuse. A.E.H.' before returning it to Richards. After the Second World War, Orr and his wife ran a bookshop in Stroud, not far from where they lived at Painswick in Gloucestershire. Increasingly deaf and feeling himself neglected, he had more or less given up composing; after 'In valleys green and still', written in 1952, he produced only five more songs, the last of them in 1957. He spent part of his remaining years compiling a list of all the musical settings of Housman he could find, a task that remained incomplete at his death in 1976.

Orr had his distinguished admirers, including Delius, Warlock, Bax, Eugene Goossens and Walter Legge, but he felt that he was insufficiently appreciated and could be spiky – he was, for example, generally dismissive of Butterworth's Housman settings and declared Vaughan Williams's 'Silent Noon' (a poem he had himself set) 'too much like a church voluntary'. In rejecting the folk-music influence that is apparent in many Housman settings for something more harmonically sophisticated, Orr was admirably ambitious, but somehow the music rarely coheres. His settings often start out well enough but they soon lose direction, being inclined merely to ramble, and have been not unfairly described by one expert in English song as 'indigestible'. 'If a composer were to take into account all the implications that can be read into Housman's verses, or indeed any other great lyric poet, I doubt he would ever set anything at all!' Orr wrote in 1973. 'For that matter, how exactly is *irony* to be conveyed in terms of melancholy and harmony?' This is a reasonable point, but most composers, with varying degrees of success, have relied upon the voice to do the work in attempting to capture the tone of the poems. Orr's setting of 'Is my team ploughing' suggests a ploughman having to turn some very heavy clods indeed; it livens up somewhat inappropriately when the friend describes the sweetheart lying down lightly; and its resolution conveys the irony of the fact that the girl is now sleeping with the dead man's friend by discordancy in the piano part, which itself stumbles on for a few inconclusive bars after the vocal part has ended. Although some of the songs are effective, Orr's musical choices, such as a determinedly unlyrical 'Loveliest of Trees, the Cherry' and the distinctly Highland flavour to his setting of 'Farewell to barn and stack and tree', can seem perverse.

Towards the end of his life Orr complained that he had 'never found any English singer manifest the slightest interest in my song efforts', which were rarely performed and even more rarely broadcast. Writing to Orr in 1935 to thank him for sending him the cycle of seven Housman songs, the conductor Eugene Goossens perhaps put his finger on why the composer was not more popular. Goossens had played violin at the first performance of Vaughan Williams's *On Wenlock Edge*, and told Orr: 'I must confess that for a long time I have considered it impossible for any other composer to realize the particular colour of Housman until your songs came along, for I consider all other settings of these poems by other composers are tawdry and unmeaning.' That said, he warned: 'There is so much in them which at first glance is lost to the reader, musically speaking I mean, of course. In other words, there are many subtleties which are not immediately apparent.' In addition he felt that

> the piano writing is terribly involved for the average, even though passably good, accompanist. I don't know what the critics have said about them, but I imagine that the difficulties offered by the piano accompaniments of the songs were, by some, severely criticised. As you know I do not approve of reducing things to the essence of simplicity and there is no earthly reason why an accompaniment should not be as complicated and involved as you have made yours in certain of these songs. But I am afraid you must resign yourself to many bad criticisms of performances lacking the brio and accuracy called for in the accompaniments of the seven songs you sent me.

He wondered whether Orr would consider orchestrating some of the songs. Orr never did, and it is only recently that his Housman settings have begun to come back into the repertoire. A recording of his complete songs was issued in 2012 by the baritone Mark Stone on his own independent label and required the combined forces of the Three Choirs Festival, the Ralph Vaughan Williams Trust, the Finzi Friends, the Housman Society and the Gloucestershire-based Langtree Trust to provide financial support for its production.

Another setting of Housman that has never quite secured its place in the repertoire is Vaughan Williams's *Along the Field* for the unusual combination of voice and solo violin. In April 1927 seven of the original nine settings were performed by the soprano Joan Elwes and the violinist Dettman Dressel in a Sunday concert of the Philharmonia Society in Bradford. Elwes repeated the performance with Marie Wilson, for whom Vaughan Williams had written *The Lark Ascending*, in October of that year. One of the songs was subsequently destroyed, and the published version consists of eight settings of poems from both *A Shropshire*

Lad and *Last Poems*. Vaughan Williams's writing here is as spare as his earlier cycle is rich, and this starkness suits the mood of Housman's poems, notably in the last song, 'With rue my heart is laden', but *Along the Field* is rarely performed or recorded.

Among the better-known composers in the inter-war period, Arnold Bax published settings of 'Far in a western brookland' and 'When I was one-and-twenty' in 1920 as components of his *Three Songs* for voice and piano. Gerald Finzi, perhaps inspired by his time in Painswick, wrote a number of Housman settings but completed none of them (fragments of ten remain). Herbert Howells also wrote several settings, but lost heart after an unfortunate encounter with Housman at High Table in Trinity:

> After regaling us for the first half of the meal with a lecture on suicide, he turned to me, knowing I was a composer, and said he hoped I'd never set any of his poems. I said I hadn't, although only that week I'd set 'Far in a Western Brookland'. There followed a vituperative dismissal of all that Vaughan Williams and Butterworth had done for all his verse in 'On Wenlock Edge' and the 'Shropshire Lad' songs and orchestral rhapsody which I did not have the courage to counter; but resolved that Housman should never see any of my settings during his lifetime, and later I destroyed them.

At a somewhat safer distance from Trinity College, the American composer Samuel Barber set 'With rue my heart is laden' in 1928 while still a student. It was published in 1934 as one of his *Three Songs for Voice and Piano*, Op. 2. Intentionally or otherwise, the opening piano chords are curiously reminiscent of Butterworth's 'Loveliest of trees'. Another renowned American composer, Bernard Herrmann, composed a piece in which the English musical idiom is deliberately evoked. *A Shropshire Lad* (1935) is one of Herrmann's five 'melodrams' for narrator and full orchestra written for the Columbia Workshop, an experimental series of radio dramas broadcast by CBS, of which Herrmann was musical director. Although unusual, this is not the first Housman setting for accompanied speaker: as early as 1915 a British composer called Kingsford Shortland composed 'Bredon Hill' for piano and reciter.

Herrmann's piece is built around three poems – 'Reveille', 'When I was one-and-twenty' and 'With rue my heart is laden' – selected by the speaker, David Ross. Herrmann 'combined these three into one melodram, which expresses the life of a man from his adolescence, through his youth, to his old age'. The music is 'based on the tone-scales of the English folk tune, and no attempt is made to follow specifically, word for word, the action of the verse'. Herrmann was born a very long way from Shropshire, in New York into a Jewish family of Russian origins, and was wholly urban. He had, however, studied music at New York University with Percy Grainger, the Australian composer who became a leading exponent of the English folk-song revival. This may explain why Herrmann's music for the melodram does indeed sound 'English'. From the same period comes John Woods Duke's rather sentimental 'Loveliest of trees', published in 1934, which is not only the best known of the American composer's many songs but remains one of the most popular of all Housman settings.

The same year that Duke's song was published, the composer Constant Lambert would declare in *Music Ho!*, his provocative and entertaining 'Study of Music in Decline', that 'since the Shropshire Lad himself published his last poem ten years ago it may without impertinence be suggested that it is high time his musical followers published their last songs. The ground might then be left clear for something less nostalgically consoling but more vital.' There was in fact a distinct decline in Housman settings from this period onwards. The most interesting of those few that were made were the *Five Housman Songs* for voice and piano composed by Lennox Berkeley in 1939 and 1940. Berkeley had fallen unrequitedly in love with Benjamin Britten and for some time lived with him in Suffolk. When Britten went to America in April 1939, Berkeley was left to pack up the house they had shared, and he began setting poems that reflected his own feelings about Britten, rather as John Ireland before him had written settings inspired by his own thwarted passions. Two of the poems were, appropriately, among those Housman had written about his parting from Moses Jackson, 'Because I liked you better' and 'He would not stay for me'. The first song in the cycle set 'The half-moon westers low, my love', a poem about two people separated by geographical distance, as both Housman and Jackson and Berkeley and Britten had been, and the two other poems had a homosexual subtext: 'The street sounds to the soldiers' tread' and 'Look not in my eyes, for fear'.

Berkeley sent four of the settings to Britten in America, ostensibly in the hope that the composer's new partner, the tenor Peter Pears, would perform them, but also perhaps to make Britten, who had treated him shabbily, realise what unhappiness he had caused. In the event, the songs remained unperformed and unpublished until after Berkeley's death, possibly because they were simply too personal or because the theme that ran through them was all too apparent. Berkeley had decided to dedicate them not to Britten, but to a promiscuous and highly unsatisfactory young airman called Peter Fraser, with whom he fell in love towards the end of 1940 and subsequently set up house. This troubled relationship lasted until Berkeley married in 1946, when the songs were put aside along with his homosexual past.

It is surprising that Britten himself did not set any Housman poems. One might have thought that their Englishness and their covert homosexuality would have held a particular appeal for him, but he may have thought that too many other composers had got there before him. This did not, however, prevent him from setting poems from the much-mined works of Thomas Hardy or Walter de la Mare. Nor did it prevent him from giving recitals with Peter Pears of Housman settings by Butterworth, Vaughan Williams and his old teacher John Ireland, or from making recordings of *On Wenlock Edge* and *The Land of Lost Content*. Of the latter cycle, which he and Pears performed at the Aldeburgh Festival in 1959, Britten wrote in a programme note: 'There have been many English composers to set Housman's poems, and none, to my mind, more sympathetically successful than Ireland. There is much in common between Ireland and Housman, who "in his strange, magical, musical, and at times sentimental way . . . seems to say good-bye to the vanishing peacefulness of the country, and to the freshness and innocence of its young men".'* It may well be that the overlap between his and Ireland's tastes and interests, as much as what he saw as the older

---

*The quotation is from a broadcast made earlier that year, by Britten's friend and sometime librettist William Plomer, to mark the centenary of Housman's birth.

composer's achievement, was precisely what prevented Britten from setting Housman himself.

Although settings of Housman's poetry had tailed off in the 1930s, the approach once more of war focused people's attention on Englishness. It seemed almost inevitable that once Britain was at war, the search for a piece of music that would evoke an 'England' once again under threat should light upon a piece inspired by *A Shropshire Lad*. Julius Harrison's *Bredon Hill* is a 'Rhapsody for Violin and Orchestra' very much in the tradition of *The Lark Ascending*. Like Housman, Harrison was a Worcestershire lad, born in 1885 at Stourport-on-Severn, around eleven miles due west of Bromsgrove. Harrison said that he was 'very much affected by the beauty of our Worcestershire countryside, and by its close association with some of the great events in our national history [. . .] to me, as with many other Worcestershire folk, this county seems to be the very Heart of England, and there is a song and a melody in each one of its lovely hills, valleys, meadows and brooks'. Harrison studied with Granville Bantock at the Birmingham and Midland Institute of Music and seemed destined for a career as a conductor, but wrote several orchestral works as a young man, including a *Worcestershire Suite* (1918), its movements named using local place-names: 'The Shawley Round', 'Redstone Rock', 'Pershore Plums' and 'The Ledbury Parson'. Having served as conductor of the Hastings Municipal Orchestra, Harrison returned to Worcestershire in the autumn of 1940 when he was appointed director of music at a local public school, Malvern College.

There are various stories about how Harrison came to write *Bredon Hill*, but the composer Elizabeth Poston, who was then director of music for the European Service of the BBC, learned that he was working on the piece and came to Malvern to listen to him playing it on the piano. Afterwards they drove off into the countryside 'on a perfect summer afternoon' to have 'a picnic tea in sight of Bredon Hill'. Poston realised that Harrison's composition would be ideal for a radio series titled *The Music of Britain*, and it received its world premiere on 29 August on the BBC's Empire Service, reminding those serving abroad of the England they had left behind. A month later it was broadcast to

America. Pearl Harbor was still several months away and a campaign of strenuous propaganda had been undertaken in the hope of persuading the United States to join the Allies. Given the popularity of Housman's poetry in America, it was a canny move to broadcast a piece of music based on *A Shropshire Lad* in support of the campaign. As Harrison said in the interview with Poston that formed part of the broadcast: 'we mustn't forget that this part of Worcestershire speaks of England at its oldest. It is the heart of Mercia, the country of Piers Plowman, and it is the spirit of Elgar's music too.' The overseas announcer, who introduced the piece as 'one of the loveliest works of the year – indeed, I would go so far as to say – of our own time', went on to make a similar point:

> It is a fact remarkable in itself that such music as this comes out of the present time. That it does, is perhaps the best witness to the eternal spirit of England. Julius Harrison, Worcestershire born of generations of countrymen, lives in sight of Bredon Hill. He has the love of our English countryside in his veins – a sense of it that you will hear in this lovely music, which springs and grows, and rises soaring – a true rhapsody – in expression of the words of Housman's poem:
>
>> Here of a Sunday morning
>> My love and I would lie,
>> And see the coloured counties,
>> And hear the larks so high,
>> Above us in the sky.

The sombre conclusion of Housman's poem is not permitted to cast its shadow over Harrison's piece. Here instead was the spirit of a timeless England, under threat but soaring triumphantly into the skies above a peaceful landscape that had to be defended at all costs.

V

ENGLISH SOLDIERS

All places, all ayres, make unto me one Country; I am in
England every where, and under any meridian.

Thomas Browne, *Religio Medici*

On 30 August 1911 Winston Churchill escaped the heat of London
to spend a few days at the old manor house of Mells in Somerset.
Although he was Home Secretary, Churchill had retained a keen
interest in international affairs since his spell in the Colonial Office,
and he had spent much of Parliament's summer recess preparing a
cabinet paper on 'Military aspects of the continental problem'. This
particular problem stemmed from what would become known as
the Agadir Crisis, the latest development in a long-running squabble
over Morocco between France and Germany that had almost led to
a European war in 1906. In a letter to Sir Edward Grey, the Foreign
Secretary, Churchill wrote that even in the beautiful surroundings
of Somerset in that famously lovely summer he 'could not think of
anything else but the peril of war': 'Sitting on a hilltop in the smiling
country which stretches round Mells, the lines I have copied [. . .] kept
running through my mind.' Those lines were the first two verses of
Housman's 'On the idle hill of summer' (XXXV). They clearly stuck
with Churchill, for he was to quote them again as the epigraph to his
chapter on Agadir in *The World Crisis 1911–1914*, published in 1923. This
was the first part of what would become a massive three-volume book

about the First World War, and when in February 1931 he published a single-volume abridgement as *The World Crisis, 1911–1918*, he used the two stanzas as the epigraph for the entire book.

Foreseeing the Somme

Though it may have sounded of the moment, Housman's poem had in fact been written in October 1895. It is one of several verses in *A Shropshire Lad* that are about the military calling and were partly inspired by the soldiering experiences of the poet's youngest brother, Herbert. 'One feels Housman foresaw the Somme,' Robert Lowell remarked, and these poems appear both to anticipate the First World War and to bridge the gap between a long English tradition of military verse and a very different way of writing about warfare that came to be known as 'war poetry'. The poem ends with Housman's hilltop idler joining the colours in full knowledge of his likely fate:

> East and west on fields forgotten,
>   Bleach the bones of comrades slain
> Lovely lads and dead and rotten;
>   None that go return again.
>
> Far the calling bugles hollo,
>   High the screaming fife replies,
> Gay the files of scarlet follow:
>   Woman bore me, I will rise.

If the line 'Lovely lads and dead and rotten' appears to anticipate the writing of such war poets as Wilfred Owen and Siegfried Sassoon, it is the 'scarlet' that places the poem in 1895, at the time of the South African wars, rather than in 1914. By the outbreak of the First World War men no longer marched away to the battlefields wearing the traditional scarlet in which earlier generations had fought. The red jackets were reputedly designed to disguise the blood of the wounded, but they made soldiers easy targets and this colourful uniform had been replaced by khaki. It is a curious fact, and a nice coincidence, that khaki dye was originally made from damsons, which were widely grown for this purpose rather than for eating in both Shropshire and Worcestershire. As the Shropshire-based gardening writer Katherine Swift put it, soldiers 'marched off to Gallipoli and the Somme with the khaki of Shropshire damsons on their backs' – though the demand was such that this natural dye was soon replaced by a chemical one.

Soldiering had traditionally been a means of escape from the daily grind for both the urban and the rural poor, and the recruiting sergeants Housman saw in the marketplace on his way to school in Bromsgrove had been familiar figures for several centuries. The most famous literary representation of this role was George Farquhar's play *The Recruiting Officer* (1706), in which two captains and a sergeant attempt to drum up army volunteers in Shrewsbury. Farquhar based his comedy on his own spell as a recruiting officer in Shropshire in 1704, and in his 'Epistle Dedicatory', which he addressed 'To all friends round the Wrekin' (a traditional Shropshire toast), he wrote:

'Twas my good fortune to be ordered some time ago into the place which is made the scene of this comedy. I was a perfect stranger to everything in Salop but its character of loyalty, the number of its inhabitants, the alacrity of the gentlemen in recruiting the army, with their generous and hospitable reception of strangers.

This character I found so amply verified in every particular, that you made recruiting, which is the greatest fatigue upon earth to others, to be the greatest pleasure in the world to me.

The kingdom cannot show better bodies of men, better inclinations for the service, more generosity, more good understanding, nor more politeness than is to be found at the foot of the Wrekin.

Given that Farquhar had used several people he had met in Shrewsbury as models for his characters, this generous tribute to the county and its people was perhaps wise; but the Salopians of his acquaintance share many of the qualities attributed to the Shropshire lads in Housman's poems.

A rather different view of military service was provided some ninety years later by Samuel Taylor Coleridge in the sermon he gave to Shrewsbury's Unitarian congregation, as reported by Hazlitt:

He made a poetical and pastoral excursion, – and to shew the fatal effects of war, drew a striking contrast between the simple shepherd boy, driving his team afield, or sitting under the hawthorn, piping to his flock, 'as though he should never be old,' and the same poor country-lad, crimped, kidnapped, brought into town, made drunk at an alehouse, turned into a wretched drummerboy, with his hair sticking on end with powder and pomatum, a long cue at his back, and tricked out in the loathsome finery of the profession of blood.

Though the tone is very far from that of Housman (Coleridge was preaching at the time of the Napoleonic Wars, when country lads were being press-ganged rather than volunteering to serve their country), the setting and vocabulary here startlingly suggest Housman Country *avant la lettre*, even down to the ever-youthful ploughboy who antic- ipates Housman's 'lads that will never be old' just down the road in Ludlow.

It was precisely the finery Coleridge so deplores that caught Housman's eye when he went on his trip to London as a schoolboy and admired the statue of Mercury in the British Museum. 'I think of all I have seen, what most impressed me is – the Guards,' he had writ- ten to his stepmother. 'This may be barbarian, but it is true.' On the cusp of sixteen, Housman was rather too old to retain the small boy's traditional enthusiasm for soldiers, and it is unclear just how innocent his interest was. It certainly seems less innocent when in 'The street sounds to the soldiers' tread' (XXII) 'A single redcoat turns his head' to look directly back at the admiring poet. One does not find this kind of glance, this kind of exchange, in Kipling.

Housman's knowledge of military life came largely from Herbert. 'The only one of the five brothers without studious inclinations', as Kate tactfully put it, Herbert gave up medical studies as soon as he reached his majority in 1889 in order to enlist as a private in the King's Royal Rifle Corps. He may not have been an intellectual – at King Edward's he won prizes for sporting events rather than for Latin – but he was a lively writer of letters, and those he sent home from postings abroad gave his brother many insights into the often hard lives of ordi- nary soldiers. Herbert was serving in Burma when in 1892 Housman sent him a copy of Kipling's just-published first volume of *Barrack-Room Ballads* as a twenty-fourth birthday present. 'The book that Alfred has sent me has been a delight to myself & comrades ever since I got it,' Herbert wrote home. 'There never was a man, & I should think never will be again, who understands "Tommy Atkins" in the rough, as he does.' Kipling was a journalist rather than a soldier, but he had moved in army circles at all levels while working in India and he did indeed thoroughly empathise with – and in these poems, which are written in an approximation of Cockney, quite literally give a voice to – 'Tommy', the professional ranker:

> I went into the theatre as sober as could be,
> They gave a drunk civilian room, but 'adn't none for me;
> They sent me to the gallery or round the music-'alls;
> But when it comes to fightin', Lord! they'll shove me in
>   the stalls . . .

'Probably you would find it difficult to understand his inimitable mixture of soldiers' slang & Hindustanee,' Herbert told his stepmother, '& it is also, of course, essentially a man's book.' A man's book it may have been, but it was hugely popular among the wider reading public, and many of the poems, such as 'Tommy', 'Gunga Din' and 'Danny Deever', became popular recital pieces. Herbert was the son of a middle-class solicitor and so did not talk in the way Kipling's soldiers do; but many of those he served alongside would have done. A large number of the poems in this first volume of *Barrack-Room Ballads* were set in India, where Herbert had also served, and these along with 'Mandalay' and 'Gentleman-Ranker', which is what he had served as, would have struck a particular chord. It was also a nice coincidence that Herbert's regiment was popularly known as the Greenjackets because their uniforms were dyed a dark camouflage colour called 'rifle-green', and this is mentioned by Kipling in another of the volume's poems, 'Soldier, Soldier'.

It is 'Soldier, Soldier' that seems faintly echoed in Housman's own most Kiplingesque poem, 'The New Mistress' (XXXIV). Whereas in Kipling's poem a returning soldier is urging the girlfriend of a dead comrade to 'go look for a new love', in Housman's the soldier, having been given the brush-off by his lover, takes the army itself as his 'new mistress'. Housman borrows the poem's metre and rhyme scheme from the verses of 'Tommy', but while he represents the speech patterns of a ranker, his Shropshire lad speaks in an accentless English:

> 'I will go where I am wanted, to a lady born and bred
> Who will dress me free for nothing in a uniform of
>   red . . . '

Elsewhere in the book, Housman adopts the viewpoint of a romantic onlooker – though one perfectly aware of the cost of war – and it is this viewpoint that particularly sets him apart from Kipling.

Housman reported that when he submitted his poems to their original publisher, the company's manager 'was particularly captivated with the military element; so much so that he wanted me at first to make the whole affair, with Herbert's assistance, into a romance of enlistment. I had to tell him this would probably take me another thirty-six years. The next thing was, he thought it would be well to have a design on the cover representing a yokel in a smock frock with a bunch of recruiting-sergeant's ribbons in his hat.' Housman resisted this notion, and the volume's military element remained small though pervasive. *Last Poems* would be far more military in its themes than *A Shropshire Lad*: its first eight poems all feature soldiers, perhaps because Herbert had been killed in action in October 1901 while serving in South Africa, but also because the volume was assembled in the wake of the First World War, in which Housman had lost a nephew. *A Shropshire Lad* itself opens with a poem about soldiers, '1887', which salutes the Salopians who have died for the Empire, those 'Shropshire names' inscribed on tombstones in Asia and 'the Severn's dead' lying beside the Nile. More specifically, these soldiers are 'Lads of the Fifty-third', which is to say the 53rd (Shropshire) Regiment of Foot, which in the Childers army reforms of 1881 had been reorganised as the King's Light Infantry (Shropshire Regiment). In 'The Recruit', which stands third in the volume, a Shropshire lad is encouraged to leave his home town of Ludlow and enlist in the colours. This urging is done in full knowledge of both the demands and the dangers of soldiering already outlined in the volume's first poem: as in '1887', the best a soldier can hope for if he dies is that he will be remembered by his friends. The heroic impulse is also urged in 'The Day of Battle' (LVI), though rather more pragmatically since it suggests that death is inevitable whether one stands to fight or runs away in the heat of battle. It begins with a bugle call echoing, as it were, from 'On the idle hill of summer'. The difference is in the response, for this lad is already and reluctantly on the battlefield rather than safely dreaming in the English countryside, where the sound of a similarly 'far' bugle causes the hearer to enlist.

While 'The New Mistress', 'The Day of Battle' and 'On the idle hill of summer' are spoken in the voices of soldiers, the more poignant poems look on from a distance with a mixture of envy and pity. The one that particularly caught the imagination of the First World War generation, and is frequently cited as if it *were* a First World War poem, is 'The lads in their hundreds to Ludlow come in for the fair' (XXIII). Its vivid concluding lines, in particular, brought some measure of comfort to those mourning the loss of young men:

> They carry back bright to the coiner the mintage of man,
>   The lads that will die in their glory and never be old.

As the bugle call in 'The Day of Battle' looks back to the one in 'On the idle hill of summer', so the Ludlow setting of this poem looks back to 'The Recruit'. Housman placed it in the volume immediately after 'The street sounds to the soldiers' tread', and in both poems the speaker stands apart from, but longs to be part of, the groups of men he describes. There is a distinct wistfulness in the glance exchanged between the speaker and the soldier in the first poem, two men separated not only by the gulf that always lies between the soldier and the civilian, but almost certainly also by class, and possibly by desire – though the ambiguity here adds to the poem's tension: 'What thoughts at heart have you and I / We cannot stop to tell'. When Housman writes 'Such leagues apart the world's ends are, / We're like to meet no more' there is perhaps an acknowledgement that the two men themselves are leagues apart already. It is also possible, particularly in view of Herbert's career, that this soldier's final destination is India, and Housman's awareness of those leagues between Britain and the subcontinent was made acute because they were what separated him from Moses Jackson. The speaker ends the poem by wishing the soldier well, just as in the poem that follows it in the volume he stands aloof from the Ludlow lads and yearns to 'wish them farewell / And watch them depart on the way that they will not return'. The tone, however, is entirely different, perhaps because these lads are still civilians, like the speaker. Indeed, although the poem is generally treated as war poetry, there is nothing specific in it to suggest that the 'glory' they will die in is military: it could simply be the glory of youth, a notion that would be very familiar to a classicist such as Housman. To that extent, the poem relates more closely to such verses as 'To an Athlete Dying Young' (XIX), which also gained an additional resonance during the First World War because many of those young men who died in it were celebrated in their obituaries as gifted sportsmen who had carried the values of the playing field onto the battlefield.

It was the war itself that made Housman a war poet. At the time he was writing, what we now think of as war poetry barely existed. This is not to say that no one wrote poems about warfare; indeed, some of the most famous poems in the language took incidents of war as their subject: Wolfe's 'The Burial of Sir John Moore after Corunna', Byron's 'The Destruction of Sennacherib', Tennyson's 'The Charge of the Light Brigade' and Newbolt's 'Vitaï Lampada'. These were not, however, poems written in the heat of battle, or even in snatched moments of peace behind the front line, as war poetry would be. Byron apart, these were not men who had seen, or would ever see, military action. Wolfe was an Irish clergyman in County Tyrone; Newbolt was a barrister at Lincoln's Inn, rather than a public-school officer in the Sudan; and Tennyson wrote his famous poem at some considerable distance from the Crimea, while living on the Isle of Wight. Even Byron had yet to do any soldiering when he wrote his poem – which in any case describes the most safely distant of all these battles: one that took place in 701 BC. This is not to accuse these poets of being armchair warriors; it is merely to say that there is a difference between 'military verse' written by distant onlookers and 'war poetry' written by people on the ground. This distance between the military poet and the action he imagines is starkly acknowledged by William Makepeace Thackeray in his Crimean War poem 'The Due of the Dead':

> I sit beside my peaceful hearth,
>   With curtain drawn and lamp trimmed bright
> I watch my children's noisy mirth;
>   I drink in home, and its delight.
>
> I sip my tea, and criticise
>   The war, from flying rumour caught;
> Trace on the map to curious eyes,
>   How here they marched, and there they fought.
>   [. . .]
> Meanwhile o'er Alma's bloody plain
>   The scathe of battle has rolled by –
> The wounded writhe and groan – the slain
>   Lie naked staring to the sky.

The First World War changed all this, chiefly because it was not, as had previously been the custom, fought in far-off places by professionals; instead, much of it was fought just across the English Channel by civilian volunteers and conscripts, most of whom were far better educated than Kipling's Tommies as a result of the Education Acts of the nineteenth century. Literacy had spread, and the founding of popular and widely available newspapers meant that the population was far more aware of what was going on in the world than had previously been the case. Most of the soldier-poets were of the officer class, expensively educated at public schools, but even an East End working-class ranker such as Isaac Rosenberg had been given the basic tools to become a writer and record his experiences.

Many of those who volunteered marched off to the front with high ideals that would be confounded by the squalid realities of modern industrialised warfare. Merciful euphemisms persisted, both in the rhetoric of commemoration and in the letters serving men wrote to the families of those killed in action. It was important to believe, both while the war was going on and during its aftermath when the cost was being counted, that the Dead should be Glorious, that they had Fallen in Battle and in doing so made the Supreme Sacrifice. It was necessary to tell families that every dead soldier had been a credit to his regiment, had been both popular and courageous, and had died instantly without suffering. The war poets, and many of those who subsequently wrote war memoirs, felt the need to tell instead what they saw as the truth: that the courage of some men had failed, that some were dangerously incompetent soldiers, that many died ignobly either in ill-planned assaults or stupid and avoidable accidents, that many more were blown to irrecoverable pieces or died in prolonged agony. Housman was not a war poet in this sense, as can be judged by his provocative assertion in 1933 that 'The Great War cannot have made much change on the opinions of any man of imagination.' This is more or less a refutation before the event of the generally agreed notion that the First World War changed everything, not least the opinions of those men of imagination such as Wilfred Owen, Siegfried Sassoon and Robert Graves, who became spokesmen for their generation. Housman undoubtedly enjoyed provoking people, but this notorious pronounce-ment was almost certainly wholly sincere. It is the remark of someone undeceived, someone who already knew the cost of war because his brother had been killed in one, someone to whom, on another front, the worst had already happened but who described himself in general terms as a 'pejorist'.

> Hope lies to mortals
>   And most believe her,
>   But man's deceiver
> Was never mine

he wrote with proud defiance in a poem drafted in September 1917, while British troops floundered in the mud of Passchendaele.

Although Housman began this poem, 'I to my perils', in 1917, he was still working on it in the 1920s and it remained unpublished during his lifetime. He published only four poems during the First World War, his main contribution to the war effort being financial rather than literary.

Too old to fight, he sent £100 to his three nephews to help them equip themselves for the trenches, and the rest of his bank balance to the Exchequer. Only one of the poems he published during the war was written in direct response to it: 'Epitaph on an Army of Mercenaries', which appeared in *The Times* on 31 October 1917 beneath the day's leader on 'The Anniversary of Ypres'. The others were all written before the war. 'As I gird on for fighting' first appeared in March 1917 in *Blunderbuss*, a magazine produced at Trinity College, Cambridge, for military cadets, but it was drafted in 1895. 'Her strong enchantments failing' was published in a variant form as 'The Conflict' in a supplement to the December 1915 edition of the *Edwardian*, the magazine of St Edward's School in Bath, in memory of Kate's son Lieutenant Clement Aubrey Symons, an alumnus of the school who had been killed in action that September; but it was written in 1894–5. 'Oh hard is the bed they have made him' was published (unsigned and as 'Illic Jacet') in the same issue of the magazine, but had already appeared, in a slightly different version, in the *Academy* in February 1900. These poems, like 'Here dead we lie because we did not choose' and several of the poems in *A Shropshire Lad*, appear to belong to the period of the First World War and have even been included in anthologies devoted to that conflict. Housman himself evidently thought the poems timeless, applicable to any conflict. When, for example, he received news of Clement's death, he sent Kate 'Illic Jacet', acknowledging that they were 'some verses that I wrote many years ago' but evidently feeling they suited the occasion. The poem has been incorrectly supposed to be about Herbert, but it was written and published before his death. *Illic jacet*, meaning 'Over there lies', is a variation on the usual tombstone inscription *Hic jacet*, 'Here lies . . . ', and so suggests death in a far-off place, and this would apply to any soldier who was buried where he fell on a far battlefield. This gave it a particular poignancy during the First World War, since the dead were not repatriated.

The title of Housman's only true First World War poem, 'Epitaph on an Army of Mercenaries', seems provocative, since he published these verses at a time when the customary rhetoric was of honour, love of country and noble self-sacrifice; but both as a scholar and a poet Housman was always attentive to the exact meanings of words.

The poem refers to the original British Expeditionary Force, made up of professional soldiers who were technically mercenaries because they took the king's shilling in exchange for fighting wherever the army sent them. At the same time, Housman was rebutting German propaganda that dismissed the BEF as nothing *but* mercenaries. The poem looks back to the autumn of 1914, when this comparatively small army of professional soldiers managed to hold the strategically vital town of Ypres against the Germans but was more or less wiped out in the process.

> These, in the day when heaven was falling,
>   The hour when earth's foundations fled,
> Followed their mercenary calling
>   And took their wages and are dead.
>
> Their shoulders held the sky suspended;
>   They stood, and earth's foundations stay;
> What God abandoned, these defended,
>   And saved the sum of things for pay.

The Scottish politician and writer William Darling declared that the poem 'does in eight lines what the official histories of the war cannot do in volumes', while Kipling described the two brief stanzas as 'the finest lines of poetry written during the war'; but it was the poems of *A Shropshire Lad* which people had taken to their hearts and would take to the trenches.

In Every Pocket

The appeal of Housman's poetry was particularly strong to those who had been classically educated at public schools, where pupils studied and learned by rote carefully selected poems from *The Greek Anthology* and would go on to become junior officers in the war. The standard edition of these poems was *Select Epigrams from the Greek Anthology*, first published in 1890 with a substantially revised edition in 1906. It was edited by Housman's friend and fellow scholar J.W. Mackail, who provided parallel prose translations for the general reader; but the book was also available in a pocket edition in which the original Greek and the English translations were placed in different volumes and sold separately. This meant that schoolboys could be given the Greek volume without its English 'crib' in order to do exercises, then be referred to the English volume to be shown how it should be done, and Mackail's edition became one of the key texts of classical education at public schools.

Mackail was the son-in-law of Edward Burne-Jones, and his book not only had a Pre-Raphaelite illustration on its title page, but a Pre-Raphaelite tinge throughout. As Cyril Connolly put it, Mackail's English translations 'exhaled pessimism and despair, an over-ripe perfection in which it was always late afternoon or the last stormy sunset of the ancient world, in which the authentic gloom of Palladas was outdone by that attributed to Simonides, Callimachus, or Plato'. As a schoolboy at Eton, Connolly 'knew all the sceptical epigrams by heart and most of those about love and death and the fate of youth and beauty'. His response to the book had been courted by Mackail in the introduction to his anthology's revised edition:

> For over all life there lay a shadow. Man, a weak and pitiable crea-ture, lay exposed to a grim and ironic power that went its own way careless of him, or only interfered to avenge its own slighted majesty [. . .] Fate seemed to take a sardonic pleasure in confounding expec-tation, making destruction spring out of apparent safety, and filling life with dramatic and memorable reversals of fortune.
>
> And beside the bolts launched by fate, life was as surely if more slowly weighed down by the silent and ceaseless tide of change against which nothing stood fixed or permanent, and which swept the finest and most beautiful things away soonest.

These words might equally apply to *A Shropshire Lad*, although Housman denied that his poetry had been particularly influenced by *The Greek Anthology*. 'Of course I have read it, or as much of it as is worth reading, but with no special heed,' he wrote in 1933. Regardless of whether or not Housman took special heed of *The Greek Anthology*, he certainly took heed of its editor. In addition to being a contemporary classical scholar Housman admired (which put him in a fairly rarefied category), Mackail was also a man whose literary taste he trusted. Housman not only sent him copies of his edition of Manilius's *Astronomica* for comment, but also consulted him as to the proposed contents of *Last Poems*.

It is scarcely surprising that with romanticised classical ideas being inculcated at their schools the Edwardians had made a cult of the fleetingness of youth. The literature of the period is suffused with an almost fatalistic sense that boys in particular are teetering upon the edges of both perfection and doom. As J.M. Barrie wrote to Arthur Quiller-Couch, whose son was about to leave Winchester College: 'An English boy has almost too good a time. Who would grudge it him, and yet he knows too well that the best is past by the time he is three-and-twenty.' This remark may owe something to Barrie's own psychology; but the idea of boys reaching their apogee during adolescence was very much in the Edwardian air, reflected not only in the huge popularity of sentimental novels of public-school life, but also (for example) in the comic yet often sinister stories of H.H. Munro, which he published under the pen name of Saki. Readers of Saki's novel *The Unbearable Bassington*, that proleptic (1912) anthem for doomed youth, would have nodded in agreement when the protagonist was described by his housemaster as one of those young men 'who are Nature's highly finished product when they are in the schoolboy stage'. Saki himself observed that 'To have reached thirty is to have failed in life.' Death seemed almost preferable to such a fate and, although well past thirty and very far from having failed in life, Munro would volunteer for active service and be killed on the Somme, his name incised on the Memorial to the Missing at Thiepval. This necessarily vast structure had been designed by Edward Lutyens, who poignantly enough had also created the sets for the first production (in 1904) of *Peter Pan*, Barrie's play about 'The Boy Who Wouldn't Grow Up'.

Barrie owed the idea for *Peter Pan* to his brother, who had died in a skating accident on the eve of his fourteenth birthday. Their mother had consoled herself with the thought that her lost boy would never grow old. A more immediate inspiration for the play was Barrie's friendship with the five sons of Arthur and Sylvia Llewelyn Davies. He had first encountered the two eldest, George and Peter, as small boys in Kensington Gardens, and he gradually befriended the entire family. When their parents died young in quick succession, Barrie adopted the boys. George would be killed in the trenches and Michael, the other son to whom Barrie was especially close, drowned with a friend when they were both undergraduates in what may have been a homosexual suicide pact or simply an accident. It is a small step from boys who wouldn't grow up to lads that will never be old, and it is no surprise to discover that Barrie read *A Shropshire Lad* 'year in, year out – over and over again'.

This fact is reported by Barrie's long-time secretary, Cynthia Asquith, in her biography of the playwright. Cynthia Asquith had herself suffered catastrophic losses in the First World War. Among the dead were her eldest and youngest brothers, Ego and Yvo Charteris, her first cousins George Wyndham, Perf Wyndham and Bim Tennant, and her brother-in-law Raymond Asquith. Her mother, Mary Elcho, had been the best friend of Frances Horner, the chatelaine of Mells, where Winston Churchill had recalled Housman's lines in the summer of 1911. One of Frances's daughters had been married to Raymond Asquith, and her elder son, Edward, was also killed in the war, along with most of the close circle of friends he had made at Eton and Balliol College, Oxford: Patrick Shaw-Stewart, Charles Lister, and Julian and Billy Grenfell. Many of these young men were the children of the Souls, a coterie of high-minded and self-regarding aristocrats and plutocrats – including the Wyndhams, the Lytteltons, the Elchos, the Tennants and the Grenfells – who congregated around the politician Arthur Balfour, and were connected by marriage, friendship, decorous flirtation and a certain amount of personal tragedy. The deaths in their early twenties of May Lyttelton (who may or may not have been secretly engaged to Balfour) and her sister-in-law Laura (née Tennant, and one of Mary Elcho's closest friends) had a profound effect on the circle, which consoled itself with frequent references to the beauty and blessedness of death and the radiance with which the expiring greeted and embraced it. The fact that May had died unprettily of typhoid and Laura as a result of giving birth to a child who succumbed to tubercular meningitis while still an infant seems not to have shaken this idealised view of death, and the slaughter of the next generation in the First World War was bathed in a similarly refulgent light. These young men may not have been the kind of lads Housman had in mind, but the notion that they had died in their glory and would never be old was one the Souls embraced wholeheartedly. Writing to Ettie Desborough about the death of her son Julian Grenfell, Cynthia Asquith commented: 'You were able to ensure him a supremely happy childhood and youth, and – in spite of the aching loneliness – it must be wonderful to think of him and all his glamour as so utterly unassailable – to know that he "carries back bright to the Coiner the mintage of man" and yet to feel that he had already found time to fulfil himself as the perfect Happy Warrior.' The line is Housman's – though it hardly needs saying that he did not allot the coiner a capital initial. It was presumably Cynthia who chose the full line ('They carry back bright to the coiner the mintage of man') to inscribe on the gravestone in the war cemetery at Sailly-Labourse of her brother Yvo, who was killed in action shortly after his nineteenth birthday having spent just five weeks at the front.

Given the losses suffered by this circle, it is hardly surprising that the legacy of the First World War is particularly palpable at St Andrew's Church at Mells. An equestrian statue of Edward Horner, modelled by Alfred Munnings on a plinth designed by Lutyens and originally intended to be placed in the nave, stands in a side chapel. Mounted on one end of the plinth is Horner's original and much-worn wooden grave-marker, brought back from the battlefield. Nearby is a memorial to Raymond Asquith consisting of a bronze wreath, also designed by Lutyens, above a Latin inscription cut into the stones of the wall by Eric Gill; Asquith's own original grave-marker hangs above a door. In the churchyard, dominated by an avenue of clipped yews again designed by Lutyens, is the grave of one of the war's leading poets, Siegfried Sassoon, buried at his request next to his spiritual advisor Ronald Knox, who had spent the last ten years of his life at the neighbouring manor house.

Before the First World War, Ronald Knox had been part of the Horner–Grenfell–Lister set at Eton and Balliol, and was particularly close to Patrick Shaw-Stewart, whose biography he wrote in 1920. Shaw-Stewart was, like Housman, widely considered one of the finest classical scholars of his generation. He was also one of those young soldiers who marched off to war with a copy of *A Shropshire Lad* in his pocket. He had long been a champion of Housman's poems, writing to a woman friend in March 1911: 'I implore you not to go about calling Housman "pretty" – all the great men wear him next to their heart, I assure you.' He served alongside another of Housman's great admirers, Rupert Brooke, in the Hood Battalion of the Royal Naval Division and, like many classically educated young men bound for Gallipoli, felt that he was following in the footsteps of the ancients. As Knox observed, 'the country he was going to was the scene of the campaign about which he probably knew more details than about any other in history', and shortly before boarding the *Grantully Castle* Shaw-Stewart wrote to a friend: 'It is the luckiest thing and the most romantic. Think of fighting in the Chersonese (hope you got the allusion from the Isles of Greece about Miltiades), or alternatively, if it's the Asiatic side they want us on, on the plains of Troy itself! I am going to take my Herodotus as a guide-book.' He had also packed his copy of the *Iliad*, and his letters home are filled with references to the classical world. It was while staying at the base camp on the island of Imbros, where he was able to look across to the site of Troy and see the sun set over Samothrace, that Shaw-Stewart would compose his only war poem. Written on the back flyleaf of his copy of *A Shropshire Lad*, which was found among his effects after his death, it has become one of the best known and most frequently anthologised poems of the First World War. Addressed to Achilles and inspired by the *Iliad*, it also clearly carries Housman's impress, as in these opening lines:

> I saw a man this morning
> > Who did not wish to die:
> I ask and cannot answer,
> > If otherwise wish I.

Next to their hearts, preferably in the breast pocket of their uniforms, was where Housman thought soldiers ought to carry their copies of his poems. The doubling in price of the book during the war, he complained to his publisher, 'diminishes the sale and therefore diminishes my chances of the advertisement to which I am always looking forward: a soldier is to receive a bullet in the breast, and it is to be turned aside from his heart by a copy of *A Shropshire Lad* which he is carrying there. Hitherto it is only the Bible that has performed this trick.' Although Housman would have needed to have published a considerably thicker volume in order for it to deflect a bullet, by 1914 those who had read and grown to love his poems far exceeded the few young men for whom he said he had written them, and if Robert Nichols's assertion that *A Shropshire Lad* was 'in every pocket' was something of an exaggeration, it nevertheless has some anecdotal support. 'We all had a copy of *The Shropshire Lad* in our pockets,' remembered Thomas Armstrong, the future director of the Royal Academy of Music who had served on the Western Front from 1917 onwards. Paying tribute in 1976 to his friend the composer Willie B. Manson, he wrote: 'Like many of our generation we were obsessed by *A Shropshire Lad*, and I have the copy that Manson gave me in 1914. The copy that I gave him was never found after his death. It must have been blown up with him.' In his chapter on 'War Books' in *The Private Papers of a Bankrupt Bookseller* (1931), William Darling described *A Shropshire Lad* as 'a favourite pocket-book'. His own copy was in fact a spoil of war, acquired at the front:

> It is the little Grant Richard's [sic] edition and I have it yet – its boards now fallen away from its 'innards'. There's no name, but the ring of a cup bottom is on the cover – a cup of tea has stood on it – by some camp bed I fancy. There is a writing though –
> 'Barrage lifts on the first objective 4.55.'
> It is written in indelible pencil which has run a little.

Darling remembered two men in particular who carried copies of the book with them: 'one – Hopper or Cooper – went out [i.e. died] in a raid some time in May up by the Vimy. The other was a Staff man, but when I saw it and remarked on it he had nothing to say. Was it too much for him or too little?' 'I first read *A Shropshire Lad* on the Messines Ridge,' another soldier recalled. 'A new officer said to me one evening, "Have you read this?", and he drew from his pocket a long, narrow, red edition of *A Shropshire Lad*. From that time I was a devotee of the great Housman.' The writer and editor A. St John Adcock was not a combatant, but he reported that when he was 'on a visit to the front in France and Belgium, during the war, the three volumes of verse that were greatly in demand among the soldiers of the new Army, down at the rest camps, were Browning's "Men and Women", Omar Khayyâm, and that excellent pocket edition of "The Shropshire Lad"'. Housman himself suggested that the book's popularity after the war was 'because so many soldiers, including at least one V.C., carried it in their pockets, and thus others got to know of it and bought it when they came home'.

After the war Housman received a letter from an American soldier that he kept for the rest of his life. The American related that he had been tending a wounded British soldier in France and had offered him his copy of *A Shropshire Lad* to read while he was recuperating. 'The man smiled and took from under his pillow a copy of his own, all tattered, torn and blood-stained. It had been in his pocket throughout the War from 1914, and he had written in it three other Housman poems' — presumably three of those published during the war. Housman's nephew Clement, who true to his uncle's poems 'had almost a hope and expectation of dying in battle', had similarly written out 'Her strong enchantments failing' (which had not at that point been published) in order to take it with him to the war.

It is easy to see why these poems were carried to the front. They were, after all, young men's poems, and the feelings they describe were intensified in wartime: close masculine friendships; a sense that life is unjust and that fate is against one; the notion that life is passing all too quickly and that death is always standing by, ready to harvest the young. As St John Adcock put it:

It is not so curious as it may seem at first blush that 'The Shropshire Lad', with its philosophically pessimistic outlook, should appeal to those men who had been in the firing line and were shortly going up again. For what is loosely called its pessimism is not so much that as a courageously stoical acceptance of the stern facts of human experience. The soldier who could find any pleasure at all in verse was in no mood, just then, for gracious sentiments or optimistic fantasies; he was up against stark realities; accustomed to the sight of death and the thought of its immanence [*sic*, for imminence], had shed nearly all his illusions, found a fearful and perhaps morbid joy in treating such things as a grim jest, and the honest facing of the truth in 'The Shropshire Lad', its wry, whimsical, indomitable realism, must have chimed with his own thoughts and strengthened him to endure that fate that is, in the long run, common to all men.

The journalist and publisher Holbrook Jackson tells an anecdote about an acquaintance who had been obliged to return to England because his business affairs in Central America had been affected by the war. When Jackson asked him how he was passing his time, the man replied: 'I am staying down at a military encampment near London, reading *A Shropshire Lad* to the soldiers, and, by gad! don't they love it!' A reason for this, Jackson suggests, is that many of the volume's poems 'move to the sound of bugles, and all of them are robust [. . .] Housman's soldier is brave in the great spirit.'

Dreams of England

Another reason that Housman's poems proved so popular during the war was that they were written not for a literary élite but for the ordinary reader. Their appeal, as Housman frequently suggested, was to the heart rather than the head, and those journeying abroad to face certain danger often wanted something to provide solace rather than intellectual stimulation. The unchanging, archetypal English landscape that Housman wrote about reminded soldiers of home, wherever that may have been. It seemed to matter little where combatants actually lived: the 'England' they were fighting for was more often than not portrayed as rural. 'They were summoned from the hillside, / They were called in from the glen' ran the opening lines of 'Keep the home fires burning', one of the war's most popular songs, rather as if no recruiting had taken place in urban areas. A well-known poster published in 1915 depicts a kilted soldier, standing beneath the slogan 'Y O U R C O U N T R Y ' S C A L L', gesturing towards an idealised landscape of small rolling hills criss-crossed with hedges and dotted with cattle, through which country lanes wind past thatched cottages covered with roses and surrounded by hollyhocks and dovecotes. 'Isn't this worth fighting for?' the poster demands: 'ENLIST NOW'. Not only was this not the kind of environment in which most potential recruits had grown up, it was also – despite the Highland soldier, who if he hadn't been raised in a city tenement would more likely have looked out over lochs and glens – a generically *English* image. Similarly, the view from the window in another well-known poster, 'WOMEN OF BRITAIN SAY – <u>GO</u>!', is of soldiers marching not through an urban street but against a backdrop of bosky downs. 'I always feel that I am fighting for England,' wrote Lieutenant Christian Carver to his brother from France in 1917. 'English fields, lanes, trees, English atmosphere, and good days in England.' As the poet Charles Hamilton Sorley put it: 'England remains the dream, the background: at once the memory and the ideal.'

In October 1914 Edward Thomas had written to his agent to say that he wanted to compile an anthology 'about England, English places and English life'. The agent thought the market was already flooded with such books, claiming that five had been published in the last week. Thomas's intention was to write 'an account of the name of England and its meaning, especially its emotional meaning [. . .] to show what is meant when a man speaks of England and especially since the war.' The book would eventually appear in 1915 under the title *This England*. 'This is an anthology from the works of English writers rather strictly so called,' Thomas wrote in a prefatory note: 'Building round a few most English poems like "When icicles hang by the wall", – excluding professedly patriotic writing because it is generally bad and because indirect praise is sweeter and more profound, – never aiming at what a committee from Great Britain and Ireland might call complete, – I wished to make a book as full of English character and country as an egg is of meat. If I have reminded others, as I did myself continually, of some of the echoes called up by the name of England, I am satisfied.'

The anthology is wide-ranging, including work by such obvious contenders as Shakespeare, Wordsworth and Dickens alongside folk songs and just two contemporary poets, Walter de la Mare and the completely unknown 'Edward Eastaway', whose 'Haymaking' and

'The Manor Farm' were in fact written by Thomas himself. True to his mission to avoid the too obviously patriotic, Thomas rejects the stirring military poems of Wolfe and Newbolt for the pastoral impressions of John Clare and Gilbert White. Although the anthology includes a section on 'London', this is by far the shortest, containing only seven pieces, whereas the principally rural section titled 'Her Sweet Three Corners' has forty-seven. ('Euston' here turns out not to be a description of the mighty railway station but an account of the park near Thetford laid out by John Evelyn.) Character and country are particularly aligned in 'The Vital Commoners', almost all of whom – Samuels Pepys and Weller apart – are country dwellers.

If this anthology provided a sense of what 'Englishness' meant in the winter of 1914, Thomas had a more concrete notion of the 'England' he would end up fighting to defend. When asked the following year why he had enlisted, he leaned down to take up a pinch of English soil and replied: 'Literally, for this.' In the first months of the war he had published an essay in *The Nation* in which he evoked a perfect rural scene in August 1914. As his anthology would be, it was titled 'This England', and in the final paragraph he described his feelings when looking at a new moon and imagining soldiers in France gazing up at the same sliver of light:

> It seemed to me that either I had never loved England, or I had loved it foolishly, aesthetically, like a slave, not having realised that it was not mine unless I were willing or prepared to die rather than leave it as Belgian women and old men and children had left their country. Something, I felt, had to be done before I could look again compos- edly at English landscape, at the elms and poplars about the houses, at the purple-headed wood-betony with two pairs of dark leaves on a stiff stem, who stood sentinel among the grasses or bracken by hedge-side or wood's-edge.

The countryside that Thomas was writing about, that stood for all England, was not in Shropshire but a neighbouring county: 'All I can say was that the name, Hereford, had somehow won in my mind a very distinct meaning; it stood out among the other county names as the most delicately rustic of them all, with a touch of nobility given it long ago, I think, by Shakespeare's "Harry of Hereford, Lancaster and Derby".' Although intended as representative, this was the real landscape of Leadington that Thomas knew well from the time he spent there. Just to the north of Dymock on the Herefordshire–Gloucestershire border, it was also the place in which he forged his friendship with Robert Frost and became a poet, somewhere that was for the Dymock Poets emblematic of the England Thomas now saw being threatened.

Siegfried Sassoon's notion of what he might shortly be fighting for also crystallised in the depths of the English countryside. On 31 July 1914, having read in *The Times* that war was now unavoidable, he set out on a long bicycle ride through the Weald of Kent, where he had spent most of his life. On the return journey, he writes, 'I found myself observing those last miles with a heightened perception of what they meant to me.' Passing two familiar hop kilns, he felt that:

In the reddening glow of the setting sun their kindly cowls were like sign-posts pointing towards the ominous continent of Europe. Those local kilns stood for England – for Kent, anyhow – rustically confronting whatever enemy might invade the freedom of the Hastings road [. . .] Lit by departing day was the length and breadth of the Weald, and the message of those friendly miles was a single chord of emotion vibrating backwards across the years to my earliest rememberings. Uplifted by this awareness, I knew that here was something deeply loved, something which the unmeasurable timelessness of childhood had made my own. I saluted it with feelings of farewell.

Taking one last lingering look across a familiar valley, 'I said to myself that I was ready to meet whatever the war might ask of me,' he continues. 'The Weald had been the world of my youngness, and while I gazed across it now I felt prepared to do what I could to defend it.'

Rupert Brooke felt something similar, though from the vantage point of Cornwall, where he was on a sailing holiday when war was declared. In an article published in the *New Statesman* on 29 August 1914, he wrote about the reaction of 'a friend' to the news that Britain and Germany were at war. Although the twenty-seven-year-old Brooke describes his protagonist as 'a normal, even ordinary man, wholly English, twenty-four years old, active and given to music', it is clearly a self-portrait. Having been told that Britain and Germany are at war, the young man climbs a gorse-covered hill and sits alone with his thoughts, gazing out across the sea:

> Something was growing in his heart, and he couldn't tell what. But as he thought 'England and Germany' the word 'England' seemed to flash like a line of foam. With a sudden tightening of his heart, he realized that there might be a raid on the English coast. He didn't imagine any possibility of it *succeeding*, but only of enemies and warfare on English soil. The idea sickened him. He was immensely surprised to perceive that the actual earth of England held for him a quality which he found in A—— ['a girl he intermittently adored'], and in a friend's honour, and scarcely anywhere else, a quality which, if he'd ever been sentimental enough to use the word, he'd have called 'holiness'. His astonishment grew as the full flood of 'England' swept over him on from thought to thought. He felt the triumphant helplessness of a lover. Grey, uneven little fields, and small, ancient hedges rushed before him, wild flowers, elms and beeches, gentleness, sedate houses of red brick, proudly unassuming, a countryside of rambling hills and friendly copses.

This is not the coastal England that the young man is sitting in, looking out to sea; it is instead the 'for ever England' of Brooke's most famous poem, 'The Soldier'. Imagining himself being buried in 'some corner of a foreign field', Brooke supposes:

> There shall be
> In that rich earth a richer dust concealed;
> A dust whom England bore, shaped, made aware,
> Gave, once, her flowers to love, her ways to roam,
> A body of England's, breathing English air,
> Washed by the rivers, blest by suns of home.

This poem is so well known, and has been so often pilloried, that its engagement with an idealised rural England, apparently inspired by walks around Dymock (it was first published in the Dymock Poets' *New Numbers 4*), has more or less vanished amid the mythologising rhetoric with which it was associated after Brooke's death.

Brooke's England is the 'England' that many soldiers imagined when fighting for it on foreign soil, perhaps particularly in the devastated landscapes of France and Belgium, but also in the very different terrains of Gallipoli and the Middle East. It is more or less identical to the one described by the hugely popular travel writer H.V. Morton in his best-selling *In Search of England* (1927), which opens with the sentence: 'I believed that I was dying in Palestine.' The scene is in fact set after the war, but Morton lures the reader into imagining that he is writing as a serving soldier. It describes him climbing a hill above Jerusalem and 'turning as accurately as I could in the direction of England', rather as a devout Muslim would face Mecca. From this vantage point

> there rose up in my mind the picture of a village street at dusk with a smell of wood smoke lying in the still air and, here and there, little red blinds shining in the dusk under the thatch. I remember how the church bells ring at home, and how, at that time of year, the sun leaves a low red bar down in the west, and against it the elms grow blacker by the minute. Then the bats start to flicker like little bits of burnt paper and you hear the slow jingle of a team coming home from the fields . . . When you think like this sitting alone in a foreign country I think you know all there is to learn about heartache.

This is not the landscape in which Morton grew up or now lived. He was born in the industrialised Lancashire town of Ashton-under-Lyne, where 'his earliest memories were of the sound of mill-girls' clogs as they clattered off to work in the morning', and moved first to Manchester at the age of five, and then to the Birmingham suburbs. At the time of writing his book he was living in London as a Fleet Street journalist, which prompts him to ask: 'does it seem strange that a townsman should in his extremity see this picture' of a quintessentially rural scene?

Would it not be more reasonable to expect him to see his own city? Why did I not think of St Paul's Cathedral or Piccadilly? I have learnt since that this vision of mine is a common one to exiles all over the world; we think of home, we long for home, but we see something greater – *we see England*.

This village that symbolizes England sleeps in the sub-consciousness of many a townsman. A little London factory hand I met during the war confessed to me when pressed, and after great mental difficulty, that he visualised the England he was fighting for – the England of the 'England wants Y O U' poster – as not London, not his own street, but as Epping Forest, the green place where he had spent Bank Holidays. And I think most of us did. The village and the English country-side are the germs of all we are and all we have become: our manufacturing cities belong to the last century and a half; our villages stand with their roots in the Heptarchy.

Looking out over Jerusalem, Morton made a pledge that would have seemed familiar to many who had served in the war: 'I took the vow that if the pain in my neck did not end for ever on the windy hills of Palestine I would go home in search of England, I would go through the lanes of England and the little thatched villages of England, and I would lean over English bridges, and lie on English grass, watching an English sky.' It is more or less a recapitulation of Rupert Brooke.

The popularity of Morton's book, which by 1932 had gone through seventeen editions in five years and would become one of the best selling books published between the wars, suggests that townspeople and city dwellers did indeed associate 'England' with green places, either because these were where they escaped at weekends or on holiday, or because it was where their forefathers had originated before the population shifts of the late nineteenth century and so lived on in their collective consciousness. Soldiers at the front did of course think of the people they had left behind, but Ronald Blythe has observed: 'The homesickness of the First World War was expressed more in terms of places than of people. In the literature which poured from the Western Front there is a passionate longing for the Cotswolds, the Welsh borders, certain villages and towns, the Malvern Hills –

a longing fashioned and taught by poets and composers.' Among those who fashioned this longing were Housman and the English composers who set his words, fixing in soldiers' minds a country that was both real and imaginary and stood for all England.

One of the reasons for volunteering early to fight in the First World War – at any rate among the officer class – was that it allowed you to select the regiment you wanted to join. Even those who enlisted in the ranks tended to do so locally and therefore, along with their friends and neighbours, joined regiments associated with the area in which they lived. The British Army was based on the old volunteer forces, which had a long history, were raised locally, and often took their names from their locality. The Childers Reforms of 1881 led to a restructuring of infantry regiments, which were given regional names and became known as 'county regiments'. Some regiments acquired additional names derived from royal patronage or the colours or facings of their uniforms. Among those that emerged from this reorganisation were the West Yorkshire Regiment (The Prince of Wales's Own), the East Kent Regiment (The Buffs), and the Shropshire Regiment (The King's Light Infantry), the last drawn from the 53rd (Shropshire) Regiment of Foot, whose soldiers were commemorated in the first poem of *A Shropshire Lad*. From the Duke of Cornwall's Light Infantry in the extreme south of England to the Border Regiment in the north, these military units had strong ties with local communities and, because they were based on the old volunteer forces, with local history. Housman's 'Lads of the fifty-third', for example, were first raised in 1755 and attached to the county of Shropshire in 1782.

By 1914 further restructuring had taken place, but England was still a country in which people often lived their entire lives in one region rather than move about in the way the population does now. The War Office capitalised on this widespread sense of being rooted in, and belonging to, a particular place to raise what became known as Pals Battalions, encouraging men from the same district to enlist together. It was a policy that in some cases had catastrophic consequences at the front. The Accrington Pals from Lancashire, to take one notorious example, went into battle on the first day on the Somme and suffered over 80 percent casualties within minutes of the attack being launched.

It had taken a mere ten days to raise the battalion and around half an hour to destroy it, and the impact upon the soldiers' home town was both devastating and long-lasting. At a less extreme level, all around the country collective pride and sorrow would draw together local communities after the Armistice as war memorials were unveiled in cities, towns and villages. Next to the war memorial at Snittersfield in Warwickshire a bench would be placed bearing the inscription: 'The noble expanse visible from this spot was Shakespeare's favourite countryside. The men whose names are inscribed on the neighbouring monument gave their lives for that England, which never did nor ever shall lie at the proud foot of a conqueror.'

Many soldiers who had volunteered for, or been conscripted into, county regiments felt that they were fighting as much for their particular part of the country as they were for a rather less clearly defined 'England'. For those who, before joining the army, had rarely strayed beyond their local town or village, these places *were* England. As Edward Thomas wrote in an article for the *English Review* in October 1914, wondering whether the thirteenth-century historian Robert of Gloucester would have found England (as he described it in his *Chronicle*) 'a right merry land' had he lived in Sussex or Northumberland: 'I take it that England then as now was a place of innumerable holes and corners, and most men loved – or, at any rate, could not do without – some one or two of these, and loved all England, but probably seldom said so, because without it the part could not exist [. . .] Throughout English history you have the two elements combined inseparably, love of the place where you "have your happiness or not at all", and a more fitfully conscious love of the island, and glory in its glories.'

Thomas was at the time reading Izaak Walton's *The Compleat Angler*: 'Since the war began I have not met so English a book, a book that filled me so with a sense of England, as this, though I have handled scores of deliberately patriotic works,' he wrote. 'In Walton's book I touched the antiquity and sweetness of England – English fields, English people, English poetry, all together.' He cites a passage in which Walton describes sitting in a field watching fish in a stream and looking beyond this to wooded hills and a meadow in which children are gathering wild flowers, as Housman's young people do in several of his poems. 'I think

England means something like this to most of us,' Thomas concludes; 'that all ideas of England are developed, spun out from such a centre into something large or infinite, solid or aëry, according to each man's nature and capacity; that England is a system of vast circumferences circling round the minute neighbouring points of home.'

As we have already seen, one soldier who spent much of the war circling in his mind round the minute neighbouring points of home was Private I.B. Gurney of the 5th Gloucestershire Regiment. In his prisoner-of-war camp, Gurney's friend Will Harvey was similarly thinking and writing about their home county. On the cover and title page of his first volume of poems, *A Gloucestershire Lad at Home and Abroad* (1916), the last four words were printed in smaller type, as if they were an afterthought or subtitle (they would subsequently be dropped altogether), and readers would immediately have recognised the allusion to Housman's volume. Like those of Gurney, Harvey's poems look back to the landscape of his youth, and while the style of most of them, and indeed their genuflections before the Almighty, set them apart from Housman, echoes of *A Shropshire Lad* are occasionally detectable, as in these lines from 'A Gloucestershire Wish at Eastertide':

> Here's luck, my lads, while Birdlip Hill is steep:–
> – As long as Cotswold's high or Severn's deep.
> Our thoughts of you will blossom and abide
> While blow the orchards about Severn side . . .

Many of Harvey's poems were first published in the battalion magazine, the *Fifth Gloucester Gazette*, and in his introduction to the volume the battalion's commander wrote:

> The poems are written by a soldier and reflect a soldier's outlook. Mud, blood and khaki are rather conspicuously absent. They are in fact the last things a soldier wants to think or talk about.
> What he does think of is his home.

Many other soldiers thought longingly of the places they had known, places that now seemed so far out of reach. A photograph of a local scene back home sent to Cyril Rawlins, serving in France as a transport officer in the 1st Welsh Battalion, brought to mind blue remembered hills as seen from Staffordshire, a couple of miles from the Shropshire border. 'How my heart ached when I pulled out your photo of Pottal Corner,' he wrote to his father, 'that sweet spot in God's own country looking just as I have so many times seen it, the long dipping road to Penkridge and far in the distance the blue dome of the Wrekin.' The photograph released in Rawlins an enormously long, homesick reminiscence of the England he had left behind him, amounting almost to a gazetteer of his home territory:

> How it brings back happy memories of the time before the war, when the world was happy and careless: the Golden Age: a summer Sunday afternoon, and I with my cycle, and some food in my saddle bag, passing this spot, cutting down through the cool perfumed plantations after the arduous climb up lovely Penkridge Bank, no sound but the drone of bees in the heather and the whirr of grouse: stopping now often to admire the distant view over the high land beyond Bowley! Swooping down the long grade into sleepy little Penkridge. Gailey; the long blue granite stretches of my favourite Watling Street: up hill and down dale on the whirring 'wheel'. Ivetsey Bank, with Boscobel away in the trees; Weston-under-Lizard, with its comfortable, respectable 'model village' air, all shaded by the tall elm trees behind the grey stone wall of the Park . . .

. . . and so on, for several pages. The place-names are almost as numerous as they are in Gurney's letters, and so detailed that it is possible a century later to follow on a map the bicycle rides Rawlins is remembering.

For other serving soldiers, it was books that brought their own landscapes to mind. 'I read Richard Jefferies to remind me of Liddington Castle and the light green and dark green of the Aldbourne Downs in summer,' Charles Hamilton Sorley wrote to his former headmaster from France in June 1915, recalling the downs above Marlborough College across which he used to run as a schoolboy. The kind of homesickness that Gurney and Rawlins suffered while at the front was clearly understood by Siegfried Sassoon. Billeted in Amiens in March 1917, he wrote in his diary:

> I wish I could write a book of 'Consolations for Homesick Soldiers in the Field' [. . .] They need someone to refresh the familiar scenes and happenings which they remember and long for. Someone to make them exclaim 'Damn it, how that takes one back to the dear old times!' [. . .] I would turn them loose in some dream gallery of Royal Academy pictures of the late-nineteenth century. I would show them bland summer landscapes, willows and meadowsweet reflected in calm waters, lifelike cows coming home to the byre with a golden sunset behind them; I would take them to gateways in garden-walls that they might gaze along dewy walls with lovers murmuring by the moss-grown sundial; I would lead them 'twixt hawthorn hedge-rows, and over field-path stiles. To old-world orchards where the lush grass is strewn with red-cheeked apples, and even the wasps have lost their stings. From the grey church-tower comes a chiming of bells, and the village smoke ascends like incense of immemorial tranquillity . . .

Sassoon's own homesickness is palpable here, and the scene he paints might well be taken from his own home in the Kentish Weald; but this is also a generic English landscape of the sort Housman wrote about in his poems. The longing in the trenches for reminders of an unspoilt pastoral England is perhaps unsurprising when one considers the kind of landscape over which most men in the front line were looking. More or less continuous bombardment had reduced some areas at the front to a featureless expanse of raw earth, from which trees, hedges, even grass had been obliterated. 'What is there out here to raise a man's mind out of the rut?' asked Second Lieutenant William Ratcliffe in a letter to his parents written a month before he was killed on the Somme at the age of nineteen. 'The countryside and the beauties of nature, which, as you know, always have a beneficial effect on a man, are all spoilt by the dust and mud of motor lorries and by huge camps.'

Sassoon's notion of a book of consolations for homesick soldiers more or less, though coincidentally, came to fruition in Ernest Rhys's anthology *The Old Country*, published in conjunction with the Young Men's Christian Association in 1917. During the war the YMCA had established huts and canteens at railway stations, in military camps and at the front where soldiers could get something to eat or relax in relatively comfortable surroundings. The organisation saw its role as supplying spiritual as well as physical sustenance, but its remit was not simply religious: 'To the average man in our forces [the YMCA] is a bit of England and the home country. It may be a big hut or a marquee, a strafed house, cellar or dug-out – no matter how poor the shanty, the familiar sign reminds him of home [. . .] In his imagination he can see his village home, which is all the world to him.' It is characteristic of the rhetoric of the war that this generic home should be a village one, and this introduction to Rhys's anthology, which is accompanied by a vignette of a thatched cottage surrounded by trees, was written by the secretary to the National Council of YMCAs, Sir Arthur Yapp, whose family had for generations farmed at Orleton in Herefordshire, a couple of miles from the Shropshire border. *The Old Country* was intended to play a similar spiritual role to that of the YMCA clubhouses. Subtitled 'A Book of Love & Praise of England', it was assembled by Rhys in response to requests for such an anthology 'from all sides: from two of our soldiers in France, from an American lady who happened to be an Ambassador's wife, from a Canadian captain, from an Australian officer with a Welsh name, and from an English Princess'. This list was intended to suggest that 'England' was something people understood and valued whichever part of the world or stratum of society they came from.

Rhys went on to explain that 'The practical use of such a kit-book or hut-book lies in its pocketable size and its effect as golden remembrance', and it was illustrated to this effect. The numerous illustrations, he wrote, were 'chosen chiefly as famous landmarks or familiar reminders. Westminster, Canterbury, St Paul's, Salisbury, Oxford and Cambridge, the Thames near its source, the Tower and Tower Bridge; the village shop; and the Tranter's cart that you read of in Hardy's Wessex Tales'. It is notable that these familiar reminders do not extend to the kind of urban streets that most of the serving men called 'home'. It is not known whether Housman was asked permission to reprint any of his poems in the anthology, and he would almost certainly have refused, as was his custom. There is, however, a coloured plate of a thatched timber-framed cottage, with a woman leaning over the gate looking out onto a lane along which a man is leading a horse and cart. The original watercolour was painted by A.R. Quinton, a hugely popular recorder of the English scene, many of whose paintings were reproduced as postcards. This example looks entirely generic, but it is captioned 'A Homestead under the Bredon Hills'.*

Rhys's anthology had been anticipated by *The Times*'s Broadsheets. Many serving soldiers, particularly those in the ranks, could not afford to have books such as *The Old Country* sent to them at the front, and would in any case have no time to read them 'from cover to cover'. So from 1915 *The Times* produced a series of so-called 'Broadsheets', in fact single sheets of ordinary notepaper on which were printed 'Six Selected Extracts from Great English Writers', as chosen by Sir Walter Raleigh, Professor of English Literature at Oxford. The sheets were inexpensive, retailing at 1d each, and could be folded into an ordinary envelope or enclosed with a letter without incurring additional postal charges. Once received at the front, they could be tucked into the pocket of a uniform, to be brought out and read during lulls in the fighting or rest periods behind the line. Explaining the scheme in a letter to *The Times*, Raleigh wrote that it had already been 'warmly welcomed and commended by many officers and men', who recognised 'that the appeal of the best things ever written, in verse and prose, is not diminished but enhanced by the new setting lent to them in war. Our fighting troops think more of England now than they thought of her when they were at home, and the familiar delights of peace have a new meaning for them. Mr Lionel Curtis, who, I believe, first suggested your scheme, has told me that for him one of the great moments of the South African War was the reading of Bacon's Essay on Gardens, from a copy of the essays which someone chanced to have by him.' There is something quintessentially English in the suggestion that

---

*Since Bredon is a single hill, it is possible that 'the Bredon Hills' is a misprint for 'the Breidden Hills', which are on the Shropshire–Montgomeryshire border.

one of 'the great moments' of a war was settling down to read about gardening – and indeed about serving, as Curtis did, as a bicyclist in the City Imperial Volunteers.

Raleigh thought that in addition to giving soldiers the best of English literature in portable form, the series would 'symbolize the cause for which we are fighting [. . .] There is no better expression of freedom, in all its senses, than English literature. I can almost imagine an intelligent German officer trembling and growing pale when he finds it in our trenches. Here is the explanation, which he has so long sought in vain, of why it is that our brothers from all the English-speaking world are at one with us, heart and soul. Here is their inheritance; why should they give it up for the bribes of a foreign drill-sergeant? By this token we shall conquer.'

As it turned out, English literature got a helping hand from other cultures and languages. Among the 'numerous and varied selection of the best passages, grave and gay, of English verse and prose' in the first series, for example, Pericles' speech to the Athenians from Thucydides' *History of the Peloponnesian War*, 'The Song of Deborah' from the biblical book of Judges, Froissart's description of the Black Prince in Spain, and Tolstoy's 'The Future Life' from *War and Peace* were included alongside extracts from Cobbett's *Rural Rides*, Dickens's *The Pickwick Papers*, Izaak Walton's *The Compleat Angler* and John Nyren's *The Cricketers of My Time*. *The Times* nevertheless felt that the distribution of such literature in the trenches would 'carry the message of English freedom, of English spontaneity, of English culture, of the great English inheritance for which England and her daughters [i.e. the colonies] are fighting'.

Although the Broadsheets were 'not designed to instruct, or to improve; but merely to give recreation to those who, in the drudgery no less than the danger of war, so sorely need rest and distraction', there was something admirably high-minded and democratic about this initiative. Not that this was appreciated everywhere. In *With Manchesters in the East* (1918), Gerald B. Hurst writes of those serving at the front in the Manchester Regiment: 'Old magazines and football editions of Saturday evening papers, published a month or two earlier in England, sufficed for their literary appetites. Lancashire boys were not brought up to read [. . .] When I once came upon a man reading the *Golden Treasury*, in Hardship Avenue, I knew he could not be a Manchester man. He was not. He came from the Isle of Man, and had joined our reserves at Southport. I found about half-a-dozen men who could enjoy *The Times* broadsheets. I am afraid *John Bull* was much more popular.' (Palgrave's *Golden Treasury* was popular trench reading among the officer class, and *John Bull* was Horatio Bottomley's populist and xenophobic weekly magazine.)

Breaking his usual rule, Housman gave Raleigh permission to reprint six poems from *A Shropshire Lad* as a Broadsheet (no. 38). Quite what Lancastrian rankers would have made of the selected poems – 'Reveille', 'The street sounds to the soldiers' tread', 'On Wenlock Edge the wood's in trouble', 'On the idle hill of summer', 'The isle of Portland' and 'Terence, this is stupid stuff' – is anyone's guess. However, whether as a result of the widespread distribution of these poems or simply because Housman's work spoke to a nation at war, yearly sales of *A Shropshire Lad* surpassed even those of the pre-war period, reaching 14,000 in 1916 and 16,000 in 1918.

Lads, We'll Remember Friends of Ours

Several of the war poets had, like Patrick Shaw-Stewart, been among those who carried the book with them to the front. Sassoon's copy was a pocket edition published in 1912 and is inscribed 'Siegfried Sassoon / 1st R.W. Fus. Nov. 1915 / 2nd R.W. Fus. March 1917 / 25th R.W. Fus. March 1918'. In other words, the book had accompanied him throughout his war service, both on the Western Front and in the Middle East. Wilfred Owen, who was himself a Shropshire lad, born near Oswestry and brought up in Shrewsbury, purchased his copy from Harold Monro's Poetry Bookshop in November 1915, shortly after he had enlisted and still feeling a little self-conscious in his brand new uniform. Gurney's copies have already been mentioned, and we can assume that one of the pockets mentioned by Robert Nichols was his own.

Even those soldier-poets who are not known to have tucked the book into their uniforms were undoubtedly influenced by *A Shropshire Lad* in what they wrote. Edward Thomas had tramped across enough of England before the war to look beyond an imaginary Shropshire, but Housman is nevertheless discernible in such wartime poems as 'A Private', 'In Memoriam (Easter 1915)' and 'The Cherry Trees'. The last, written in May 1916, inevitably brings to mind 'Loveliest of trees, the cherry now', and its reference to 'the old road where all that passed are dead' is distinctly Housman-like. 'A Private', written in January 1915, describes a soldier-ploughman who in death 'sleeps' out of doors in a place no one can find, just as he did in life. Exchanging a protecting hawthorn bush on the Wiltshire Downs for his bed of clay on the battlefields of France, 'he sleeps / More sound', just as Housman's dead lads do. Housman is most obviously present, both in form and content, in 'In Memoriam (Easter 1915)', a single compressed stanza of four lines in which unpicked flowers in a wood at 'Eastertide' remind the poet of the war's dead, who are no longer there to join their sweethearts in gathering the blooms. This is the traditional springtime recreation that Housman described in such poems as 'Oh see how thick the goldcup flowers', 'March', 'The Lent Lily' and, most particularly, ''Tis time, I think, by Wenlock town', where the speaker, detained by exile rather than death, is no longer able to join the assembled couples.

More generally, both the irony and the plangency that are characteristic of Housman's poetry suited the mood of those writing about the war. The gap between the high ideals with which many young men enlisted and the experiences they and their fellow soldiers underwent in the trenches produced a mood of disillusionment. There were, of course, others whose idealism and belief in the justice of the war survived even the most ghastly front-line experiences, and it is notable that Sassoon, having made a public protest against the war that almost got him court-martialled, went back to lead his men into battle. As Housman had demonstrated, irony was a way – and a very English way – of assimilating and recording unpalatable daily reality, and it became the dominant mode of much of the writing about the First World War. If 'On the idle hill of summer' captures the kind of romantic enthusiasm for soldiering that caused young men to volunteer for service as soon as war was declared in 1914, then other poems on non-military themes show a way of responding to the implacable workings of fate.

Like Rupert Brooke, Charles Hamilton Sorley had drawn the

attention of his schoolfellows to *A Shropshire Lad*, in a talk he gave to the Marlborough College Literary Society in May 1913, a few days shy of his eighteenth birthday. He judged that 'as a language-maker alone, apart from what he expresses, [Housman] is second to none of his contemporaries and can sit beside almost any other English poet, except Shakespeare'. '1887' and 'On the idle hill of summer' were, he felt, 'as fine as anything I know', and although he saw Shropshire as the wellspring of Housman's poetry, he added: 'I do not know much about the Greeks: perhaps something less than I ought to: but it has struck me that Housman would have pleased them very much. His perfect restraint and refinement of obloquy or irony: no less than his limited and reasonable conclusions about the universe: would have charmed many lesser Greek philosophers with the charm that it produced by reflecting "That's exactly what I think too: and if I had had to express it, I should have expressed it in exactly the same way."'

In its rhymes, rhythms, vocabulary and equivocal tone, Sorley's best-known poem, 'All the hills and vales along', follows Housman's lead:

> All the hills and vales along
> Earth is bursting into song,
> And the singers are the chaps
> Who are going to die perhaps.

Frequently anthologised (sometimes under the unauthorised title 'Marching Song' and in one anthology of war poetry in a section titled 'Visions of Glory'), this poem has more in common with Housman's 'On the idle hill of summer' than it does with Brooke's 'The Soldier'. The countryside through which the soldiers march merely sends back a hollow echo of their song and is wholly indifferent to their fate, just as nature tends to be in Housman:

> Earth that never doubts nor fears,
> Earth that knows of death, not tears,
> Earth that bore with joyful ease
> Hemlock for Socrates,
> Earth that blossomed and was glad

'Neath the cross that Christ had,
Shall rejoice and blossom too
When the bullet reaches you.
　　Wherefore, men marching
　　On the road to death, sing!
　　Pour your gladness on earth's head,
　　So be merry, so be dead.

That final line, as with the 'perhaps' at the end of the first extract, combined with what we know about Sorley's attitude to the war from his remarkable letters, suggests that to class this poem as an unequivocal celebration of the warrior spirit would be misguided. Like Housman's soldiers, Sorley's are 'marching, all to die'.

A less well-known poet, Frank Prewett, was Canadian, but was educated at Christ Church, Oxford and served with the Royal Field Artillery in France until he was wounded in 1917. It was while convalescing in London that he met Sassoon and the two men became close friends, though Sassoon's physical attraction to Prewett was not reciprocated. 'The Soldier', published in his 1921 volume of *Poems*, suggests that Prewett knew his Housman. (Having returned to Ontario after the war, he would complain: 'Thomas Hardy cannot be bought in Toronto, nor *The Shropshire Lad*'.) The first verse more or less recapitulates 'Is my team ploughing', even down to the rhyming of 'plough' and 'now':

My years I counted twenty-one
Mostly at the tail of plough:
The furrow that I drove is done,
To sleep in furrow now.

The third verse, though containing a sexual image wholly alien to Housman, also sounds familiar:

A lad to life has paid his debts
Who bests and kills a foe,
A man upon his sweetheart gets
To reap as well as sow.

Though he later had a more complicated literary relationship with Housman, whom he thought unreliable because homosexual (with the proviso that 'this was "all right" because he'd hated being one'), Robert Graves seems to have known *A Shropshire Lad* when he went off to war. His second volume of poems, *Fairies and Fusiliers* (1917), contains some distinct Housman echoes, as in the couplet 'Rhyme and music flow in plenty / For the lad of one-and-twenty' in 'Babylon' and the line 'Shot, poor lad, so bold and young' in 'When I'm Killed'. Similarly, the first stanza of 'To Lucasta on Going to the War – for the Fourth Time', in which the Fusiliers are self-described as 'lads' who are both proud and true, owes as much to Housman as it does to Lovelace, while 'An Old Twenty-Third Man', ostensibly about a Roman legion but clearly with application to the present war, both refers to 'brave lads that die' and more generally cries kinship with 'On Wenlock Edge the wood's in trouble'.

Then as now, soldiers were often referred to collectively as 'lads' by their comrades and in the popular press, with no intended nod to Housman. Paul Fussell has nevertheless argued that 'Housman's greatest contribution to the war was the word *lad*, to which his poems had given the meaning "a beautiful brave doomed boy".' He goes on to suggest: 'In Great War diction there are three degrees of erotic heat attaching to three words: *men* is largely neutral; *boys* is a little warmer; *lads* is very warm [. . .] As *men* grow more attractive, they are seen as *boys*, until finally, when they are conceived as potential lovers, they turn into *lads* [. . .] The lads who populate the poems and memoirs of the Great War have about them both the doom of Housman's lads and the pederastic allure of John Gambrill Nicholson's.'

Nicholson (1866–1931) was one of the self-styled Uranian poets who had, in their own subterranean way, flourished from the late 1880s, publishing enough volumes of verse celebrating boyhood to fill an entire prep-school library. Most of these books were 'Privately Printed' and recklessly frank about their authors' appreciation of the finer points of 'boys' and 'lads' both ancient and modern, from diminutive Greek gods, through anguished juvenile saints, to bold modern striplings in (or sometimes out of) hotel-page or telegraph-office uniforms. The Uranians were extremely fond of the word 'lad', perhaps because its very ambiguity cast a gossamer veil of decency over their verses. 'Lad' had more of a stretch in terms of age than 'boy', extending beyond child-hood and adolescence to encompass young men of the sort Housman wrote about. It all, however, depended on context: the Church Lads' Brigade, for example, seems straightforwardly above board; a volume of poems titled *Ladslove Lyrics* (1918) by 'Philebus' less so.*

Although Housman had no association with these poets, and would have regarded both their prosody and their approach to their subject matter as incontinent, *A Shropshire Lad* was included in F.E. Murray's *A Catalogue of Selected Books from the Private Library of a Student of Boyhood, Youth and Comradeship* (1924), where it keeps company with such titles as the Rev. E.E. Bradford's *Passing the Love of Women* (1913), Cuthbert Wright's *One Way of Love* (1915) and *A Boy's Absence* 'By a Schoolmaster' (1919). 'Look not in my eyes, for fear' (XV), with its final lines about the 'Grecian lad' Narcissus turning into a downward-glancing 'jon-quil', and 'The Merry Guide' (XLII), in which the poet is beguiled by the figure of a youthful Mercury, are the only poems in *A Shropshire Lad* that might fit the canon of Uranian verse, but both of them are far more subtle and austerely chaste than most of the literary effusions of the movement's clergymen and schoolmasters. Given that the circula-tion of Uranian books was a great deal less widespread than that of *A Shropshire Lad*, Fussell is right to attribute the flowering of 'lad' in First World War poetry to Housman rather than to these poetic pederasts, although there is occasionally some overlap.†

The very close bonds that developed between soldiers at the front have often been written about, and the love and loss recorded in war

---

*The original Philebus was the defender of hedonism in one of Plato's Socratic dia-logues; this one was a medic serving in the merchant navy. 'Ladslove' or 'lad's love', conveniently enough, is one of the English names for the pungent-leafed plant *Artemisia abrotanum*, which led to a certain amount of covert Uranian punning. Among J.G. Nicholson's publications are not only *A Garland of Ladslove* (1911) but also *A Chaplet of Southernwood* (1896), southernwood being an alternative name for the plant.

†He is wrong, however, to suggest that 'As a name especially of a beloved boy who is dead (cf Sassoon's "The Effect": "When Dick was killed last week he looked like that. / Flapping along the fire-step like a fish"), "Dick" may derive from Housman's "The Night is Freezing Fast".' The poem he refers to was not published until after the war, in 1922 as no. XX of *Last Poems*; Sassoon's poem was written in the summer of 1917.

poetry tends more often to be about comrades killed in the trenches than girls left behind at home. It was as if Housman's laments for doomed lads, 'handsome of face and [. . .] handsome of heart', not only showed a younger generation of poets how to write elegies for dead friends that sometimes read like love poetry, but also gave them permission to do so. Gurney, for example, unselfconsciously gave the title 'To His Love' to the poem he wrote about Will Harvey. It is a poem in which landscape, love and loss are all bound up in a way that would be wholly familiar to readers of *A Shropshire Lad*. Part of the reason Housman was a useful model for such elegies is that he avoided the archness and furtiveness of the Decadents and Uranians that – particularly in the wake of the Wilde trials – made much of the poetry written about young men seem highly suspect, choosing instead a style that was classically restrained but none the less affecting for that. 'The one [poet] who most moves me to tears – when poetry can – is Housman,' wrote Robert Lowell. 'His iron quatrains are sometimes like the tomb-inscriptions for the Athenian youths who died at Marathon' – and it was both Housman and his classical predecessors who provided models for poetry mourning the English youths who died at Loos, in the Ypres Salient and on the Somme.

The notion Housman proposed in such poems as '1887' and 'The Recruit' that the best a soldier could hope for, given that he was likely to die in battle, was to be remembered by his friends was realised in countless poetic tributes written by soldiers to dead young comrades. Second Lieutenant H. Rex Freston, whose parents were living in the Shropshire village of Worthen when he was killed in action in January 1916, was the author of two volumes of poetry. *The Quest of Truth*, published posthumously in 1916, contained two poems titled 'To A.M. (*Killed in Flanders*)', one of which clearly takes Housman as its model:

> Time was in summer weather,
>   By Cherwell's wandering streams,
> We loved to walk together
>   To where the iris gleams.

Now in French fields are blowing
  Wild flowers about your hair;
And gentle streams are flowing
  But you no longer care.

It is not simply that the form of the poem recalls Housman: the walk through the countryside, the summer weather, the wandering streams, the contrast between past happiness and the forlorn present, of love interrupted by death and of the inevitable though unwilled indifference of the dead friend or lover, are all familiar from such poems as 'Bredon Hill', 'This time of year a twelvemonth past', 'Along the field as we came by', 'When last I came to Ludlow' and 'With rue my heart is laden'. Another of Freston's poems, 'The Garden of Death', seems to borrow its first line from this last poem: 'Now the golden lads are lying / Under the grass and under the sky . . . '

Other poets seemed even less guarded when mourning the deaths of their fellow soldiers. Robert Nichols's distinctly overwrought but astonishingly popular *Ardours and Endurances* (1917) is one of several volumes of war poetry included with some justification in Murray's catalogue: *Sorrow of War* by Louis Golding (now best known as a writer of novels on Jewish themes), James S. Yates's *War Lyrics and Other Poems*, T.P. Cameron Wilson's *Magpies in Picardy* (all published in 1919) and Fabian S. Woodley's *A Crown of Friendship* (1921) each find their place there. There is clearly some correspondence between poems celebrating the transient beauty of boys and those commemorating the deaths of young men in battle, a correspondence that becomes clear in Woodley's volume, where the theme unblushingly outlined in such poems as 'The Vision' and 'To G.O'C.' is returned to in the section of 'Verses Written During the War'.

Something similar is apparent in the far more sophisticated poems of Wilfred Owen, several of which would not seem out of place in the *Artist and Journal of Home Culture*, where a good deal of Uranian literature appeared. Verses such as 'It was a navy boy', 'To the Bitter Sweet-Heart: A Dream' and 'Who is the god of Canongate?' were not at first regarded as canonical, but their relationship to such war poems as 'I saw his round mouth's crimson', 'Arms and the Boy',

'Greater Love' and 'Futility' now seems obvious. Born and brought up in Housman Country, in 1913 Owen had written a long poem titled 'Uriconium: An Ode', which brings to mind Housman's about Wenlock Edge, with its similar setting and its elision of past and present. In addition, the sense of ancient violence in Owen's poem recalls 'The Welsh Marches' (XXVIII), which is set in Owen's home town of Shrewsbury. Owen, however, unlike Housman, was a frequent and fascinated visitor to the excavations of Uriconium (or Viroconium) at Wroxeter, and his inspiration may simply have been local history rather than a literary elder.

Owen too, though from a different direction, looked out across the landscape that formed Housman's childhood horizon: 'The hills of Cheshire and Shropshire, steep grassy ridges rising abruptly from the plain to flat tops covered in "herb and heather", were always where his imagination felt most at home,' his biographer Dominic Hibberd observed. 'His attic room in Shrewsbury looked towards Haughmond Hill and the Wrekin, and beyond them to Caer Caradoc and the Long Mynd, those "landscapes whereupon my windows lean" which feature from time to time in his verse and letters and which seem to be reflected in the setting of "Spring Offensive".' While serving in France in 1917, Owen told his mother that the letters he received from his sixteen-year-old brother, Colin (whom he once addressed as 'Darling Lad'), 'bring me Shropshire as yours bring me Home', and 'Spring Offensive', ostensibly set in Picardy, clearly incorporates a memory of the poet's frequent walks in the Shropshire countryside. In his family memoir, Owen's other brother, Harold, recalled the family returning from an evening service in the village of Uffington to their home in Shrewsbury through water meadows spangled with buttercups. The wet petals from the flowers stuck to their boots, and seeing this Owen exclaimed that 'Harold's boots are blessed with gold', an image that is carried directly into the poem, with the added poignancy that the blessing the natural world bestows upon soldiers takes place in a tranquil landscape that will shortly erupt into a murderous and annihilating battle. As for Blunden and Sassoon, the beauties of nature provide Owen with a stark contrast to the death and destruction amidst which he finds himself at the front; he was, like Housman, a keen botanist and once wrote that 'bluebells, it may be, more than Greek iambics, fitted me for my job'.

It is not known if Owen had read *A Shropshire Lad* when he wrote 'Uriconium' in 1913, though given the book's popularity, its element of 'local colour' for a young man brought up in Shropshire, and its distinct sensibility, it would be astonishing if he had not encountered the poems before he bought a copy in 1915. Temperamentally he would certainly count as one of the 'young men' whom Housman envisaged as his primary readers, and he readily embraced the word 'lad' in his poetry. He had already used the word in poems he wrote before enlisting, mostly in a homoerotic context, as when addressing the 'prim and trim' navy boy encountered on a train as 'lad', kissing the 'brown hands of a server-lad' in 'Maundy Thursday', or asking a youthful male prostitute 'What shall I pay for you, lily-lad?' in 'Who is the god of Canongate?' The word 'lad' also crops up in his pre-war correspondence, tending to generate the kind of warmth Fussell noted. The two boys he began tutoring in France towards the end of 1914 (one of whom he describes as 'pretty rather than handsome') turned out to be 'dear, clever lads'. A fifteen-year-old French 'lad' first encountered at the Union Chrétienne in Bordeaux later produces a postcard Owen had sent him, 'preciously preserved among the *billet-doux* and secret photographs of his pocket book!' In a letter from the spring of 1915, subsequently much mutilated by the overly protective Harold, Owen writes to their mother that 'Perseus was a sailor lad; and never, I take it, bore epaulets on his brown shoulders or gold-braid on his bare chest.'

Young men who seem especially vulnerable and evoke the 'pity' that Owen declared the principal inspiration for his war poetry are often referred to as 'lads'. Coming back from a night patrol, he observes that his men were 'all half dead with fatigue & some quite, poor lads', and when a shell explodes near a dugout, he tells his mother that 'one lad was blown down and, I am afraid, blinded', an incident he re-created in his poem 'The Sentry'. Another of Owen's 'lads' exposed to danger was a railway clerk called Browne, who had 'stood by' the poet at the front before it was discovered he was underage and so was sent back to England. At Craiglockhart War Hospital, where he was being treated for shell shock and first met Sassoon, Owen thought often of those left behind at the front and in particular of 'the bleeding lad's cheeks I have wiped'. Having rejoined his regiment in Scarborough, he describes a waiter in the mess as 'the best lad for work I've got – wounded in the leg'. Also at Scarborough, with a knowing nod to Housman, Owen refers to 'Shropshire lads whose speech bewrayed them to me.'

Back in France, he is greatly cheered to see among the members of his regiment marching into camp 'at least two lads [who] instantly recognize me. They were, strangely enough, the very two I most hoped would survive.' Similarly, in the poems men become 'lads' when they are most under threat or deserving of pity, whether it is Isaac about to be sacrificed by Abraham, who ignores God's order 'Lay not thine hand upon the lad' and slaughters him anyway, or 'The Dead-Beat', who is accounted a 'stout lad' before shell shock and exhaustion reduce him to breakdown and result in his death. In 'S.I.W.' another 'lad', pressured into joining up by his family, is unable to stand the trenches and ends up shooting himself dead, like the Woolwich cadet. A supposedly luckier soldier in the unfinished poem 'Beauty' is congratulated by his comrades when he is hit in the arm by a shrapnel ball – 'What a beauty! What a beauty, lad!' – because the wound is a 'blighty', a minor one that will result in a man being sent back to England; but the wound festers and the soldier dies on board the ship taking him across the Channel. Perhaps the most sensuous, and most Housman-like, image occurs in 'Arms and the Boy', where Owen refers to bullets 'Which long to nuzzle in the hearts of lads'.

Another poem which does not use the word 'lad' is nevertheless clearly indebted to Housman – and was written after Owen had purchased his copy of A Shropshire Lad in 1915. 'Disabled' both echoes and subverts 'To an Athlete Dying Young' (XIX). Both poems portray a sporting hero, Housman's now dead, Owen's legless and missing one arm. Owen's image of the young man 'After the matches, carried shoulder-high' more or less paraphrases the opening lines of Housman's poem:

> The time you won your town the race
> We chaired you through the market-place;

Man and boy stood cheering by,
And home we brought you shoulder-high.

The principal difference is that Housman's athlete has died in his glory, whereas Owen's has survived, an embittered amputee who recalls (in another echo of Housman's poem) that 'Some cheered him home, but not as crowds cheer Goal'.

The fact that Housman tended to write about the doomed youth in his poetry more in sorrow than in anger provided Owen and other poets with a model. Owen's friend and mentor Siegfried Sassoon became known for his angrily satirical poems about the callousness and indifference to individual suffering he thought characterised both the general staff and those on the home front. There was, however, a more tender side to his war poetry and, like Owen, he made strategic use of the word 'lad' when in this mood, perhaps because Housman was so much of a presence during his war service. Sassoon not only carried *A Shropshire Lad* with him throughout the war, sometimes quoting lines from the poems in his diaries, but visited Housman Country while on leave in Liverpool in September 1915, stopping at a hotel in Church Stretton for tea with some fellow officers, with one of whom he had been in love rather in the manner of Housman and Moses Jackson. He returned to the hotel almost exactly nine years later, driving from Ludlow over Wenlock Edge and walking in the Shropshire Hills alone with his memories. 'Strange to think that on that day [in 1915] I knew so few of my present circle of friends. But the *difference* between then and now' – at which point a half-page has been torn out of the diary. Even incomplete, this entry has what Laurence Housman would have called 'the authentic note of the "Shropshire Lad"' – as do some of Sassoon's poems.

In 'Song-Books of the War', for example, Sassoon imagines a time fifty years after the war when 'Adventurous lads will sigh and cast / Proud looks upon the plundered past', a couplet that, read 'blind', might well be ascribed to Housman. Occasionally Sassoon uses the word 'lad' conventionally, as when a man in a London club in 'The Fathers' refers to his 'eldest lad', but 'lads' are more usually seen from the perspective of the officer-poet as innocent young men either in danger or already dead. The difference between these two usages is apparent in 'To Any Dead Officer', in which the salute 'Good-bye, old lad!' is in marked contrast to the pitiful image of 'lads [. . .] left in shell-holes dying slow'. In 'Night on the Convoy', the deck of a troopship is 'heaped and spread with lads in sprawling strength', who lie there 'prostrate and defenceless, head to head'. 'Editorial Impressions' is one of Sassoon's satirical poems, in which a journalist who has had 'a glorious time' visiting the trenches is depicted in conversation with a cheerful 'lad' who has been badly wounded in 'some wiped-out impossible Attack'. In another angry poem, 'Suicide in the Trenches', the poet hopes that the crowds 'who cheer when soldier lads march by' will 'never know / The hell where youth and laughter go', while one of the things we are urged not to forget in 'Aftermath' is 'those ashen-grey / Masks of the lads who once were keen and kind and gay'. Sassoon certainly never will: 'Oh lad that I loved, there is rain on your face,' he exclaims with dismay in 'I Stood with the Dead', written in France in June 1918.

Long after the hostilities ended Housman would continue to have a particular association with the First World War. For those mourning the loss of a generation, four lines published in *More Poems* in 1936 spoke with simple eloquence for the youthful dead. They were in fact written between 1895 and 1900, and so commemorated the dead of the South African wars, but, as so often with Housman, they proved universal:

> Here dead we lie because we did not choose
>> To live and shame the land from which we sprung.
> Life, to be sure, is nothing much to lose,
>> But young men think it is, and we were young.

For those who survived, the world Housman had created in *A Shropshire Lad* reminded them of what they had nevertheless lost. The grandfather of the writer Maggie Fergusson was brought up in what she describes as 'a kind of rural idyll' in Claughton, a small village between the Calder and Brock valleys in Lancashire. 'An album of old photographs evokes an apparently endless, carefree, Edwardian summer,' she writes. 'Men with turned-up trousers and rolled-up shirtsleeves carry cricket bats and tennis racquets. Women in ankle-length skirts and pin-tucked blouses laugh from the shade of parasols. A farmer cuts a field of hay with a horse-drawn scythe.' In the summer of 1918, at the age of nineteen, her grandfather was commissioned in the Coldstream Guards and set off for the Western Front. In September, while leading his men over the top, he was wounded by a hand grenade, a jagged piece of which 'penetrated his cheekbone just below his left eye, passed through the narrow space between the bottom of his brain and the roof of his mouth, and broke his right jaw'. His mother had already lost her eldest son, a brother and four of her five nephews, and when she received news that another son had been wounded, perhaps fatally, she took her own life.

Her son in fact survived, but doctors were unable to remove the fragment of metal, which remained in his head for the rest of his life, and his face was left permanently scarred. In later life he was, unsurprisingly, easily moved to tears. He would often spend evenings listening to Vaughan Williams's *On Wenlock Edge* in the famous recording made by Gervase Elwes. The song that particularly moved him was 'Bredon Hill'. Fergusson remembers her grandfather in old age, sitting in the twilight, a tumbler of whisky at his elbow, playing the record over and over as tears streamed silently down his ruined face. The words and music may have been written and composed before his war, but their evocation of young people relaxing on a perfect summer's day on a peaceful English hill, unaware of what lies in store for them, represented for this old soldier a whole irrecoverable world.

THE REDISCOVERY OF ENGLAND

Never before have so many people been searching for England

H.V. Morton, 1927

O ne of the most striking things about England in the years immediately after the war was the overwhelming quotidian presence,
and the resulting psychological burden, of 'the Glorious Dead'. As
the war memorials erected in every city, town and village in the land
proclaimed all too clearly, Housman had indeed foreseen the Somme
and lads in their hundreds and thousands would never be old. Ludlow
Tower was still standing, but beneath it a roll of honour would record
137 names, including those of the three sons of Thomas and Sarah
Halford, who lived in the centre of the town at 9 Raven Lane: Private
John Robert Halford of the 7th Battalion, the King's Shropshire Light
Infantry, killed at Mametz in July 1916, aged twenty-four; Private
William Henry Halford of the Army Service Corps, who died aged
twenty-seven when his troopship was torpedoed in the Aegean in
April 1917; and Private George Halford of the 8th Battalion, the King's
Shropshire Light Infantry, who died of wounds aged twenty-four in
Salonika in September 1918. The names of those who might have
'come in for the fair' from outlying districts are recorded on their own
village memorials at nearby Bromfield, Caynham, Stokesay, Onibury
and Ashford Carbonell.

Twenty-four of the war dead are recorded on a plaque in Clunbury church, twelve on one at Clungunford, and thirty-one beneath a large granite cross rearing out of the churchyard wall at Clun. Thirty-two lads who ended up 'a long way further than Knighton' are marshalled on the cenotaph in the centre of that town. The roll of officers and men killed, printed in double columns in *The History of the King's Shropshire Light Infantry in the Great War 1914–1918*, runs to sixty-six pages, and the book has as its epigraph 'They carry back bright to the Coiner the mintage of man'. The regiment was also commemorated by John Ernest Auden, uncle of the poet: the 1918 revised edition of his guide to Shropshire is dedicated

TO MY OLD COMRADES

THE OFFICERS, NON-COMMISSIONED

OFFICERS AND MEN

OF THE

4TH BATT. K.S.L.I. (T.)

Over the Herefordshire border, in the village of Cradley, is a memorial to four men from the same family, among them Captain Ivan Clarkson Maclean and Lieutenant Alec Clarkson Maclean, the two younger brothers of Harry Maclean, the Woolwich cadet, who is buried in the adjoining churchyard. Thirty-eight names of students and staff at the Royal College of Music are recorded on the war memorial there, among them George Butterworth and Ernest Farrar, both of whom were further commemorated when two prizes were founded in their names. Among the six men who formed the English Folk Dance Society's first Morris side, three – Butterworth, George Jerrard Wilkinson and Perceval Lucas (younger brother of the editor of *The Open Road*) – were killed on the Somme within weeks of each other in August 1916, as was R.J.E. Tiddy, an occasional member of the side who was also the author of *The Mummers' Play*, a collection of thirty-three folk plays published posthumously in 1923.

There is no record that he was aware of the fact, but in 1916 Housman had himself appeared in a design for a war memorial. When it became clear that the thousands of people killed in action would require some form of commemoration after the war, Henry Wilson,

President of the Arts & Crafts Exhibition Society, mounted an exhibition of designs for future war memorials at the Royal Academy of Art. When he asked Housman's friend William Rothenstein to contribute something, the artist immediately recalled a degree ceremony he had witnessed at Oxford University:

> The sight of a number of youths, booted and spurred, with their gowns over their khaki, kneeling before the Chancellor to receive their degrees, put me in mind of the age of chivalry, so touching and beautiful were these young figures; and I thought what a fine subject for a memorial painting this would make [. . .] I therefore painted a group of representative figures, Vice-Chancellors, scholars and men of science surrounding a Chancellor conferring a degree upon a young soldier, with a group of undergraduates, Rupert Brooke, Julian Grenfell, Raymond Asquith, John Manners and others, walking up, hand in hand, to receive symbolically what could never now be given them.

In the event the exhibition was postponed, but Rothenstein's three huge panels, 'Designed as a Memorial for Members of the English Universities who have served in the War', were exhibited at the Royal Academy in the autumn of that year. Rothenstein had worked on the painting with the assistance of the war artist Eric Kennington, who helped square out the canvases and transfer Rothenstein's original drawing onto them, as well as painting some of the architectural details and the decorations on the Chancellor's robe. 'I was glad of his help,' Rothenstein recalled, 'for there were sixty feet of canvas to be covered with life-size figures.' These figures included representatives of 'university types' (including Housman, M.R. James, A.C. Benson, Sir Joseph Thomson, Sir Walter Raleigh and Robert Bridges) whose portraits Rothenstein had already drawn at Oxford and Cambridge or when they came to stay at his Gloucestershire home, alongside 'Rupert Brooke and other heroic young men who had lost their lives in the war', whom he painted from photographs supplied by Edward Marsh. Rothenstein recalled that when the exhibition ended, 'my 60 feet of canvas were rolled up and forgotten'; but after his death his son

John found the panels and in 1959 presented them to the University of Southampton. The central panel, depicting Housman and the other gowned academics, is displayed in the university's Senate Room, while the two flanking panels depicting the war dead are on loan to Taplow Court in Buckinghamshire, the former home of Julian and Billy Grenfell.

In spite of the proliferation of war memorials, the English countryside itself seemed little changed after the war – particularly when compared with the more or less erased landscapes over which many of the returning soldiers had fought in France and Belgium. In 1922 Grant Richards published a collection of articles by the journalist S.P.B. Mais under the title *Oh! To Be in England* – a sentiment very familiar to those who had served in the war. The phrase comes from 'Home-Thoughts, from Abroad', Robert Browning's popular poem of 1845 celebrating the arrival of the English spring and written while the poet was travelling in Italy. Browning's poem had, unsurprisingly, been included in Rhys's *The Old Country*, and Mais evidently expected his readers to recognise his reference to it since he did not use the poem as an epigraph to his book. Instead he selected lines from Shakespeare and Rupert Brooke, two poets who were now considered exemplars of Englishness – not least because of the coincidence that, almost exactly three centuries apart, both men had died on 23 April, St George's Day.

Mais was a prolific journalist, who had previously been employed as an English teacher in several public schools and now worked at the *Daily Express* as a book reviewer. In the Preface to *Oh! To Be in England* he writes: 'This book is a debt that I owe, a long-standing debt, to England, which to me is not the Fleet Street where I work, but the country-side to which I belong.' Like H.V. Morton, who was also employed by the *Express* at this period, Mais was not a countryman by birth, having been born in Birmingham. Shortly afterwards, however, his father was appointed rector of the mining village of Tansley in Derbyshire, on the southern edge of the Peak District, and during his youth Mais became a keen walker and runner in the surrounding hills. Unlike Morton, Mais disdained motorised transport and believed that the only way to appreciate the countryside was by walking in it. He even followed Alfred Hyatt, editor of *The Footpath Way*, in considering exploration by bicycle, a recreation that had become very popular, too speedy for a properly immersive encounter with the English landscape. 'I am told that I may perhaps set other men wandering to discover England, the England who refuses to disclose her naked beauty in its full glory to any but the devout worshipper on foot,' he wrote. 'The best is hidden from all except the few who follow in the footsteps of George Borrow, Richard [sic] Cobbett, Edward Thomas, W.H. Davies, W.H. Hudson, Gilbert White, Richard Jefferies, William Hazlitt, the youthful Belloc and their like.'

Mais thus places himself in a high literary tradition of writing about the English countryside, but he also wanted to encourage ordinary people to set off on foot and find the kind of spiritual tranquillity he did before an office job curtailed his ramblings: 'If any of these descriptions rouse a single reader to explore for himself an unknown plot of rural England where he finds this peace I shall be happy [. . .] I long to start a new religion . . . "This England of yours, have you seen it? Leave your books and your games, your work and your worries, escape by yourself to the lonely places and there you shall find unutterable joy and profound peace."' Mais insists that he is not averse to foreign travel, but this can wait: as the title of a later book instructed, *See England First* – an appeal that would have seemed particularly inviting to those who had been obliged to spend time abroad during the recent war in places where joy and peace were in very short supply. This had not been Mais's lot, since a near-fatal appendectomy had kept him from active service, but at one point he had 'stood under the shadow of the Jungfrau and longed for the hop-fields of Kent', a civilian version of the kind of yearning for home felt by many soldiers at the front.

The frontispiece of *See England First*, published by Grant Richards in 1927, was a photograph of the Shropshire landscape by Edgar Ward; at Richards's suggestion Ward had sent this to Housman, who declared it 'very magnificent'. What Housman thought about Mais captioning the photograph with lines from 'Into my heart an air that kills' is unrecorded. Housman Country would also feature in Mais's *This Unknown Island* (1932), based on 'seventeen haphazard excursions made at high speed at the request of the B.B.C. for the purpose of stimulating in listeners a desire to explore and rediscover their own island'. High speed obliged Mais to make use of a hired car, 'an expensive and (to me) more or less distasteful way of exploring new ground', but it allowed him to cover an astonishing 15,000 miles during the four months he made his weekly broadcasts. The broadcasts proved hugely popular, Mais claiming that: 'I had more letters after my first talk than I have had in twenty years after writing forty books.' He began his talk on 'The Welsh Marches' by quoting a traditional poem:

> Happy is the eye
> Between Severn and Wye,
> But thrice happy he
> Between Severn and Clee.

'Happiness is not the first word one associates with the novels of Mary Webb or the poems of A.E. Housman,' Mais commented, 'though both were inspired by this part of Shropshire.' For Mais, Housman is the more significant of the two writers. Staying overnight at the Feathers Hotel in Ludlow, he encounters at breakfast a young married woman who is reading *A Shropshire Lad*. Mais asks her what she thinks of Mary Webb and receives the succinct answer 'Not much.' 'I have a feeling that the future will endorse her judgment in preferring Housman,' he says. In the village church at Minsterley he finds a collection of 'maiden's garlands', which were traditionally placed on the coffins of young unmarried girls and afterwards hung on the pews in which they had sat. 'This seemed to me an outward and visible sign of the whole content of Mr Housman's poetic vision,' Mais remarks. If not encompassing the whole poetic vision, these garlands certainly bring to mind the high proportion of young women who die before their time in *A Shropshire Lad* and may even have suggested to Housman, had he read about them somewhere, 'The garland briefer than a girl's' in the final line of 'To an Athlete Dying Young'. Mais inevitably quotes the traditional rhyme with which Housman prefaced 'In valleys of springs of rivers' and suggests that the war memorial at Clun is 'another very vivid reminder of *A Shropshire Lad*' before going on to quote the fifth verse of '1887' about the 'Shropshire names' incised on tombstones from an earlier war.

This Unknown Island was published two years after the formation of the Youth Hostels Association and three years before the foundation of the Ramblers' Association. Both organisations encouraged the discovery of the English countryside, the first by providing accommodation for young walkers, the second by campaigning for the right to roam over land that had hitherto been regarded as private and was often fiercely guarded by landowners' employees. Such rights were promoted by the popular philosopher C.E.M. Joad in *A Charter for Ramblers* (1934), in which he described the by now widespread enthusiasm for walking. 'The Central Station at Manchester early on a Sunday morning is an unforgettable sight,' he wrote, 'with its crowd of ramblers, complete with rucksacks, shorts, and hob-nailed boots.' When he observed that 'this generation has replaced beer by "hiking" as the shortest cut out of Manchester', he evoked the spirit of *A Shropshire Lad*, with its invitation 'come out to ramble' and its suggestion that beer had often been used as an escape from life's problems. While the Ramblers' Association had a political dimension, and had grown out of an organised 'mass trespass' on Kinder Scout in the Peak District in 1932, the YHA was rather more traditional and conservative in its outlook, formed to 'help all, especially young people of limited means, to a greater knowledge, love and care of the countryside'. Walking had become a national and highly popular pastime and well-equipped individuals or groups, with their rucksacks and sticks, were now a common sight in the landscape.

Some walkers took their copies of *A Shropshire Lad* with them. The Rt Rev. Mervyn Charles-Edwards, a retired Bishop of Worcester who had been brought up in Shrewsbury, recalled that in the 1920s, 'long before I owned a car, a copy of *A Shropshire Lad* was always in my pocket or haversack, for the advantage of a home where money was scarce was that as expensive holidays were out of the question I early learnt the joy of walking, and in company with four friends climbed every hill Shropshire. On the Stiperstones, Long Mynd, Caradoc and the Clees, during the lunch interval we used to take turns in reading the poems to each other.' These friends felt that Housman had 'caught the atmosphere of the country-side which we knew and loved. "Far in a western brookland", for us this was the little stream that ran by the

Bridge Inn near Ratlinghope where we drank beer and ate ham and eggs on our way from Church Stretton to Minsterley. In a mystical sense Housman's poems bound us to the past, we became involved in the very soil of Shropshire and were united with other lads before us who, "in their hundreds to Ludlow came in for the fair".'

After Charles-Edwards moved away from Shrewsbury, his pocket edition of *A Shropshire Lad* remained his 'constant companion'. He bought his first car, a second-hand Morris Cowley costing twenty-five pounds, in 1929, and the book became 'part of its essential equipment (and the same applied to all the cars I have owned)'. Even 'fifty-two years later, amid maps, the Highway Code and the car handbook, a copy of the poems has its place.'

Although many people, like the Manchester hikers, reached their rural destinations by rail, others increasingly got there by road. 'The remarkable system of motor-coach services which now penetrates every part of the country has thrown open to ordinary people regions which even after the coming of the railway were remote and inaccessible,' H.V. Morton observed in 1927. 'The popularity of the cheap motor-car is also greatly responsible for this long-overdue interest in English history, antiquities and topography.' While this is undoubtedly true, it is also the case that such interests were kindled in the trenches, where soldiers had spent time thinking about what it was they were fighting for. When they got home, they wanted to look at the things they had come to value when it occurred to them that they might lose them, and Edmund Blunden noticed 'a strong desire' among returning soldiers 'to see something of our own country, considered in many aspects, external and spiritual, personal and geographical, artistic and institutional'. The number of privately owned cars did indeed rise sharply after the First World War, from some 109,000 in 1919 to around a million by 1931 and two million by the outbreak of the Second World War. It was in 1919 that the Ordnance Survey produced its first set of one-inch-to-one-mile 'Tourist Maps'. The OS's hitherto austere and utilitarian maps were repackaged for the general public, with colourful pictorial covers by Ellis Martin, designed to entice people not only to well-known areas of outstanding natural beauty but also to *Burns' Country* and *Scott's Country*, as two of the Scottish maps were romantically renamed. In 1921 the OS recorded its highest ever sales, with profits up by 56 percent.

Guidebooks were now carried as often as not in glove compartments rather than in the bulging pockets of Norfolk jackets. Morton's *In Search of England* started out as a series of articles in the *Daily Express* that were announced on the paper's front page on St George's Day in 1926. Morton would set out from London in a two-seater 'Bullnose' Morris Cowley. 'I suppose many a man has stood at his window above a London square in April hearing a message from the lanes of England,' he wrote. 'The Georgians [of the eighteenth century] no doubt fancied that Aegipans and Centaurs kicked their hoofs in Berkeley Square, and I, above my humbler square, dreamt a no less classic eclogue of hedges lit with hawthorn, of orchards ready for their brief wave of pink spray, of fields in which smoky-faced lambs pressed against their dams, of new furrows over which moved slowly the eternal figure bent above a plough [. . .] Now I will go, with spring before me and the road calling me out into England. It does not matter where I go, for it is all England.' This excursion would fulfil the pledge he made to himself while standing on the hill above Jerusalem. 'It was the only religious moment I experienced in Jerusalem,' he recalled, rather as Mais described his urging of people out into the English countryside as 'a new religion'.

Morton's journey through England was not comprehensive, missing out several richly bucolic counties such as Kent, Sussex and Suffolk. More tellingly he tends to bypass the industrial heartlands of England. Crossing the Cheshire–Lancashire border, he steers a careful passage 'between Liverpool on the left and Manchester on the right, and about sixteen miles from both cities'. From this distance Liverpool is safely reduced to 'red smoke-stacks rising above the flat lands by the sandy shore' of the Mersey estuary, while Manchester is merely 'an ominous grey haze in the skies'. 'For months I have motored through a green England which might never have known the Industrial Revolution. Round Bristol, it is true, I saw factories. I left Birmingham on my right, and saw no trace of that monster as I went on into Old England. Here was new England: an England of crowded towns, of tall chimneys, of great mill walls, of canals of slow, black water; an England of grey, hard-looking little houses in interminable rows; the England of coal and chemicals; of cotton, glass, and iron.'

This, it is clear, is not the England Morton has come in search of, even though it is an England in which many of his readers were living, particularly those who read his account in the *Express* rather than between hard covers. He acknowledges that industrial architecture has its own 'grim power' when seen from a distance, but takes consolation from the fact that 'these monster towns and cities of the north of England are a mere speck in the amazing greenness of England; their inhabitants can be lost in green fields and woodlands within a few minutes.'

The book ends not with Morton back in London, but in a small, unnamed and presumably emblematic country church at Harvest Festival:

A Sunday hush lay over field and wood: a silence broken only by the song of birds and the drone of insects. The church bell rang.

The little church was full of corn sheaves. Apples, picked for their size and colour, washed and polished, stood in a line against the altar rails. Above the empty pew of the absent squire, barley nodded its golden head. The church smelt of ripe corn and fruit. Some one, I wonder if consciously or just by chance, had placed a posy of flowers in the stiff, stone hands of Sir Gervais. He lay there with his thin, mailed toes to the vaulting, his sword at his side and in his hands this offering from his own land to warm his heart in a Norman heaven.

When the service ends, Morton walks out into the churchyard and performs the same gesture as Edward Thomas did after he had enlisted: 'I took up a handful of earth and felt it crumble and run through my fingers, thinking that as long as one English field lies against another there is something left in the world for a man to love.' The book ends with an exchange between Morton and a clergyman:

'Well,' smiled the vicar, as he walked towards me between the yew trees, 'that, I am afraid, is all we have.'

'You have England,' I said.

Morton's England is recognisably the England of Stanley Baldwin, who served three terms as Britain's Prime Minister between the wars (1923–4, 1924–9, 1935–7). Like Housman, Baldwin was born in Worcestershire, at Bewdley, the original destination of the Severn in 'The Welsh Marches' before Housman changed it to Buildwas in Shropshire. Until Baldwin's great-grandfather moved to Stourport-on-Severn to set up a foundry in 1788, the family had been yeoman and tenant farmers in Shropshire for almost two centuries, and when Baldwin retired he acknowledged both Shropshire and Worcestershire in the titles he took, becoming Viscount Corvedale as well as Earl Baldwin of Bewdley. 'There could have been no more typical English surroundings in which to cherish the earliest memories,' he said of Bewdley.

> I remember as a child looking up the river from the bridge into that mysterious and romantic land of Shropshire, so close to us, from which my people came only three generations before, and watching the smoke of the train running along the little railway through places bearing names like Wyre Forest, Cleobury Mortimer, Neen Sollars and Tenbury – names steeped in romance and redolent of the springtime in an England long ago passed, but whose heritage is ours. Those names must have been familiar to Langland as he lay on the slopes of the Malvern Hills while the great poem of *Piers Plowman* shaped itself in his brain.

These names would have been familiar to Langland because he is thought to have been born in Shropshire, between the Wyre Forest and the Clee Hills.

A large part of Baldwin's popular appeal was that he presented himself as a dependable, straightforward English countryman, setting himself apart from the sleekly metropolitan personae of other leading politicians. He was rarely seen without his pipe, and he favoured baggy suits, stout footwear and old hats. He had little time for the smart set in London and appeared to regard the capital rather as Housman's Lad did, as a place of exile from the beloved countryside of his youth. He even had his own blue remembered hills, the ones he could see from the garden of his Worcestershire home. It was a view that often came to mind when he was in his Whitehall office, as he told members of the Worcestershire Association at one of their annual London dinners:

> I see the hills known to you all, beginning in the north-east, the Clents; and beyond, in Warwickshire, Edgehill, where the English squire passed with horse and hounds between the two armies; Bredon, the beginning of the Cotswolds, like a cameo against the sky, and the wonderful straight blue line of the Malverns, little shapes of Ankerdine and Berrow Hill, and, perhaps most beautiful and graceful, his two neighbours, Woodbury and Abberley; and Clee Hill, opening up another beautiful and romantic world and pre-senting a circle of beauty which I defy any part of England to match.

Housman, too, often came to Baldwin's mind. The two men had met on only three occasions. Appropriately enough, they had acted as pallbear-ers at the funeral of Thomas Hardy in Westminster Abbey on 16 January 1928. Some time later Baldwin was taken to visit Housman in his rooms, where he was 'not made very welcome', and in 1933 sat next to him at a Cambridge dining club, where he found him 'most unclubbable'. If he did not know or much care for the man, Baldwin certainly knew the work and clearly expected his audience to do so when he quoted it in his speeches. It was a knowledge he shared with Churchill, with whom he also felt a certain kinship because 'although not a Worcestershire man, he is sprung from the soil of Oxfordshire, which is not very far off, and has some of our happy characteristics. We country people have, by the mere fact of our birth and sojourn in the heart of England, learned something which stands us in good stead in the strange life of politics in which we are both immersed.' The context for this was another speech Baldwin made to the Worcestershire Association, this one delivered in February 1929 during his second term as Prime Minister, when Churchill was serving as Chancellor of the Exchequer:

> It is, as the Chancellor said, the background – the constant, con-sistent, persistent background – of the old country life that is so strength-giving and so refreshing. Picture to yourselves the House

of Commons on one of those rare occasions when things are not going well, when tempers are rising, and when observations which had better not be reported are flashing across from one side of the House of Commons to the other: when possibly those who dwell beside the Clyde seem so different from those one had known on the banks of the Severn. It is in those moments that the lines of the poet which I have quoted so often before in connection with our county come back to mind:

'In valleys of springs of rivers
By Ony and Teme and Clun,
The country for easy livers,
The quietest under the sun.'

The contemplation of that takes one far away from the turmoil in which one is, and enables one to pass through the fire unscathed.

The banks of the Clyde had been anything but quiet during Baldwin's political career, becoming a byword for industrial unrest among engineers and shipbuilders ever since the mass strike and subsequent establishment of the Clyde Workers' Committee in 1915. Baldwin never names Housman in his speeches, merely referring to 'the poet' or 'the beautiful lines which I am sure you all know', and these same lines came to his mind when, for instance, he was delivering a speech at the annual dinner of the Fly Fishers' Club in 1927. The theme of the speech was that fishing promoted social unity, that no matter what their station in life, 'the mere fact that a man is a fisherman, whether it is on the Ony, the Teme or Severn, all these men are brothers', and that these men were further bonded by 'love of the open air and open spaces' suggested by Housman's poem: 'That is all we want; it is such little things we want to make with pleasant livers and all around us peace and quiet, and it is just what so few of us can get.' A famous 1937 cartoon by Bernard Partridge marking Baldwin's departure from office depicts him as a ploughman being congratulated by John Bull on 'a long day and a rare straight furrow': it was captioned 'The Worcestershire Lad'.

Baldwin was not of course quite the simple countryman he presented himself as. He was very attached to his Scottish mother, who came from a highly literary and artistic family: her parents moved in Pre-Raphaelite circles, and one of her sisters married Burne-Jones, another E.J. Poynter, while the third was the mother of Kipling. Louisa Baldwin wrote novels, poetry and children's books, and brought up her only son with a keen appreciation of English language and literature. Baldwin would famously champion the works of that other author closely connected with Shropshire, Mary Webb, turning her from what he regarded as a neglected genius into a best-selling writer – he even wrote the preface to *Precious Bane* in the collected edition of her works. All that said, the persona Baldwin adopted was not created for him by political advisors but was an intrinsic part of his character. One would expect a prime minister to be patriotic, but Baldwin's love of his country was entirely bound up in his love of the English countryside. As he said in a speech delivered at the annual dinner of the Royal Society of St George in May 1924:

> To me, England is the country and the country is England. And when I ask myself what I mean by England, when I think of England when I am abroad, England comes to me through my various senses – through the ear, through the eye, and through certain imperishable scents. I will tell you what they are, and there may be those among you who feel as I do.
>
> The sounds of England, the tinkle of the hammer on the anvil in the country smithy, the corncrake on a dewy morning, the sound of the scythe against the whetstone, and the sight of a plough team coming over the brow of a hill, the sight that has been seen in England since England was a land, and may be seen in England long after the Empire has perished and every works in England has ceased to function, for centuries the one eternal sight of England. The wild anemones in the woods in April, the last load at night of hay being drawn down a lane as the twilight comes on, when you can scarcely distinguish the figures of the horses as they take it home to the farm, and above all, most subtle, most penetrating and most moving, the smell of wood smoke coming up in an autumn

evening, or the smell of the scutch fires [. . .] These things strike down into the very depths of our nature, and touch chords that go back to the very beginning of time and the human race, but they are chords that with every year of our life sound a deeper note in our innermost being.

Some have dismissed such speeches as both sentimental and irrelevant in a country that was still in the grip of an agricultural depression and in any case highly industrialised. To some extent Baldwin was aware that he was open to such criticisms, but while acknowledging that 'we have become largely an urban folk', he persisted in believing that the true spirit of England continued to reside in fields, woods and villages, and that this was something that everyone recognised. As he put it in one speech: 'there lies, deep down in the hearts even of those who have toiled in our cities for two or three generations, an ineradicable love of country things and country beauty, as it may exist in them traditionally and subconsciously; and to them, as much as and even more to ourselves, the country represents the eternal values and the eternal traditions from which we must never allow ourselves to be separated'. He may well have been right. It is hard to imagine a British politician today managing to reach out to a wide public in the way Baldwin did – or indeed to have his speeches not only put between hard covers but becoming best sellers. Published in April 1926, *On England* was in its fifth edition by October of that year. Such was the demand for the book that a 'Cheap edition' was published in April 1927 and a 'Popular' one in March 1933, by which time it had sold over 26,000 copies. The *Manchester Guardian* felt that the book 'reveals and expresses a love of England that goes [. . .] far to explain the hold [its author] has so quickly won over his fellow-countrymen. It is no political theory, but a healthy concrete attachment to the soil and fields, the hedges and buildings of the countryside and to the men and women who draw their life from it.' J.C. Squire in the *Observer* identified the book's particular appeal: 'This is the work of a thoroughly representative Englishman; not the common man, but one expressing . . . what the common man feels and cannot say for himself.' There were all manner of practical things people wanted in the 1920s and 1930s in a country still reeling from a devastating war and beset by unemployment, industrial unrest and the rise of fascism in Europe; but equally they needed reassurance and a sense that the essential nature of England persisted in spite of such upheavals and threats.

Publishers were keen to tap into this renewed sense of what England stood for and how it should be appreciated. J.C. Squire and Viscount Lee of Fareham were joint editors of the 'English Heritage Series' published between 1929 and 1936. Individual volumes were dedicated to such national pastimes as *Cricket* (1930), *Fox-Hunting* (1935) and *English Folk-Song and Dance* (1935), such national institutions as *The English Public School* (1929), *The English Inn* (1930), *The English Parish Church* (1930), and *The English Country House* (1935), and such cultural phenomena as *English Humour* (written by J.B. Priestley, with an introduction by Baldwin, 1929) and *English Music* (1931), while Edmund Blunden contributed to the series a more general, topographical volume on *The Face of England* (1932). In an article titled 'On Pilgrimage in England: Voyages of Discovery', Blunden cited Katharine A. Esdaile's survey of *Monuments in English Churches* (1937) and Colonel M.H. Grant's *Chronological History of the Old English Landscape Painters*, which appeared in three lavishly illustrated folio volumes from 1926, as instances of the way in which England was being catalogued and appreciated. 'At no time have some of our national treasures been reconsidered with half the gusto or half the living scholarship that has been witnessed during the past quarter of a century,' he wrote.

Among the many books on the countryside that appeared between the wars, the best known were Arthur Mee's *The King's England* series, the Shell County Guides and the series of volumes published by B.T. Batsford. Mee was a journalist who had become well known for his phenomenally popular *Children's Encyclopaedia*, originally published in fifty fortnightly parts between 1908 and 1910. *The King's England*, which began publishing in 1936, was advertised as 'A New Domesday Book of 10,000 Towns and Villages'. It would eventually run to forty volumes, each dedicated to an individual county, with the addition of an introductory one, *Enchanted Land* (1936), which in its revised edition was subtitled 'The Very Essence of England and the English Character'. Mee claimed of the series that 'There has been nothing like it before:

it is the first census of the ancient and beautiful and curious historic possessions of England since the motor car came to make it possible.' He and a team of researchers travelled the land recording not only cities, towns, villages, notable buildings, monuments, natural features and 'enchanting vistas', but also local history, legends and anecdotes. The books were illustrated with sepia photographs, included a fold-out map, and were written in a relaxed conversational style aimed at 'ordinary' people. The *Shropshire* volume, subtitled 'County of the Western Hills', first appeared in 1939, and refers to 'Mr Housman' or quotes his poetry in its descriptions of Clun, Hughley, Ludlow, Shrewsbury and Wenlock Edge.

The Shell County Guides were intended to appeal to a rather different market. The idea for them came from John Betjeman, at that time an assistant editor at the *Architectural Review*, and it was he who approached Jack Beddington, the publicity director of the petroleum company Shell-Mex & BP Ltd. Beddington had been working for Shell for a decade, having apparently got the job after he had criticised the company's advertisements, which were striking but concentrated entirely on its products. He was determined instead to promote the company itself, inventing slogans and commissioning painters and graphic artists to create posters for hoardings. As motor cars became more affordable, they were increasingly used for leisure activities, notably following H.V. Morton's lead in exploring the countryside, and among Beddington's most successful campaigns were those depicting landscape, buildings or other notable structures and urging motorists to 'See Britain First on Shell' or assuring them that 'To Visit British Landmarks You Can Be Sure of Shell' and even 'Everywhere You Go You Can Be Sure of Shell'.

The images were commissioned from both established artists and those starting out in their careers, and Beddington was inclined to give his designers a free hand. This resulted in a wide range of styles: John Piper's dark image of Stonehenge beneath the stars, Graham Sutherland's airy, almost surreal rendering of the Great Globe at Swanage, Paul Nash's Cubist-inspired vision of the Rye Marshes, and Rex Whistler's lush green view across Aylesbury Vale. The series both encouraged tourism and provided a genuinely public art gallery which promoted the works of, among others, Duncan Grant, Vanessa Bell, Leonard Rosoman, Frank Dobson, Edward Bawden, E. McKnight Kauffer, Barnett Freedman, Edward Bawden and Denton Welch. Betjeman felt that Beddington's innovative approach to design, and his policy of letting those he commissioned get on with it without undue interference, would make Shell the perfect commercial sponsors for a series that would be quite unlike any guidebook previously published.

Betjeman himself wrote the first volume, on Cornwall, in 1934. Its idiosyncratic text, drawing attention to unfashionable periods of architecture, its inclusion of local recipes, its use of old and new photographs, collage and both modern and Victorian typefaces, and its overall impression of enthusiastic amateurism rather than dry scholarship, set the tone for the entire series. Another feature that set the guides apart was that they were spiral-bound, which meant that they could be opened flat – far more convenient for motorists than traditionally bound guidebooks. During the 1930s a further twelve guides would be published, often written by Betjeman's friends and fellow enthusiasts: John Piper on Oxfordshire, Lord Clonmore on Kent, Robert Byron on Wiltshire, Peter Quennell on Somerset. Few of the books were the work of professional historians, and in commissioning instead artists such as Piper, Paul Nash (Dorset), John Nash (Buckinghamshire) and Stephen Bone (the West Coast of Scotland), Betjeman was continuing the policy Beddington had already established with the Shell posters. The series has been described as 'the largest essay on the relationship between our physical environment and British identity in the twentieth century'.

The books published by Batsford during this period also encouraged readers to explore their own country, but were intended to be read at home rather than on the road. They were distinguished by their stylised and brightly coloured dust-jackets, designed by 'Brian Cook', otherwise Brian Batsford, nephew of, and eventually successor as chairman to, the firm's founder. His first jacket design was for A.K. Wickham's *The Villages of England* in 1932, and overall the books gave a contemporary graphic look to timeless English landscapes. As the books multiplied, Batsford marshalled them into 'libraries' with such titles as 'The Face of Britain', 'The Pilgrim's Library' and the

'Home-Front Handbooks', which appeared during the Second World War. The books were written by a wide variety of authors and were illustrated with photographs. Volumes in 'The Face of Britain' series were regionally specific (*English Lakeland*, *English Downland*, *Welsh Border Country*, *Shakespeare's Country*) and written by individual authors, but those in 'The Pilgrim's Library' were collections of essays by individual hands, attracting such well-known writers as J.B. Priestley, Edmund Blunden, Henry Williamson, H.E. Bates, Adrian Bell and G.M. Young (who would go on to become Stanley Baldwin's official biographer). The Pilgrim's Library was launched in April 1935 with *The Beauty of Britain* (1935), followed by *The Legacy of England* ('An Illustrated Survey of the Works of Man in the English Country'), *Nature in Britain* and *The English Countryside*.

The 'Handbooks' first appeared in the autumn of 1939 and were 'designed to meet the needs of those who, through wartime circumstances, must seek their own entertainment instead of finding it readymade to hand'. The series, according to the publisher's blurb, was 'intended particularly for people now living in the country for the first time', by which it was presumably meant those who had moved there to escape threatened air raids, 'that they might use their leisure constructively for their own benefit and for the benefit of the nation in general'. While it was easy to see how a book on *How to Grow Food* might benefit both individuals and the nation, other titles seemed rather less practical: *How to See Nature*, *How to Look at Old Buildings* and *How to See the Countryside*. Presumably these titles were intended to boost morale and remind people what the country was fighting to protect.

In this they resembled 'There'll Always Be an England', a song composed in the summer of 1939 by Ross Parker and Hughie Charles and first performed by a boy soprano in a midshipman's uniform in the film *Discoveries*. It became one of the most popular songs of the Second World War, particularly when sung by the 'Forces' Sweetheart', Vera Lynn, and its chorus proclaimed, in words that echoed the sentiments of Stanley Baldwin:

> There'll always be an England
> While there's a country lane,

Wherever there's a cottage small
Beside a field of grain.

Within two months of the declaration of war some 200,000 copies of the sheet music had been sold, and S.P.B. Mais appropriated the song's title for a morale-boosting volume about the English landscape published in 1940.

Mais's earlier suggestion that people should 'Leave your books and your games, your work and your worries, escape by yourself to the lonely places and there you shall find unutterable joy and profound peace' was taken up by the protagonist of Francis Brett Young's *Mr Lucton's Freedom*. The novel was written and published in 1940 but is set in a timeless England during the last summer of peace, and is saturated in Housman. The book's American publisher acknowledged this when retitling it *The Happy Highway*, a phrase borrowed from 'Into my heart an air that kills'. Brett Young draws together those enduring notions of the countryside as a repository of true English values into which urban people can escape. In particular, the English landscape that lies between the River Severn and the Welsh Marches is portrayed as a place where spiritual peace and happiness can be found and briefly grasped before the onset of another world war.

Brett Young is one of those prolific English novelists of the interwar years whose work was widely read at the time but has since been largely forgotten. Born in 1884 in the Worcestershire town of Halesowen, he had looked longingly to the westward hills as a child. His own 'Pisgah' was the nearby Walton Hill, as he wrote in some notes for an uncompleted autobiography: 'Even today, I doubt if I could ever wholly overcome the awe of that prospect, for it is one of the widest and fairest in all England: the dreamy, green expanse of the Severn Plain; the level line of the Cotswolds – pale blue as the chalk hill butterfly; Bredon (beloved hill!), a half-strung bow; Malvern, peaked and fantastic like scenery on a stage; Abberley, with its tower; two waves of Clee; and, beyond it all, a tangle of unnamed hills.'

While studying medicine at Birmingham University he met his future wife, the daughter of a local gentleman-farmer, but they were temporarily separated after a couple of months when she took a job in

Somerset. Having paid her a visit on the eve of her departure, Brett Young walked the eleven miles back to his home: 'I don't believe I saw two inches of the road – I just trudged along with my head full of love and hope and anxieties, reviewing, as a drowning man sees his whole life in the flash of a moment, our wonderful experience of the last two months – till the steady swing of my walk resolved itself into the metre of a poem by A.E. Housman, and I mentally repeated it a hundred times.' That poem was 'White in the moon the long road lies', but the pair would be reunited and would marry after Brett Young had gained a first-class medical degree and begun practising as a GP in Devon. In his spare time he wrote music, setting the words of English poets, including Housman, and embarked on his career as a novelist.

He served with the RAMC in South Africa during the First World War, but was invalided out and gave up medicine to become a full-time writer, embarking on a series of novels set in the West Midlands and the Welsh Marches and known, after Hardy's model, as the Mercian Novels. They would eventually be published in a uniform 'Severn Edition'. The first of them were written on Capri, where he had gone in 1919 to recover his health and where he remained until 1928. As with the Shropshire Lad, exile from the landscape of his youth increased his longing for it. 'Ever since my childhood, my soul has wandered over these beloved hills, and brooded over them, tenderly,' he wrote, and this yearning fed into the Mercian novels, which made his reputation and sold in large numbers. In almost all of them the western horizon, seen from somewhere approximating Birmingham, represents contentment and freedom.

At the time he wrote *Mr Lucton's Freedom*, Brett Young had returned to Worcestershire and was living in Craycombe House in the ancient village of Fladbury, midway between Evesham and Pershore. During the war the BBC had moved their headquarters to Wood Norton, a couple of miles away, and Brett Young played host to many of those who broadcast from there, including Stanley Baldwin. He had sent Baldwin a copy of *Portrait of Clare*, the novel that made his reputation in 1927, and a cordial friendship based on a shared love of literature, cricket and Worcestershire had eventually resulted. It is perhaps no coincidence that Baldwin stayed at Craycombe while Brett Young was writing *Mr Lucton's Escape*, since the two men's vision of England is essentially the same.

In the novel a successful but discontented fifty-year-old business-man called Mr Lucton leaves his home in North Bromwich (otherwise Birmingham) one beautiful summer's evening to drive out into the countryside, with no particular purpose in mind except to escape 'the grimy tentacles' of his home town. Having accidentally driven his car into a deep pond, he decides to abandon it and head west on foot. Despite undergoing some alarming experiences, he finds in the countryside the kind of 'authentic' life denied him in the city. He helps a farming family bring in the hay, teams up with an enthusiastic Black Country member of the Ramblers' Association, reluctantly takes part in a local cricket match, and ends up in the small village of Chapel Green as handyman to a pair of spinster sisters. The precise location of Chapel Green is not revealed, but it is in south Shropshire, and people do their shopping and consult their solicitors in nearby Ludlow.

By an unlikely coincidence, Mr Lucton's secretary comes from this district, and it is her mention of it in the book's opening pages that brings Housman to her employer's mind. Like Housman and Brett Young himself, Mr Lucton 'had often wistfully gazed on [distant west-ward hills] when he was a boy', and the first four lines of 'In valleys of springs of rivers' run through his mind after his secretary refers to her family home, transporting him from his oppressive office into the idyllic English landscape he knew in his youth: 'Ah Shropshire,' he exclaims. 'When I was a lad, Miss Jenkins, I rode all through that part of the country on a bicycling-tour [. . .] Nothing to beat it!' A few pages later, he recalls the long-gone happiness he experienced when first married, and the intolerable passing of irrecoverable time since then: 'Twenty-five years ago,' he thinks. 'That's more than a third of a lifetime. *And take from seventy springs three score* — two and a half score to be precise — *It only leaves me twenty more*. Only twenty years more, after thirty of drudgery.' It is these feelings that decide him to set off on his journey. What he needs is 'a landscape warm and green and soothing to his nerves; and so, as he canvassed the possibilities, there came to his mind – led thither, unconsciously perhaps, by the lines of Housman he had quoted to his secretary that morning – a vision of Bredon Hill (Bredon Cloud, as the old maps called it) rising gently out of the orchard lands of the Severn Plain with the slow Avon meandering about its feet and larks overhead.'

He heads west out of North Bromwich, 'beyond which the line of the Clees and the dome of the Wrekin marked the ultimate skyline', and travels through 'the green brooklands of the Severn' towards Housman Country: 'It was odd, he reflected, how, all through his life, that prospect had drawn his imagination westward.'

The novel contains frequent further allusions to Housman's poems. Mr Lucton twice refers to hawthorn blossom as 'tarnished', for instance, and during his spell as a haymaker listens appreciatively to 'the jingle of harness' as the horses toss their heads and swish their tails. Mr Lucton has never really found a proper confidant, and so is delighted when an attractive young hiker he briefly encounters at a remote spot invites him to open his heart to her, a moment that in its setting and mood recalls 'From far, from eve and morning'. Mr Lucton tells the young woman his life story: 'All through this prolonged narration he was encouraged and warmed by the certainty that, for once, his emotions and motives – however small, unimportant, or even childishly ridiculous – were being acknowledged with a deeper understanding and sympathy than he had ever hoped for. From the first his heart had assured him that this would be so, yet the actuality moved him nonetheless. In that high and misty solitude a miracle had removed his loneliness.' Tellingly, the young woman turns out to be the daughter of Lord Clun, and she tarries with Mr Lucton for no more than a breath, vanishing during the night.

Although the Black Country rambler had not known Housman's poetry ('never bought a book in my life'), it is the immediate recognition of lines from *A Shropshire Lad* that draws Mr Lucton to one of the sisters for whom he ends up working at Chapel Green, and 'had marked the beginning of their companionship'. When he drives the two women to Ludlow for an ominous meeting with their solicitor, he whiles away the time wandering around the town and recalls that Milton's *Comus* was first performed there (in 1634). 'It was odd how, in periods of emotion such as this, great poetry seemed to gain in intensity and even in beauty,' he thinks.

> He walked to and fro, trying to dredge from his imperfect memory of *Comus* the lines he loved best, and, failing these, with better success, the poems in *A Shropshire Lad* that had Ludlow for a scene – pretty melancholy they were on the whole, and most of them connected with the idea of war. Fifty years had passed, he reflected, since Housman wrote them, and here we were again, thinking of war again! *Danzig: New Nazi Moves . . . Poles Mobilize*, the blood-red news-bills shrieked at him from the stationers over the way.

At the end of the novel Mr Lucton returns to North Bromwich to take up his responsibilities once more, and the book marks the point at which escaping into the countryside is no longer an option, at which people will once again march off to war to defend the values these landscapes had come to embody, the ancient, unspoilt rural beauty now under threat from the industrialised Nazi war machine.

When war was finally declared, propaganda posters once again drew upon that English countryside, urging 'Your Britain – Fight For It Now'. Although Abram Games, born and raised in London's East End, produced forward-looking images of Modernist façades behind which lay bomb-damaged urban streets, far more familiar are the posters of his assistant at the War Office, Frank Newbould. Born in Bradford and working mainly in London, Newbould nevertheless produced posters for the same series in which a shepherd and his dog drive sheep across the rolling landscape of the South Downs, a village pub and church are framed by an ancient oak, people enjoy swingboats and roundabouts on the green at Alfriston, and Salisbury Cathedral is seen not across the city's rooftops but through lushly foliaged trees from the opposite bank of the River Nadder. Though Newbould's images are mostly particular, they are also emblematic, a feature they share with Housman's Shropshire.

By this time, Housman's poetry was available in a collected edition, edited by John Carter and published in Britain in 1939 and in America in March 1940. Although running to only 128 pages, it was issued at a standard size rather than in the 'waistcoat pocket' format that proved so popular when used for *A Shropshire Lad* in the First World War. In America, however, *The Selected Poems of A.E. Housman* (numbered M-1) became one of the first of the Armed Services Editions published by the Council on Books in Wartime, distributed free to American servicemen and designed specifically for battledress pockets. The format was landscape, measuring just 5½ by 3¾ inches, and the book was staple-bound in paper covers. The poems themselves were printed in double columns and arranged by published volume. This edition contained all but five of the poems that appeared in *The Collected Poems*, as well as Carter's 'Notes on the Text' and an additional note on the author by Louis Untermeyer, reprinted from his 1920 anthology of *Modern British Poetry*. The poems omitted were 'On the idle hill of summer' and 'The Day of Battle' from *A Shropshire Lad*, 'The chestnut casts his flambeaux, and the flowers' and 'Epitaph on an Army of Mercenaries' from *Last Poems*, and 'Farewell to a name and number' from *More Poems*. No acknowledgement is made of these exclusions: poems are merely renumbered, using Arabic rather than the original Roman numerals, so that 'White in the moon the long road lies' simply moves back a place to become no. 35 rather than no. XXXVI, which is what it should be. It was presumably felt that references to 'dead and rotten' soldiers, slaughtered mercenaries and combatants 'cheap to the King' were scarcely good for front-line morale, while the advice that it makes little difference to the inevitable fate of combatants whether they fight or run away might even be regarded as seditious.

The odd one out among the omitted poems is 'The chestnut casts his flambeaux, and the flowers', which unlike the others does not have a dispiriting or alarming military theme. One can only assume that it was Housman's reference to 'Whatever brute or blackguard made the world' that caused difficulties in a country where the national anthem included the words 'And this be our motto: "In God is our trust"' and which stamped a variation of this motto ('In God We Trust') on all its coins. Paul Fussell has written of anthologies issued by the Council on Books in Wartime that 'it is unthinkable that any materials of a pacifistic, subversive, or even very skeptical tendency would find an entrance', but Housman's distrust of God is quite apparent in other poems. Perhaps it was the vehemence of expression that led to the omission of these few verses from the Armed Services volume. Equally, other poems that were not excluded provide a less than cheerful account of military service, so perhaps it was the particular expression of doom and dissent in the four that were dropped that caused the authorities qualms.

Those poems that had escaped the cull came strongly recommended, reflecting the high regard in which Housman had always been held in America. 'When he died in 1936, A.E. Housman was universally acknowledged the greatest English poet of our day,' it was proclaimed on the book's wrapper. Untermeyer's note was equally certain: 'Purely as writing, *A Shropshire Lad* is incomparable,' he had written. 'It is as a poet that Housman will live, and his verse already seems marked for permanence.' If the American novelist Walker Percy is to be believed, some US soldiers also took Housman's first volume with them to war. In *The Moviegoer* (1961) the protagonist's father, an American from New Orleans, 'was commissioned in the RCAF in 1940 and got himself killed before his country entered the war. And in Crete. And in the wine dark sea [. . .] And with a copy of *The Shropshire Lad* in his pocket.'

If, back in England, *A Shropshire Lad* was no longer in every pocket by the time war broke out, it was still being widely bought in the pocket edition, 5000 copies of which were reprinted in 1935, with two further reprints the following year, one more in 1937, two more in 1938 and another in 1940. As in the First World War, the poems served to remind soldiers of the England they had left behind them. 'When I was posted by Coastal Command to Africa in 1942,' recalled the novelist J.L. Carr, '*A Shropshire Lad* was one of the two books I took with me and throughout their war service his very *English* poems greatly consoled many thousands of servicemen sent abroad.' (The emphasis is Carr's.)

Among those soldiers who knew the poems by heart and so did not need to pack the book itself was Anthony Chenevix-Trench. An outstanding classicist, he had been educated at Shrewsbury School, where he would spend his free time exploring the Shropshire Hills by bicycle and on foot, and had won a scholarship to Oxford; but his education was interrupted by the outbreak of war. Taken prisoner by the Japanese, he ended up working on the Burma railway, and although he lost one eye and suffered kidney failure he survived his experiences to become head-master of Eton. During his wartime ordeal, his biographer records: 'His family, his friends and his education acted as a sturdy shield as he sought solace in the serenity of his past, central to which were his literary pursuits. He summoned up his awesome powers of memory to translate all the poetry he knew into Latin and Greek. A particular occupational therapy was translating *A Shropshire Lad* into Latin while stonebreaking on the railway – a very Salopian thing to do, one of Tony's friends later remarked.' Indeed, it recalls *Sabrinae Corolla*, the volume Housman had been given at the age of seventeen containing English poetry translated into Latin and Greek by scholars from that school. Some of Chenevix-Trench's translations found their way back to Shrewsbury and were published anonymously in the school's magazine, the *Salopian*. The poems in question were 'If truth in hearts that perish', 'When last I came to Ludlow' and 'Into my heart an air that kills' (*'Ei mihi! quam flatus per pectora letifer inflat / Illic spectanti qua procul arva nitent!'*). 'Access to books he had none,' the magazine noted, 'and there were minor inaccuracies in the English that he had by heart, and even a slip or two in the Latin [. . .] but it seemed more interesting to publish them practically as they reached his former Headmaster in the Schools. Not often can Latin verses have been composed in such untoward circumstances.' This last comment was the kind of English understatement that Housman himself might have enjoyed, and Chenevix-Trench's biography was given the title *Land of Lost Content*.

One of Chenevix-Trench's fellow prisoners of war in the Far East was a young solicitors' clerk from Northamptonshire called Geoffrey Ipgrave. When he sailed with the Transport Corps on one of the last troopships bound for Singapore, he took the 1940 pocket edition of *A Shropshire Lad* with him. By the time the ship arrived in Singapore, the base had fallen to the Japanese and almost as soon as he disembarked Ipgrave became one of the 85,000 Allied troops taken prisoner there. He was sent to work on the railways in Thailand, moving from camp to camp, and remained a prisoner until the end of the war. *A Shropshire Lad* was the only one of his books that he refused to give up so that its pages could be used to make roll-up cigarettes, the customary fate of such volumes in POW camps. Like Salley Vickers's father in

Germany, Ipgrave was holding on to a little piece of England, a book that reminded him of the long walks he had taken with his dog in the Northamptonshire countryside, walks he also recalled in the letters he wrote home. Particular poems reminded him of particular places, not in Shropshire but in his own county, a hundred miles or so due east of Ludlow. In his copy of the book he has pencilled in his own local place-names: 'Bulwick' against the line 'See how thick the goldcup flowers'; 'Newton' under the poem 'March'; 'Blatherwycke Lake' between the first and second stanzas of 'Oh fair enough are sky and plain', in which Housman describes trees and clouds reflected in water. Elsewhere individual phrases, lines and verses of the poems are underlined or encircled, most of them descriptions of landscape, but he sometimes marked Housman's references to loneliness or exhortations to stoicism. Perhaps most poignantly, against the lines 'Here I lie down in London / And turn to rest alone' in 'Far in a western brookland' he has simply written 'T H A I L A N D' against 'London'. Given the harsh and monotonous cycle of his days on the railways, it is perhaps unsurprising that he should highlight the dispiriting first stanza of 'The Immortal Part' (XLIII):

> When I meet the morning beam,
> Or lay me down at night to dream,
> I hear my bones within me say,
> 'Another night, another day . . . '

To counterbalance this, however, under his signature and the inscription 'Singapore. 1942. Feb. 24th' on the book's flyleaf, he has written out the final stanza of 'Twice a week the winter thorough' (XVII), in which the Lad determines to be glad in spite of his circumstances. Ipgrave has also written out a couplet from 'Loitering with a vacant eye' (LI) on the leaf facing the title page, which has been marked in red with the Japanese censor's stamp:

> Courage, lad, 'tis not for long;
> Stand, quit you like stone, be strong.

Housman would no doubt have been delighted to learn that the Bible was the first book Ipgrave had sacrificed to roll-ups, although the wafer-thin pages proved unsuited to this use. *A Shropshire Lad* was evidently more effective than the scriptures in providing spiritual comfort to this prisoner far from home. In the words of his son Michael, who became Bishop of Woolwich, 'It obviously spoke really powerfully to him as a young man at the beginning of his life going off as a soldier to a pretty bleak situation – it really spoke direct to his heart.' The situation when Geoffrey Ipgrave arrived in Singapore was even bleaker than he could possibly have envisaged, but wherever he was sent, the increasingly battered little book – its pages torn and loose, its buckram cover worn right down to the linen so that the title and the author's name have been wholly erased – went with him. It provided him both with a model of endurance and the means of escape from the grim circumstances of his daily life into a familiar English landscape of the imagination.

VII

AFTERMATHS

So up and down I sow them
    For lads like me to find . . .

A Shropshire Lad LXIII

On a beautiful June day in 1951 a young army cadet called Julian Hurd took a gun from his parents' house near Marlborough in Wiltshire, walked into a nearby wood, and shot himself dead. Finding the empty gun case, and their son's commonplace book lying open on his desk at a page where he had written some lines from Sophocles, his parents feared the worst and went in search of him. They found him in the wood, 'down in the most beautiful corner – stretched out with the filtering sunlight playing over him'. He was just nineteen and the family had spent the previous day driving around the local countryside, stopping from time to time to take walks and look out over the Vale of Pewsey. 'Quite exhausted by so much loveliness J and I both slept on the way home,' his mother had written in her diary.

This sudden, violent death was a mystery. Julian was not much enjoying the rough and tumble of National Service, but had recently been enrolled at the Cadet School in Aldershot and had a place waiting for him at Cambridge University. He seemed, his older brother thought, 'in good form'. Unlike that other nineteen-year-old army cadet who shot himself in 1895, there was no evidence that Julian was experiencing any romantic or sexual troubles. His mother decided that the contrast between army life and the day he had just spent soaking up the beauty of the English landscape had simply proved too much for him: 'Julian died from what might be called an overdose of beauty after having been starved of it for so long.'

The family nevertheless looked for other clues to the tragedy. The quotation Julian had left on his desk was taken from *Antigone*, in which the play's protagonist, under threat of death, justifies her decision to defy Creon's order that her brother's body should lie unburied on the battlefield: 'That I must die some time I knew, edict or no edict, and if I am to die before my time that I count a gain. When one lives as I do in the midst of a sorrow surely one were better dead.' Julian's own sorrows may have been related to an unspoken feeling that the army was training him to kill, and that he was at heart a conscientious objector, but there was no specific evidence for this theory. For his brother Douglas, the future Conservative politician and writer, there was 'one other literary clue. During the short time he was at Aldershot Julian bought the *Collected Poems* of A.E. Housman, the green hard-back edition published by Jonathan Cape. I have it in front of me; it is in excellent condition. Interleaved is a mauve eightpenny bus ticket issued at Aldershot on 28 May 1951. I suppose that Julian bought the book on that day and read it when he came home for the last time the following weekend. Housman's repeated messages of despair addressed to young men in language of powerful, carefully contrived simplicity fitted exactly Julian's mood.'

Douglas Hurd concluded that the immediate cause of his brother's decision to end his life was the one his mother had identified. 'The damage was done by the immediate contrast between the beauty and loving kindness of a weekend spent at home and the ugly misery of army life to which he had to return that Sunday night. This contrast played on the strong emotions of a romantic nineteen-year-old keyed up by a sentimental education. Deep down in Julian's nature must have been a strain of sadness which suddenly overpowered him.'

Julian Hurd was one of those troubled young men whom Housman imagined reading his poems in some distant future. The melancholy of the poems that had so particularly appealed to young men in the early years of the twentieth century remained potent, but it also continued to have a much wider appeal. A century after that generation marched away to their battlefronts, Housman remains a pervasive presence in what we read, watch and listen to. The assertion by Edmund Wilson in 1938 that the poems of *A Shropshire Lad* 'went on vibrating for decades' is borne out by the book's continuing longevity. It is not so much that it has remained in print and been read generation after generation, but that its vibrations have persisted in the collective mind. As Ted Hughes put it: 'His poems have entered the national consciousness, or perhaps one should say national subconsciousness, with a deeper kind of familiarity and subjective intimacy, more unforgettably, than even, say, Hardy's poems.'

In 'Tell me not here, it needs not saying', Housman used the word 'aftermaths' in its original, agricultural sense. Aftermaths were the new growth that appeared in fields after they had been mown or harvested, and it seems an appropriate word to use for the many different manifestations of Housman's continuing presence in our culture some eighty years after his death.

And Fields Will Yearly Bear Them

Housman's first volume of poems seemed fresh and forward-looking when it appeared in 1896, but his second was published the same year as *The Waste Land*. As the tides of Modernism washed around him, Housman remained firm upon his little rock, and as they receded he came to be valued as a representative of an older but still vital tradition. It was a tradition particularly appreciated by such poets as Siegfried Sassoon and Edmund Blunden, who in both their life and their work felt a deep attachment to England and its landscape, and to a world that had been swept away by the war that made their literary reputations. When in 1940 F.R. Leavis declared Eliot 'the greatest living English poet', Blunden protested that 'my feeling is that to this day T.S.E. is an American and his verse is not part of our natural production'. Sassoon agreed, replying that whatever the merits of Eliot's poetry, it was 'not the same thing that comes from essentially English feeling. A Herefordshire apple is itself, and so is a Burgundy vine. We write our lines out of our bones, and out of the soil our forefathers cultivated. Let

Eliot write out of his New England ancestry.' Over a decade later, the two poets placed Housman alongside Thomas Hardy, Robert Bridges and Walter de la Mare as the leading twentieth-century figures in what Sassoon called 'the authentic procession of English poetry'.

Writers of a later generation agreed. 'I consider A.E. Housman a great English poet, one of our greatest since Matthew Arnold,' Kingsley Amis wrote in the *TLS* in 1991. 'In my compilation *The Amis Anthology* (1988) I included thirteen of his poems, a total not surpassed by any other poet in the book.' (Amis in fact slips a fourteenth poem into the anthology's notes, where Housman's 'R.S.L.' appears in the commentary on Robert Louis Stevenson's 'Requiem'.) For Amis, Housman had 'nothing to do with the great modernist development in poetry', a development more or less ignored in his anthology, but belonged instead to the 'older, home-grown tradition of Matthew Arnold, Hardy, Edward Thomas and, in poems like "First Sight" and "Cut Grass", Philip Larkin'. Larkin shared Amis's respect for this tradition and his 1973 edition of *The Oxford Book of Twentieth-Century English Verse* attracted considerable controversy for what was felt to be its anti-Modernist selection: Hardy was represented by twenty-seven poems, Kipling by thirteen, Betjeman by twelve, Graves by eleven, Edward Thomas by nine, and de la Mare and Housman by eight each (which was one more than Eliot).

Looking forwards rather than backwards, Louis MacNeice had written in 1938 that 'Housman has left no followers.' In the strictest sense of the term, he was probably right. 'Housman is easy to parody and hard to imitate,' noted John Carey in *Pure Pleasure* (2000), in which Housman's *Collected Poems* was one of fifty books he selected to represent twentieth-century literature. Housman nevertheless left his mark on other writers – not least on MacNeice himself. Like many of his generation, MacNeice was introduced to *A Shropshire Lad* at school, and a short list of his principal characteristics drawn up by a close friend in the 1960s included 'Housman by heart'. In the 1940s he was delighted to be living for a while in Byron Cottage, where Housman had written most of his first book, and his 1949 radio play *The Queen of Air and Darkness* was both inspired by and took its title from 'Her strong enchantments failing'. His friend and collaborator W.H. Auden disagreed about followers and felt, rather, that Housman provided a good model for the young poet: 'Art for him will be something infinitely precious, pessimistic and hostile to life. If it speaks of love, it must be love frustrated, for all success seems to him noisy and vulgar; if it moralizes, it must counsel a stoic resignation, for the world he knows is well content with itself and will not change.' Auden had spent his own apprentice years reading and learning from older poets, and among his earliest poems, written at school and university, are several that are both modelled upon and echo Housman. A poem such as 'Envoi', for example, is almost entirely made up of lines and phrases more or less lifted from Housman. It begins 'Take up your load and go, lad / And leave your friends behind', and its verse form, prosody and vocabulary – sin, dust, bearing sorrows, dark roads, broken vows – are all Housman's. As Auden later admitted, verses written early in a poet's career are often 'made up of magical phrases that seem to have risen involuntarily to the consciousness'.

Although Housman's influence upon Auden's poetry was compara-tively short-lived – the discovery of T.S. Eliot in the summer of 1926 changed everything – Auden returned to this early literary godfather not only in several essays but also in the well-known but biographically contentious poem 'A.E. Housman', written in December 1938. As late as 1971 Auden would open his poem 'A Shock' with the declaration: 'Housman was perfectly right. / Our world rapidly worsens'. This observation was prompted by Auden's reading of Housman's letters, in his review of which he quoted and glossed Housman's claim to be a pejorist, and the poem goes on to recall a childhood in 'leafy dells', echoing the cuckoo in 'Tell me not here, it needs not saying', which 'shouts all day at nothing / In leafy dells alone'.

Of the same generation as Auden, John Betjeman was a poet whose work achieved a similar popularity to Housman's among general readers. He 'learned most of *A Shropshire Lad* and *Last Poems* by heart' while at school with MacNeice, and, as a result, Housman had a great influence on his 'ear and eye'. Betjeman's own poetry came to repre-sent a distinctive kind of Englishness; less complex than Housman's, and more concerned with buildings and cities than with landscape, it was nevertheless replete with place-names and the occasional note of suppressed homoeroticism, and was written with an acute awareness of time passing, youth fading, and death lying in wait. Betjeman nods specifically to Housman by giving the title 'A Shropshire Lad' to a poem he wrote about Captain Matthew Webb, a Salopian (born in Dawley) who in 1875 became the first man to swim the English Channel. When asked to define the role of the poet, Betjeman's answer was one Housman himself might have given: 'I think primarily it's to say things simply, shortly, rhythmically, memorably. And if it's true that my poetry's read by a lot of people who don't ordinarily read poetry, that's all I could want to happen.'

Place-names and a different, more primal sense of England are a feature of Geoffrey Hill's poetry. Hill seems an unlikely debtor to Housman, but the two poets share a childhood with deep roots in the soil of Worcestershire. Hill was born some two miles north of Housman's birthplace, and he was educated in Bromsgrove. With a nod to 'To an Athlete Dying Young', he has acknowledged Housman as a 'fellow townsman' both in an interview and in the title poem of his 2006 collection *Without Title*, in which Housman is held up as a model for the expression of grief. Housman's *Collected Poems* and Oliver Hill's *Little Treasury of Modern Poetry* (1946) were the two books that introduced Hill to modern poetry at the age of fifteen, when they were bought for him by his father. Hill's childhood may have taken place some seventy years after Housman's, and in very different social circumstances, but the view west from Bromsgrove had not changed. 'Before I knew anything at all about the psychology of Housman, I knew what his "Shropshire" meant to him at an intuitive level,' he has said in an interview, 'because the Shropshire Hills were the western horizon of the village landscape of my childhood. If you stood at the top of the field opposite our house you looked right across the Severn Valley to the Clee Hills and the Welsh hills very faint and far off behind them, and this was the landscape of Housman's own childhood.' As in Housman's, place-names in Hill's poetry evoke a lost past – Shrawley, Burcot, Romsley, Waseley, Walton, Lickey, Ipsley, Hurcott – and Hill made his own selection of his 'local' poems to publish alongside those of Housman and Molly Holden in *Three Bromsgrove Poets* (2003).

Housman surfaces most intriguingly in the poem 'A Cloud in

Aquila', published in Hill's 2007 collection *A Treatise of Civil Power*. The subject of the poem is Alan Turing, the brilliant mathematician, computer scientist and wartime codebreaker, who fell foul of 'the laws of God, the laws of man' when he was prosecuted for homosexuality in 1952 and subsequently committed suicide. It would hardly be surprising if Turing's fate did not bring Housman to mind, but there were further links between the two men. While at his public school Turing met Christopher Morcom, who became his best friend and first love – a love that was undeclared and unreciprocated. Morcom was another lad who would never be old, dying suddenly in his teens from bovine tuberculosis. The two schoolboys shared Housman's interest in astronomy, and Morcom's death caused Turing to think about the separation of mind and body, which in turn led the way to his most significant work, on computing and artificial intelligence, rather as Housman's memories of his friendship with Moses Jackson had led to the writing of *A Shropshire Lad*. As Hill put it elsewhere: 'Morcom was Turing's muse.' Not only that: Morcom lived at 'The Clock House', otherwise Fockbury House, where Housman had spent his teens. Hill's poem ends with the reflection that Turing too is now dead and the Clock House demolished, but that the nearby road still leads to 'Housman's Pisgah'.

One of Philip Larkin's poems that Amis singled out as belonging to the older, home-grown tradition, 'Cut Grass' was written in 1971 and consists of three four-line stanzas. In subject as well as form it is recognisably set in Housman Country, with its allusions to the death-haunted natural cycle of blooming and fading, while its image of June hedgerows seemingly strewn with snow appears to be borrowed from ''Tis time, I think, by Wenlock town'. If this is a rare example of Larkin deliberately following Housman, the two poets nevertheless had a good deal in common both in their personalities and their writing. As Wendy Cope has noted, Clive James's observation that Larkin 'faces the worst on our behalf, and brings it to order' might equally apply to Housman. Introducing himself to the novelist Barbara Pym, Larkin wrote: 'I have a great shrinking from publicity – think of me as A.E. Housman without the talent, or the scholarship, or the soft job, or the curious private life.' Both poets belong to the long tradition of English melancholia, which is often mistaken for mere gloom, and it was with a certain amount of fellow-feeling that Larkin's review of Richard Perceval Graves's 1979 biography of Housman was titled 'All Right When You Knew Him'. More accurately, Larkin described Housman as 'the poet of unhappiness', adding: 'no one else has reiterated his single message so plangently.' The two poets hold a similar place in the English imagination and inspire the same kind of affection among readers.

The Names and Nature of Books

One of the more remarkable and unobtrusive ways in which Housman's poems have entered the culture is that a large number of authors have borrowed lines and phrases from them for the titles of their books. In 1967 it was estimated that more titles had been taken from the collected poems of A.E. Housman than any other source apart from the Bible and Shakespeare, and if the gap between second and third place remains large, a vast number of additional Housman-derived titles have appeared in the almost fifty years since then. Edmund Wilson suggested that one reason authors light upon Housman when searching for book titles is that they 'assume that his poems are so well known that it is almost like quoting Shakespeare'. Among renowned writers working in a wide range of genres who, in search of a striking title, have reached for their copies of Housman's poems are James T. Farrell (*A World I Never Made*, 1936, and *No Star Is Lost*, 1938), Nevil Shute (*The Far Country*, 1952), Patrick White (*The Tree of Man*, 1955), Ursula K. Le Guin (*The Wind's Twelve Corners*, 1976) and James Ellroy (*Blood's a Rover*, 2009). While it seems natural that an account of Ludlow in the First World War should go to 'The Recruit' for the title *Till Ludlow Tower Shall Fall*, other books that have nothing to do with Housman's poems nevertheless bear titles derived from them. Some of these, such as *Brooks Too Broad for Leaping*, *With One Coin for Fee* and *The Sky Suspended*, could only have come from Housman. Others, such as *Drums of Morning*, *The Careless People* and *End of Roaming*, might have been chosen without particular reference to his poems, but in almost every case the borrowing is acknowledged and the poem from which it is taken is reproduced in part or in full, either in the text or as an epigraph.

'Into my heart an air that kills' appears to have provided more titles than any other Housman poem, not only because it contains striking phrases that have become very well known, but also because its references to an irrecoverable past have provided writers with a kind of emotional shorthand. When Dennis Potter called his 1979 television play about childhood *Blue Remembered Hills*, he expected viewers both to recognise the reference and appreciate its irony. Far from depicting childhood as a land of lost content, the play echoes William Golding's *Lord of the Flies* in emphasising the innate barbarity and cruelty of children (all of whom are played by adult actors), and it ends with the most vulnerable and unhappy of them being burned to death in a barn while the author himself intones Housman's poem in voice-over. The same poem is similarly read in the coda to Nicolas Roeg's 1971 film *Walkabout*, in which a woman recalls a scene of primal innocence when, some years earlier, she and her little brother, lost at the time in the Australian outback, swam naked in a waterhole with the Aboriginal boy who had saved them before killing himself. That Housman's poem has travelled a long way from Shropshire or Highgate is also suggested when it is quoted (but not identified) in Chimamanda Ngozi Adichie's *Half of a Yellow Sun* (2006). An English writer in Nigeria during the civil war in the 1960s thinks about his parents' house in Wentnor, a Shropshire village just to the west of The Long Mynd, and recalls his father reading this poem, which has further resonance in the novel because the secessionist Republic of Biafra lasted only two and a half years before being reintegrated into Nigeria. For the Igbo people who had fought for independence, Biafra became a lost homeland that 'will not come again'.

Like Housman's Shropshire, the magical kingdom of Gramarye in T.H. White's great Arthurian novel, *The Once and Future King* (1939–58), is a far (and partly imaginary) country that stands for all England. The revised second volume of this quartet was titled *The Queen of Air and Darkness* and took as its epigraph the final stanza of 'The Welsh Marches' (XXVIII), a poem of unusual violence that seems to have haunted White, probably because he felt some of his own troubles related back to his being the child of ill-matched and viciously warring parents. During his revisions, White wrote to a friend that the character of Morgause in the novel 'is now pure melodramatic WITCH (rather fun) who goes about boiling black cats alive and so forth. Housman wrote a poem about her. (Her strong enchantments failing, Her towers of fear in wreck, Her limbecks dried of poison, etc.)'. The character of Lancelot, first introduced as a fifteen-year-old smitten with Arthur, also owes something to Housman: 'The boy thought there was something wrong with him. All through his life – even when he was a great man with the world at his feet – he was to feel this gap: something at the bottom of his heart of which he was aware and ashamed, but which he did not understand. There is no need for us to try to understand it. We do not have to dabble in a place which he preferred to keep secret.'

Rather more unexpectedly, Housman's poetry is at the centre of Alice Munro's story 'Wenlock Edge' (2005), in which a young woman in Canada is persuaded to remove all her clothes in order to read aloud *A Shropshire Lad* to an older man, while in Kingsley Amis's *One Fat Englishman* (1963), the protagonist attempts to ward off orgasm by repeatedly reciting to himself 'The weeping Pleiads wester'. Allusions to Housman and his poetry in fiction more often turn up in a homosexual context, however. A distinct *Shropshire Lad* atmosphere pervades the journals of the cult English writer Denton Welch, in which he records bicycling around the Kentish countryside in the 1940s, watching lads stripping off to bathe in rivers and reflecting upon their likely fate in the war. The editor of these journals, Jocelyn Brooke, devoted most of his own writing to an attempt to capture a land of lost content, and both his semi-autobiographical novel, *The Orchid Trilogy* (1948–50), and the botanical volume *The Flower in Season* (1952, its title taken from 'Ho, everyone that thirsteth') are replete with references to Housman.

Mary Renault's pioneering homosexual novel *The Charioteer* (1953) also alludes to Housman in an appropriately covert way. Wounded at Dunkirk, Laurie Odell is torn between his love for a naval officer called Ralph and a conscientious objector called Andrew. Lying in bed during an air raid, he worries whether the two men are safe, while attempting to reassure a small boy in the next bed, who is recovering from a burst appendix. Laurie recalls (inaccurately) lines from 'The chestnut casts his flambeaux, and the flowers', which he feels he might have recited to the boy had he been a few years older – 'But he looked a little fragile, yet, to shoulder the sky; and, besides, he had fallen asleep'. The source of these lines remains unidentified, but Renault was counting on her readers to recognise them – not least because, along with Plato's *Phaedrus* (from which the novel derives its title), Housman's poetry would be part of the supportive intellectual equipment a sensitive young homosexual such as Laurie would be likely to carry around with him.

This is the kind of literature that the playwright Alan Bennett sought out as a shy, bookish, homosexual, working-class teenager in Leeds in the early 1950s: 'I study as if they are code books the works of writers I have been told are homosexual, though of course they cannot at this time openly admit it. Most satisfactorily, though, there is A.E. Housman, whose affections are unspoken (or spoken of as unspoken), which is what mine always are, and who regards love as a doomed enterprise right from the start. Of his life and the object of his affections I know nothing, but as I roam the streets of Headingley in 1950 I feel he is the one I might tell it to, though what the "it" was I would have been hard put to say.' This is a strikingly similar reaction to that of the young E.M. Forster some forty years before.

Housman was one of the poets Bennett selected for a television series, *Poetry in Motion*, broadcast by Channel 4 in 1990. This was a 'personal anthology' of *Six Poets: Hardy to Larkin* (the title under which the accompanying book was republished in 2014), the other three being Betjeman, Auden and MacNeice. The poems Bennett chose were 'all in differing degrees accessible' and expressed a distinctive kind of Englishness, often manifesting itself in 'that very English fault: an overdose of irony'. Irony is certainly characteristic of Bennett himself, whose 1968 play *Forty Years On* is a kind of cavalcade of Englishness, at once critical and affectionate, performed as a play at a public school called Albion House. Bennett described his play (which contains references to Housman) as 'an elegy for the passing of a traditional England', and admitted that his 'heart was very much in [the headmaster's] final speech in which he bids farewell to Albion House and this old England. And yet the world we lost wasn't one in which I would have been happy, though I look back on it and read about it with affection.' There is a distinct note of *A Shropshire Lad* in these remarks, which (Bennett notes) were written on the fiftieth anniversary of the Armistice.

Housman's dictum that 'All knowledge is precious whether or not it serves the slightest human use' is quoted by a popular (and homosexual) teacher in Bennett's later school play, *The History Boys* (2004), the principal theme of which is similar to that of Housman's Introductory Lecture of 1892 about the purpose of learning and education. Housman himself steps onto the stage in Tom Stoppard's *The Invention of Love* (1997), in which he is played by two different actors, one representing him as an old man, the other as an Oxford undergraduate. This provides the same double perspective that gives *A Shropshire Lad* much of its emotional power, youthful hope in dialogue with rueful maturity – literally so in the play, in which the two Housmans have extended conversations with each other about poetry, love and the Classics.

But perhaps the perfect example of the way in which Housman's poetry has been absorbed and refracted by a writer of a later generation is J.L. Carr's novel *A Month in the Country* (1980). Housman's were the poems Carr 'loved best', the poems he took with him to the Second World War. He subsequently became headmaster of Highfields Primary School in Kettering, Northamptonshire, and every year he would march all 200 of his pupils through a local housing estate when spring blossom was on the trees, leading them in a mass recitation of 'Loveliest of trees, the cherry now', a poem some of them still had by heart forty years later. *A Month in the Country* is amongst other things a beautifully wrought study of England and Englishness. Although set in the North Riding of Yorkshire, it was written at least in part in Housman Country: the words '*Stocken, Presteigne / September, 1978*' are printed on its last page, referring to the place in the Welsh Marches where Carr had lived in a caravan while working on one of the series of illustrated county maps he published. The novel is narrated by Tom Birkin, who in old age recalls the summer of 1920, when, as a shell-shocked young veteran of the First World War who has been deserted by his wife, he spends several recuperative weeks uncovering a medieval wall painting in an isolated church.

The novel suggests Housman in its brevity, its lyricism, and its mood of nostalgia and regret. The second stanza of 'From far, from eve and morning' (XXXII) is used as one of its epigraphs, and is more or less paraphrased in the crucial central scene in which Birkin fails to make his feelings known to the young wife of the local vicar, with whom he has fallen in love. 'That was the missed moment. I should have put out a hand and taken her arm and said "Here I am. Ask me. Now. The real question! Tell me. While I'm here. Ask me before it is too late."' Both Housman and Elgar, and their place in the English landscape of the Clee Hills and the Malverns, are imagined at the novel's close, and the final paragraph carries a similar charge to that of *A Shropshire Lad*: 'We can ask and ask but we can't have again what once seemed ours for ever – the way things looked, that church alone in the fields, a bed on a belfry floor, a remembered voice, the touch of a hand, a loved face. They've gone and you can only wait for the pain to pass.'

It is not just in literary fiction that Housman's presence is felt. As early as 1930 a knowledge of Housman's poetry helps Lord Peter Wimsey solve the murder case at the centre of Dorothy L. Sayers' *Strong Poison* (1930). The particular poem ('Terence, this is stupid stuff') is not mentioned by name, presumably because Sayers imagined her readers to be as literate as Wimsey's butler, for whom the mere presence of *A Shropshire Lad* in his employer's library is clue enough.

A more recent fictional detective who knows his Housman is Inspector Morse, who first appeared in Colin Dexter's *Last Bus to Woodstock* in 1975 and solved cases in twelve further novels over the following twenty-four years. Although these books were best-sellers, it was when *The Dead of Jericho* (1981) was adapted for television in 1987, inaugurating a series of thirty-three two-hour episodes broadcast over thirteen years, that Morse became arguably the most popular fictional English detective of all time. Morse's love of Wagner is a constant feature of both the books and the television series, but his love of Housman is equally marked. Dexter suggests an equivalence for Morse between the two men in *The Wench Is Dead* (1989), at the beginning of which the detective experiences a spell in hospital in the same ward as a character who dies. 'Had Morse known how the man could never abide a chord of Wagner, he would have felt much aggrieved,' Dexter writes; 'yet had he known how the Colonel had committed to memory virtually the whole of Housman's poetic corpus, he would have been profoundly gratified.' *The Life of Richard Wagner* and *Selected Prose of A.E. Housman* are among the 'small pile of books' on Morse's bedside table in the second of the novels, *Last Seen Wearing* (1976), the latter informing the inspector about the dilemma he finds himself in during his investigation into the disappearance of a schoolgirl. Housman is referred to in several of the other novels, most notably in *The Remorseful Day* (1999), which takes its title from 'How clear, how lovely bright'. Although the novel contains several mentions of Housman, the title is intended to suggest the dying Morse's feelings about past mistakes, omissions, deceptions and things badly done, and it evokes the general mood of the book rather than anything more specific. In the television adaptation by Stephen Churchett, however, Morse recites the last verse of Housman's poem as he watches a spectacular sunset.

Dexter, who bought a copy of the first edition of Housman's *Collected Poems* while reading Classics at Cambridge in 1950 and claims since then to have 'collected everything written by Housman and about Housman', sometimes relies upon his readers having an equal knowledge of the poet and his work. In *Death Is Now My Neighbour* (1996), for instance, Morse recalls that he had kept the photograph of a young woman he had loved and lost 'pressed between pages 88–89 of his *Collected Poems of A.E. Housman*'. The reader needs to know which edition of the book Morse owns, because in the standard edition available in 1996 the 'Epithalamium' Housman wrote for Moses Jackson appears on those pages, but in the first edition (the one Morse is more likely to own) it would be 'The True Lover'. Even more obscure are the lines 'Dry the azured skylit water / Sky my everlasting tent', which appear in a poem received by the police purporting to provide information about the location of a body in *The Way Through the Woods* (1992). The poem is attributed to 'A. Austin (1853–87)', which as the novel's more literary readers will recognise from the dates cannot be the man who was Poet Laureate when *A Shropshire Lad* was published. They might also, if they really know their Housman, recognise that the poem has not merely appropriated two lines from 'In my own shire, if I was sad' (XLI) – 'And like a skylit water stood / The bluebells in the azured wood' – but has additionally cannibalised the cancelled quatrain from 'He looked at me with eyes I thought'. This is not merely a rarefied literary in-joke; it also provides a clue to the identity of the person who wrote the mysterious poem.

After the *Inspector Morse* television series came to an end, the detective's sidekick Sergeant Lewis returned with his own series, and both *Lewis* and *Endeavour* (a 'prequel' set in the 1960s when Morse was embarking on his career in the police force) have continued to honour Housman. While Lewis still struggles with cultural references, his new sergeant, James Hathaway, is almost as well read as Morse was. In *Dead of Winter* (2010), a childhood friend who is being obliged to marry someone she doesn't love in order to save her family's finances is discovered looking up 'Into my heart an air that kills', a poem that Hathaway naturally knows by heart. The same poem is read when the ashes of a murder victim are scattered in a non-religious ceremony in *Down Among the Fearful* (2003), while the pilot episode of *Endeavour* (2012) involves an investigation into the death of a fifteen-year-old girl, during which the fact that she has a volume of Housman's poems among other first editions on her bedside table provides a clue.

The presence of Housman in these globally successful television series shows how far the poet has penetrated popular culture. Another sure sign that one has become part of the mainstream is to feature in *The Simpsons*, a cartoon series distinguished by its knowing references to both high and low culture. In an episode from 1998 titled 'The Last Temptation of Krust' (itself a nod to a Martin Scorsese film), Bart persuades his favourite comedian, Krusty the Clown, to appear at a comedy festival. Krusty's dated and offensive material is so fiercely criticised that the clown announces his retirement and quotes 'To an Athlete Dying Young' in his farewell speech. Housman's poetry is also read or recited in such mainstream Hollywood films as *Titanic* (1953) and *Out of Africa* (1985), while John Irvine's film adaptation of Frederick Forsyth's *The Dogs of War* (1980), in which a group of soldiers are hired to stage a coup in a West African country, has Geoffrey Burgon's setting of 'Epitaph on an Army of Mercenaries' sung over its end titles. Housman even features in *The Twilight Zone*, which originally ran on

American television between 1959 and 1964, in a much-loved episode titled 'The Changing of the Guard' (1962). A disillusioned teacher at a boys' high school gives a class on Housman and is later saved from suicide when visited by the grateful ghosts of former pupils. Housman has also been saluted on the radio by the BBC's hugely popular agricultural soap opera *The Archers*, which has been running since 1951 and is set in the fictional West Midlands county of Borsetshire. Bert Fry is a retired farm worker and part-time gardener who also fancies himself as a poet, and in an episode broadcast in January 2014, he asks one of his employers for some washing-up liquid: '"Loveliest of trees, the cherry now . . . " I'm going to clean the dirt and the algae off. I always thinks of Housman when I looks at it. In fact it's sparked off a few lines of me own if you'd care to hear them.' People, on the whole, would rather not hear Bert's poetry, which is written in a style closer to that of William McGonagall than Housman; undaunted by this lack of enthusiasm, Bert has long been planning to publish a volume of his verses which he intends to call *A Borsetshire Boy*.

One way of judging the continuing appeal of Housman among the young is to look at YouTube, where he has a surprisingly strong presence. If not currently on the British school curriculum, Housman's poems are certainly being studied at schools in America and other parts of the world as far away from Shropshire as South Korea. Many of the videos posted on YouTube are class assignments in which students 'interpret' Housman's poems, usually in the form of a recital of an individual poem, sometimes accompanied by a dramatic or animated presentation. Other YouTube postings seem to be unrelated to school work, or are at any rate persuasively extra-curricular: a young black man with dreadlocks recites 'When I was one-and-twenty' while standing in a back yard; a young Chinese-American, beneath his bedclothes, sings unaccompanied what appears to be his own rather beautiful setting of 'Loveliest of trees, the cherry now'; four students from the Universitas Slamet Riyadi in Java, two of them in hijabs, sing the words of 'The Olive' translated into their own language.

The poems that appear most frequently on YouTube are 'When I was one-and-twenty', 'Loveliest of trees, the cherry now' and 'To an Athlete Dying Young'. The last of these is often used to commemorate classmates or sportsmen who have died prematurely – or, by stretching a point, celebrities such as the film actor Paul Walker, who was killed in a car crash at the age of forty. (The use of the poem in this way stretches back to 1949, when lines from it were printed beneath a *New York Tribune* editorial on the death of Jack Lovelock, the New Zealand Olympic runner who had died at the age of thirty-nine when he fell under a subway train.) Videos of ninth grade African-American New Media students reciting 'When I was one-and-twenty', dance interpretations of Housman's poems being performed by pupils at the Buenlag National High School at Calasiao in the Philippines, and a supine Mumbai-based Indian poet reciting 'Here dead we lie because we did not choose' to illustrate his disgust with those who do not treat soldiers with proper respect, show just how far Housman's poems have travelled, just how widely and variously they are appreciated, interpreted and employed. Even those who scoff at the lack of quality control on YouTube could hardly fail to be moved by a performance of 'Look not in my eyes' in American Sign Language or a man celebrating his 103rd birthday with a recitation from memory of 'Think no more, lad; laugh, be jolly'.

Come, Pipe a Tune to Dance to, Lad

The Internet has also become one of the principal platforms for music, and music remains one of the main ways in which people first encounter Housman's poetry, both in classical and contemporary settings. It seems only right that John France's invaluable blog on British classical music is called 'The Land of Lost Content', but Housman is no longer the preserve of English pastoralists. He has nevertheless remained a point of reference in instrumental pieces written in the tradition of Butterworth and Julius Harrison, such as James Langley's *The Coloured Counties: Idyll for Orchestra* from the 1960s and Edward Watson's *Blue Remembered Hills* (1994) for flute, cor anglais and string trio. More importantly, Housman has also maintained a place in the continuing English song tradition. This tradition was in decline for many years after the Second World War, but interest in it is now fast growing thanks to societies devoted to individual composers, music festivals at which the songs are performed, and the availability on CD of previously neglected works.

There are those who think, as Constant Lambert did back in 1934, that contemporary composers should now leave Housman alone, that his language and mood belongs to a specific period and that there are already so many good settings of his poems in the catalogue that no more are needed. One composer who disagreed was John R. Williamson (1929–2015), who achieved the distinction of having set more of Housman's poems than any other composer. Three years before he died, he claimed to have set 'all of Housman's verse, excepting the long poems', and while this may be something of an exaggeration, the LiederNet Archive lists 121 Housman settings by him, almost all of them for baritone and piano. Other composers have written settings more likely to remain in the repertoire. Some, such as Peter Pope and Ian Venables, have followed in the earlier lyric tradition of pre-war settings; others, such as Michael Berkeley, Ronald Corp and Martin Bussey, have attempted to forge a new musical style far removed from the nostalgic English pastoral mode. Venables argues that although his cycle of four *Songs of Eternity and Sorrow* (2004) consciously uses the same forces as Vaughan Williams and Gurney, what made the piece contemporary was his choice of such poems as 'Oh who is that young sinner with the handcuffs on his wrists?', which earlier composers had shunned because of its subject matter. This poem has also been given a rollicking setting by Stephen Hough as part of *Other Love Songs* (2009), a cycle intended to accompany Brahms's two sets of *Liebeslieder Walzer* and explore different kinds of love than the romantic heterosexual variety celebrated by the older composer. An earlier setting of the poem (1994) by the Australian composer Gordon Kerry reached a wide audience when it was taken up by the Sydney Gay & Lesbian Choir, who featured it in concerts and recordings alongside Cilla Black's 'Anyone Who Had a Heart' and Abba's 'Dancing Queen'.

There have been many other settings of Housman's poems by Australian and American composers as well as English ones, and the continuity between the earliest Housman settings and those being written a century later tends to have less to do with geography and landscape than with the enduring troubles suffered by young people wherever they might be. The American composer Jake Heggie has described his 2005 song cycle *Here and Gone* for tenor, baritone, piano and string trio as 'a deeply personal journey of missed connections and unrequited love between two men', and it sets Housman's poetry alongside that of Vachel Lindsay. Heggie's music draws upon the traditions of both the art song and music theatre, and it is his sure sense of narrative that makes this one of the most successful and moving recent cycles based on Housman's poetry, one in which both the topographical and emotional landscapes of the poems have become universal.

While composers such as Heggie honour the classical tradition of Housman settings, elsewhere in the musical world the poetry has been radically reimagined. In August 2008 Shpetim Zogaj, later a contestant on *Albanians Got Talent*, posted a video on YouTube 'from the newest country in the world', the Republic of Kosovo, which had declared its independence from Serbia six months earlier. Dedicated 'to all those that are scared of being In Love', Zogaj's performance of his own setting of 'When I was one-and-twenty' for voice and electric guitar is accompanied by written onscreen exhortations to accept that relationships are often difficult but to persist with them anyway – something with which Housman might mournfully have agreed. As elsewhere, this particular poem has attracted popular musicians working in a wide variety of genres, and among other people who have set and sung it are Michael Nesmith (formerly of The Monkees), the young English indie singer-songwriter Joe Booley, the German band Black Eye, and the veteran Minnesotan folk singer Billey R. Rubble.

It is unsurprising that poems linked to both the English pastoral tradition and old ballads should have attracted the attention of folk singers, but in some cases, the folk element more or less takes over. Dave Webber and Anni Fentiman's 2002 album of unaccompanied songs *Away from It All* includes a track titled 'Is Me Team a-Ploughing', in which Housman's poem is so thoroughly absorbed into the folk tradition that the friend is not 'my friend' but 'me old friend' and his answers to the dead lad's questions all begin with the traditional chorus-introduction 'It's ay . . . ' rather than the poem's 'Ay'. Purists may blench, but this setting and performance show just how close the poem is to traditional folk song – so much so that it would not seem out of place on one of the albums of Fred Jordan (1922–2002), a Ludlow farm worker and singer of the kind Vaughan Williams or Butterworth might have tracked down, and whose discography inevitably includes a compilation album titled *A Shropshire Lad* (2012). Fewer liberties were taken by the Shropshire-based Polly Bolton Band, whose album *Loveliest of Trees* (1996) alternated readings of Housman's poems by the actor Nigel Hawthorne with settings of them which employ piano, saxophone and synthesisers alongside more customary folk instruments such as guitar, violins and violas and Northumbrian pipes.

Two years earlier the veteran folk duo Michael Raven and Joan Mills produced an album titled *A Shropshire Lad*. Also based in Shropshire, Raven (1938–2008) was a prolific writer, poet, photographer, publisher and musician, who wrote many books on local topography and folklore as well as collections of folk songs arranged for guitar, one of them titled *Land of Lost Content* (1999). Raven composed his own music for two of the poems on his *Shropshire Lad* album, but the rest are set to traditional Welsh tunes arranged for voice and guitar. For Raven there was an obvious fit between Housman's poetry and the traditional music of Wales. 'In the Dark Ages Shropshire was ruled by the Princes of Powys,' he wrote, 'and Welsh blood still flows through the veins of many a Salopian. There is a link, too, between the poetry of *A Shropshire Lad* and the pre-Celtic Iberians from over the border, namely a melancholy mood. Sombre, brooding melodies are as typical of the Welsh as jigs and reels are of the Irish.' The Welsh band Fernhill included a setting of 'Bredon Hill' on their 1998 album *Llatai*, as did Hilary James on her 2011 album *English Sketches*, and this poem has, perhaps predictably, particularly appealed to folk singers.

Jazz settings of Housman are, unsurprisingly, rather rarer, though there have been some notable examples. June Tabor's recording of 'The lads in their hundreds' (2013), in which Butterworth's tune is beautifully arranged by Iain Ballamy for voice, piano and saxophone, might be described as transitional: the song sits neatly between jazz and folk and does honour to both Butterworth and Housman. The Bulgarian opera singer Stanislava Stoytcheva's wonderfully bluesy rendition of Samuel Barber's 'With rue my heart is laden' (2014) similarly treads a borderline between jazz and classical music. Two decades earlier, the vocalist Jacqui Dankworth commissioned a major piece, *Five Housman Settings*, for herself and a jazz septet and classical wind quintet performing under the name New Perspectives. Among those who provided the songs was Dankworth's father, Johnny, who had already set 'When I was one-and-twenty' for voice and clarinet for his wife Cleo Laine, and now set 'Sinner's Rue' for his daughter. The other songs are Patrick Gowers's setting of 'Terence, this is stupid stuff', a poem which for understandable reasons, not least its length, has been almost entirely left alone by composers (the only other known setting being Stanley Wilson's in 1929 for men's voices); Andrea Vicari's 'On the idle hill of summer'; and John Williams's 'When summer's end is nighing' – all of them showing Housman's adaptability to a musical style far removed from that of the English art song. Less successful are more recent settings of three Housman poems for 'a unique combination of extended composition and jazz instrumentation' on Anne Mette Iversen's 2012 album *Poetry of Earth*, in which Housman's words seem wholly incidental to the music.

Housman has also been reinterpreted in what might broadly be described as the rock music tradition, sometimes becoming the inspiration for entire albums. Matt Perzinski first came across *A Shropshire Lad* while teaching British Literature at a Catholic boys' school in Baltimore. 'The moods of the poems, the narratives, the cynical beauty, and inherent comical tragedy of The Melancholy Thinking Man's Life really got to me,' he recalls, and so he began setting them to music. He recorded ten songs in 2006 and, as The Agrarians, released them online as *Selections from Housman's A Shropshire Lad*. The arrangements are relatively simple, with guitar and percussion accompaniment and the voice double-tracked. The Pennsylvanian singer-songwriter Peter Kurie was introduced to Housman's work in 2001 while attending classes with the American poet Jeffrey Carson: 'I was curious about the differences between lyrics-for-singing and poems-for-reading. I wanted to write verse that could be both sung and read. Jeffrey pointed me to Housman.' Over ten years later, as a graduate student of anthropology at Princeton, Kurie met the Irish poet Paul Muldoon, who had written some lyrics for a local rock band. 'He got me thinking again about the possibilities, and problems, of setting poems to song. Remembering

Housman, I started rereading him. I realised there was an opportunity to "update"/reinvent/reinterpret Housman's verse in the modern musical styles I enjoy: rock, pop, jazz, folk, electronica, etc.' In the summer of 2013 Kurie took time off from writing his dissertation to spend two months composing and recording an album released later that year as *Housman Revisited*. Musically the album is both sophisticated and engagingly eclectic, running indeed through several musical styles but remaining true to the poems, demonstrating how they are open to a variety of musical interpretations.

Back in England, Wild Billy Childish & The Spartan Dreggs included a song titled 'A Shropshire Lad' (a setting of 'To an Athlete Dying Young') on their 2012 album *Coastal Command*, and released it as a single that same year. Childish's music is hard to categorise, since he tends to move from genre to genre, but this song has a raw, garage feel to it. This may not seem the most obvious genre for setting Housman, but Childish went on to record a six-track EP of songs derived from *A Shropshire Lad. A Tribute to A.E. Housman* (2013) features the Van der Weyde portrait of Housman on the sleeve, and its tracks are fairly similar in their approach to the earlier setting, propelled by driving rhythms on guitar and drums against which Housman's words are chanted just as if they were rock lyrics.

There are many other examples of Housman rocking around the world. In 2013 Quieter than Spiders, a synthpop band based in Shanghai, freely adapted 'Into my heart an air that kills' for a number titled 'The Land of Lost Content', while the first track on the Swedish rock-noir band Les Fleurs Du Mal's *Concrete Ravings* (2013) is 'A Remorseful Day', prefaced by a reading of the last stanza of 'How clear, how lovely bright' and incorporating phrases from the poem ('Oh, I drove off a cliff alright / past human touch and sound and sight') throughout. The Russian electronica musician Barrytone's 2011 album *Argonauts* contains an instrumental track titled 'Land of Lost Content', and the acoustic German group Treigbut perform their own version of 'Loveliest of Trees'. Most unlikely of all, in 2015 'a group of dudes (currently in high school) that just want to make boring school projects a little fun and interesting', and calling themselves Ghoul Industries, posted a video on YouTube in which a beret-wearing youth introduces performances of two songs he dubs 'A.E. Housemusic'. It's a nice pun, and while the setting of 'When I was one-and-twenty' is nearer energetic hillbilly bluegrass, 'To an Athlete Dying Young' shows that if the words are read in an exaggerated rhythm and to the right accompaniment it is possible to rap Housman.

The latter poem inspired a different kind of tribute when an American rock group that had started out as Army of Strippers changed its name to Housman's Athletes. This was done on the grounds that Housman's poem 'is about an athlete that wins all of his races and abruptly dies at the top of his game; never defeated, never growing old, never fading away'. As the band's guitarist D.J. Foley puts it: 'Our goal as a band is for our music to have some longevity. We want to never get old. We want our music to stick around forever.' Given the band's name, it seems wholly appropriate that their 2008 debut album, *Race to the Finish*, should include a track titled 'Unrequited'.

While Housman's words are used by a wide variety of bands, the musician who most embodies the poet's spirit is Morrissey. In 1995 The Smiths released a compilation album, *Singles*, with an image of Diana Dors on its sleeve. The images for the band's albums were always chosen by Morrissey, becoming a gallery of his personal icons, and the image he selected of Dors was a still from *Yield to the Night*, a 1956 film in which she plays a convicted murderer called Mary Hilton. The film was based on Joan Henry's best-selling 1954 novel of the same name, through which 'Loveliest of trees, the cherry now' runs as a constant motif, and lines from the poem become Mary's last thought as she is hanged. This motif is carried over into the film, in which at one point Mary picks up her lover's copy of *A Shropshire Lad* and reads the poem in full, and so the still Morrissey selected for *Singles* salutes Housman as well as Dors.

Morrissey was himself one of those troubled lads for whom Housman's poems held a special appeal. Growing up in working-class Manchester, he was a book-loving boy who felt that he didn't fit in, didn't make friends easily, and stood apart from his easy-going peers. Asked in August 1998 during a phone-in on KCXX Radio, San Bernardino which poets had influenced his songs, Morrissey replied: 'Well, the poet who means the most to me is a poet called

A.E. Housman. Have you ever heard of him?' The listener, who had been taking a literature class at the California State University in Los Angeles, replied that indeed he had: 'I am a fan of A.E. Housman as well, so that's great to know. What poems in particular?' Morrissey did not answer this directly, but described the poems in general as 'really, really sad and really powerful but beautiful'. The listener recognised at once why such poems might appeal to Morrissey, replying: 'Well, I think it would be an understatement to say that your lyrics are very sad and very powerful.'

The bands appearing on small, independent record labels in the 1980s produced what became known as 'music for misfits' because it found its audience among young people who stood apart from the mainstream, tended to be introspective, and were often fluid or confused in their sexuality. The Smiths rapidly emerged as the most popular and enduring representatives of the Indie scene, and the songs Morrissey and Johnny Marr wrote for the band have occupied a similar position in the youth culture of the past thirty years that the poems of Housman did for W.H. Auden's generation: they seemed 'perfectly to express the sensibility of a male adolescent'. As a young Scottish admirer put it in an online fanzine, using an appropriately Housman-like metaphor: 'As a teenager, I had felt at times that I was ploughing a lonely furrow, but Morrissey's music became my constant companion.'

That Morrissey should embrace Housman is no surprise, since the singer has always toyed publicly with the idea of his own buried emotional and sexual life. He has described Housman as 'Vulnerable and complex [. . .] a complete mystery even to those who knew him', and this is precisely what Morrissey himself projected both on and off stage while with The Smiths. Morrissey has always divided opinion, but whether you loved him or loathed him, you could see exactly why he was drawn to Housman when he wrote of him in his *Autobiography*: 'A stern custodian of art and life, he shunned the world and he lived a solitary existence of monastic pain, unconnected to others [. . .] The pain done to Housman allowed him to rise above the mediocre and find the words that most of us need help in order to say. The price paid by Housman was a life alone; the righteous rhymer enduring each year unloved and unable to love.' This is more or less how Morrissey has portrayed himself in the book. His refusal to declare himself sexually led to a great deal of speculation about his love life, or lack of it, just as Housman's reticence had provoked curiosity; but his fans were always very well informed about other aspects of his life, and while he was touring America in 1992 to promote his solo album *Your Arsenal* a devotee hurled a copy of *A Shropshire Lad* onto the stage. Thereafter Morrissey's musical collaborator Boz Boorer would sometimes read aloud from the book during concerts. In an online fanzine in 2013 Morrissey chose the words 'If by chance your eye offend you' as the headline of an announcement that a proposed tour of South America was being cancelled for lack of funding. This led a fan to post the entire poem, presumably to provide a context for such a puzzling appropriation.

It is evident that Morrissey has done a good deal for Housman's popularity, since eager fans seek out any literary work their idol recommends. Some of these fans might have avoided poetry altogether until led to Housman. 'I thought his poems would be drivel about babies and flowers,' one fan wrote, 'but it's really good stuff about suicide.' The image of the young Morrissey assuaging his loneliness with literature and music has struck a chord with many of his followers. 'When I was growing up, books and records had always been my refuge, and again I shared this in common with Morrissey,' wrote the Scottish ploughboy of that lonely teenage furrow. 'And, through the years, he has encouraged me to read so many writers whose work I now love and admire, such as Oscar Wilde and A.E. Housman.' There is plenty of evidence that Morrissey has spread Housman's fame far and wide. One fan posted 'Loveliest of trees, the cherry now' online on the grounds that Morrissey had 'quoted the last line – more or less – while appearing live in Japan', while another posted one of Housman's most comically despondent poems, 'Yonder see the morning blink', because Morrissey had quoted lines from it during a concert in Honolulu. For some, Housman and Morrissey have become inextricably and distractingly entangled: 'Whilst sitting in my English Literature exam this morning,' one young fan wrote, 'I came across a poem which I had not read before (even though I have been studying the book all year) entitled "Here Dead We Lie", containing the line "Life, to be sure, is nothing much to lose". I had "Mama Lay Softly On The Riverbed" stuck in my head for the rest of the exam. If I fail, I blame Morrissey.' The song in question, from Morrissey's 2009 album *Years of Refusal*, contains an abbreviated version of Housman's line. Such is Morrissey's assumed expertise in Housman Studies that it has even been proposed that he turn his hand to biography: 'I wish he'd write biographies on his faves,' writes Eurydice. 'I couldn't put down the *Autobiography* when he wrote about Housman.'

The Morrissey-Solo website is particularly abuzz with Housman. Two regular contributors post comments under the handles 'The spirit of A.E. Housman (once a writer)' and 'A.E. Housman (A Shropshire Lad)'. Other fans simply post Housman's poems, and the reasons for doing so are sometimes not hard to guess: 'Baker Street Queen' selects 'He would not stay for me'. It is on this forum that one Morrissey devotee recommends Housman's work as 'Incredibly poignant verse if conventional in form. Like all great poetry, it expresses the seemingly unexpressible.' Morrissey appears to have done something similar in his songs, putting into words feelings that some of his fans have had difficulty articulating, and in doing so eliciting the same kind of recognition and gratitude among his generation's 'luckless lads' that Housman did.

Farewell to Barn and Stack and Tree

On 22 March 1985 a statue of Housman was unveiled in Bromsgrove High Street. Having been pedestrianised, the street was not as Housman had known it, but the weather seemed about right, the skies dark, the rain falling heavily and steadily. By the time of the unveiling, the downpour had stopped and large crowds had gathered to witness the Duke of Westminster pull on the cord that would release Kenneth Potts's statue from its Union flag shroud. Standing on a rock, Housman is dressed for walking, his cap and walking stick in one hand, his other hand thrust casually into his trouser pocket. He looks down the High Street, which is now undergoing regeneration after a period of sad decay, with nail parlours and pound shops occupying premises that once served more traditional uses. Bromsgrove remains proud of its son, who is commemorated by five individual plaques on buildings associated with him, including Perry Hall, now a boarding house for Bromsgrove (formerly King Edward's) School and renamed Housman Hall. The district council in association with the Housman Society publishes a well-designed and informative leaflet which latter-day pilgrims can use to follow 'The Housman Trail' in the area.

Shropshire too has embraced its adopted son in the knowledge that many people are attracted to the region because of Housman and his poems. As Brian J. Bailey writes in a chapter of his *Portrait of Shropshire* titled 'Those Blue Remembered Hills': 'Rural Shropshire is known the world over, not because of geography text-books or cheap package-tours but because of A.E. Housman.' Acknowledging this, books about the county frequently mention or quote Housman, sometimes pointing out discrepancies between what he wrote and what the tourist might find, as at Hughley. Bailey rightly insists that 'The purpose of art is exaltation, not topography, and what suited Housman's poetic purpose has exalted this county', and most guidebooks concur. H.W. Timperley's account of Wenlock Edge in his *Shropshire Hills* is suffused with Housman. He notes the blooming of the wild cherries – the tree Housman had in mind rather than the pink-flowered hybrids that have in places been planted in mistaken tribute to him – and writes, in what is essentially a prose version of ''Tis time, I think, by Wenlock town':

> When it is far away the Edge is often vividly remembered because of flower, tree blossom, or berry, once seen, or maybe usually seen at its best there. Not only the flower, but all the Edge round it is clear to the inward eye, and not coldly as something casually remembered and nothing more, but kindling the imagination, setting it aglow, until an old joy is revived as fresh as new, and one becomes a partly wondering, partly accusing self-questioner, saying: 'Why am I not there now?'

Since Housman actually visited Wenlock Edge, Timperley has some justification for describing him as 'among the Edge's willing bondsmen and their [sic] poet above all'. The sense of an ancient and mysterious

384

past that is present in 'On Wenlock Edge the wood's in trouble' strikes Timperley while he stands among the remains of the Bronze Age stone circle on another eminence, Stapeley Hill in the south-west of the county:

> There is one moment of the day when the solitude of the circle on its hill, the feeling it rouses that of all we should know about its significance the greater part will never be clearly known, and the far reach of the views to those remote mountain tops make me remember A.E. Housman's
>
> Comrade, look not on the west . . .

Edmund Vale, in his 1949 book on Shropshire for Robert Hale's 'County Books' series, believes that the works of both Housman and Mary Webb embody a prevalent Salopian characteristic: 'gaiety and sadness going hand in hand is in the people and in their scenery. You feel it by the Wrekin, and on the Clee Hills' – apparently blown there from the neighbouring Welsh hills. If this seems somewhat fanciful, it is as nothing to Vale's account of the burial of Housman's ashes at St Laurence's Church in Ludlow. Many guidebooks mention that Housman found his final resting place here, but Vale believes that it was requested that the ashes 'should be lodged within the fabric of the church. This was done. The place selected was the north wall of the nave [. . .] The ashes of the poet were injected through a joint in the masonry on the outside of the wall and sealed with a grouting of liquid cement. A brass plate marks the site on the outside of the church.' How Vale came across this preposterous, macabre and wholly untrue story is not known. Anyone less likely than Housman to wish to become part of the fabric of a church is hard to imagine, and his ashes were in fact buried in the ground outside the church, between two buttresses on the north wall. Soil from his two childhood homes in Bromsgrove had not only been mixed with the ashes but was also sprinkled on top of the casket, rather as the Unknown Warrior was buried in Westminster Abbey in soil imported from the battlefields of the First World War. The tablet on the wall (which is of stone, not brass, and quotes the poem Moses Jackson remembered in his final illness) was already in place, and a simple stone plaque bearing the legend HIC JACET / A.E.H. was placed over the grave itself. The cherry tree subsequently planted near the spot died, as did several successors before it was decided to plant one (a pink hybrid, alas) in another part of the grave-yard. In the church itself is a brightly coloured wall-hanging made by the Borderers' Patchwork and Quilting Group to mark the centenary of *A Shropshire Lad*.

Elsewhere Housman's most popular book has been commemorated on railways and canals and in breweries and nurseries. At the turn of the twenty-first century the British Rail Class 67 mainline locomotives were introduced on Britain's railway network, among them No. 67012, 'A Shropshire Lad', which operated on several lines, including the Wrexham and Shropshire Railway, until the company closed in 2011. In its elegant silver and dark grey W&SR livery, the train was also produced as a 1:76-scale electric model by the well-known Hornby toy company. The real train ended its life with Chiltern Railways, and after it had been taken out of service its nameplate was auctioned for charity. 'A Shropshire Lad' far outclassed the other three nameplates at the sale at Pershore in Worcestershire in July 2015 – even 'Thomas Telford'. Whereas the other plates sold for between £1400 and £3600 (excluding the additional buyer's premium), a report of the sale stated that 'A Shropshire Lad' 'pulled in a whopping £7,100 plus premium, costing the buyer just under £8,000 and setting a class record by a huge margin. The nameplate was highly fought for in the room but if you're a Shropshire lad, worked for Wrexham and Shropshire railways and passed out your driving career on 67012 then it must have been worth every penny.'

The winning bidder would have been able to celebrate with a pint or two of 'Shropshire Lad', an ale brewed by Wood's Shropshire Beers at Craven Arms – a town in which you can also find Land of Lost Content, otherwise the National Museum of Popular Culture. 'Shropshire Lad' is a traditionally brewed spring bitter, first introduced in 1996 to mark the centenary of Housman's volume. According to the manufacturers the flavour is 'evocative of the county and a bucolic lifestyle' – and it has proved one of their most popular beers. While Housman – and Terence Hearsay – would surely have approved of this beer, he might have balked at 'Shropshire Lass', 'a blonde stunner [. . .] lighter in strength as well as style', which was introduced in 2007 in response to requests for 'a golden ale to complement the strong and traditional virtues of Shropshire Lad'.

As someone who watched beacons burn for his own monarch and whose youngest brother was a professional soldier, Housman might also have been pleased that a narrowboat called *Shropshire Lad*, manned by military personnel seriously injured in Afghanistan, took part in the Thames pageant organised for the present Queen's Diamond Jubilee in June 2012. Gardeners, meanwhile, can plant a rose named 'A Shropshire Lad', a peach-pink climber introduced by the nurseryman David Austin in 1996 to mark the book's centenary. Austin has patented a collection of 'English Roses', bred to retain all the advantages of old roses but without their drawbacks, and this one is vigorous, repeat flowering, highly scented, and (unlike Housman) almost thornless.

Housman's spirit and words have been invoked as the centenary of the First World War is being marked around the world, a four-year act of commemoration that has resulted in all manner of events, exhibitions, books, films, concerts and recordings. Regardless of chronology, Housman continues to be associated with the national trauma of 1914–18. In the run-up to the ninetieth anniversary of the Armistice on 11 November 2008, one of the poems displayed in London's tube carriages as part of the 'Poems on the Underground' initiative was 'Here dead we lie because we did not choose', written about the fallen of the Boer War, but like much of Housman's poetry, both timeless and saying in a few words all that needs to be said. New settings of 'The lads in their hundreds to Ludlow come in for the fair' have appeared on centenary albums, and in new anthologies of First World War poetry Housman frequently takes his place alongside the soldier-poets. This is perhaps as it should be, for he was the supreme elegist of and for his age. He may not have been a combatant like Owen, Rosenberg and Sassoon, reporting back from the front line the shocking cost of modern industrialised warfare, but he understood those young men who had marched away in 1914. He knew, and could convey in poems that anyone could understand and appreciate, their moods, their fears, and what they had in their hearts. He also understood the world they had left behind them and distilled in his poems the essence of a rural England that was already passing in 1896. This may not be a real place, but it was one that people recognise and for which they still search. We all have our lands of lost content.

And we all have our Moses Jacksons, people we have loved unwisely, secretly, consumingly, and with little prospect of reciprocation. 'I suppose you have read A.E. Housman,' the Second World War poet Keith Douglas wrote in 1939 to a young woman he was unsuccessfully wooing. 'If you will take as from me the saddest and most moving love poem he ever wrote, and read it well, you will have much better what I want to say than I could tell you.' This is one of the roles poetry plays in our lives: to put into words what we cannot, or at any rate not so effectively and memorably. For those who care about academic league tables, Housman may be a minor poet rather than a major one, but, as Auden pointed out, this 'does not mean that his poems are inferior in artistic merit to those of a major poet, only that the range of theme and emotion is narrow, and that the poems show no development over the years. On the evidence of the text alone, it would be very difficult to say whether a poem appeared in *A Shropshire Lad*, published when he was thirty-seven, or in *Last Poems*, published when he was sixty-three.' Another way of putting this would be to say that Housman's poetry constitutes a coherent, consistent and instantly recognisable body of work.

Housman's notion that poetry should provide 'that thrilling utterance which pierces the heart and brings tears to the eyes' is what his own poems have done over many generations. The 'peculiar function of poetry', he said in his Leslie Stephen Lecture, was 'to transfuse emotion – not to transmit thought but to set up in the reader's sense a vibration corresponding to what was felt by the writer'. This direct connection between poet and reader, producing vibrations like those of a tuning fork that has been gently struck, is one of the principal reasons why Housman's poetry has been taken into people's hearts. A contemporary commentator described Housman's lecture as 'notably independent of current fashion', and it was delivered at a period when the current fashion was for intellectualism in poetry, for the complex and allusive poems of T.S. Eliot and the rising generation headed by

W.H. Auden. We know, however, that Auden rated Housman highly, while Eliot, who sent Housman an advance copy of *Journey of the Magi* inscribed with his 'respectful homage', is reported to have remarked: 'We should all write like Housman – if only we could.'

Fashion, literary or otherwise, was not something that greatly interested Housman. *A Shropshire Lad* had stood apart from the modish urban poetry of the period in which it was published and has survived many other fluctuations of literary taste since then. As the decades have passed, the book's reputation has ebbed and flowed among our cultural arbiters, who are perhaps more swayed by fashion than the ordinary readers for whom Housman wrote his poems. And it is those ordinary readers who have done something much more important. They have continued to respond to the poems as Housman hoped they would, have felt that vibration he wanted to set up in them, and have continued to read *A Shropshire Lad* for 120 years.

ACKNOWLEDGEMENTS

Twenty years ago John Walsh commissioned me to write an article for the *Independent* about the centenary of *A Shropshire Lad*, and my first thanks go to him for planting the seed of this book in my mind. My agent, David Miller, watered that seed and contributed numerous ideas and suggestions for its cultivation. As always, Christopher Potter is my first editor, and my thanks go to him for this and for much else. Richard Beswick at Little, Brown was a model of enthusiasm, patience and editorial ruthlessness, while Iain Hunt provided considerable help compiling the source notes and saw the book through to press with great speed and efficiency. I'd also like to thank Steve Gove for his meticulous copy-editing. At FSG, I would like to thank Jonathan Galassi, Ileene Smith, Jackson Howard, Jeff Seroy, Maya Binyam, Charlotte Strick and Claire Williams.

Many other individuals and institutions have contributed towards this book and my particular thanks go to Jim Page of the Housman Society for innumerable kindnesses; Iain Burnside, and all those involved in the Ludlow English Song Weekend; Salley Vickers, Maggie Fergusson and Michael Ipgrave, Bishop of Woolwich, for providing me with family stories of *A Shropshire Lad* in wartime; Richard Davenport-Hines for drawing my attention to Willa Cather's letters and Douglas Hurd's memoirs; and the late Elizabeth Jane Howard for remembering she had an unpublished letter from Housman somewhere in her files and allowing me to reproduce it here. Several biographies and other studies of Housman, all of which are listed in the bibliography, have proved invaluable, but special mention should be made of Archie Burnett's editions of the *Poems* and the *Letters*, both of which have been on my desk throughout the writing of this book. Among others who have provided assorted material, interviews, information, leads, suggestions, advice, accommodation, encouragement and occasional welcome distraction, I thank Nicholas Allen, Adam Bager, Prasun Banerjee, Sarah

Acknowledgements

Baxter (the Society of Authors), Edward Behrens, Judith Bingham, Thomas Blaikie, Polly Bolton, Mark Bostridge, John Bridcut, Robin Brooke-Smith (Shrewsbury School), Martin Bussey, Richard Canning, Niladri Chatterjee, Barry Cheeseman, Alex Clark, Peter Conradi, Ronald Corp, Minoo Dinshaw, Maggie Elkin, Paul Fincham, Brendan Finucane, Chris Fletcher, Jonathan Gibbs, David Graham, Georgina Hammick, Linda Hart, Selina Hastings, Alison Hennegan, Jonathan Hunt, Jennifer Ingleheart, Graham Johnson, Lyndon Jones, Peter Kurie, Philip Lancaster, Chris Lawrey, Julius Lunn, John Matheson, Jennie McGregor-Smith, Diana McVeagh, Candia McWilliam, Edward Mendelson, Michael Meredith (Eton College), Jean Moorcroft-Wilson, Michael Parkinson, Matt Perzinski, Ros Porter, Simon Rowland-Jones, Alice Sielle, Peter Sisley (the Housman Society), Nicola Starks, Adrian Symons, Ian Venables, Edward Watson, Sarah Watts (University of Southampton) and David Wheeler. My thanks also go to Jonathan Smith and the staff at Trinity College Library, Cambridge, and to the staff of the London Library and the British Library. If I have overlooked anyone, I hope that this will be put down to inattention rather than ingratitude.

Additional thanks go to Trinity College Library, Cambridge, for permission to reproduce material from their holdings and the photograph of Housman used as the frontispiece. Unpublished writing by Katharine E. Symons is reproduced by kind permission of the Housman Society; the letter from A.E. Housman to Arthur Somervell is reproduced by permission of the Society of Authors as the Literary Representative of the Estate of A.E. Housman; the lines from John Masefield's 'London Town' are also reproduced by permission of the Society of Authors as the Literary Representative of the Estate of John Masefield. It has not always been possible to trace copyright holders, and the publishers would be pleased to hear from any who have proved elusive or been overlooked.

I was fortunate enough to be born and brought up on the fringes of Housman Country within easy reach of many of the places mentioned in *A Shropshire Lad*. Having, however, twice failed my driving test in Ludlow, I am eternally grateful to my late father and mother and to my sister, who severally chauffeured me round Housman sites in both Shropshire and Worcestershire. This book is for them.

NOTES

A Note on Sources

References to quoted material are listed by page number and in order, identified by a brief phrase. Published sources are referred to by the author's surname, followed by an abbreviated title where necessary. Books and individuals who occur frequently are referred to using the following abbreviations:

AEH – A.E. Housman
GR – Grant Richards
KES – Katharine E. Symons
LH – Laurence Housman
MJJ – Moses Jackson
TCC – Trinity College, Cambridge

A.E.H. – Laurence Housman, *A.E.H.* (1937)
AP – Additional Poems
ASL – A Shropshire Lad
ASLOP – A Shropshire Lad and Other Poems, ed. Archie Burnett (2010)
Bromsgrove – *Alfred Edward Housman* (Bromsgrove School, 1936)
CH – A.E. Housman: The Critical Heritage, ed. Philip Gardner (1992)
CP&SP – Collected Poems and Selected Prose, ed. Christopher Ricks (1988)
GRH – Grant Richards, *Housman: 1897–1926* (1941)
HSJ – Housman Society Journal
Letters I and *Letters II* – the two volumes of *The Letters of A.E. Housman* (2007)
LP – Last Poems

Notes

MP — *More Poems*

Poems — *The Poems of A.E. Housman*, ed. Archie Burnett (1997)

Recollections — Katharine E. Symons et al., *Alfred Edward Housman: Recollections* (1937)

TN&NP — 'The Name and Nature of Poetry', 1933 lecture

Preface

ix   *not a complete biography* GRH, p. xi

I. England in Your Pocket

1   epigraph Birch, *Westminster Abbey*, p. 29

1   *sweetness of country life* The Times, 27 March 1896, *CH*, p. 58

2   *a very real poet* Review of Reviews, Vol. 14, Aug 1896, p. 187

2   *the one I most wanted* Richards, *Author Hunting*, p. 92

2   *Vanity, not avarice* To GR, 22 June 1903, *Letters I*, p. 149

2   *I only stipulate* To GR, 22 July 1898, ibid., p. 109

2   *perhaps the largest sum* To GR, 24 July 1898, ibid., p. 109

2   *a pocket edition* To GR, 11 Dec 1899, ibid., p. 114

2   *gave full weight* GRH, p. 33

3   *bound to say* To GR, 27 July 1904, *Letters I*, p. 159; GRH, p. 33

3   *It was not for its reputation* Quoted GRH, p. 34

3   *in every pocket* Nichols, p. 29

4   *the last thirty years* To John Coghlan, 8 Feb 1934, *Letters I*, p. 405

4   *The particular psychology* To C.W. Orr, 23 Jan 1935, Foreman, From Parry, p. 182

4   *No contemporary poet* American Services edition of *Selected Poems*, back jacket

4   *no book of poetry* Quoted Weber, p. 124

4   *Yardley could use* See New Yorker, 7 Nov 1931, p. 29

4   *I was born* Letters II, pp. 327–8

6   *considered inferior* A.E.H., p. 211

6   *of a lower standard* Ibid.

6   *rescued from periodicals* Carter and Sparrow, p. 165

7   *My chief object* To Witter Bynner, 3 June 1903, *Letters I*, p. 147

7   *I don't know how* Auden, *Forewords*, p. 332

7   *the writer who had* Orwell and Angus, pp. 552, 550, 551

8   *stood for* Ibid., pp. 553, 554

8   *more healing than prose* To KES, 5 Oct 1915, *Letters I*, pp. 346–7

8   *Nothing is less poetical* Quoted *Letters I*, p. 347

9   *The blind* To GR, 10 Jan 1923, ibid., p. 533

9   *not to personal experience* To M. Pollet, 5 Feb 1933, *Letters II*, p. 329

Notes

9   *Pray who gave* To GR, 29 June 1907, *Letters I*, p. 211

9   *the pompous edition* *Letters II*, p. 114

9   *while the book was printing* *Letters I*, p. 612

9   *If he reminds us* *Fortnightly Review*, 1 Aug 1898, *CH*, p. 77

9   *cried kinship* *Chap-Book* (Chicago), 1 Feb 1897, *CH*, p. 70

10   *no Arcadia* *CH*, p. 76

10   *full of the charm* Orwell and Angus, p. 551

10   *Like a true Englishman* Anon, *Citizen* (Philadelphia), 9 Nov 1897, *CH,* p. 74

11   *A theme or note* Barker, *National*, p. 229

11   *Anglo-Saxon genius* Ker, quoted ibid., p. 229

11   *Best Is Yet to Come* 'The Best Is Yet to Come' (1959) by Cy Coleman and Carolyn Leigh

12   *I followed England* Preface, quoted Schwarz, p. 72

13   *Amid the uncertainties* Froude, p. 17

13   *Alfred's laws* Quoted Schwarz, p. 72

13   *Englishman proper* Quoted Samuel, p. 58

15   *high-days and holidays* 'Merry England' in Rhys, p. 67

15   *Indian summer* The phrase is used by Girouard, p. 17

15   *age of chivalry* Edmund Burke, *Reflections on the Revolution in France* (1790), quoted Girouard, p. 19

16   *ideal of chivalry* Norwood, p. 19

17   *Poets of England* Palgrave, Preface

17   *deepened our sense* C.H. Herford in *Bulletin*, Sept 1918, quoted Doyle, p. 27

17   *mere chatter* Quoted in *Oxford Dictionary of National Biography* article on A.C. Bradley

17   *radiantly legitimised* Arthur Quiller-Couch, *On the Art of Writing* (1916), pp. 139–40, quoted Doyle, p. 21

18   *Colonisation* Quoted Doyle, p. 30

18   *has been deeply affected* Barker, *Character*, p. 3

19   *Towns came late* Ibid., pp. 3–4

19   *I feel very sorry* Question Time, BBC1, 14 June 2012

20   *peculiarly 'English' poet* Birch, *Westminster Abbey*, p. 16

20   *Englishness of Housman's poetry* Ibid., p. 26

20   *a great statement* Ibid., p. 24

20   *a piece of England* Vickers to author, 18 Dec 2013

II. The Man and His Book

22   epigraph *Letters II*, p. 377

23   *alderman* Keats (Rollins), p. 88

23   *There is death* Coleridge, p. 184

23   *in a very sad state* *Letters I*, p. 76

24   *with whom any* Quoted Stallworthy, p. 469

Notes

25   *Sodomites* To GR, 9 Oct 28, *Letters II*, p. 93

26   *Housman is one* Plimpton, p. 299

26   *self-loathing* Maas, *Spoken and Unspoken*, p. 14

27   *He always seemed* Quoted R.P. Graves, p. 142

27   *I read Gentlemen* Mark Twain Quarterly, Winter 1936, p. 10

27   *very pleasant* Page, pp. 105–6

27   *as he got easier* Ibid., p. 107

27   *only abominable* Ibid., p. 104

28   *a good raconteur* The Times, 2 May 1936, p. 9

28   *odd affectionateness* Quoted Page, p. 152

30   *damp your ardour* To GR, 21 Feb 1898, *Letters I*, pp. 105–6

30   *after the book* To GR, 24 July 1898, ibid., p. 109

30   *I should like* To GR, 11 Dec 1898, ibid., p. 114

30   *I enclose* To GR, 27 July 1904, ibid., p. 159

30   *unbecoming* To Messrs Alexander Mooring, 17 Aug 1906, ibid., p. 198

30   *how atrociously* To GR, 17 Aug 1906, ibid., p. 199

30   *atrocious production* To GR, 27 June 1908, ibid., p. 223

31   *usual blunders* To GR, 28 Aug 1911, ibid., p. 273

31   *more likely to remember* See GRH, p. 223

32   *flee the country with* To GR, 12 Dec 1920, *Letters I*, p. 457

32   *Naturally* To GR, 20 Oct 1921, ibid., p. 474

33   *As matters stand* To GR, 1 Oct 1924, ibid., p. 573

33   *exact* To GR, 17 Dec 1926, ibid., p. 641

33   *Dijon* Title of Chapter XXVI of GRH

33   *Even deflections* A.E.H., p. 105

33   *bains de vapeur* See AEH to GR, 9 Oct 1928, *Letters II*, p. 93 and 22 May 1922, *Letters I*, p. 494

33   *puts a stigma* GRH, p. 297

34   *There is no single* Ibid.

34   *a shy, proud* A.E.H., p. 13

34   *This is me* Quoted ibid., p. 99

35   *He was not a man* Ibid., p. 13

35   *We may seem* CP&SP, p. 263

35   *extracted from life* A.E.H., p. 13

35   *implicit in his poetry* GRH, p. 395

35   *Well, William* Rothenstein 1900–1922, p. 39

35   *an absconding cashier* Quoted R.P. Graves, p. 116

35   *grim and dry* Rothenstein, 1900–1922, p. 39

36   *had never met* Mendelson, *Later Auden*, p. 440

36   *more physical* TN&NP in *ASLOP*, p. 254

36   *when the trees* GRH, p. 289

37   *strangely moved* Encounter, October 1967, p. 39

37   *Only those who* Ibid.

Notes

38 *The English poet* Barker, *Character*, p. 304

38 *It ought to be* To Withers, 28 Dec 1928, *Letters II*, p. 102

39 *the best portrait* *MP*, p. 10

39 *very unlike* To Alice Rothenstein, 16 Jan 1927, *Letters II*, p. 5

39 *oblige the artist* To KES, 18 March 1934, *Letters II*, p. 409

40 *an undertaker's mute . . . maiden aunts* Middleton: quoted Watson, p. 190; Benson: quoted Peter Green, *New Republic*, 13 Feb 2008

40 *aged 35* A.E.H., plate facing p. 84

40 *early manhood* To Percy Withers, 24 Nov 1934, *Letters II*, p. 450

41 *the year when* To GR, 28 Sept 1920, *Letters I*, p. 452

42 *all clever boys* LH, *Unexpected*, p. 88

42 *fell into my hands* To Maurice Pollet, 5 Feb 1933, *Letters II*, p. 328

42 *dark, twisted* LH, *Unexpected,* p. 23

43 *Was there ever* Ibid., pp. 19–20

43 *I was the sun* A.E.H., pp. 22–3

43 *a science which* *CP&SP*, p. 260

44 *roused within him* Bromsgrove, p. 10

46 *Country influences* Ibid., p. 10

46 *very pretty streams* Ibid., p. 12

46 *Many years later* A.E.H., p. 29

46 *there used to be* To Alice Rothenstein, 16 Jan 1927, *Letters II*, p. 5

47 *Summer!* *Poems*, p. 203

47 *Yesterday I went* To Lucy Housman, 29 Jan 1895, *Letters I*, p. 8

48 *has in it* A.E.H., p. 27

48 *Give me a land* *MP* VIIIA

48 *depth of feeling* LH, *Unexpected*, p. 73

48 *Now and then* Ibid., p. 74

48 *western horizon* To M. Pollet, 5 Feb 1933, *Letters II*, p. 328

49 *spent most* To Lucy Housman, 9 Jan 1875, *Letters I*, p. 6

50 *increasing restriction* Bromsgrove, p. 24

50 *Tristram* Pollard in ibid., p. 30

50 *generally recognized* Ibid.

51 *a perfect Philistine* Quoted in Page, p. 41

51 *lively* Woudhuysen, p. 41

51 *I believe that* c. Nov/Dec 1893, *Letters I*, p. 75

51 *15-mile walks* MJJ to AEH, 23 Nov 1922, in *HSJ* 36 (2010), p. 45

51 *simplicity* Woudhuysen, p. 41

51 *After we had* Bromsgrove, pp. 30–1

52 *absolutely safe first* Ibid., p. 31

52 *vowed that* Quoted R.P. Graves, p. 49

52 *came away* Gow, p. 5

52 *abstract thought* Ibid., p. 7

52 *There are few* 11 Dec 1885, *Letters I*, p. 58

Notes

52 *Deliberately* 'A.E. Housman' in Auden, *Collected Poems*, p. 182

52 *that voice* Ricks, *Critical Essays*, p. 23

53 *Propertius* Gow, p. 7

53 *emendation* 11 Dec 1885, *Letters I*, p. 58

53 *marriage of logic* HSJ 1 (1974), p. 28

53 *facile and frivolous* Gow, p. 13

53 *Housman's chief love* Ibid., p. 12

53 *a society . . . intimate comradeship* Quoted Dowling, pp. 85–6

54 *Every pious parent* Quoted Parker, p. 90

54 *atheist at 21* To Pollet, 5 Feb 1933, *Letters II*, p. 328

54 *went on believing* To KES, 10 Nov 1935, ibid., p. 504

55 *abandoned Christianity* Ibid.

55 *towards the end* Ibid.

55 *bewilderment* Bromsgrove, p. 31

56 *refused to consider* Quoted R.P. Graves, p. 54

56 *on whom he* Quoted *Letters I*, pp. 261–2

57 *During those years* LH, *Unexpected*, p. 95

57 *He returned home* GRH, p. xv

57 *blamable* Ibid., p. xiv

57 *When summer's end* LP XXXIX

58 *On miry meads* MP XXXIV

58 *This failure* John Sparrow, *TLS*, 16 Aug 1957

58 *lay me down and die* MP XXI

59 *Diffugere Nives* MP V

59 *told him he* LH to Gow, 15 June 1936, TCC, Add MS a. 71–126

60 *did not much love* To A.F. Scholfield, 16 June 1936,
     TCC, Add MS a. 71–188

60 *most familiar friends* F.W. Hodges to Gow, n.d., quoted Page, p. 51

60 *a photograph of Jackson* Reproduced in Watson, facing page 88

60 *a Thames oarsman* Page, p. 51

60 *When he goes* AEH to Lucy Housman, 29 March 1885, *Letters I*, pp. 55–6

61 *a most delightful* To Gow, n.d. TCC, Add MS a. 71–191

62 *Though he would* A.E.H., p. 60

62 *an irregular life* R.P. Graves, p. 64

63 *Whether the worst* Encounter, Oct 1967, p. 35

63 *met daily* Ibid.

63 *three poems* MP XXX, XXI; AP VII

63 *The Mills and Boon* Birch, *Bibliography*, p. 3

63 *I still think* Encounter, Oct 1967, p. 41

64 *He looked at me* MP XLI

64 *Turn East* Poems, p. 139

64 *I doubt whether* Encounter, Oct 1967, p. 41

64 *that straight look* MP XLII

Notes

65   *wishful thinking*   Naiditch, *Problems*, p. 140

65   *My fate*   Propertius, p. 16

65   *Housman would not*   GRH, p. 449

66   *Most of the pages*   The diaries are now in the British Library (Add MS 45861), but have been transcribed, with varying degrees of accuracy, by LH in *Encounter* (October 1967) and P.D. Eaton in *HSJ* 8 (1982), pp. 8–12

68   *After leaving Karachi*   This account of MJJ's life and career owes much to P.G. Naiditch's 'Notes on the Life of M.J. Jackson', *HSJ* 12 (1986), pp. 93–114, collected in Naiditch, *Problems*, pp. 132–44

69   *held his character*   6 Feb 1911, quoted *HSJ* 36 (2010), p. 40

69   *I do not want*   AEH to MJJ, 12 June 1911, in ibid., p. 41

69   *cramped*   Andrew Jackson, 'A Pivotal Friendship', *HSJ* 36 (2010), p. 41

69   *grown up*   To MJJ, 24 Aug 1918, quoted Jackson, p. 171

70   *largely responsible*   AEH to MJJ, 4 Jan 1923, in *HSJ* 36, p. 46

70   *I wrote verse*   5 Feb 1933, *Letters II*, p. 328

70   *in his twentieth year*   *A.E.H.*, p. 114

70   *it smacked*   Ibid.

71   *That thing*   MJJ to AEH, 23 Nov 1922, in *HSJ* 36 (2010), p. 43

71   *I never was*   AEH to MJJ, 4 Jan 1923, in ibid., p. 46

72   *I am going on*   MJJ to AEH, 10 Dec 1922, in ibid., p. 44

72   *As I cannot*   AEH to MJJ, 4 Jan 1923, in ibid., p. 46

73   *Epithalamium*   *LP* XXIV

73   *Propertius*   in Ricks, *Critical Essays*, p. 22

73   *the voice of*   Ibid., p. 23

73   *dactylic hexameters*   I owe this point to A.E. Stallings in the notes to his translation of the poem published in *Poetry* in March 2012: http://www.poetryfoundation.org/poemcomment/243608

74   *the love of comrades*   Cf dedicatory poem in *CP&SP*, p. 253–5 and *AP* V

76   *He said that*   Quoted Naiditch, *Problems*, p. 142

76   *I did not begin*   *Letters II*, p. 329

76   *I promise nothing*   *MP* XII

77   *Literature as Compensation*   Forster, *Commonplace Book*, p. 47

77   *continuous excitement*   Prefatory note to *Last Poems*

77   *came to him*   GRH, p. 436

77   *thirteen times*   TN&NP in *ASLOP*, p. 256

77   *easy reading*   *Athenaeum*, 8 Oct 1898, quoted GRH, p. 27

78   *Housman is perhaps*   *New Statesman*, 1 Jan 1938, p. 19

78   *During the last*   To the Council of UCL, 19 April 1892, *Letters I*, p. 72

78   *picked him out*   Quoted R.P. Graves, p. 79

78   *Having drunk*   TN&NP in *ASLOP*, pp. 255–6

79   *The leader of*   20 May 1933, *Letters II*, p. 347

80   *Poetry is not*   TN&NP in *ASLOP*, p. 248

80   *opinions and beliefs*   Ibid., p. 247

80 *Nymphs and shepherds* Ibid., p. 254

81 *Experience has taught me* Ibid.

81 *only describe* Ibid., pp. 254–5. AEH is slightly misquoting a letter Keats wrote to Charles Brown, dated 1 Nov 1820: see Keats (Colvin), p. 374

81 *one passion* Quoted *Oxford Dictionary of National Biography* entry on Frances Brawne

82 *seldom written* TN&NP in *ASLOP*, p. 255

82 *rather out of health* Quoted Page, p. 78

82 *most prolific* To Maurice Pollet, 5 Feb 1933, *Letters II*, p. 329

82 *Punctuality* Bromsgrove, p. 23

82 *had from the first* Ibid., p. 30

82 *starry sky* Ibid., p. 24

82 *That his daily* Gow, p. 51

83 *To burn always* Pater, pp. 210–11

84 *I am always* 'Preface: Being a word on behalf of Patchouli', in Symons, *Silhouettes*, p. xv

84 *no very salutary* Ibid., p. xiv

85 *the High Priest* National Observer, 6 April 1895, quoted Hyde, p. 156

86 *Here is a writer* CH, p. 65

86 *pleasant* Ibid., p. 67

86 *Mr Housman has* Ibid., p. 69

86 *The little volume* Ibid., pp. 59–60

86 *the best review* To Houston Martin, 22 March 1936, *Letters II*, p. 528

86 *people who had* Rothenstein, *1872–1900*, p. 281

87 *Its narrow measure* Epigraph to *More Poems*

88 *a biography* Review of Reviews, Vol. 14, August 1896, p. 187

89 *a persona* Leggett, *Housman's Land*, p. 124

89 *progressively tragic* Ibid., p. 107

89 *Very little* Letters II, p. 329

90 *The 'Enigma'* Quoted Rushton, p. 65

90 *It is evident* Idler ix, June 1896, p. 727

91 *Only the archangel* To LH, 16 Feb 1929, *Letters II*, p. 111

91 *Some of the gentlemen* Musical Times, 1 Dec 1930, p. 1094

92 *an imaginary figure* To Pollet, 5 Feb 1933, *Letters II*, p. 329

92 *an imaginary character* Undated draft of letter to Pollet, ibid., p. 326

93 *wanting in the note* CH, p. 61

93 *The Funereal Muse* Ibid., pp. 88, 90

94 *moves our compassion* Ibid., p. 74

96 *Mr Housman writes* Ibid., p. 76

98 *He saved others* Matthew 17:42; Mark 15:31

102 *Shakespeare's songs* To M. Pollet, 5 Feb 1933, *Letters II*, p. 329

103 *I suppose that* To Witter Bynner, 3 June 1903, *Letters I*, p. 147

103 *merely a necessary* Marlow, Preface

Notes

103   *a nursing home*   See *Letters I*, p. 554; *Letters II*, p. 504

103   *The other day*   To Witter Bynner, 28 Feb 1910, *Letters I*, p. 248

103   *Echoes of Gray*   See Burnett, *Poems*, pp. 327, 348

104   *How jocund*   Thomas Gray, 'Elegy written in a Country Churchyard', line 27

104   *The sigh that heaves*   *LP* XXVII

104   *On acres*   *LP* XL

104   *Now to her lap*   *MP* VIII

104   *His favourite*   Bromsgrove, p. 30

104   *For Hardy*   To Pollet, 5 Feb 1933, *Letters II*, p. 330

105   *Hardy has surely*   Quoted in *HSJ* 8 (1982), p. 32

105   *To tell the truth*   Quoted ibid., p. 33

105   *Echoes of this*   Cf Arnold's poem 'The Buried Life', lines 9–11

105   *Homespun collars*   *MP* XXIX

106   *Deutsche Treue*   See Marlow, p. 96

107   *lyrical achievement*   TN&NP in *ASLOP*, p. 250

107   *In an extraordinary*   Norman Gale, *Academy*, 11 July 1896, in *CH*, p. 69

107   *To my knowledge*   Lynn Gardner, 'Stuff & Nonsense' blog, 3 April 2012: www.lynngardner.name/2012_04_01_archive.html

107   *My dad*   Comment from JaneGS, ibid.

108   *You may read it*   William Archer, *Fortnightly Review*, 1 Aug 1898, in *CH*, p. 76

108   *the removal*   KES to GR, 7 March 1939, quoted R.P. Graves, p. 102

108   *it could not*   *GRH*, p. 313

108   *As Sarpedon says*   *CP&SP*, pp. 262–3

109   *contemplated suicide*   *St James's Gazette*, 10 August 1896, p. 12

109   *a service weapon*   Ibid.

109   *lying on the floor*   *Evening News*, 10 August 1895, p. 3

110   *had carefully destroyed*   J.M. Nosworthy, 'A.E. Housman and the Woolwich Cadet', *Notes and Queries*, New Series 17, September 1970, p. 351

110   *I wish it to be*   Reproduced in *St James's Gazette*, 10 August 1896, p. 12

112   *whoso shall offend*   Matthew 18:6

112   *Wherefore if thy*   Matthew 18:8

112   *Lock your heart*   Haber, *Making*, p. 249

113   *there may yet*   *A.E.H.*, pp. 104–5

115   *The queen of air*   To Geoffrey Wethered, 13 Sept 1933, *Letters II*, p. 377

115   *believed the poem*   Marlow, p. 101

116   *Ho, everyone that*   *MP* XXII

116   *a transitional period*   LH to Gow, 26 May 1936, TCC, Add MS a. 71–139

116   *though somewhat lacking*   *A.E.H.*, p. 105

118   *what they say*   Dickinson to AEH, 22 Nov 1922, quoted Page, p. 3

118   *The chestnut casts*   *LP* IX

119   *few young men*   To Witter Bynner, 3 June 1903, *Letters I*, p. 147

Notes

120   *It always pleases*   LH to Geoffrey Wethered, 29 Dec 1937, in *HSJ* 4 (1978), p. 7

120   *great and real*   To Percy Withers, 24 Nov 1934, *Letters II*, p. 450

120   *The thoughts of others*   MP VI

121   *The world goes*   MP XXI

121   *Sinner's Rue*   LP XXX

122   *filthiest book*   AEH to LH, 25 Feb 1929, *Letters II*, p. 112

122   *intellectually frivolous*   TN&NP in *ASLOP*, p. 236

123   *dream-fed beauty*   Carpenter, p. 4

124   *Like fragrant ashes*   Reade, p. 228

124   *But I loved*   Wilde, *Complete Works*, p. 864

125   *Do the British*   Fussell, *Great War*, p. 272

126   *I have lately*   Wilde to LH, 9 Aug 1897, Wilde, *Complete Letters*, p. 923

126   *above Wilde's average*   To Seymour Adelman, 21 June 1928, *Letters II*, p. 78

127   *I've made two*   Forster, *Journals*, Vol. 1, p. 130

127   *A copy with*   Forster, *Creator*, p. 126

127   *not yet looking*   Ibid.

127   *I had a rush*   Ibid.

128   *My obscure admiration*   Ibid.

128   *ventured to hazard*   Ibid.

128   *When I read*   Forster to AEH, 22 Feb 1923, Forster, *Letters*, Vol. 2, p. 33

129   *perhaps this letter*   To Forster, 25 Feb 1923, *Letters I*, p. 537

129   *literary criticism*   To J.J. Thomson, 22 Feb 1925, ibid., p. 585

129   *Housman came to*   Forster, *Commonplace*, p. 22

129   *Neither memory*   Forster, *Aspects*, p. 36

130   *unrespectable company*   Forster, *Creator*, p. 127

130   *ventured to climb*   Ibid.

130   *somewhat warmly*   Forster to AEH, 28 March 1928, Forster, *Letters*, Vol. 2, p. 85

130   *I don't know whether*   Ibid.

130   *I did not conceal*   Forster, *Creator*, pp. 127–8

131   *half-educated public*   Forster, *Eternal*, p. 71

131   *forcing the pace*   Forster, *Creator*, p. 128

131   *I value the good*   13 Sept 1933, *Letters II*, p. 377

131   *but he liked*   LH to Geoffrey Wethered, 29 Dec 1937, in *HSJ* 4 (1978), p. 7

131   *Mortified*   Forster, *Creator*, p. 128

132   *Good-night, my lad*   LP XVIII

132   *It seems to me*   Forster to Florence Barger, 18 July 1917, Forster, *Letters*, Vol. 1, p. 263

132   *such a triumph*   Forster to Florence Barger, 25 August 1917, ibid., pp. 268–9

133   *my gondolier*   To Lucy Housman, 15 Oct 1900, *Letters I*, p. 129

133   *rushed off*   Withers, in GRH, p. 395

133   *I cannot offer*   To GR, 18 May 1932, *Letters II*, p. 293

133   *a nice young man* To KES, 18 Aug 1933, ibid., p. 371
133   *I do know something* To GR, 22 May 1922, *Letters I*, p. 494
134   *This was offered* Forster, *Creator*, p. 127
134   *any way preferable* To GR, 9 Oct 1928, *Letters II*, p. 93
134   *an anal passive* New Yorker, 19 Feb 1972, in Auden, *Forewords*, p. 327
134   *Ho, everyone* *MP* XXII
134   *Stolen waters* Proverbs 9:17
135   *Perhaps he had* Forster, *Prince's*, p. 122
135   *tasted some* R.P. Graves, p. 151
136   *His powers of* GRH, p. 446
137   *He was capable* Ibid., p. 448
137   *ashamed of* Ibid., pp. 448–9
137   *The emotions* GRH, p. 395
137   *go forth* Forster, *Abinger*, pp. 4–5
138   *deeply or not* Ibid., pp. 5–6
138   *It is a strong* Quoted Turner, p. xv
139   *The intensity* Withers, pp. 129–30
139   *We can't get* Forster, *Abinger*, p. 7
140   *The answer must* Barker, *Character*, pp. 304–5; the lines of poetry are from
      Wordsworth's 'A Complaint' (1806)
140   *implicit in* GRH, p. 395
140   *a beautiful ruin* Reade, p. 49
140   *they tell more* KES to Gow, 24 Sept 1937, TCC, Add MS a. 7132
140   *would never talk* Barker, *Character*, p. 306
141   *his most intimate friend* Page, p. 51
141   *I am as delighted* Letter and envelope reproduced in facsimile in Adelman, pp.
      30–1
144   *Temp. 80* *HSJ* 8 (1982), pp. 10–11
144   *carries a promise* De Cleene and Lejeune, Vol. 2, pp. 174, 175
146   *He would not stay* *AP* VII
147   *The weeping Pleiads* *MP* X
148   *The cheerful* To MJJ, 19 Oct 1922, *Letters I*, pp. 516–18
148   *extraordinary exhibition* MJJ to AEH, 21 Nov 1922, in *HSJ* 36 (2010), p. 45; for
      Larry, see David McKie, 'Jacksoniana', *HSJ* 37 (2011), pp. 139–40
148   *a fellow who thinks* To MJJ, 4 Jan 1924, in *HSJ* 36 (2010), p. 46
149   *Now I can die* 17 Jan 1923, *Letters II*, pp. 533–4
149   *owing to the cost* GRH, p. 160
149   *The working classes* To GR, 6 June 1918, *Letters I*, p. 389
149   *to make as certain* GRH, p. 200
150   *Oh, Alfred* Punch, 25 October 1922, reproduced in ibid., p. 203
150   *a continuation* The Times, 17 October 1922, p. 13
150   *extra numbers* CH, p. 125
150   *TLS* Ibid., p. 112; Gosse, *Sunday Times*, 22 Oct 1922, ibid., p. 116

150 *Spectator* Ibid., p. 128; *Bookman*, ibid., p. 130

151 *Dodd* Ibid., p. 135

151 *that rare being* Ibid., p. 126

151 *a large number* Weber, p. 84

151 *examined twenty-five* Ibid., p. 105

152 *huge and important circulation* Quoted ibid., p. 120

152 *knew by heart* GRH, p. 55

152 *Housman came as* Quoted Weber, p. 123

152 *I have seldom* Quoted ibid., p. 124

152 *I had a visit* To Basil Housman, 29 Dec 1927, *Letters II*, p. 48

153 *I remember* http://law2.umkc.edu/faculty/projects/ftrials/leoploeb /darrowclosing.html

154 *I care not* Ibid.

154 *my poems are misquoted* To Basil Housman, 29 Dec 1927, *Letters II*, p. 48

154 *guttering low* http://law2.umkc.edu/faculty/projects/ftrials/leoploeb /darrowclosing.html

154 *I should have written* CP&SP, p. 448

154 *The printers have* Ibid.

155 *In the course of* 22 Dec 1932, *Letters II*, p. 320

155 *I suppose* 15 June 1933, ibid., p. 354

155 *now behaving* To Percy Withers, 7 June 1933, ibid., p. 352

155 *My real trouble* Ibid.

155 *In previous visitations* To Percy Withers, 10 Aug 1933, ibid., p. 369

155 *violently painful* To GR, 28 Sept 1933, ibid., p. 380

155 *honeymoon mixture* To Percy Withers, 10 Nov 1933, ibid., p. 386

156 *all his life* A.E.H., p. 118

156 *The doctor does not* 9 June 1935, *Letters II*, p. 476

156 *The continuation* 27 July 1935, ibid., p. 486

156 *Do not expect* To KES, 28 Aug 1935, ibid., pp. 490–1

156 *breathlessness* To KES, 24 Oct 1935, ibid., p. 500

156 *with a bathroom* To Denis Symons, 11 Dec 1935, ibid., p. 508

156 *but I wake up* Ibid.

157 *The other night* To KES, 27 Dec 1935, ibid., p. 513

157 *but with no strength* To GR, 20 Jan 1936, ibid., p. 517

157 *I have no idea* To Houston Martin, 22 March 1936, ibid., p. 527

157 *terribly ill* Quoted *Letters II*, p. 533

157 *Ugh!* To KES, 25 April 1936, ibid., p. 533

157 *defying it* Recollections, pp. 81–2

III. English Landscape

158 epigraph Forster, *Howards*, p. 250

159 *a land of boughs* MP VIIIa

Notes

159   *I know Ludlow* To M. Pollet, 5 Feb 1933, *Letters II*, p. 328

159   *neatly tended graves* Recollections, p. 48

159   *to gain local colour* Withers, p. 67

159   *I ascertained* To LH, 5 Oct 1896, *Letters I*, p. 90

160   *Shropshire no longer* CH, p. 75

160   *In [Housman]* Peele, p. 95

160   *Wenlock . . . Buildwas* Haber, *Making*, pp. 197, 151

161   *Of the beauties* Nightingale, p. 1

162   *not offer any* Murray's Handbook, p. 13

162   *reputation for* Ibid.

162   *treatment of neurasthenia* www.malvernwaters.co.uk

164   *In midnights* LP XIX

164   *Nature meant* To Gundred Savory, 15 April 1931, *Letters II*, p. 242

164   *the southern half* To Houston Martin, 14 April 1934, ibid., p. 416

164   *The greater part* Murray's Handbook, p. 29

165   *smooth green miles* LP XLI

165   *traditional . . . popular doggerel* To Houston Martin, 14 April 1934, *Letters II*, p. 416; *Murray's Handbook*, p. 33

165   *virtually enshrined* Murray's Handbook, p. 51

165   *Dead Man's Fair . . . Hell Gate* Ibid., pp. 48, 13

165   *There is so much* Ibid., p. v

165   *is conspicuous* Ibid., pp. 47–8

166   *Shropshire was* To Houston Martin, 14 April 1934, *Letters II*, p. 416

166   *was to reach* Recollections, pp. 12–13

166   *How clear* MP XVI

168   *The past is* Hartley, p. 9

170   *If a tuft* Southgate, p. 19

172   *One guessed* Forster, *Howards*, p. 109

173   *the tide of time* James, pp. 251–2

174   *For some years* Masefield, *Grace*, p. 1

175   *Then hey* Masefield, *Poems*, p. 59

175   *I had a very great* [footnote] *Mark Twain Quarterly*, Winter 1936, p. 7

175   *Never was there* CH, p. 76

176   *may create some* To GR, 22 July 1898, *Letters I*, p. 109

176   *Tell me not* LP XL

176   *How compare* Quoted Rothenstein, *1900–1922*, p. 343

177   *temperamental sunlessness* Larkin, *Required*, p. 143

179   *every man his* Quoted Hewitt, p. 209

179   *I accompanied him* Quoted Hazlitt, p. 8

180   *I observed that* Ibid., p. 9

180   *I can enjoy* Ibid., p. 141

180   *truly poisonous* Seamus Perry, 'Coleridge's Scotland', *Coleridge Bulletin*, New Series 17, Summer 2001, pp. 61–2

Notes

180	*Give me* Hazlitt, pp. 141–2	
181	*four massive* Hewitt, p. 163	
181	*forty days' wages* Ibid., p. 166	
182	*With limbs all* Davies, *The Soul's Destroyer*, pp. x–xi	
183	*I would rather* Davies, *Autobiography*, p. 148	
184	*enjoyed, without perceiving* Fitzgerald, *Knox*, p. 70	
184	*while traversing* Palgrave, p. 3	
185	*Poetry gives* Ibid., p. 8	
185	*a small octavo* Quoted Alysoun Sanders, '150 Anniversary of *The Golden Treasury*', *Connected* Issue 3 (Nov 2011)	
185	*Bast recommends* Forster, *Howards*, p. 111	
185	*aims at nothing* 'Argument' in Lucas	
186	*speechless* To GR, 2 July 1907, *Letters I*, p. 212	
186	*This little selection* 'Editor's Note' in Hyatt	
186	*she flies* Ibid., p. 3	
187	*Let us get* Thomas, *Childhood*, p. 134	
187	*A walk in Housman Country* www.bbc.co.uk/shropshire/content/articles/2009/01/30/housman_feature.shtml	
187	*it reposes* To Denis Symons, 25 Feb 1932, *Letters II*, p. 281	
187	*did not apprehend* To LH, 5 Oct 1896, *Letters I*, p. 90	
188	*You might as well* Quoted John Betjeman, *HSJ* 7 (1981), p. 16	
188	*but he indicates* CH, p. 117	
188	*with a plea* Tallents, p. 149	
188	*The Shropshire Lad had* Ibid., p. 152	
189	*some six years ago* Cather, p. 73	
189	*As soon as I* Ibid., p. 62	
189	*in green pastures* Ibid., p. 63	
189	*to all the places* Ibid., p. 73 [I have corrected the spelling of place-names since this letter was published from a transcript and contains such obvious misreadings as 'Ouy' for Ony. In other letters, Cather's spelling of Shrewsbury, for example (rendered here three times as 'Shrewesbury'), is correct.]	
190	*rhyme with morn* Ibid., p. 62–3	
190	*I'll not quit Shropshire* Ibid., p. 64	
190	*You must not carry* Ibid., p. 63	
190	*Somehow it makes* Ibid., pp. 62–3	
191	*an awful suburb* Ibid., p. 73	
191	*safe and impersonal channels* Ibid., p. 673	
192	*besieged by demands* Ibid., p. 526	
192	*Several rather mushy* Ibid., p. 673	
192	*charged with emotion* Quoted Moffatt, p. 72	
193	*Unspoilt and alive* Forster, *Journals*, Vol. 1, p. 150	
193	*sitting in the* Forster, *Creator*, p. 126	
193	*Wet walk* Forster, *Journals*, Vol. 1, pp. 49, 50	

194   *Incurious at a window* Forster, *Creator*, pp. 729–30

194   *the wrong part* Forster, *Howards*, p. 194

194   *How lovely* 20 Nov 1963, Forster, *Letters*, Vol. 2, p. 287

194   *Day and night* Forster, *Howards*, p. 233

195   *the graver sides* Ibid., p. 250

195   *favourite characters* Forster, *Creator*, p. 126

195   *How can he be* Forster, *Room*, p. 31

195   *I only know* Ibid., p. 32

196   *Everything is fate* Ibid., p. 136

196   *Never heard of it* Ibid., pp. 132–3

196   *What these unannotated* See Summers, p. 101

197   *I do not really* To Edward Marsh, 1 Oct 1912, *Letters I*, p. 297

197   *we are awake* 'The Georgian Renaissance' in *Rhythm* II (March 1913), quoted Hollis, p. 10

197   *to know Nature* Hale, p. 16

197   *the star poem* Orwell and Angus, p. 552

197   *the only proper* To Geoffrey Fry, July [1907], R. Brooke, *Letters*, p. 90

198   *with Lascelles Abercrombie* Hassall, p. 250

198   *Emmanuel, and* R. Brooke, *Letters*, p. 277

199   *But the years* R. Brooke, *Poems*, p. 275

199   *He was obsessed* Waugh, pp. 25–6

199   *on an autumn morning* Quoted Hassall, p. 95

200   *close cousins* See *ASL* I, XXIII, XXXVII, LXI, L

200   *valuable document* Orwell and Angus, p. 552

201   *the love she needed* Hassall, p. 376

201   *and at last* Beckett, p. 43

202   *lay nude* Delaney, p. 53

202   *The South Seas* R. Brooke, *Letters*, p. 538

202   *One starts* Ibid., p. 539

203   *Here in our quiet* quoted Hart, p. 15

203   *the most beautiful* R. Brooke, *Letters*, p. 598

IV. English Music

204   epigraph 'Mr Housman and the Composers', *Sunday Times*, 29 Oct 1922, p. 7

204   *wonderful air* Barry Marsh, 'Borderland Interlude: E.J. Moeran in Herefordshire' (1994) at www.moeran.net

205   *played at* Lionel Hill, p. 50

205   *He took us* Ibid.

205   *with whom any* Quoted Stallworthy, p. 469

205   *I am tempted* *Evening Standard* on 17 June 1938, quoted GRH, p. 88

205   *I wish they* To P.G.L. Webb, 17 June 1896, *Letters I*, p. 88

Notes

206   *all but about* 'Mr. Housman and the Composers', *Sunday Times*, 29 Oct 1922, quoted William White in *Music & Letters* Vol. 24, No. 4 (Oct 1943), p. 218

206   *He cared little* GRH, p. 394

207   *Good critical taste* Ibid., p. 448

207   *I am sorry* To Oliver Robinson, 23 Nov 1933, *Letters II*, p. 390

207   *Considering the evidence* Music & Letters, Vol. 25, No. 1 (Jan 1944), p. 60

208   *had a pleasant* Ibid., p. 61

209   *My dear Sir* To Arthur Somervell, 19 Sept 1904, private collection

210   *I always give* 18 Aug 1906, *Letters I*, p. 199

210   *helped themselves* GRH, p. 88

210   *mattered nothing* Withers, p. 69

210   *Hell Gate* LP XXXI

211   *the orchestra* To LH, 11 March 1936, *Letters II*, p. 526

211   *I don't allow* 9 Feb 1927, ibid., p. 10

211   *Never before* Sunday Times, 29 Oct 1922, p. 7

212   *It has more* J.A. Westrup in Barker, *Character*, p. 399

212   *The choral festivals* Ibid., p. 404

213   *the only cultured* http://www.musicweb-international.com/dasland .htm#ixzz2Pltm1Yht

213   *His black hair* Hardy, Vol. 1, p. 286

214   *the English are not* Haweis, pp. 483, 486

214   *until music is* Ibid., pp. 486, 485

214   *We must not* Ibid., pp. 553–4

215   *the only English composer* David Wright, 'The South Kensington Music Schools and the Development of the British Conservatoire in the Late Nineteenth Century', *Journal of the Royal Musical Association*, Vol. 130, No. 2 (2005), p. 242

215   *To establish* Ibid., p. 241

215   *not remember* Ibid., p. 238

215   *when a principal* Ibid., p. 251

216   *more and better* Hughes and Stradling, p. 32

216   *pastures of Berkshire* Music in England, pp. 11–12

217   *Although the rural* Introduction to the Study of National Music, p. 173

218   *and circulated* Hullah, Preface

219   *English musicians* Engel, pp. 99–100

220   *primary object* 'A Folk-Song Function', *Musical Times*, 1 March 1899, p. 168

220   *where the jerry-builder* Ibid.

221   *after a long illness* Karpeles, *Cecil Sharp*, p. 23

221   *a strange procession* Ibid., p. 25

222   *good, strong* Ibid., p. 26

222   *dances, also* Sharp, p. 173

Notes

222 *English folk songs* Ibid., p. 172

222 *simple ditties* Ibid., pp. 173–4

223 *When Miss Carrie* Ashwell, p. 27

223 *the quickening* Sharp, 'The Country Dance', *Musical Times*, 1 November 1915, p. 660

223 *At one point* Ashwell, pp. 178–9

223 *The spiritual essence* Hughes and Stradling, p. 180

223 *not many of the men* Karpeles, *Cecil Sharp*, p. 173

224 *had been put* Ibid., p. 32

225 *I had that sense* Quoted in booklet for CD *Vaughan Williams Folksong Arrangements* (EMI B0018OAP34, 2008)

226 *Such a wealth* Sharp, p. vii

228 *Since the war* 6 May 1916, quoted in Colls and Dodd

229 *I am still at heart* Quoted in Marshall, p. 19

229 *biographical sketch* 'Edward Elgar', *Musical Times*, Vol. 41, No. 692 (1 Oct 1900), pp. 641–8

230 *descended from* Ibid.

230 *worthy to be* Langland, p. xxviii

230 *his home* Quoted ibid., p. xxiv

231 *draw their inspiration* Elgar, p. 51

231 *Don't play it* Quoted Marshall, p. 35

231 *it's only me* Quoted ibid., pp. 32, 34

232 *cursed* Barry Marsh, 'Borderland Interlude: E.J. Moeran in Herefordshire' (1994) at www.moeran.net

232 *It was in his* Quoted Marshall, p. 49

232 *truly lyrical qualities* Edwin Evans, 'English Song and "On Wenlock Edge"', *Musical Times*, 1 June 1918, p. 147

233 *Mr. Housman's book* Ernest Newman, 'Concerning "A Shropshire Lad" and other matters', *Musical Times*, 1 Sept 1918, p. 393

233 *I have no objection* To GR, 22 June 1903, *Letters I*, p. 149

234 *amongst the best* *Musical Times*, 1 March 1905, p. 188

234 *would seem to* Ibid.

235 *The lads* The usually reliable Stephen Banfield, notes for the CD *Somervell: Maude & A Shropshire Lad* (Hyperion Helios CDH55089, 2001)

235 *broad and manly treatment* 'New Songs', *The Times*, 8 Sept 1905, p. 2

237 *a miniature tragedy* *The Times*, 26 Jan 1909, quoted Banfield, pp. 234–5

237 *remarkable for accurate* *The Times*, 16 Nov 1909, p. 14

239 *I wonder* To GR, 20 Dec 1920, *Letters I*, p. 458

239 *the composer has* Quoted GRH, p. 221

239 *Vaughan Williams's setting* Newman, *Musical Times*, 1 Sept 1918, p. 397

240 *he could no more* Smith, p. 91

243 *a pastime for cranks* Karpeles, *Cecil Sharp*, p. 173

243 *It has often been* Smith, pp. 90–1

Notes

244   *the emphasis shifts* Stephen Banfield, '*A Shropshire Lad* in the making: A Note on the composition of George Butterworth's Songs', *The Music Review* XLII (1981), p. 263

245   *Only those who* 'Memoir by R.O.M.' in Smith, p. 17

246   *seems only to* Johnson, p. 43

246   *much too flippant* Letter, 5 June 1905, quoted Murphy, p. 41

246   *a quiet little heaven* Morton, p. 257

246   *I remember* Ibid.

248   *in the nature* Butterworth's programme note for the first London performance of the piece, quoted in Barlow, p. 99

248   *the title has* Butterworth to Herbert Thompson, 1 June 1913, in Foreman, *From Parry*, p. 55

248   *be careful of* Butterworth to Herbert Thompson, n.d., in ibid., p. 56

248   *our one really* Quoted Barlow, p. 106

250   *Midsummer 1916* Dated MS: John Talbot, booklet for Chandos CD *E.J. Moeran: Complete Solo Songs* (2010), CHAN 10596 (2)

251   *altered the way* Quoted Banfield, p. 131

251   *to breathe the* Quoted Roy Palmer, booklet for British Music Society CD *E.J. Moeran: Folksong Arrangements* (2010), BMS438CD

252   *A 'national' movement* Newman, *Musical Times*, 1 Sept 1918, p. 394

253   *These poems are* Ibid.

253   *it varies, of course* Ibid.

254   *musical sentiment* Ibid.

254   *There is in modern* Ibid., p. 249

255   *Purely English* Quoted by Philip Lancaster in booklet for Linn Records CD of *On Wenlock Edge* sung by James Gilchrist (CKD 296, 2007)

256   *Mr I.B. Gurney* 16 May 1908, *Letters I*, p. 219

257   *something of great importance* M. Hurd, p. 24

257   *Why does he bother?* Quoted ibid., p. 28

257   *For one thing* Music and Letters, Vol. 19, No. 1 (Jan 1938), p. 3

257   *a view of* Quoted M. Hurd, p. 45

257   *Potentially he is* Music and Letters, Vol. 19, No. 1 (Jan 1938), p. 14

258   *I have done 5* Quoted M. Hurd, p. 37

258   *the special Glory* Gurney, *Collected Letters*, p. 8

258   *appeals and scorn* Quoted M. Hurd, p. 53

258   *I suppose you* 8 April 1915, Gurney, *Collected Letters*, p. 17. The quotation is from Thomas Hood

258   *the beauty of my* Ibid., pp. 40, 43

258   *When I can lie* Letter to Matilda Chapman, Oct 1915, ibid., p. 53

259   *When I am old* To Marion Scott, Sept 1915, Gurney, *War Letters*, pp. 36–7

259   *If you could write* June 1916, Gurney, *Collected Letters*, p. 96

259   *This autumnal morning* Ibid., p. 144

259   *I wait for* 13 Feb 1917, ibid., p. 208

Notes

260 *once in England* Ibid., p. 289

260 *Here I am* Ibid., p. 145

260 *He's gone* Gurney, *Poems*, p. 41

260 *Western* See, for example, Gurney, *Collected Letters*, pp. 192, 208

261 *The beautiful Cotswold* TLS, 22 Nov 1917, issue 827, p. 570

261 *I find a store* Gurney, *Collected Letters*, p. 46

261 *You are right* Ibid., p. 180

261 *Another Gloucestershire Lad* Quoted ibid., p. 381

262 *Do you know* To Marion Scott, 10 March 1917, ibid., pp. 223–4

262 *once again I feel* To M. Scott, 30 April 1917, Gurney, *War Letters*, p. 158

262 *In my head* To M. Scott, 11 June 1917, ibid., p. 168

262 *Well, here comes* To M. Scott, 24 Dec 1917, Gurney, *Collected Letters*, p. 385

265 *English at the core* To M. Scott, 11 Jan 1918, Gurney, *War Letters*, p. 238

265 *had just rediscovered* *Music & Letters*, Vol. 19, No. 1 (Jan 1938)

265 *had the same sickness* To M. Scott, 29 Nov 1917, ibid., p. 234

266 *This proved* Quoted M. Hurd, p. 168

268 *a pleasant country place* Quoted Lewis Foreman, booklet for Chandos CD *Ireland: A Downland Suite, etc* (1995), CHAN 9376

268 *In the verse* J. Brooke, *Orchid*, p. 256

269 *Ireland's music* Jocelyn Brooke, *London Magazine*, April 1965, in Foreman, *Ireland*, p. 350

269 *a country of the mind* J. Brooke, *Dog*, p. 100

271 *an old French nursery rhyme* To Charles Williams, 8 March 1930, *Letters II*, p. 175

273 *Schubert might have approved* Quoted Banfield, p. 302

273 *Refuse.* To GR, 6 Oct 1930, *Letters II*, 209

274 *too much like* Banfield, p. 306

274 *indigestible* Ibid., p. 304

274 *If a composer* Quoted ibid., p. 399

274 *never found any* Quoted ibid., p. 301

275 *I must confess* Eugene Goossens to C.W. Orr, 23 Jan 1935, Foreman, *From Parry*, p. 182

275 *in October of that year* The London performance is usually listed as the work's (partial) premiere, but the Bradford performance is recorded in the *Musical Times*, 1 May 1927, p. 458.

276 *After regaling us* Quoted in Palmer, p. 16

277 *combined these three* Introduction to 1935 CBS broadcast from the Columbia Workshop, available on YouTube: https://www.youtube.com/watch?v=bwqyrYNr_ts

277 *since the Shropshire Lad* Lambert, p. 205

278 *There have been many* Kildea, *Britten on Music*, p. 402

279 *very much affected* John France, 'Julius Harrison & Bredon Hill' (2007) on MusicWeb-International: http://www.musicweb-international.com/classrev/2007/Jan07/Harrison.htm

Notes

279   *on a perfect summer* BBC broadcast in the North American Transmission, 29 Sept 1941, in Foreman, *From Parry*, p. 240

280   *we mustn't forget* Ibid., pp. 240–1

280   *It is a fact remarkable* Transcript of BBC Overseas Service Transmission, 29 September 1941, ibid., p. 241

V. English Soldiers

281   *epigraph*, Browne, p. 84

281   *could not think* Quoted Bonham-Carter, p. 234

281   *he was to quote them again* Churchill, *1911–1914*, p. 42

282   *One feels Housman* Encounter, May 1973, p. 68

283   *marched off to Gallipoli* Swift, p. 140

283   *'Twas my good fortune* Farquhar, p. 3

284   *He made a poetical* Hazlitt, p. 3

284   *I think of all* To Lucy Housman, 9 Jan 1875, *Letters I*, p. 7

284   *The only one* Bromsgrove, p. 26

285   *The book that Alfred* Bourne, *Soldier*, p. 67

285   *I went into* 'Tommy', *Barrack-Room Ballads* (First Series)

285   *Probably you would* Bourne, *Soldier*, p. 67

286   *was particularly captivated* To LH, 20 March 1896, *Letters I*, p. 85

289   *I sit beside* Silkin, p. 119

290   *The Great War* To M. Pollet, 5 Feb 1933, *Letters II*, p. 329

290   *Hope lies to mortals* MP VI

291   *Too old to fight* KES in *Recollections*, p. 34

291   *Epitaph on an Army* LP XXXVII

291   *As I gird on* LP II

291   *Her strong enchantments* LP III

291   *Oh hard is the bed* LP IV

291   *Here dead we lie* MP XXXVI

291   *some verses that I wrote* To KES, 5 Oct 1915, *Letters I*, p. 346

292   *does in eight lines* Darling, p. 216

292   *the finest* Quoted Lycett, p. 582

293   *knew all the sceptical* Connolly, pp. 233, 239

293   *For over all life* Mackail, pp. 64–5

293   *Of course I have* To M. Pollet, 5 Feb 1933, *Letters II*, p. 329

294   *An English boy* Quoted Birkin, p. 175

294   *who are Nature's* Saki, p. 579

294   *To have reached thirty* Quoted Parker, p. 93

295   *year in, year out* Quoted Birkin, p. 262

296   *You were able to* Quoted Fletcher, p. 265

296   *They carry back* See Fletcher, plate 31

297   *I implore you* Knox, p. 154

297 *the country* Ibid., p. 114

297 *It is the luckiest* 24 Feb 1915, quoted ibid., p. 112

297 *diminishes the sale* To GR, 5 Dec 1916, *Letters I*, p. 371

298 *We all had* Interview recorded for the Imperial War Museum: http://www.iwm.org.uk/collections/item/object/80009542

298 *Like many of our generation* Quoted *HSJ* 30 (2004), p. 140

298 *favourite pocket-book* Darling, pp. 215–16

298 *Hopper or Cooper* Ibid., p. 216

298 *I first read* Evan Pughe, quoted Weber, p. 121

299 *on a visit to the front* Adcock, p. 120

299 *because so many soldiers* To MJJ, 19 Oct 1922, *Letters I*, p. 517

299 *The man smiled* GRH, p. 155

299 *had almost a hope* To KES, 5 Oct 1915, *Letters I*, p. 346

299 *It is not so curious* Adcock, pp. 120–1

300 *move to the sound* Quoted Weber, p. 122

301 *I always feel* LH, *War Letters*, p. 68

301 *England remains* Sorley, *Letters*, p. 275

301 *an account of* Quoted Hollis, p. 171

301 *This is an anthology* Thomas, *This England*, p. iii

302 *Literally, for this* Quoted Hollis, p. 287

302 *It seemed to me that* The Nation, 7 November 1914, p. 171

302 *All I can say* Ibid., p. 170

303 *I found myself observing* Sassoon, *Weald*, pp. 275–8

304 *normal, even ordinary man* R. Brooke, *Prose*, p. 195

304 *Something was growing* Ibid., p. 199

305 *there rose up* Morton, pp. 1–2

305 *his earliest memories* Bartholomew, p. 2

306 *Would it not be* Morton, p. 2

306 *I took the vow* Ibid., pp. 2–3

306 *The homesickness* Blythe, p. 62

308 *The noble expanse* Turner, p. 132

308 *I take it that England* Thomas, *Last Sheaf*, pp. 102–3

308 *Since the war* Ibid., p. 109

308 *I think England* Ibid., p. 111

309 *Here's luck* Harvey, p. 6

309 *The poems are written* Ibid., p. viii

310 *How it brings back* 15 August 1915, in Tapert, pp. 26–7. [I have corrected a misreading of 'Penkridge', which is reproduced by Tapert as 'Penbridge'.]

310 *I read Richard Jefferies* To the Master of Marlborough, 25 June 1915, Sorley, *Letters*, p. 281

311 *I wish I could* 30 March 1917, Sassoon, *Diaries 1915–1918*, pp. 146–7

311 *What is there* LH, *War Letters*, p. 225

Notes

312   *To the average man* Rhys, p. v

312   *The practical use* 'Editor's Note' in ibid., p. viii

312   *chosen chiefly* Ibid., pp. viii–ix

313   *from cover to cover* The Times, 30 Aug 1915, p. 7

314   *symbolize the cause* Ibid.

314   *carry the message* The Times, 3 Sept 1903, p. 9

314   *not designed to* Ibid.

314   *Old magazines* Hurst, pp. 59–60

315   *yearly sales* Figures quoted in R.P. Graves, p. 174

315   *Siegfried Sassoon* Moorcroft-Wilson, *Sassoon*, p. 555

315   *purchased his copy from Harold Monro's* Hibberd, *Wilfred Owen*, pp. 212–13

316   *the old road where* Thomas, *Collected Poems*, p. 120

316   *A Private* Ibid., p. 50

317   *as a language-maker* Sorley, *Letters*, p. 49

317   *I do not know much* Ibid., p. 50

318   *Thomas Hardy cannot* Prewett, p. 13

318   *A lad to life* Ibid., p. 59

319   *this was 'all right'* Seymour-Smith, p. 432

319   *distinct Housman echoes* R. Graves, *Fairies*, pp. 14, 28, 5; Graves, *Selected Poems*, p. 32

319   *Housman's greatest contribution* Fussell, *Great War*, pp. 282–3

321   *His iron quatrains* Encounter, May 1973, p. 68

321   *Time was in summer* Freston, p. 52

322   *The Garden of Death* Ibid., p. 77

323   *The hills of Cheshire* Hibberd, *Owen the Poet*, p. 2

323   *bring me Shropshire* To Colin Owen, 10 Aug 1914, Owen, *Letters*, p. 428; to Susan Owen, 16 May 1917, ibid., p. 462

323   *Harold's boots* Harold Owen, p. 176. For the poem, see Owen, *Poems* (Stallworthy), p. 170

324   *bluebells, it may be* To Susan Owen, 21 February 1918, Owen, *Letters*, p. 535

324   *god of Canongate* Poems (Stallworthy), pp. 56, 86

324   *dear, clever lads* To Susan Owen, 2 December 1914 and 16 June 1915, Owen, *Letters*, pp. 300, 340

324   *preciously preserved* To Susan Owen, 18 Aug 1915, ibid., p. 356

324   *Perseus was a sailor* To Susan Owen, 10 April 1915, ibid., p. 334

324   *pity* 'Preface' to Owen, *Poems* (1920), p. vii

324   *all half dead* To Susan Owen, 6 or 8 April 1917 and 16 Jan 1917, Owen, *Letters*, pp. 450 and p. 428

324   *stood by* To Susan Owen, 12 Feb 1917, ibid., p. 434

325   *the bleeding lad's* To Susan Owen, 13 Aug 1917, ibid., p. 483

325   *the best lad* To Susan Owen, 3 Dec 1917, ibid., p. 514

325   *Shropshire lads whose* To Susan Owen, 21 June 1918, ibid., p. 560

325 *at least two lads* To Susan Owen, 15 Sept 1918, ibid., p. 577

325 *stout lad* 'The Parable of the Old Man and the Young' and 'The Dead-Beat', *Poems* (Stallworthy), pp. 151, 121

325 *like the Woolwich Cadet* 'S.I.W.', ibid., p. 137

325 *Beauty* Ibid., p. 180

325 *Which long to nuzzle* 'Arms and the Boy', ibid., p. 131

326 *Some cheered him home* Ibid., p. 152

326 *Strange to think* 12 Sept 1924, Sassoon, *Diaries 1923–1925*, p. 197

326 *Adventurous lads* Sassoon, *War Poems*, p. 126

327 *shell-holes dying slow* Ibid., p. 83

327 *head to head* Ibid., p. 121

327 *some wiped-out impossible Attack* Ibid., p. 89

327 *kind and gay* Ibid., pp. 119, 143

327 *Oh lad that I loved* Ibid., p. 123

327 *Here dead we lie* MP XXXVI

327 *An album of* 'My Grandfather' in Morpurgo, p. 283

328 *penetrated his cheekbone* Ibid., p. 292

VI. The Rediscovery of England

329 epigraph Morton, p. vii

331 *The sight of a number* Rothenstein 1900–1922, pp. 298–9

331 *Designed as a Memorial* Exhibition catalogue, p. 238

331 *my 60 feet of canvas* Rothenstein 1900–1922, p. 310

332 *This book is a debt* Mais, *Oh! To Be in England*, p. 9

333 *I am told that* Ibid., p. 10

333 *If any of these* Ibid., p. 11

333 *stood under* Ibid., pp. 12–13

333 *very magnificent* To GR, 5 Feb 1927, *Letters II*, p. 9

333 *seventeen haphazard excursions* Mais, *Unknown*, p. vii

334 *an expensive* Ibid., p. viii

334 *I had more letters* Ibid., p. ix

334 *Happiness is not* Ibid., p. 177

334 *I have a feeling* Ibid., pp. 184–5

334 *Shropshire names* Ibid., p. 188

335 *this generation has replaced* Joad, p. 12

335 *help all, especially* Quoted Matless, p. 72

335 *long before I owned* HSJ 8 (1982), p. 1

336 *The remarkable system* Morton, p. vii

336 *a strong desire* 'On Pilgrimage in England', *TLS*, 28 March 1942

336 *number of privately owned cars* Figures from Wild, p. 120

337 *I suppose many* Morton, pp. 3–4

337 *only religious moment* Ibid., p. 3

337   *For months I have*   Ibid., pp. 185–6

338   *A Sunday hush*   Ibid., p. 279

338   *I took up a handful*   Ibid., p. 280

339   *There could have been*   Baldwin, *On England*, pp. 8–9

340   *I see the hills*   Quoted Cannadine, pp. 105–6

340   *most unclubbable*   Jones, p. 207

340   *as the Chancellor said*   Baldwin, *Torch*, pp. 124–5

341   *That is all we want*   Ibid., pp. 304–5, 306

342   *And when I ask myself*   Baldwin, *On England*, pp. 5–6

343   *there lies, deep down*   Baldwin, *Torch*, p. 120

343   *reveals and expresses . . . This is the work*   Quotes from jacket of Baldwin, *On England*

344   *At no time*   TLS, 28 March 1942

344   *There has been nothing*   Quoted on The King's England Press website: http://www.kingsengland.com/PBCPPlayer.asp?ID=773748

346   *the largest essay*   Heathcote, p. 1

348   *Leave your books*   Mais, *Oh!*, p. 11

348   *Even today*   Quoted Cannadine, p. 108

349   *I don't believe*   Quoted Jessica Brett Young, p. 27

349   *Ever since my childhood*   Quoted Cannadine, p. 109

350   *the grimy tentacles*   Francis Brett Young, p. 50

350   *had often wistfully*   Ibid., p. 193

350   *Ah Shropshire*   Ibid., p. 4

350   *Twenty-five years ago*   Ibid., p. 8

350   *a landscape warm*   Ibid., p. 50

351   *beyond which*   Ibid.

351   *the green brooklands*   Ibid., p. 49

351   *It was odd*   Ibid., p. 50

351   *tarnished... jingle*   Ibid., pp. 54, 84, 91

351   *All through this*   Ibid., p. 204

351   *never bought a book*   Ibid., p. 140

351   *had marked*   Ibid., p. 328

351   *It was odd how*   Ibid., p. 317

353   *dead and rotten*   MP XL

353   *it is unthinkable*   Fussell, *Wartime*, p. 247

354   *When he died*   Armed Services edition, pp. 127–8

354   *was commissioned*   Percy, p. 25

354   *When I was posted*   Birch, *Westminster Abbey*, p. 15

355   *His family, his friends*   Peel, p. 57

355   *Access to books*   The Salopian, June 1946, p. 231

357   *It obviously spoke*   Michael Ipgrave, Bishop of Woolwich, in *Soul Music: A Shropshire Lad*, BBC Radio 4, 11 November 2014

Notes

VII. Aftermaths

358   *down in the most beautiful* The account of his brother's death is in D. Hurd, *Memoirs*, pp. 79–87

360   *went on vibrating* Ricks, *Critical Essays*, p. 23

360   *His poems have entered* Birch, *Westminster Abbey*, p. 29

360   *my feeling is that* Blunden to Sassoon, 30 Sept 1940, Sassoon, *Letters*, Vol. 2, p. 265

360   *not the same thing* Sassoon to Blunden, 20 Oct 1940, ibid., p. 266

361   *the authentic procession* Sassoon to Blunden, 21 Jan 1954, ibid., p. 57

361   *I consider A.E. Housman* Amis, *Letters*, p. 1106

361   *Housman has left no* MacNeice, *Modern Poetry*, p. 83

361   *Housman is easy to* Carey, p. 96

361   *Housman by heart* MacNeice, *Letters*, p. 591

362   *Art for him* Auden, *Prose 1939–1948*, p. 43

362   *are all Housman's* Auden, *Juvenilia*, p. 13

362   *made up of magical* Auden, *Prose 1939–1948*, p. 155

362   *'A Shock'* Auden, *Collected Poems*, p. 866

362   *ear and eye* HSJ 7 (1981), p. 16

363   *I think primarily* Parkinson, ITV, date unknown

363   *fellow townsman* Haffenden, p. 79; Hill, *Broken Hierarchies*, p. 484

363   *Before I knew anything* Haffenden, p. 79

364   *Morcom was Turing's muse* Quoted in Lyon and McDonald, p. 85

364   *'Cut Grass'* Larkin, *Poems*, p. 183

364   *faces the worst* Poet on Poet of the Week: www.carcanet.co.uk/cgi-bin /scribe?showdoc=43

364   *I have a great shrinking* Larkin to Pym, 8 April 1963, in Larkin, *Letters*, p. 351

365   *the poet of unhappiness* Larkin, *Required Writing*, p. 264

365   *In 1967 it was estimated* Haber, *A.E. Housman*, p. 177

365   *assume that his poems* Quoted T.B. Haber, *Papers of the Bibliographical Society of America* 62 (1968), p. 448

367   *pure melodramatic WITCH* T.H. White to L.J. Potts, 8 Jan 1941, White, *Letters*, p. 122

367   *The boy thought* White, *The Once and Future King*, p. 353

368   *I study as if* Bennett, *Untold Stories*, p. 140

368   *all in differing degrees* Bennett, *Poetry in Motion*, p. 1

368   *an elegy for* Bennett, *Writing Home*, pp. xii, 259

369   *All knowledge is precious* Bennett, *The History Boys*, p. 5

369   *loved best* Carr, p. ix

370   *the missed moment* Ibid., p. 60

370   *We can ask* Ibid., p. 85

371   *Had Morse known* Dexter, *Wench*, p. 12

Notes

371   *In the television adaptation* ITV, 15 Nov 2000

371   *collected everything* HSJ 30 (2004), p. 8

371   *pressed between pages* Dexter, *Death Is Now*, p. 89

372   *He looked at me with eyes* MP XLI; Dexter, *The Way*, p. 38

373   *if you'd care to hear them* The Archers (omnibus edition), BBC Radio 4, 11 Jan 2014

373   *the words of 'The Olive'* AP XXIII

375   *all of Housman's verse* Interview with Rob Barnett on MusicWeb International, March 2012: www.musicweb-international.com/classrev/2012/Mar12 /Williamson_interview.htm#ixzz3tdkvhdoo

376   *deeply personal journey* Heggie, programme note for concert 'Theater in Song: Music by Jake Heggie and Ricky Ian Gordon' held at the Herz Theater, UC Berkeley, 29 April 2007

377   *In the Dark Ages* Booklet for CD *A Shropshire Lad* (Michael Raven, 1994)

378   *a unique combination* http://annemetteiversen.com/Poetry-of-Earth/poetry -of-earth.html

378   *The moods of the poems* Matt Perzinski to author, 4 May 2013

378   *I was curious* Peter Kurie to author, 8 Feb 2015

379   *a group of dudes* www.youtube.com/watch?v=UiyeYgciO74&index= 16&list=FLB68oL4POTlM6NqZsPHMYpQ

380   *Our goal as a band* www.sonicbids.com/band/housmansathletes/

381   *Well, I think it* http://motorcycleaupairboy.com/interviews/1998/radio.htm

381   *As a teenager* http://true-to-you.net/article_040120_01

381   *Vulnerable and complex* Morrissey, p. 93

381   *A stern custodian* Ibid., pp. 93, 95

382   *If by chance* http://true-to-you.net/morrissey_news_130719_01; www .morrissey-solo.com/content/1350

382   *I thought his poems* www.morrissey-solo.com/threads/1059-Morrissey-s-books

382   *When I was growing up* http://true-to-you.net/article_040120_01

382   *quoted the last line* www.morrissey-solo.com/entries/3508

382   *Yonder see* www.morrissey-solo.com/content/774 (page 2); LP XI

383   *Whilst sitting* www.morrissey-solo.com/archive/index.php/t-83338-p-4.html

383   *I wish he'd write* www.morrissey-solo.com/archive/index.php/t-134296.html

383   *Incredibly poignant* http://www.morrissey-solo.com/threads/65098 (page 3)

384   *Rural Shropshire* Bailey, p. 146

384   *The purpose of art* Ibid.

384   *among the Edge's* Timperley, p. 21

385   *There is one moment* Ibid., pp. 126–7

385   *gaiety and sadness* Vale, p. 31

385   *should be lodged* Ibid., p. 108

386   *pulled in a whopping* 'Auction Reports 2015' on *Modern Railwayana* website: http://hst43029.moonfruit.com/home/4581422849

386   *The winning bidder* Shropshire Star, 3 Feb 2014

Notes

386   *evocative of the county* www.woodbrewery.co.uk

388   *I suppose you have* Douglas to Betty Sze, n.d. (1939), *Douglas*, p. 71

388   *does not mean* Auden, *Forewords*, pp. 331–2

388   *that thrilling utterance* TN&NP in *ASLOP*, p. 247

388   *peculiar function* Ibid., p. 235

388   *notably independent* *Manchester Guardian Weekly*, 9 June 1933, in *CH*, p. 235

389   *We should all write* Quoted Michael Henderson, 'Those I have loved', *Spectator*, 17 Dec 2011

BIBLIOGRAPHY

Books by A.E. Housman

The Poems of A.E. Housman, ed. Archie Burnett (OUP, 1997)
The Letters of A.E. Housman, ed. Archie Burnett, 2 vols (OUP, 2007)
A Shropshire Lad and Other Poems, ed. Archie Burnett (Penguin, 2010)
Poems, selected by Alan Hollinghurst (Faber, 2001)
The Collected Poems, ed. John Carter (Jonathan Cape, 1939)
Collected Poems and Selected Prose, ed. Christopher Ricks (Penguin, 1988)
The Letters of A.E. Housman, ed. Henry Maas (Rupert Hart-Davis, 1971)
Introductory Lecture (CUP, 1937)
Selected Poems of A.E. Housman (Armed Services edition, n.d.)
A Shropshire Lad, with Notes and a Bibliography, ed. Carl J. Weber (Colby College Library, 1946)
More Poems (Jonathan Cape, 1936)

Secondary Sources

Books are listed in their first editions; where other editions have been used for the purposes of quotation, the publisher (if different) and date follow in square brackets.

Books

J.R. Ackerley, *The Letters of J.R. Ackerley*, ed. Neville Braybrooke (Duckworth, 1975)
A. St John Adcock, *The Glory That Was Grub Street* (Sampson Low, Marston and Co, 1928)

Bibliography

Seymour Adelman, *The Name and Nature of A.E. Housman* (Bryn Mawr College Library, 1986)

Chimamanda Ngozi Adichie, *Half of a Yellow Sun* (Fourth Estate, 2006)

Kingsley Amis, *One Fat Englishman* (Gollancz, 1963)

—— *The Amis Anthology* (Hutchinson, 1988)

—— *The Amis Collection* (Hutchinson, 1990)

—— *Memoirs* (Hutchinson, 1991)

—— *The Letters of Kingsley Amis*, ed. Zachary Leader (HarperCollins, 2000)

Ruth Artmonsky, *Jack Beddington: The Footnote Man* (Artmonsky Arts, 2006)

Lena Ashwell, *Modern Troubadours* (Gyldenal, 1922)

J.H. Auden, *The Little Guides: Shropshire* (Methuen, 1912; third edition, 1921)

W.H. Auden, *Forewords and Afterwords* (Faber, 1973)

—— *W.H. Auden: Juvenilia*, ed. Katherine Bucknell (Faber, 1994)

—— *Auden Studies 3*, ed. Katherine Bucknell and Nicholas Jenkins (OUP, 1995)

—— *W.H. Auden: Prose 1939–1948*, ed. Edward Mendelson (Faber, 2002)

—— *Collected Poems*, ed. Edward Mendelson (Random House, 2007)

W.H. Auden and John Garrett (ed.), *The Poet's Tongue* (G. Bell and Sons, 1935)

Simon Baatz, *For the Thrill of It* (Harper, 2008)

A.L. Bacharach (ed.), *British Music of Our Time* (Pelican, 1946)

Brian J. Bailey, *Portrait of Shropshire* (Robert Hale, 1981)

Stanley Baldwin, *On England* (Philip Allan, 1926, Popular edition, 1933)

—— *This Torch of Freedom* (Hodder and Stoughton, 1935)

Stephen Banfield, *Sensibility and English Song* (CUP, 1985)

Ernest Barker, *National Character and the Factors in Its Formation* (Methuen, 1927)

—— (ed.) *The Character of England* (Clarendon Press, 1947)

Michael Barlow, *Whom the Gods Love: The Life and Music of George Butterworth* (Toccata Press, 1997)

Michael Bartholomew, *In Search of H.V. Morton* (Methuen, 2006)

William Barton, *When Heaven Fell* (Grand Central Publishing, 1995)

John Bayley, *Housman's Poems* (Clarendon Press, 1992)

Lorna C. Beckett, *The Second I Saw You: The True Love Story of Rupert Brooke and Phyllis Gardner* (British Library, 2015)

Adrian Bell (ed.), *The Open Air: An Anthology of English Country Life* (Faber, 1939)

Alan Bennett, *Forty Years On and Other Plays* (Faber, 1985)

—— *Poetry in Motion* (Channel 4 Television, 1990)

—— *Writing Home* (Faber, 1994)

—— *The History Boys* (Faber, 2004)

—— *Untold Stories* (Faber, 2005)

Bibliography

Roy Birch (ed.), *A.E. Housman, Poet and Scholar, Westminster Abbey, September 1996* (The Housman Society, 1996)

—— *A.E. Housman: A Select Bibliography* (Housman Society, 2001; revised 2010)

Andrew Birkin, *J.M. Barrie and the Lost Boys* (Constable, 1979)

Ronald Blythe (ed.), *Private Words: Letters and Diaries from the Second World War* (Viking, 1991)

Violet Bonham-Carter, *Winston Churchill As I Knew Him* (Eyre and Spottiswoode and Collins, 1965)

Jeremy Bourne, *The Westerly Wanderer* (The Housman Society, 1996)

—— *Soldier, I Wish You Well* (The Housman Society, 2001)

—— *Housman and Heine: A Neglected Relationship* (The Housman Society, 2011)

Francis Brett Young, *The Happy Highway* (Reynal and Hitchcock, 1940)

Jessica Brett Young, *Francis Brett Young: A Biography* (Heinemann, 1962)

Bromsgrove School, *Alfred Edward Housman* (Bromsgrove School, 1936)

Jocelyn Brooke, *The Flower in Season* (The Bodley Head, 1952)

—— *The Dog at Clambercrown* (The Bodley Head, 1955)

—— *The Orchid Trilogy* (Secker and Warburg, 1981)

Rupert Brooke, *Collected Poems* (Sidgwick and Jackson, 1918)

—— *The Prose of Rupert Brooke*, ed. Christopher Hassall (Sidgwick and Jackson, 1956)

—— *The Letters of Rupert Brooke*, ed. Geoffrey Keynes (Faber, 1968)

—— *Friends and Apostles: The Correspondence of Rupert Brooke and James Strachey, 1905–1914*, ed. Keith Hale (Yale, 1998)

Piers Browne, *Elegy in Arcady* (Ashford, 1989, revised edition, 1990)

Thomas Browne, *Religio Medici, Urn Burial, Christian Morals and Other Essays* (Walter Scott, 1886)

Angus Calder, *The Myth of the Blitz* (Jonathan Cape, 1991)

David Cannadine, 'Politics, Propaganda and Art: The Case of Two "Worcestershire Lads"' in *Midland History* (1978)

John Carey, *Pure Pleasure* (Faber, 2000)

Edward Carpenter, *Narcissus and Other Poems* (Henry S. King and Co., 1873)

J.L. Carr, *A Month in the Country* (Harvester, 1980) [Penguin, 2000]

John Carter and John Sparrow, *A.E. Housman: A Bibliography*, second edition, revised by William White (St Paul's Bibliographies, 1982)

Willa Cather, *The Selected Letters of Willa Cather*, ed. Andrew Jewell and Janis Stout (Alfred A. Knopf, 2013)

Francis James Child, *The English and Scottish Popular Ballads*, 5 vols (Houghton, Mifflin & Co., 1884–98)

Winston Churchill, *The World Crisis 1911–1914* (Thornton Butterworth, 1923)

—— *The World Crisis 1911–1918* (Thornton Butterworth, 1931)

Bibliography

Humphrey Clucas, *Through Time and Place to Roam* (University of Salzburg, 1995)

Samuel Taylor Coleridge, *The Table Talk and Omniana of Samuel Taylor Coleridge* (George Bell and Sons, 1884)

Robert Colls and Philip Dodd (ed.), *Englishness: Politics and Culture 1880–1920* (Croom Helm, 1986)

Cyril Connolly, *Enemies of Promise* (Routledge and Kegan Paul, 1938) [Penguin, 1961]

Wendy Cope, *Life, Love and The Archers* (Two Roads, 2014)

Ian Copley, *George Butterworth and His Music* (Thames Publishing, 1985)

Julian Critchley and David Paterson, *Borderlands* (Peak Publishing, 1993)

William Darling, *The Private Papers of a Bankrupt Bookseller* (Oliver and Boyd, 1931)

W.H. Davies, *The Soul's Destroyer and Other Poems* (Alston Rivers, 1907)

—— *Autobiography of a Super-Tramp* (A.C. Fifield, 1908) [OUP, 1980]

Marcel De Cleene and Marie Claire Lejeune, *Compendium of Symbolic and Ritual Plants in Europe*, 2 vols (Man and Culture Publishers, Ghent, 1999–2003)

Paul Delaney, *The Neo-pagans* (Macmillan, 1987)

Colin Dexter, *Last Seen Wearing* (Macmillan, 1976)

—— *The Riddle of the Third Mile* (Macmillan, 1983)

—— *The Wench is Dead* (Macmillan, 1989)

—— *The Jewel That Was Ours* (Macmillan, 1991)

—— *The Way Through the Wood* (Macmillan, 1992)

—— *The Daughters of Cain* (Macmillan, 1994)

—— *Death Is Now My Neighbour* (Macmillan, 1996)

—— *The Remorseful Day* (Macmillan, 1999)

Keith Douglas, *The Letters*, ed. Desmond Graham (Carcanet, 2000)

Linda Dowling, *Hellenism and Homosexuality in Victorian Oxford* (Cornell University Press, 1994)

Brian Doyle, *English and Englishness* (Routledge, 1989)

Edward Elgar, *A Future for English Music and Other Lectures*, ed. Percy M. Young (Dennis Dobson, 1968)

Carl Engel, *An Introduction to the Study of National Music* (Longmans, Green, Reader and Dyer, 1866)

—— *The Literature of National Music* (Novello, Ewer, 1879)

George Farquhar, *The Recruiting Officer* (Bloomsbury, 2011)

Penelope Fitzgerald, *The Knox Brothers* (Macmillan, 1977) [Fourth Estate, 2002]

—— *A House of Air: Selected Writings* (Flamingo, 2003)

The Letters of Penelope Fitzgerald, ed. Terence Dooley (Fourth Estate, 2008)

Anthony Fletcher, *Life, Death and Growing Up on the Western Front* (Yale University Press, 2013)

Lewis Foreman, *From Parry to Britten: British Music in Letters, 1900–1945* (Batsford, 1987)

—— (ed.) *The John Ireland Companion* (Boydell Press, 2011)

E.M. Forster, *A Room with a View* (Edward Arnold, 1908) [Penguin, 1955]

—— *The Longest Journey* (Edward Arnold, 1907)

—— *Howards End* (Edward Arnold, 1910) [Penguin, 1941]

—— *Aspects of the Novel* (Edward Arnold, 1927) [Penguin, 1962]

—— *The Eternal Moment* (Sidgwick and Jackson, 1928)

—— *Abinger Harvest* (Edward Arnold, 1936) [Abinger Edition, André Deutsch, 1996]

—— *Maurice* (Edward Arnold, 1971) [Abinger Edition, André Deutsch, 1999]

—— *The Prince's Tale and Other Uncollected Writings* (André Deutsch, 1998)

—— *Commonplace Book*, ed. Philip Gardner (Scolar Press, 1981)

—— *Selected Letters of E.M. Forster: Volume One 1879–1920*, ed. Mary Lago and P.N. Furbank (William Collins, 1983)

—— *Selected Letters of E.M. Forster: Volume Two, 1921–1970*, ed. Mary Lago and P.N. Furbank (William Collins, 1985)

—— *The Creator as Critic and Other Writings by E.M. Forster*, ed. Jeffrey M. Heath (Dundurn Press, 2008)

—— *The Journals and Diaries of E.M. Forster*, ed. Philip Gardner, 3 Vols (Pickering and Chatto, 2011)

H. Rex Freston, *The Quest of Truth and Other Poems* (Blackwell, 1916)

J.W. Froude, *Oceana* (Longmans, Green and Co., 1886)

Sophie Fuller and Lloyd Whitesell (ed.), *Queer Episodes in Music and Modern Identity* (University of Illinois Press, 2002)

Paul Fussell, *The Great War and Modern Memory* (OUP, 1975)

—— *Wartime* (OUP, 1989)

Philip Gardner (ed.), *A.E. Housman: The Critical Heritage* (Routledge, 1992)

Mark Girouard, *The Return to Camelot* (Yale University Press, 1981)

Bryan N.S. Gooch and David S. Thatcher, *Musical Settings of Late Victorian and Modern British Literature: A Catalogue* (Garland, 1976)

A.S.F. Gow, *A.E. Housman: A Sketch* (CUP, 1936)

Richard Perceval Graves, *A.E. Housman: The Scholar Poet* (OUP, 1979)

Robert Graves, *Fairies and Fusiliers* (William Heinemann, 1917)

—— *Selected Poems*, ed. Paul O'Prey (Penguin, 1986)

Steven J. Green and Katharina Volk (ed.), *Forgotten Stars: Rediscovering Manilius' Astronomica* (OUP, 2011)

Ivor Gurney, *War Letters*, ed. R.K.R. Thornton (Hogarth Press, 1984)

—— *Collected Poems of Ivor Gurney*, ed. P.J. Kavanagh (OUP, 1982)

—— *Stars in a Dark Night: The Letters of Ivor Gurney to the Chapman Family*, ed. Anthony Boden (Alan Sutton, 1986)

—— *Collected Letters*, ed. R.K.R. Thornton (The Mid-Northumberland Arts Group and Carcanet Press, 1991)

Thomas Burns Haber, *The Manuscript Poems of A.E. Housman* (University of Minnesota Press, 1955)

—— *The Making of A Shropshire Lad* (University of Washington Press, 1966)

—— *A.E. Housman* (Twayne, 1967)

John Haffenden, *Viewpoints* (Faber, 1981)

Keith Hale (ed.) *Georgian Poetry* (Watersgreen House, 2014)

Thomas Hardy, *The Life of Thomas Hardy* (Macmillan, 1994)

Alexandra Harris, *Weatherland* (Thames and Hudson, 2015)

Linda Hart, *Once They Lived in Gloucestershire: A Dymock Poets Anthology* (revised edition, Green Branch Press, 2000)

L.P. Hartley, *The Go-Between* (Hamish Hamilton, 1953)

F.W. Harvey, *A Gloucestershire Lad* (Sidgwick and Jackson, 1917)

Christopher Hassall, *Rupert Brooke* (Faber, 1964)

H.R. Haweis, *Music and Morals* (Longmans, Green and Co., 1871)

William Hazlitt, *Selected Essays*, ed. George Sampson (CUP, 1917)

David Heathcote, *A Shell Eye on England* (Libri Publishing, 2011)

Simon Heffer, *Like the Roman: The Life of Enoch Powell* (Weidenfeld and Nicolson, 1998)

Joan Henry, *Yield to the Night* (Victor Gollancz, 1954)

Rachel Hewitt, *Map of a Nation* (Granta, 2010)

Dominic Hibberd, *Owen the Poet* (Macmillan Press, 1986)

—— *Wilfred Owen* (Weidenfeld and Nicolson, 2002)

Geoffrey Hill, *Collected Critical Writings* (OUP, 2008)

—— *Broken Hierarchies: Poems 1952–2012* (OUP, 2013)

Lionel Hill, *Lonely Waters* (Thames Publishing, 1985)

Alan W. Holden and J. Roy Birch (ed.), *A.E. Housman: A Reassessment* (Macmillan Press, 2000)

Anthony and Ben Holden (ed.), *Poems That Make Grown Men Cry* (Simon and Schuster, 2014)

Matthew Hollis, *Now All Roads Lead to France* (Faber, 2011)

Laurence Housman, *A.E.H.* (Jonathan Cape, 1937)

—— *The Unexpected Years* (Jonathan Cape, 1937)

—— (ed.) *War Letters from Fallen Englishmen* (Victor Gollancz, 1930)

Alun Howkins, *The Death of Rural England* (Routledge, 2003)

Meirion Hughes and Robert Stradling, *The English Musical Renaissance 1840–1940: Constructing a National Music* (Manchester University Press, 2001)

John Hullah (ed.) *The Song Book* (Macmillan, revised edition, 1892)

Douglas Hurd, *Memoirs* (Little, Brown, 2003)

Bibliography

Michael Hurd, *The Ordeal of Ivor Gurney* (OUP, 1978)

Gerald B. Hurst, *With Manchesters in the East* (Manchester University Press, 1918)

Alfred H. Hyatt, *The Footpath Way* (T.N. Foulis, 1906)

H. Montgomery Hyde, *The Trials of Oscar Wilde* (Dover, 1973)

Clyde K. Hyder, *A Concordance of the Poems of A.E. Housman* (Peter Smith, 1966)

Andrew Jackson, *A Fine View of the Show* (Lulu, 2009)

Henry James, *The Tragic Muse* (Macmillan, 1890)

Keith Jebb, *A.E. Housman* (Seren Books, 1992)

C.E.M. Joad, *A Charter for Ramblers* (Hutchinson, 1934)

Graham Johnson, *Britten, Voice and Piano* (Ashgate/Guildhall School of Music and Drama, 2003)

Thomas Jones, *A Diary with Letters, 1931–1950* (OUP, 1954)

Maude Karpeles, *Cecil Sharp: His Life and Work* (Routledge and Kegan Paul, 1967)

—— *An Introduction to English Folk Song* (OUP, 1973)

John Keats, *The Letters of John Keats 1814–1821*, Vol. 2, ed. Hyder Edward Rollins (Harvard University Press, 1958)

—— *Letters of John Keats*, ed. Sidney Colvin (Macmillan, 1891)

Michael Kennedy and Joyce Bourne (ed.) *Concise Oxford Dictionary of Music* (OUP, 1996)

W.P. Ker, *The Dark Ages* (Charles Scribner, 1904)

Paul Kildea, *Benjamin Britten: A Life in the Twentieth Century* (Allen Lane, 2013)

—— (ed.) *Britten on Music* (OUP, 2003)

Rudyard Kipling, *Barrack-Room Ballads* (Methuen, 1892)

Ronald Knox, *Patrick Shaw-Stewart* (William Collins, 1920)

Constant Lambert, *Music Ho!* (Faber, 1934) [Penguin, 1948]

William Langland, *Piers the Plowman*, ed. W.W. Skeat (OUP, tenth edition, 1923)

Philip Larkin, *Required Writing: Miscellaneous Pieces 1955–1982* (Faber, 1983)

—— (ed.) *The Oxford Book of Twentieth-Century English Verse* (OUP, 1973)

—— *Collected Poems*, ed. Anthony Thwaite (Faber, 1988)

—— *Selected Letters of Philip Larkin, 1940–1985*, ed. Anthony Thwaite (Faber, 1992)

B.J. Leggett, *Housman's Land of Lost Content* (University of Tennessee Press, 1970)

—— *The Poetic Art of A.E. Housman: Theory and Practice* (University of Nebraska Press, 1978)

E.V. Lucas, *The Open Road* (Grant Richards, 1899)

Andrew Lycett, *Rudyard Kipling* (Weidenfeld and Nicolson, 1999)

John Lyon and Peter McDonald (ed.), *Geoffrey Hill: Essays on His Later Work* (OUP, 2012)

Bibliography

Henry Maas, *A.E. Housman: Spoken and Unspoken Love* (Greenwich Exchange, 2012)

J.W. Mackail, *Select Epigrams from the Greek Anthology* (revised edition, Longmans, Green and Co., 1906)

Louis MacNeice, *Modern Poetry* (OUP, 1938) [second edition, OUP, 1968]

—— *Letters of Louis MacNeice*, ed. Jonathan Allison (Faber, 2010)

S.P.B. Mais, *Oh! To Be in England* (Grant Richards, 1922)

—— *This Unknown Island* (Putnam, 1932)

Norman Marlow, *A.E. Housman: Scholar and Poet* (Routledge and Kegan Paul, 1958)

Em Marshall, *Music in the Landscape* (Robert Hale, 2011)

John Masefield, *The Collected Poems of John Masefield* (William Heinemann, 1923)

—— *Grace Before Ploughing* (William Heinemann, 1966)

David Matless, *Landscape and Englishness* (Reaktion, 1998)

David Matless, Andrew Leyshon and George Revill (ed.), *The Place of Music* (The Guilford Press, 1998)

Arthur Mee, *Enchanted Land* (Hodder and Stoughton, 1936)

—— *Shropshire: County of the Western Hills* (Hodder and Stoughton, 1939)

Vera Mendel, Francis Meynell and John Goss (ed.), *The Week-End Book* (The Nonesuch Press, 1928 revised edition)

Edward Mendelson, *Early Auden* (Faber, 1981)

—— *Later Auden* (Faber, 1999)

Wendy Moffatt, *E.M. Forster: A New Life* (Bloomsbury, 2010)

Jean Moorcroft-Wilson, *Siegfried Sassoon: The Making of a War Poet. A Biography (1886-1918)* (Duckworth, 1998)

—— *Edward Thomas: From Addlestrop to Arras* (Bloomsbury, 2015)

Michael Morpurgo (ed.) *Only Remembered* (Jonathan Cape, 2014)

Morrissey, *Autobiography* (Penguin, 2013)

H.V. Morton, *In Search of England* (Methuen, 1927)

Alice Munro, *Too Much Happiness* (Chatto and Windus, 2009)

Anthony Murphy, *Banks of Green Willow* (Cappella Archive, 2012)

Murray's Handbook for Shropshire, Cheshire and Lancashire (John Murray, 1870)

Music in England. The Proposed Royal College of Music (John Murray, 1882)

P.G. Naiditch, *Problems in the Life and Writings of A.E. Housman* (Krown and Spellman, 1995)

—— *The Centenary of 'A Shropshire Lad': The Life and Writings of A.E. Housman* (University College, London, 1996)

—— *An Index to Archie Burnett's Commentary on 'The Poems of A.E. Housman'* (The Housman Society, 1998)

Bibliography

—— *Additional Problems in the Life and Writings of A.E. Housman* (Sam: Johnson's Publishers, 2005)

Robert Nichols (ed.), *Anthology of War Poetry, 1914–1918* (Nicholson and Watson, 1943)

Rev. J. Nightingale, *The Beauties of England and Wales*, Vol. XIII, Part I (J. Harris, Longman and Co, etc., 1813)

Cyril Norwood, *The English Tradition in Education* (John Murray, 1929)

Sonia Orwell and Ian Angus (ed.), *The Collected Essays, Journalism and Letters of George Orwell*, Volume 1 (Secker and Warburg, 1968)

Harold Owen, *Journey from Obscurity*, Vol. 1 (OUP, 1963)

Wilfred Owen, *Poems* (Chatto and Windus, 1920)

—— *Collected Letters*, ed. Harold Owen and John Bell (OUP, 1967)

—— *The Poems of Wilfred Owen*, ed. John Stallworthy (Chatto and Windus, 1985)

Norman Page, *A.E. Housman: A Critical Biography* (Macmillan, 1983)

F.T. Palgrave, *The Golden Treasury* (Macmillan, 1891 ed.) [Penguin, 1991]

Christopher Palmer, *Herbert Howells: A Study* (Novello, 1978)

Peter Parker, *The Old Lie* (Constable, 1987)

Walter Pater, *Studies in the History of the Renaissance* (Macmillan, 1873)

Mark Peel, *Land of Lost Content: The Biography of Anthony Chenevix-Trench* (The Pentland Press, 1996)

Michael Peele, *Shropshire in Poem and Legend* (Wilding and Son, 1923)

Walker Percy, *The Moviegoer* (Alfred A. Knopf, 1961) [Methuen, 2004]

Nikolaus Pevsner, *The Buildings of England: Shropshire* (Penguin, 1958)

John Piper and John Betjeman (ed.), *Shropshire: A Shell Guide* (Faber, 1951)

George Plimpton (ed.), *Writers at Work: The Paris Review Interviews*, 4th Series (1976) [Penguin, 1977]

Frank Prewett, *Selected Poems of Frank Prewett*, ed. Bruce Meyer and Barry Callaghan (Exile Editions, 2000)

Propertius, *The Poems*, translated by Guy Lee (OUP, 1994)

John Pugh, *Bromsgrove and the Housmans* (The Housman Society, 1974)

Brian Reade (ed.), *Sexual Heretics* (Routledge and Kegan Paul, 1970)

Mary Renault, *The Charioteer* (Longmans, Green and Co, 1953) [Virago, 2013]

Ernest Rhys (ed.), *The Old Country* (J.M. Dent, 1917)

Grant Richards, *Author Hunting* (Hamish Hamilton, 1934)

—— *Housman: 1897–1926* (OUP, 1941)

Clive Richardson, *Till Ludlow Tower Shall Fall: Ludlow's Sacrifice in World War One* (Ludlow Historical Research Group, 2010)

Christopher Ricks (ed.), *A.E. Housman: A Collection of Critical Essays* (Prentice-Hall, 1968)

Maisie Robson, *An Unrepentant Englishman* (The King's England Press, 2005)

Bibliography

Byron Rogers, *The Last Englishman: The Life of J.L. Carr* (Aurum Press, 2003)

William Rothenstein, *Men and Memories: Recollections of William Rothenstein 1872–1900* (Faber, 1931)

—— *Men and Memories: Recollections of William Rothenstein 1900–1922* (Faber, 1932)

Trevor Rowley, *The Shropshire Landscape* (Hodder and Stoughton, 1972)

Julian Rushton, *Elgar: 'Enigma' Variations* (CUP, 1999)

Saki, *The Complete Works of Saki* (Bodley Head, 1980)

Raphael Samuel, *Island Stories* (Verso, 1998)

Siegfried Sassoon, *The Weald of Youth* (Faber, 1942)

—— *Meredith* (Constable, 1948)

—— *The War Poems*, ed. R. Hart-Davis (Faber, 1983)

—— *Diaries 1915–1918*, ed. Rupert Hart-Davis (Faber, 1983)

—— *Diaries 1923–1925*, ed. Rupert Hart-Davis (Faber, 1985)

—— *Selected Letters of Siegfried Sassoon and Edmund Blunden, 1919–1967*, ed. Carol Z. Rothkopf (3 vols, Pickering and Chatto, 2012)

Dorothy L. Sayers, *Strong Poison* (Victor Gollancz, 1930)

Camilla Schofield, *Enoch Powell and the Making of Postcolonial Britain* (CUP, 2013)

Bill Schwarz, *The White Man's World* (OUP, 2011)

Tony Scotland, *Lennox and Freda* (Michael Russell, 2010)

Martin Seymour-Smith, *Robert Graves: His Life and Works* (Hutchinson, 1982)

Cecil Sharp, *English Folk Song: Some Conclusions* (fourth edition, E.P. Publishing, 1965)

Robin Shaw, *Housman's Places* (The Housman Society, 1995)

—— (ed.) *Three Bromsgrove Poets* (The Housman Society, 2003)

Jon Silkin (ed.), *The Oxford Book of War Poetry* (OUP, 1984)

Wayne Smith (ed.), *George Butterworth: Memorial Volume* (Centenary Edition, YouCaxton Publications, 2015)

Charles Sorley, *The Letters of Charles Sorley* (CUP, 1919)

—— *Marlborough and Other Poems* (CUP, 1919)

Walter Southgate, *That's the Way It Was* (New Clarion Press, 1982)

Jon Stallworthy, *Louis MacNeice* (Faber, 1995)

Tom Stoppard, *The Invention of Love* (Faber, 1997)

Claude J. Summers, *E.M. Forster* (Frederick Ungar, 1983)

Katherine Swift, *The Morville Hours* (Bloomsbury, 2008)

Arthur Symons, *Days and Nights* (Macmillan, 1889)

—— *Silhouettes* (revised edition, Leonard Smithers, 1896)

Katharine E. Symons et al., *Alfred Edward Housman: Recollections* (Henry Holt and Co, 1937)

Bibliography

Stephen Tallents, *Man and Boy* (Faber, 1943)

Annette Tapert (ed.), *Despatches from the Heart* (Hamish Hamilton, 1984)

Edward Thomas, *Richard Jefferies* (Hutchinson, 1909)

—— *This England* (OUP, 1915)

—— *The Last Sheaf* (Jonathan Cape, 1928)

—— *The Childhood of Edward Thomas* (Faber, 1938)

—— (ed.) *The Pocket Book of Poems and Songs for the Open Road* (E. Grant Richards, 1907) [Jonathan Cape, 1928]

—— *The Annotated Collected Poems*, ed. Edna Longley (Bloodaxe, 2008)

H.W. Timperley, *Shropshire Hills* (J.M. Dent, 1947)

Alwyn W. Turner, *The Last Post* (Aurum Press, 2014)

Edmund Vale, *Shropshire* (Robert Hale, 1949)

Elizabeth Vandiver, *Stand in the Trench, Achilles* (OUP, 2010)

Vincent Waite, *Shropshire Hill Country* (Dent, 1970)

Sylvia Townsend Warner, *T.H. White: A Biography* (Jonathan Cape/Chatto and Windus, 1967)

George L. Watson, *A.E. Housman: A Divided Life* (Rupert Hart-Davis, 1957)

Arthur Waugh, *Tradition and Change: Studies in Contemporary Literature* (Chapman and Hall, 1919)

Denton Welch, *The Denton Welch Journals*, ed. Jocelyn Brooke (Hamish Hamilton, 1952)

—— *Denton Welch: A Selection from his Published Works*, ed. Jocelyn Brooke (Chapman and Hall, 1963)

—— *The Journals of Denton Welch*, ed. Michael De-la-Noy (Alison and Busby, 1984)

T.H. White, *The Once and Future King* (William Collins, 1958) [HarperCollins, 2013]

—— *T.H. White: Letters to a Friend*, ed. François Gallix (Alan Sutton, 1984)

Kevin Robert Whittingham, '*A Shropshire Lad* in British Music Since 1940: Decline and Renewal' (University of South Africa, 2008)

Trevor Wild, *Village England: A Social History of the Countryside* (I.B. Tauris, 2004)

Oscar Wilde, *Complete Works of Oscar Wilde* (Collins, 1966)

—— *The Complete Letters of Oscar Wilde*, ed. Merlin Holland and Rupert Hart-Davis (Fourth Estate, 2000)

Raymond Williams, *The Country and the City* (Chatto and Windus, 1973)

Percy Withers, *A Buried Life* (Jonathan Cape, 1940)

H.R. Woudhuysen (ed.), *A.E.H. A.W.P.: A Classical Friendship* (The Foundling Press and Bernard Quaritch, 2006)

Websites

The Housman Society: www.housman-society.co.uk

British Classical Music: The Land of Lost Content: landofllostcontent.blogspot.
co.uk

The First World War Poetry Digital Archive: www.oucs.ox.ac.uk/ww1lit

The LiederNet Archive: www.lieder.net

Ludlow English Song Weekend: http://ludlowenglishsongweekend.com

MusicWeb International: www.musicweb-international.com

The Ralph Vaughan Williams Society: www.rvwsociety.com

INDEX

Index

A SHROPSHIRE LAD

by
A.E. Housman

I

1887

From Clee to heaven the beacon burns,
    The shires have seen it plain,
From north and south the sign returns
    And beacons burn again.

Look left, look right, the hills are bright,
    The dales are light between,
Because 'tis fifty years to-night
    That God has saved the Queen.

Now, when the flame they watch not towers
    About the soil they trod,
Lads, we'll remember friends of ours
    Who shared the work with God.

To skies that knit their heartstrings right,
    To fields that bred them brave,
The saviours come not home to-night:
    Themselves they could not save.

It dawns in Asia, tombstones show
    And Shropshire names are read;
And the Nile spills his overflow
    Beside the Severn's dead.

We pledge in peace by farm and town
    The Queen they served in war,
And fire the beacons up and down
    The land they perished for.

'God save the Queen' we living sing,
  From height to height 'tis heard;
And with the rest your voices ring,
  Lads of the Fifty-third.

Oh, God will save her, fear you not:
  Be you the men you've been,
Get you the sons your fathers got,
  And God will save the Queen.

II

Loveliest of trees, the cherry now
Is hung with bloom along the bough,
And stands about the woodland ride
Wearing white for Eastertide.

Now, of my threescore years and ten,
Twenty will not come again,
And take from seventy springs a score,
It only leaves me fifty more.

And since to look at things in bloom
Fifty springs are little room,
About the woodlands I will go
To see the cherry hung with snow.

III

The Recruit

Leave your home behind, lad,
    And reach your friends your hand,
And go, and luck go with you
    While Ludlow tower shall stand.

Oh, come you home of Sunday
    When Ludlow streets are still
And Ludlow bells are calling
    To farm and lane and mill,

Or come you home of Monday
    When Ludlow market hums
And Ludlow chimes are playing
    'The conquering hero comes,'

Come you home a hero,
    Or come not home at all,
The lads you leave will mind you
    Till Ludlow tower shall fall.

And you will list the bugle
    That blows in lands of morn,
And make the foes of England
    Be sorry you were born.

And you till trump of doomsday
    On lands of morn may lie,
And make the hearts of comrades
    Be heavy where you die.

Leave your home behind you,
    Your friends by field and town:
Oh, town and field will mind you
    Till Ludlow tower is down.

IV

Reveille

Wake: the silver dusk returning
　　Up the beach of darkness brims,
And the ship of sunrise burning
　　Strands upon the eastern rims.

Wake: the vaulted shadow shatters,
　　Trampled to the floor it spanned,
And the tent of night in tatters
　　Straws the sky-pavilioned land.

Up, lad, up, 'tis late for lying:
　　Hear the drums of morning play;
Hark, the empty highways crying
　　'Who'll beyond the hills away?'

Towns and countries woo together,
　　Forelands beacon, belfries call;
Never lad that trod on leather
　　Lived to feast his heart with all.

Up, lad: thews that lie and cumber
　　Sunlit pallets never thrive;
Morns abed and daylight slumber
　　Were not meant for man alive.

Clay lies still, but blood's a rover;
　　Breath's a ware that will not keep.
Up, lad: when the journey's over
　　There'll be time enough to sleep.

V

Oh see how thick the goldcup flowers
  Are lying in field and lane,
With dandelions to tell the hours
  That never are told again.
Oh may I squire you round the meads
  And pick you posies gay?
— 'Twill do no harm to take my arm.
  'You may, young man, you may.'

Ah, spring was sent for lass and lad,
  'Tis now the blood runs gold,
And man and maid had best be glad
  Before the world is old.
What flowers to-day may flower to-morrow,
  But never as good as new.
— Suppose I wound my arm right round —
  ''Tis true, young man, 'tis true.'

Some lads there are, 'tis shame to say,
  That only court to thieve,
And once they bear the bloom away
  'Tis little enough they leave.
Then keep your heart for men like me
  And safe from trustless chaps.
My love is true and all for you.
  'Perhaps, young man, perhaps.'

Oh, look in my eyes then, can you doubt?
  — Why, 'tis a mile from town.
How green the grass is all about!
  We might as well sit down.

— Ah, life, what is it but a flower?
  Why must true lovers sigh?
Be kind, have pity, my own, my pretty, —
  'Good-bye, young man, good-bye.'

VI

When the lad for longing sighs,
    Mute and dull of cheer and pale,
If at death's own door he lies,
    Maiden, you can heal his ail.

Lovers' ills are all to buy:
    The wan look, the hollow tone,
The hung head, the sunken eye,
    You can have them for your own.

Buy them, buy them: eve and morn
    Lovers' ills are all to sell.
Then you can lie down forlorn;
    But the lover will be well.

VII

When smoke stood up from Ludlow,
   And mist blew off from Teme,
And blithe afield to ploughing
   Against the morning beam
   I strode beside my team,

The blackbird in the coppice
   Looked out to see me stride,
And hearkened as I whistled
   The trampling team beside,
   And fluted and replied:

'Lie down, lie down, young yeoman;
   What use to rise and rise?
Rise man a thousand mornings
   Yet down at last he lies,
   And then the man is wise.'

I heard the tune he sang me,
   And spied his yellow bill;
I picked a stone and aimed it
   And threw it with a will:
   Then the bird was still.

Then my soul within me
   Took up the blackbird's strain,
And still beside the horses
   Along the dewy lane
   It sang the song again:

'Lie down, lie down, young yeoman;
    The sun moves always west;
The road one treads to labour
    Will lead one home to rest,
    And that will be the best.'

VIII

'Farewell to barn and stack and tree,
   Farewell to Severn shore.
Terence, look your last at me,
   For I come home no more.

'The sun burns on the half-mown hill,
   By now the blood is dried;
And Maurice amongst the hay lies still
   And my knife is in his side.

'My mother thinks us long away;
   'Tis time the field were mown.
She had two sons at rising day,
   To-night she'll be alone.

'And here's a bloody hand to shake,
   And oh, man, here's good-bye;
We'll sweat no more on scythe and rake,
   My bloody hands and I.

'I wish you strength to bring you pride,
   And a love to keep you clean,
And I wish you luck, come Lammastide,
   At racing on the green.

'Long for me the rick will wait,
   And long will wait the fold,
And long will stand the empty plate,
   And dinner will be cold.'

IX

On moonlit heath and lonesome bank
    The sheep beside me graze;
And yon the gallows used to clank
    Fast by the four cross ways.

A careless shepherd once would keep
    The flocks by moonlight there,*
And high amongst the glimmering sheep
    The dead man stood on air.

They hang us now in Shrewsbury jail:
    The whistles blow forlorn,
And trains all night groan on the rail
    To men that die at morn.

There sleeps in Shrewsbury jail to-night,
    Or wakes, as may betide,
A better lad, if things went right,
    Than most that sleep outside.

And naked to the hangman's noose
    The morning clocks will ring
A neck God made for other use
    Than strangling in a string.

And sharp the link of life will snap,
    And dead on air will stand
Heels that held up as straight a chap
    As treads upon the land.

---

*Hanging in chains was called keeping sheep by moonlight.

So here I'll watch the night and wait
    To see the morning shine,
When he will hear the stroke of eight
    And not the stroke of nine;

And wish my friend as sound a sleep
    As lads' I did not know,
That shepherded the moonlit sheep
    A hundred years ago.

X

March

The Sun at noon to higher air,
Unharnessing the silver Pair
That late before his chariot swam,
Rides on the gold wool of the Ram.

So braver notes the storm-cock sings
To start the rusted wheel of things,
And brutes in field and brutes in pen
Leap that the world goes round again.

The boys are up the woods with day
To fetch the daffodils away,
And home at noonday from the hills
They bring no dearth of daffodils.

Afield for palms the girls repair,
And sure enough the palms are there,
And each will find by hedge or pond
Her waving silver-tufted wand.

In farm and field through all the shire
The eye beholds the heart's desire;
Ah, let not only mine be vain,
For lovers should be loved again.

XI

On your midnight pallet lying,
    Listen, and undo the door:
Lads that waste the light in sighing
    In the dark should sigh no more;
Night should ease a lover's sorrow;
Therefore, since I go to-morrow,
    Pity me before.

In the land to which I travel,
    The far dwelling, let me say —
Once, if here the couch is gravel,
    In a kinder bed I lay,
And the breast the darnel smothers
Rested once upon another's
    When it was not clay.

XII

When I watch the living meet,
    And the moving pageant file
Warm and breathing through the street
    Where I lodge a little while,

If the heats of hate and lust
    In the house of flesh are strong,
Let me mind the house of dust
    Where my sojourn shall be long.

In the nation that is not
    Nothing stands that stood before;
There revenges are forgot,
    And the hater hates no more;

Lovers lying two and two
    Ask not whom they sleep beside,
And the bridegroom all night through
    Never turns him to the bride.

XIII

When I was one-and-twenty
   I heard a wise man say,
'Give crowns and pounds and guineas
   But not your heart away;
Give pearls away and rubies
   But keep your fancy free.'
But I was one-and-twenty,
   No use to talk to me.

When I was one-and-twenty
   I heard him say again,
'The heart out of the bosom
   Was never given in vain;
'Tis paid with sighs a plenty
   And sold for endless rue.'
And I am two-and-twenty,
   And oh, 'tis true, 'tis true.

XIV

There pass the careless people
    That call their souls their own:
Here by the road I loiter,
    How idle and alone.

Ah, past the plunge of plummet,
    In seas I cannot sound,
My heart and soul and senses,
    World without end, are drowned.

His folly has not fellow
    Beneath the blue of day
That gives to man or woman
    His heart and soul away.

There flowers no balm to sain him
    From east of earth to west
That's lost for everlasting
    The heart out of his breast.

Here by the labouring highway
    With empty hands I stroll:
Sea-deep, till doomsday morning,
    Lie lost my heart and soul.

XV

Look not in my eyes, for fear
    They mirror true the sight I see,
And there you find your face too clear
    And love it and be lost like me.
One the long nights through must lie
    Spent in star-defeated sighs,
But why should you as well as I
    Perish? gaze not in my eyes.

A Grecian lad, as I hear tell,
    One that many loved in vain,
Looked into a forest well
    And never looked away again.
There, when the turf in springtime flowers,
    With downward eye and gazes sad,
Stands amid the glancing showers
    A jonquil, not a Grecian lad.

XVI

It nods and curtseys and recovers
    When the wind blows above,
The nettle on the graves of lovers
    That hanged themselves for love.

The nettle nods, the wind blows over,
    The man, he does not move,
The lover of the grave, the lover
    That hanged himself for love.

XVII

Twice a week the winter thorough
    Here stood I to keep the goal:
Football then was fighting sorrow
    For the young man's soul.

Now in Maytime to the wicket
    Out I march with bat and pad:
See the son of grief at cricket
    Trying to be glad.

Try I will; no harm in trying:
    Wonder 'tis how little mirth
Keeps the bones of man from lying
    On the bed of earth.

XVIII

Oh, when I was in love with you,
    Then I was clean and brave,
And miles around the wonder grew
    How well did I behave.

And now the fancy passes by,
    And nothing will remain,
And miles around they'll say that I
    Am quite myself again.

XIX

To an Athlete Dying Young

The time you won your town the race
We chaired you through the market-place;
Man and boy stood cheering by,
And home we brought you shoulder-high.

To-day, the road all runners come,
Shoulder-high we bring you home,
And set you at your threshold down,
Townsman of a stiller town.

Smart lad, to slip betimes away
From fields where glory does not stay
And early though the laurel grows
It withers quicker than the rose.

Eyes the shady night has shut
Cannot see the record cut,
And silence sounds no worse than cheers
After earth has stopped the ears:

Now you will not swell the rout
Of lads that wore their honours out,
Runners whom renown outran
And the name died before the man.

So set, before its echoes fade,
The fleet foot on the sill of shade,
And hold to the low lintel up
The still-defended challenge-cup.

And round that early-laurelled head
Will flock to gaze the strengthless dead,
And find unwithered on its curls
The garland briefer than a girl's.

XX

Oh fair enough are sky and plain,
    But I know fairer far:
Those are as beautiful again
    That in the water are;

The pools and rivers wash so clean
    The trees and clouds and air,
The like on earth was never seen,
    And oh that I were there.

These are the thoughts I often think
    As I stand gazing down
In act upon the cressy brink
    To strip and dive and drown;

But in the golden-sanded brooks
    And azure meres I spy
A silly lad that longs and looks
    And wishes he were I.

XXI

Bredon* Hill

In summertime on Bredon
    The bells they sound so clear;
Round both the shires they ring them
    In steeples far and near,
    A happy noise to hear.

Here of a Sunday morning
    My love and I would lie,
And see the coloured counties,
    And hear the larks so high
    About us in the sky.

The bells would ring to call her
    In valleys miles away:
'Come all to church, good people;
    Good people, come and pray.'
    But here my love would stay.

And I would turn and answer
    Among the springing thyme,
'Oh, peal upon our wedding,
    And we will hear the chime,
    And come to church in time.'

But when the snows at Christmas
    On Bredon top were strown,
My love rose up so early
    And stole out unbeknown
    And went to church alone.

---

*Pronounced Breedon.

They tolled the one bell only,
    Groom there was none to see,
The mourners followed after,
    And so to church went she,
    And would not wait for me.

The bells they sound on Bredon,
    And still the steeples hum.
'Come all to church, good people,' —
    Oh, noisy bells, be dumb;
    I hear you, I will come.

XXII

The street sounds to the soldiers' tread,
    And out we troop to see:
A single redcoat turns his head,
    He turns and looks at me.

My man, from sky to sky's so far,
    We never crossed before;
Such leagues apart the world's ends are,
    We're like to meet no more;

What thoughts at heart have you and I
    We cannot stop to tell;
But dead or living, drunk or dry,
    Soldier, I wish you well.

XXIII

The lads in their hundreds to Ludlow come in for the fair,
  There's men from the barn and the forge and the mill and
    the fold,
The lads for the girls and the lads for the liquor are there,
  And there with the rest are the lads that will never be old.

There's chaps from the town and the field and the till and the
    cart,
  And many to count are the stalwart, and many the brave,
And many the handsome of face and the handsome of heart,
  And few that will carry their looks or their truth to the
    grave.

I wish one could know them, I wish there were tokens to tell
  The fortunate fellows that now you can never discern;
And then one could talk with them friendly and wish them
    farewell
  And watch them depart on the way that they will not
    return.

But now you may stare as you like and there's nothing to scan;
  And brushing your elbow unguessed-at and not to be told
They carry back bright to the coiner the mintage of man,
  The lads that will die in their glory and never be old.

XXIV

Say, lad, have you things to do?
   Quick then, while your day's at prime.
Quick, and if 'tis work for two,
   Here am I, man: now's your time.

Send me now, and I shall go;
   Call me, I shall hear you call;
Use me ere they lay me low
   Where a man's no use at all;

Ere the wholesome flesh decay,
   And the willing nerve be numb,
And the lips lack breath to say,
   'No, my lad, I cannot come.'

XXV

This time of year a twelvemonth past,
  When Fred and I would meet,
We needs must jangle, till at last
  We fought and I was beat.

So then the summer fields about,
  Till rainy days began,
Rose Harland on her Sundays out
  Walked with the better man.

The better man she walks with still,
  Though now 'tis not with Fred:
A lad that lives and has his will
  Is worth a dozen dead.

Fred keeps the house all kinds of weather,
  And clay's the house he keeps;
When Rose and I walk out together
  Stock-still lies Fred and sleeps.

XXVI

Along the field as we came by
A year ago, my love and I,
The aspen over stile and stone
Was talking to itself alone.
'Oh who are these that kiss and pass?
A country lover and his lass;
Two lovers looking to be wed;
And time shall put them both to bed,
But she shall lie with earth above,
And he beside another love.'

And sure enough beneath the tree
There walks another love with me,
And overhead the aspen heaves
Its rainy-sounding silver leaves;
And I spell nothing in their stir,
But now perhaps they speak to her,
And plain for her to understand
They talk about a time at hand
When I shall sleep with clover clad,
And she beside another lad.

XXVII

'Is my team ploughing,
　　That I was used to drive
And hear the harness jingle
　　When I was man alive?'

Ay, the horses trample,
　　The harness jingles now;
No change though you lie under
　　The land you used to plough.

'Is football playing
　　Along the river shore,
With lads to chase the leather,
　　Now I stand up no more?'

Ay, the ball is flying,
　　The lads play heart and soul;
The goal stands up, the keeper
　　Stands up to keep the goal.

'Is my girl happy,
　　That I thought hard to leave,
And has she tired of weeping
　　As she lies down at eve?'

Ay, she lies down lightly,
　　She lies not down to weep:
Your girl is well contented.
　　Be still, my lad, and sleep.

'Is my friend hearty,
    Now I am thin and pine,
And has he found to sleep in
    A better bed than mine?'

Yes, lad, I lie easy,
    I lie as lads would choose;
I cheer a dead man's sweetheart,
    Never ask me whose.

XXVIII

The Welsh Marches

High the vanes of Shrewsbury gleam
Islanded in Severn stream;
The bridges from the steepled crest
Cross the water east and west.

The flag of morn in conqueror's state
Enters at the English gate:
The vanquished eve, as night prevails,
Bleeds upon the road to Wales.

Ages since the vanquished bled
Round my mother's marriage-bed;
There the ravens feasted far
About the open house of war:

When Severn down to Buildwas ran
Coloured with the death of man,
Couched upon her brother's grave
The Saxon got me on the slave.

The sound of fight is silent long
That began the ancient wrong;
Long the voice of tears is still
That wept of old the endless ill.

In my heart it has not died,
The war that sleeps on Severn side;
They cease not fighting, east and west,
On the marches of my breast.

Here the truceless armies yet
Trample, rolled in blood and sweat;
They kill and kill and never die;
And I think that each is I.

None will part us, none undo
The knot that makes one flesh of two,
Sick with hatred, sick with pain,
Strangling – When shall we be slain?

When shall I be dead and rid
Of the wrong my father did?
How long, how long, till spade and hearse
Put to sleep my mother's curse?

XXIX

The Lent Lily

'Tis spring; come out to ramble
    The hilly brakes around,
For under thorn and bramble
    About the hollow ground
    The primroses are found.

And there's the windflower chilly
    With all the winds at play,
And there's the Lenten lily
    That has not long to stay
    And dies on Easter day.

And since till girls go maying
    You find the primrose still,
And find the windflower playing
    With every wind at will,
    But not the daffodil,

Bring baskets now, and sally
    Upon the spring's array,
And bear from hill and valley
    The daffodil away
    That dies on Easter day.

XXX

Others, I am not the first,
Have willed more mischief than they durst:
If in the breathless night I too
Shiver now, 'tis nothing new.

More than I, if truth were told,
Have stood and sweated hot and cold,
And through their reins in ice and fire
Fear contended with desire.

Agued once like me were they,
But I like them shall win my way
Lastly to the bed of mould
Where there's neither heat nor cold.

But from my grave across my brow
Plays no wind of healing now,
And fire and ice within me fight
Beneath the suffocating night.

XXXI

On Wenlock Edge the wood's in trouble;
    His forest fleece the Wrekin heaves;
The gale, it plies the saplings double,
    And thick on Severn snow the leaves.

'Twould blow like this through holt and hanger
    When Uricon the city stood:
'Tis the old wind in the old anger,
    But then it threshed another wood.

Then, 'twas before my time, the Roman
    At yonder heaving hill would stare:
The blood that warms an English yeoman,
    The thoughts that hurt him, they were there.

There, like the wind through woods in riot,
    Through him the gale of life blew high;
The tree of man was never quiet:
    Then 'twas the Roman, now 'tis I.

The gale, it plies the saplings double,
    It blows so hard, 'twill soon be gone:
To-day the Roman and his trouble
    Are ashes under Uricon.

XXXII

From far, from eve and morning
    And yon twelve-winded sky,
The stuff of life to knit me
    Blew hither: here am I.

Now — for a breath I tarry
    Nor yet disperse apart —
Take my hand quick and tell me,
    What have you in your heart.

Speak now, and I will answer;
    How shall I help you, say;
Ere to the wind's twelve quarters
    I take my endless way.

XXXIII

If truth in hearts that perish
   Could move the powers on high,
I think the love I bear you
   Should make you not to die.

Sure, sure, if stedfast meaning,
   If single thought could save,
The world might end to-morrow,
   You should not see the grave.

This long and sure-set liking,
   This boundless will to please,
– Oh, you should live for ever
   If there were help in these.

But now, since all is idle,
   To this lost heart be kind,
Ere to a town you journey
   Where friends are ill to find.

XXXIV

The New Mistress

'Oh, sick I am to see you, will you never let me be?
You may be good for something but you are not good for me.
Oh, go where you are wanted, for you are not wanted here.
And that was all the farewell when I parted from my
     dear.

'I will go where I am wanted, to a lady born and bred
Who will dress me free for nothing in a uniform of red;
She will not be sick to see me if I only keep it clean:
I will go where I am wanted for a soldier of the Queen.

'I will go where I am wanted, for the sergeant does not
     mind;
He may be sick to see me but he treats me very kind:
He gives me beer and breakfast and a ribbon for my cap,
And I never knew a sweetheart spend her money on a
     chap.

'I will go where I am wanted, where there's room for
     one or two,
And the men are none too many for the work there is to
     do;
Where the standing line wears thinner and the dropping
     dead lie thick;
And the enemies of England they shall see me and be
     sick.'

XXXV

On the idle hill of summer,
  Sleepy with the flow of streams,
Far I hear the steady drummer
  Drumming like a noise in dreams.

Far and near and low and louder
  On the roads of earth go by,
Dear to friends and food for powder,
  Soldiers marching, all to die.

East and west on fields forgotten
  Bleach the bones of comrades slain,
Lovely lads and dead and rotten;
  None that go return again.

Far the calling bugles hollo,
  High the screaming fife replies,
Gay the files of scarlet follow:
  Woman bore me, I will rise.

XXXVI

White in the moon the long road lies,
 The moon stands blank above;
White in the moon the long road lies
 That leads me from my love.

Still hangs the hedge without a gust,
 Still, still the shadows stay:
My feet upon the moonlit dust
 Pursue the ceaseless way.

The world is round, so travellers tell,
 And straight though reach the track,
Trudge on, trudge on, 'twill all be well,
 The way will guide one back.

But ere the circle homeward hies
 Far, far must it remove:
White in the moon the long road lies
 That leads me from my love.

XXXVII

As through the wild green hills of Wyre
The train ran, changing sky and shire,
And far behind, a fading crest,
Low in the forsaken west
Sank the high-reared head of Clee,
My hand lay empty on my knee.
Aching on my knee it lay:
That morning half a shire away
So many an honest fellow's fist
Had well nigh wrung it from the wrist.
Hand, said I, since now we part
From fields and men we know by heart,
For strangers' faces, strangers' lands, –
Hand, you have held true fellows' hands.
Be clean then; rot before you do
A thing they'd not believe of you.
You and I must keep from shame
In London streets the Shropshire name;
On banks of Thames they must not say
Severn breeds worse men than they;
And friends abroad must bear in mind
Friends at home they leave behind.
Oh, I shall be stiff and cold
When I forget you, hearts of gold;
The land where I shall mind you not
Is the land where all's forgot.
And if my foot returns no more
To Teme nor Corve nor Severn shore,
Luck, my lads, be with you still
By falling stream and standing hill,
By chiming tower and whispering tree,
Men that made a man of me.

About your work in town and farm
Still you'll keep my head from harm,
Still you'll help me, hands that gave
A grasp to friend me to the grave.

XXXVIII

The winds out of the west land blow,
    My friends have breathed them there;
Warm with the blood of lads I know
    Comes east the sighing air.

It fanned their temples, filled their lungs,
    Scattered their forelocks free;
My friends made words of it with tongues
    That talk no more to me.

Their voices, dying as they fly,
    Loose on the wind are sown;
The names of men blow soundless by,
    My fellows' and my own.

Oh lads, at home I heard you plain,
    But here your speech is still,
And down the sighing wind in vain
    You hollo from the hill.

The wind and I, we both were there,
    But neither long abode;
Now through the friendless world we fare
    And sigh upon the road.

XXXIX

'Tis time, I think, by Wenlock town
    The golden broom should blow;
The hawthorn sprinkled up and down
    Should charge the land with snow.

Spring will not wait the loiterer's time
    Who keeps so long away;
So others wear the broom and climb
    The hedgerows heaped with may.

Oh tarnish late on Wenlock Edge,
    Gold that I never see;
Lie long, high snowdrifts in the hedge
    That will not shower on me.

XL

Into my heart an air that kills
    From yon far country blows:
What are those blue remembered hills,
    What spires, what farms are those?

That is the land of lost content,
    I see it shining plain,
The happy highways where I went
    And cannot come again.

XLI

In my own shire, if I was sad,
Homely comforters I had:
The earth, because my heart was sore,
Sorrowed for the son she bore;
And standing hills, long to remain,
Shared their short-lived comrade's pain.
And bound for the same bourn as I,
On every road I wandered by,
Trod beside me, close and dear,
The beautiful and death-struck year:
Whether in the woodland brown
I heard the beechnut rustle down,
And saw the purple crocus pale
Flower about the autumn dale;
Or littering far the fields of May
Lady-smocks a-bleaching lay,
And like a skylit water stood
The bluebells in the azured wood.

Yonder, lightening other loads,
The seasons range the country roads,
But here in London streets I ken
No such helpmates, only men;
And these are not in plight to bear,
If they would, another's care.
They have enough as 'tis: I see
In many an eye that measures me
The mortal sickness of a mind
Too unhappy to be kind.
Undone with misery, all they can
Is to hate their fellow man;
And till they drop they needs must still
Look at you and wish you ill.

XLII

The Merry Guide

Once in the wind of morning
    I ranged the thymy wold;
The world-wide air was azure
    And all the brooks ran gold.

There through the dews beside me
    Behold a youth that trod,
With feathered cap on forehead,
    And poised a golden rod.

With mien to match the morning
    And gay delightful guise
And friendly brows and laughter
    He looked me in the eyes.

Oh whence, I asked, and whither?
    He smiled and would not say,
And looked at me and beckoned
    And laughed and led the way.

And with kind looks and laughter
    And nought to say beside
We two went on together,
    I and my happy guide.

Across the glittering pastures
    And empty upland still
And solitude of shepherds
    High in the folded hill,

By hanging woods and hamlets
    That gaze through orchards down
On many a windmill turning
    And far-discovered town,

With gay regards of promise
    And sure unslackened stride
And smiles and nothing spoken
    Led on my merry guide.

By blowing realms of woodland
    With sunstruck vanes afield
And cloud-led shadows sailing
    About the windy weald,

By valley-guarded granges
    And silver waters wide,
Content at heart I followed
    With my delightful guide.

And like the cloudy shadows
    Across the country blown
We two fare on for ever,
    But not we two alone.

With the great gale we journey
    That breathes from gardens thinned,
Borne in the drift of blossoms
    Whose petals throng the wind;

Buoyed on the heaven-heard whisper
    Of dancing leaflets whirled
From all the woods that autumn
    Bereaves in all the world.

And midst the fluttering legion
    Of all that ever died
I follow, and before us
    Goes the delightful guide,

With lips that brim with laughter
    But never once respond,
And feet that fly on feathers,
    And serpent-circled wand.

XLIII

The Immortal Part

When I meet the morning beam
Or lay me down at night to dream,
I hear my bones within me say,
'Another night, another day.

'When shall this slough of sense be cast,
This dust of thoughts be laid at last,
The man of flesh and soul be slain
And the man of bone remain?

'This tongue that talks, these lungs that shout,
These thews that hustle us about,
This brain that fills the skull with schemes,
And its humming hive of dreams, –

'These to-day are proud in power
And lord it in their little hour:
The immortal bones obey control
Of dying flesh and dying soul.

''Tis long till eve and morn are gone:
Slow the endless night comes on,
And late to fulness grows the birth
That shall last as long as earth.

'Wanderers eastward, wanderers west,
Know you why you cannot rest?
'Tis that every mother's son
Travails with a skeleton.

'Lie down in the bed of dust;
Bear the fruit that bear you must;
Bring the eternal seed to light,
And morn is all the same as night.

'Rest you so from trouble sore,
Fear the heat o' the sun no more,
Nor the snowing winter wild,
Now you labour not with child.

'Empty vessel, garment cast,
We that wore you long shall last.
– Another night, another day.'
So my bones within me say.

Therefore they shall do my will
To-day while I am master still,
And flesh and soul, now both are strong,
Shall hale the sullen slaves along,

Before this fire of sense decay,
This smoke of thought blow clean away,
And leave with ancient night alone
The stedfast and enduring bone.

XLIV

Shot? so quick, so clean an ending?
    Oh that was right, lad, that was brave:
Yours was not an ill for mending,
    'Twas best to take it to the grave.

Oh you had forethought, you could reason,
    And saw your road and where it led,
And early wise and brave in season
    Put the pistol to your head.

Oh soon, and better so than later
    After long disgrace and scorn,
You shot dead the household traitor,
    The soul that should not have been born.

Right you guessed the rising morrow
    And scorned to tread the mire you must:
Dust's your wages, son of sorrow,
    But men may come to worse than dust.

Souls undone, undoing others, –
    Long time since the tale began.
You would not live to wrong your brothers:
    Oh lad, you died as fits a man.

Now to your grave shall friend and stranger
    With ruth and some with envy come:
Undishonoured, clear of danger,
    Clean of guilt, pass hence and home.

Turn safe to rest, no dreams, no waking;
   And here, man, here's the wreath I've made:
'Tis not a gift that's worth the taking,
   But wear it and it will not fade.

XLV

If it chance your eye offend you,
  Pluck it out, lad, and be sound:
'Twill hurt, but here are salves to friend you,
  And many a balsam grows on ground.

And if your hand or foot offend you,
  Cut it off, lad, and be whole;
But play the man, stand up and end you,
  When your sickness is your soul.

XLVI

Bring, in this timeless grave to throw,
No cypress, sombre on the snow;
Snap not from the bitter yew
His leaves that live December through;
Break no rosemary, bright with rime
And sparkling to the cruel clime;
Nor plod the winter land to look
For willows in the icy brook
To cast them leafless round him: bring
No spray that ever buds in spring.

But if the Christmas field has kept
Awns the last gleaner overstept,
Or shrivelled flax, whose flower is blue
A single season, never two;
Or if one haulm whose year is o'er
Shivers on the upland frore,
— Oh, bring from hill and stream and plain
Whatever will not flower again,
To give him comfort: he and those
Shall bide eternal bedfellows
Where low upon the couch he lies
Whence he never shall arise.

XLVII

The Carpenter's Son

'Here the hangman stops his cart:
Now the best of friends must part.
Fare you well, for ill fare I:
Live, lads, and I will die.

'Oh, at home had I but stayed
'Prenticed to my father's trade,
Had I stuck to plane and adze,
I had not been lost, my lads.

'Then I might have built perhaps
Gallows-trees for other chaps,
Never dangled on my own,
Had I but left ill alone.

'Now, you see, they hang me high,
And the people passing by
Stop to shake their fists and curse;
So 'tis come from ill to worse.

'Here hang I, and right and left
Two poor fellows hang for theft:
All the same's the luck we prove,
Though the midmost hangs for love.

'Comrades all, that stand and gaze,
Walk henceforth in other ways;
See my neck and save your own:
Comrades all, leave ill alone.

'Make some day a decent end,
Shrewder fellows than your friend.
Fare you well, for ill fare I:
Live, lads, and I will die.'

XLVIII

Be still, my soul, be still; the arms you bear are brittle,
    Earth and high heaven are fixt of old and founded
        strong.
Think rather, – call to thought, if now you grieve a little,
    The days when we had rest, O soul, for they were long.

Men loved unkindness then, but lightless in the quarry
    I slept and saw not; tears fell down, I did not mourn;
Sweat ran and blood sprang out and I was never sorry:
    Then it was well with me, in days ere I was born.

Now, and I muse for why and never find the reason,
    I pace the earth, and drink the air, and feel the sun.
Be still, be still, my soul; it is but for a season:
    Let us endure an hour and see injustice done.

Ay, look: high heaven and earth ail from the prime foundation;
    All thoughts to rive the heart are here, and all are vain:
Horror and scorn and hate and fear and indignation –
    Oh why did I awake? when shall I sleep again?

XLIX

Think no more, lad; laugh, be jolly:
    Why should men make haste to die?
Empty heads and tongues a-talking
Make the rough road easy walking,
And the feather pate of folly
    Bears the falling sky.

Oh 'tis jesting, dancing, drinking
    Spins the heavy world around.
If young hearts were not so clever,
Oh, they would be young for ever:
Think no more; 'tis only thinking
    Lays lads underground.

L

Clunton and Clunbury,
Clungunford and Clun,
Are the quietest places
Under the sun.

In valleys of springs of rivers,
    By Ony and Teme and Clun,
The country for easy livers,
    The quietest under the sun,

We still had sorrows to lighten,
    One could not be always glad,
And lads knew trouble at Knighton
    When I was a Knighton lad.

By bridges that Thames runs under,
    In London, the town built ill,
'Tis sure small matter for wonder
    If sorrow is with one still.

And if as a lad grows older
    The troubles he bears are more,
He carries his griefs on a shoulder
    That handselled them long before.

Where shall one halt to deliver
    This luggage I'd lief set down?
Not Thames, not Teme is the river,
    Nor London nor Knighton the town:

'Tis a long way further than Knighton,
    A quieter place than Clun,
Where doomsday may thunder and lighten
    And little 'twill matter to one.

LI

Loitering with a vacant eye
Along the Grecian gallery,
And brooding on my heavy ill,
I met a statue standing still.
Still in marble stone stood he,
And stedfastly he looked at me.
'Well met,' I thought the look would say,
'We both were fashioned far away;
We neither knew, when we were young,
These Londoners we live among.'

Still he stood and eyed me hard,
An earnest and a grave regard:
'What, lad, drooping with your lot?
I too would be where I am not.
I too survey that endless line
Of men whose thoughts are not as mine.
Years, ere you stood up from rest,
On my neck the collar prest;
Years, when you lay down your ill,
I shall stand and bear it still.
Courage, lad, 'tis not for long:
Stand, quit you like stone, be strong.'
So I thought his look would say;
And light on me my trouble lay,
And I stept out in flesh and bone
Manful like the man of stone.

LII

Far in a western brookland
    That bred me long ago
The poplars stand and tremble
    By pools I used to know.

There in the windless night-time,
    The wanderer, marvelling why,
Halts on the bridge to hearken
    How soft the poplars sigh.

He hears: no more remembered
    In fields where I was known,
Here I lie down in London
    And turn to rest alone.

There, by the starlit fences,
    The wanderer halts and hears
My soul that lingers sighing
    About the glimmering weirs.

LIII

The True Lover

The lad came to the door at night,
    When lovers crown their vows,
And whistled soft and out of sight
    In shadow of the boughs.

'I shall not vex you with my face
    Henceforth, my love, for aye;
So take me in your arms a space
    Before the east is grey.

'When I from hence away am past
    I shall not find a bride,
And you shall be the first and last
    I ever lay beside.'

She heard and went and knew not why;
    Her heart to his she laid;
Light was the air beneath the sky
    But dark under the shade.

'Oh do you breathe, lad, that your breast
    Seems not to rise and fall,
And here upon my bosom prest
    There beats no heart at all?'

'Oh loud, my girl, it once would knock,
    You should have felt it then;
But since for you I stopped the clock
    It never goes again.'

517

'Oh lad, what is it, lad, that drips
    Wet from your neck on mine?
What is it falling on my lips,
    My lad, that tastes of brine?'

'Oh like enough 'tis blood, my dear,
    For when the knife has slit
The throat across from ear to ear
    'Twill bleed because of it.'

Under the stars the air was light
    But dark below the boughs,
The still air of the speechless night,
    When lovers crown their vows.

LIV

With rue my heart is laden
    For golden friends I had,
For many a rose-lipt maiden
    And many a lightfoot lad.

By brooks too broad for leaping
    The lightfoot boys are laid;
The rose-lipt girls are sleeping
    In fields where roses fade.

LV

Westward on the high-hilled plains
    Where for me the world began,
Still, I think, in newer veins
    Frets the changeless blood of man.

Now that other lads than I
    Strip to bathe on Severn shore,
They, no help, for all they try,
    Tread the mill I trod before.

There, when hueless is the west
    And the darkness hushes wide,
Where the lad lies down to rest
    Stands the troubled dream beside.

There, on thoughts that once were mine,
    Day looks down the eastern steep,
And the youth at morning shine
    Makes the vow he will not keep.

LVI

The Day of Battle

'Far I hear the bugle blow
To call me where I would not go,
And the guns begin the song,
"Soldier, fly or stay for long."

'Comrade, if to turn and fly
Made a soldier never die,
Fly I would, for who would not?
'Tis sure no pleasure to be shot.

'But since the man that runs away
Lives to die another day,
And cowards' funerals, when they come,
Are not wept so well at home,

'Therefore, though the best is bad,
Stand and do the best, my lad;
Stand and fight and see your slain,
And take the bullet in your brain.'

LVII

You smile upon your friend to-day,
    To-day his ills are over;
You hearken to the lover's say,
    And happy is the lover.

'Tis late to hearken, late to smile,
    But better late than never:
I shall have lived a little while
    Before I die for ever.

LVIII

When I came last to Ludlow
    Amidst the moonlight pale,
Two friends kept step beside me,
    Two honest lads and hale.

Now Dick lies long in the churchyard,
    And Ned lies long in jail,
And I come home to Ludlow
    Amidst the moonlight pale.

LIX

The Isle of Portland

The star-filled seas are smooth to-night
    From France to England strown;
Black towers above the Portland light
    The felon-quarried stone.

On yonder island, not to rise,
    Never to stir forth free,
Far from his folk a dead lad lies
    That once was friends with me.

Lie you easy, dream you light,
    And sleep you fast for aye;
And luckier may you find the night
    Than ever you found the day.

LX

Now hollow fires burn out to black,
    And lights are guttering low:
Square your shoulders, lift your pack,
    And leave your friends and go.

Oh never fear, man, nought's to dread,
    Look not left nor right:
In all the endless road you tread
    There's nothing but the night.

LXI

Hughley Steeple

The vane on Hughley steeple
    Veers bright, a far-known sign,
And there lie Hughley people,
    And there lie friends of mine.
Tall in their midst the tower
    Divides the shade and sun,
And the clock strikes the hour
    And tells the time to none.

To south the headstones cluster,
    The sunny mounds lie thick;
The dead are more in muster
    At Hughley than the quick.
North, for a soon-told number,
    Chill graves the sexton delves,
And steeple-shadowed slumber
    The slayers of themselves.

To north, to south, lie parted,
    With Hughley tower above,
The kind, the single-hearted,
    The lads I used to love.
And, south or north, 'tis only
    A choice of friends one knows,
And I shall ne'er be lonely
    Asleep with these or those.

LXII

'Terence, this is stupid stuff:
You eat your victuals fast enough;
There can't be much amiss, 'tis clear,
To see the rate you drink your beer.
But oh, good Lord, the verse you make,
It gives a chap the belly-ache.
The cow, the old cow, she is dead;
It sleeps well, the horned head:
We poor lads, 'tis our turn now
To hear such tunes as killed the cow.
Pretty friendship 'tis to rhyme
Your friends to death before their time
Moping melancholy mad:
Come, pipe a tune to dance to, lad.'

Why, if 'tis dancing you would be,
There's brisker pipes than poetry.
Say, for what were hop-yards meant,
Or why was Burton built on Trent?
Oh many a peer of England brews
Livelier liquor than the Muse,
And malt does more than Milton can
To justify God's ways to man.
Ale, man, ale's the stuff to drink
For fellows whom it hurts to think:
Look into the pewter pot
To see the world as the world's not.
And faith, 'tis pleasant till 'tis past:
The mischief is that 'twill not last.
Oh I have been to Ludlow fair
And left my necktie God knows where,
And carried half way home, or near,
Pints and quarts of Ludlow beer:

Then the world seemed none so bad,
And I myself a sterling lad;
And down in lovely muck I've lain,
Happy till I woke again.
Then I saw the morning sky:
Heigho, the tale was all a lie;
The world, it was the old world yet,
I was I, my things were wet,
And nothing now remained to do
But begin the game anew.

   Therefore, since the world has still
Much good, but much less good than ill,
And while the sun and moon endure
Luck's a chance, but trouble's sure,
I'd face it as a wise man would,
And train for ill and not for good.
'Tis true, the stuff I bring for sale
Is not so brisk a brew as ale:
Out of a stem that scored the hand
I wrung it in a weary land.
But take it: if the smack is sour,
The better for the embittered hour;
It should do good to heart and head
When your soul is in my soul's stead;
And I will friend you, if I may,
In the dark and cloudy day.

   There was a king reigned in the east:
There, when kings will sit to feast,
They get their fill before they think
With poisoned meat and poisoned drink.
He gathered all that springs to birth
From the many-venomed earth;
First a little, thence to more,
He sampled all her killing store;

And easy, smiling, seasoned sound,
Sate the king when healths went round.
They put arsenic in his meat
And stared aghast to watch him eat;
They poured strychnine in his cup
And shook to see him drink it up:
They shook, they stared as white's their shirt:
Them it was their poison hurt.
— I tell the tale that I heard told.
Mithridates, he died old.

LXIII

I hoed and trenched and weeded,
    And took the flowers to fair:
I brought them home unheeded;
    The hue was not the wear.

So up and down I sow them
    For lads like me to find,
When I shall lie below them,
    A dead man out of mind.

Some seed the birds devour,
    And some the season mars,
But here and there will flower
    The solitary stars,

And fields will yearly bear them
    As light-leaved spring comes on,
And luckless lads will wear them
    When I am dead and gone.

THE END